Away for the WEEKEND®

NORTHERN CALIFORNIA

Revised and Updated

Away for the WEEKEND®

NORTHERN CALIFORNIA

Great Getaways for
Every Season of the Year

ELEANOR BERMAN

Revised and Updated

Crown Trade Paperbacks
New York

For Alan, who made this possible . . .
and made it a pleasure

Published by Crown Trade Paperbacks, 201 East 50th Street, New York, New York
10022. Member of the Crown Publishing Group.

Random House, Inc. New York, Toronto, London, Sydney, Auckland

CROWN TRADE PAPERBACKS and colophon are trademarks of Crown Publishers,
Inc.

Originally published by Clarkson N. Potter, Inc. in 1992.

Manufactured in the United States of America

Library of Congress Cataloging-in-Publication Data
Berman, Eleanor
   Away for the weekend, Northern California : great getaways for every season of the
year / by Eleanor Berman.—Rev. and updated.
   Includes index.
   1. California, Northern—Tours.   I. Title.
F867.5.B47   1996
917.9404'53—dc20   95-30648

ISBN 0-517-88519-0

10   9   8   7   6   5   4   3   2   1

Revised Edition

Contents

CONTENTS

FALL

WINTER

Acknowledgments

My sincere thanks to the many local tourist offices that helped me along the way, to my editor, Katie Workman and her assistant Allison Hanes, and to my diligent researcher, Terry Klewan.

Introduction

Everything in Northern California comes in superlatives—the tallest trees, the highest mountains, the most dramatic meetings of land and sea. The wine is world class, and so is the skiing. From the rustic romance of gold country to the gabled Victorians of San Francisco, irresistible charm is found everywhere. Five national parks and even more national monuments are packed into the remarkable upper half of this one fortunate state.

With so many choices, the question is where to start. Should you head for the waters of Lake Tahoe or Clear Lake, the crashing surf of Big Sur or the rocky coast of Mendocino? Should you follow the crowds to Yosemite or discover the more solitary wonders of Lassen National Park? Take in the towering redwoods or the stupendous sequoias?

Away for the Weekend® *Northern California* invites you to sample them all, one at a time, as memorable weekend trips. The pages that follow offer the best of the getaways, ideas for every season of the year. Included are beaches and mountains, gala festivals and quiet retreats, hideaway places for lovers and forays for families. Some of the weekends focus on a special event; others are simply an introduction to a special place.

"Northern California" here has been stretched to take in some of the central part of the state, places that are within reasonable weekending range of the Bay Area and/or Sacramento.

It should be said at the start that this is a somewhat personal and selective guide to places I have visited and liked. I've not tried to list every lodging or even every sightseeing attraction in each area, sticking instead to those I found to be best. For dining, I've either sampled the food or depended upon reliable local recommendations, particularly from innkeepers, who know firsthand which places their guests most enjoy.

Since changing seasons may bring different attractions in the same area, you will find repeat mentions of some destinations. The trips themselves are arranged by season, not only because activities change with the calendar but to allow you time to read ahead about upcoming events and reserve rooms early. Advance information enables you to make the most of a festival or special event, planning a relaxing and leisurely weekend of sightseeing rather than a tiring day trip.

Don't feel bound by my calendar, however. Many of these destinations are equally appealing and less crowded when nothing special is going on. In fact, you'll find that some of my suggestions are for "out of season" visits. Until you've seen Yosemite in the snow or visited the coast in the crisp sunshine of late fall, you haven't seen either in its full beauty.

For Bay Area residents, some of these suggestions may seem too close to home for a weekend. Too often it is faraway places that beckon most alluringly, causing us to overlook treasures in our own backyards. In this case, the backyard is a beauty, so don't pass up the quick getaways that can make for a refreshing change of pace. Instead of a day trip, take a weekend and really get to know your fascinating neighbors.

HOW TO USE THIS BOOK

The format for the trips in *Away for the Weekend*® assumes that you have a normal two-day weekend to spend, leaving on Friday night, returning late on Sunday. Each chapter suggests an itinerary for a two-day stay, with added suggestions to accommodate varying tastes and time schedules. Mileages are given from both San Francisco and Sacramento, but driving directions give the general location, so that they can be used from any part of the state.

When there is enough to do to warrant a longer stay, a symbol at the start of each trip will tell you so. When you do have more than a weekend to spend, use these symbols and also check the map at the back to combine nearby weekends to fill out an extended stay. The coastline, the mountains, gold country, and the wine country of Napa and Sonoma counties all invite longer exploration.

Symbols also indicate trips that seem appropriate for children, though you are the best judge of what your family might enjoy.

Another symbol marks a few trips that can be done entirely via public transportation. These are destinations where air transportation, bus, or Amtrak make it possible to extend your weekend range or to cut down on winter driving.

The symbols for these various categories are as follows:

   🧸 = recommended for children

   🚌 = accessible at least in part via public transportation

   💼 = recommended for long weekends

Lodging prices indicated are for a double room; dining listings indicate the cost of main courses only rather than a whole dinner, since not everyone chooses to order a three-course meal.

For lodgings:

I (inexpensive)	= under $70
M (medium)	= $70 to $100
E (expensive)	= $100 to $135
EE (extra expensive)	= over $135

When meals are included in the rates, these letters are used:

CP = continental plan (breakfast only)
MAP = modified American plan (breakfast and dinner)
AP = American plan (all three meals)

For dining, the letters are as follows:

I = most entrées under $12 per person
M = most entrées between $12 and $20
E = most entrées between $20 and $30
EE = most entrées over $30 (often a prix fixe menu)

When prices bridge two categories, a combination of letters is used.

Bed-and-breakfast registry services are sometimes included among the area lodgings. No rates are given because of the abundance of listings and the wide price range. An overall list of these services follows at the end of this section. Since AAA, Mobil, and other similar guides do so well by motel listings, I've omitted motels here unless they are the only available lodgings or have a special appeal. You can get a listing of motels by writing to the local tourist office at the end of each chapter. Throughout, (800) telephone numbers are toll free.

Camping information is not included here, but the telephone number for California state park reservations is included in the information section.

Rates frequently increase, often before a book makes it from author to publisher to bookstore. The same is true of admission prices. Rates and prices here are as accurate as could be determined at the time of publication, and are included as a *general indication* of what to expect. Please use them just that way, as a general guide *only*. Always use the telephone numbers included to check for current prices when you plan your trip. It is well to verify current hours and holiday closings, too.

When it comes to restaurants and lodgings, remember that a new owner or new chef can make a big difference, and changes and closings cannot always be predicted. If you find that any information here has become seriously outdated, that a place has closed or gone downhill, I hope that you will let me know in care of Clarkson N. Potter, Inc., 201 East 50th Street, New York, New York 10022, so that the entry can be corrected. If you discover new places, or some appealing ones that I have missed, I hope you will let me know about these as well.

The maps in this book are simplified to highlight locations of suggested destinations. They are not necessarily reliable as road maps. You can get an excellent overall map free from the California Office of Tourism at the address listed below.

One last tip: Reserve well ahead if you want to stay in country inns or visit beach or ski resorts in high season. Most lodgings offer refunds on deposits if you cancel with reasonable notice, so write ahead and take your pick instead of settling for leftovers.

For this easterner, traveling in California to research and update this book has been a special privilege. I have been enlightened by the western history I learned, regaled with wonderful food and wine. From mud baths to garlic feasts, I've had a wonderful time. Most of all, I've been awed and amazed by the variety and the abundance of beauty gracing this most exceptional part of our country.

I hope that my enthusiasm for these places and pleasures comes through, inspiring you to share my discoveries—and to make some of your own.

INFORMATION SOURCES

California Division of Tourism, P.O. Box 1499, Sacramento, CA 95812-1499. Phone (800) 462-2543. Request a map, guides for hotel and motel lodgings and bed-and-breakfast services, a comprehensive statewide guidebook, and a guide to California skiing, all free.

Redwood Empire Association, 785 Market Street, 15th Floor, San Francisco, CA 94103, (415) 543-8334. A guide is available to redwood country from San Francisco to the Oregon border, covering Marin, Sonoma, Napa, Lake, Mendocino, Humboldt, and Del Norte counties. $3.

Amtrak, (800) USA-RAIL. Northern California service is offered along the coast, in the Central Valley, and from the Bay Area to Truckee—Lake Tahoe. Phone for schedules and rates.

California Department of Parks and Recreation. For general information, write P.O. Box 942896, Sacramento, CA 94296, or call (916) 445-6477. For camping reservation information, forms, and reservations, call MISTIX, in California (800) 444-7275. The Official Guide to California State Parks may be ordered by mail by sending $2 to the Publications Office at the address above.

National Park Service, Western Region Information Office, Fort Mason, Building 201, San Francisco, CA 94123, (415) 556-0560. Can supply information on the state's 17 national parks, monuments, historic sites, and recreational areas.

BED-AND-BREAKFAST REGISTRY SERVICES

The following are information sources for bed-and breakfast lodgings and small inns in the locations listed. Where no telephone number is listed, there is no permanent office, so write for the local guide.

Accommodations Referral
(Napa Valley)
P.O. Box 59
St. Helena, CA 94574
(800) 240-8466

Bed & Breakfast Exchange
(Wine country, north coast,
gold country, and Mendocino)
1407 Main Street, Suite 102
St. Helena, CA 94574
(707) 942-5900

*Bed & Breakfast Exchange of
Marin County*
45 Entrata
San Anselmo, CA 94960
(415) 485-1971

*Bed & Breakfast Inns of
Amador County*
P.O. Box 1347
Sutter Creek, CA 95685
(800) 726-INNS

*Bed & Breakfast Inns of the
Gold Country*
(Tuolumne County)
P.O. Box 462
Sonora, CA 95370
(209) 533-1845

*Bed & Breakfast Inns of the
Mother Lode*
P.O. Box 106
Placerville, CA 95667

Bed & Breakfast International
(Bay Area, wine country, Monterey peninsula, and entire state)
P.O. Box 282910
San Francisco, CA 94128
(415) 696-1690 or
(800) 872-4500

*Bed and Breakfast San
Francisco*
(Bay Area, wine country,
Monterey/Carmel, Pacific coast
north and south of San Francisco)
P.O. Box 420009
San Francisco, CA 94142
(415) 479-1913 or
(800) 452-8249

*California Association
of Bed and Breakfast Inns*
(Entire state)
2715 Porter Street
Soquel, CA 95073
(800) 284-INNS

Country Inns of the Russian River
P.O. Box 2416
Guerneville, CA 95446
(800) 927-4667

*The Guide to California Bed &
Breakfast Inns*
Statewide listings, available free
from the California Division of
Tourism at the address above.

Inns of Point Reyes
P.O. Box 145
Inverness, CA 94937
(415) 663-1420 or
(707) 664-6606

*Mendocino Coast Innkeepers
Association*
P.O. Box 1141
Mendocino, CA 95460

*Wine Country Inns of Sonoma
County*
P.O. Box 51
Geyserville, CA 95441
(707) 433-INNS

SPRING

Wining and Dining in Healdsburg

Success has not spoiled Healdsburg. This unpretentious little town has everything to recommend it—a pretty, shady town plaza dating back to 1852, inviting inns, superb restaurants, lots of outdoor recreation nearby. Three important growing areas, the Alexander, Dry Creek, and Russian River valleys, are all within easy striking distance, with more than 50 wineries to be sampled.

Yet, though the word is spreading and the venerable plaza has been spruced up for the company that comes in increasing numbers, Healdsburg has remained a relaxed country town at heart. You can still see signs that not very long ago this was a farm center, surrounded by fruit orchards. Since the more lucrative grapevines replaced most of the fruit trees and the tourists began arriving, the shops have upgraded considerably, but they are interesting rather than touristy. And you can still browse or go to a concert at the gazebo in the plaza without being jostled by crowds. What's more, the country roads to the vineyards are wonderfully wide open compared to the busy highways in the Napa Valley or southern Sonoma County.

Healdsburg is at its most appealing in spring, when the vineyards are carpeted with golden wild mustard plants and the remaining orchards blossom in their best pink-and-white finery. Time your visit for mid-May and you can attend the annual Russian River Wine Festival, with 40 vintners offering tastings in the town plaza.

The first difficult decision is where to stay. If you want to be within walking distance of shops and three top restaurants, try the Healdsburg Inn on the Plaza, a live-in art gallery with nicely done old-fashioned rooms and a roof-garden solarium. Just a few blocks away, the Camellia Inn draws Victoriana lovers; the elegant 1869 Italianate town house has marble fireplaces, chandeliers, antique-filled rooms, and an outdoor pool in case the days turn warm. Grape Leaf Inn is another in-town charmer, an imaginatively restored 1900 Queen Anne Victorian with skylights, weathered paneling, and stained glass, decorated with lovely posters and photos of the wine country. The smaller George Alexander House has Victorian decor and notable breakfasts. Each of the latter inns offers some rooms with whirlpools or Jacuzzis for two.

The most elaborate lodging in town is Madrona Manor, a mansion in the country with a pool, spacious grounds, and a rather formal, gloomy air. My favorite spot is the Belle de Jour, just outside town, where four cottages provide privacy, a light and airy French country feel, and matchless views of the vineyards.

One final possibility for those who want to be out in the country is the homey Campbell Ranch Inn in Geyserville, about eight miles to the north. There are vineyard views, flower gardens surrounding the pool, and a private tennis court for guests. The hosts here take pride in the homemade pies served with coffee every evening; often the filling comes from the 22 fruit trees on the property.

You might want to start a Healdsburg stay with a stroll around the plaza. The little shops on all sides are full of temptations. On Matheson Street, for example, they range from quilts in Fabrications to home accessories at Friends in the Country to paintings at Innpressions Gallery, downstairs from the Inn on the Plaza. There's an excellent bookstore on the block, as well. Turn down Healdsburg Avenue and walk north just beyond the plaza for a couple of other interesting stops. Palladio specializes in intriguing furniture, and Evans Ceramics at 355 Healdsburg Avenue is a leading producer of raku pottery.

Wander a few blocks farther to the local library at Center and Piper streets to look through the impressive Sonoma County Wine Library, with just about everything you'd want to know about wine including some 1,000 volumes from the Vintner's Club Library of San Francisco.

If you are curious about the early history of the area, the local museum will oblige with original photos and newspapers going back to 1878. Check out the four churches that are part of town history; they date from 1868 to 1892.

After you've browsed away the morning and have built up an appetite, there are several possibilities for a food break. Healdsburg Coffee Company Café on Center Street has homemade soups and sandwiches for a light lunch. The Downtown Bakery and Creamery has delectable desserts. Or stop at the Healdsburg Charcuterie and Deli or the Salami Tree Deli for the fixings for a picnic to be enjoyed on the plaza or in the vineyards.

Alternatively, you can have an elegant lunch by driving just north of town to the impressive twin-towered Chateau Souverain winery. You'll enjoy some of the best food to be found anywhere in wine country, accompanied by delicious wine and an unbeatable vineyard view. Lunch here is a happy way to avoid footing the hefty tab for dinner. Then you can save your dinner splurge for the other gourmet choice in town, Madrona Manor.

Those who can't afford either place need not despair. Three excellent and more moderately priced choices are right on the town plaza: cozy Bistro Ralph with a diverse menu, Samba Java with lively decor and eclectic offerings with a Caribbean flavor, and Tre Scalini for Tuscan specialties that have pleased many reviewers.

You'll certainly want to sample some of the area wineries. One of the better tours is the Simi Winery, one of the oldest establishments in the region. The original 1890 stone winery is still used as an aging cellar.

No tours are offered at Chateau Souverain, though visitors are welcome at the handsome tasting room, and it's worth a stop just to see the building. Two other well-known local wineries, Piper Sonoma (the California headquarters of the renowned French champagne maker) and Clos du Bois, do offer tours, but only by advance appointment. This is the policy at many of the small wineries in the area, so it's always best to call ahead if you want to tour. Most places are happy to have you drop in anytime for tastings.

For an attractive drive through vineyard and orchard country, try West Dry Creek Road. The Dry Creek Valley is noted for Zinfandel, and Dry Creek Vineyards, a turnoff from West Dry Creek Road on Lambert Bridge Road north of Healdsburg, is one place to try it. Farther north above Geyserville, and not to be missed, is Ferrari-Carano, with a lavish Italian villa and magnificent gardens.

If you follow the road south of Healdsburg, the name will eventually change to Westside Road. The Hop Kiln Winery on Westside Road is one of the most popular with photographers. The distinctive three chimneys were actually used in the past to roast hops for beer. Visitors are welcome to picnic on the grounds.

Westside runs into the River Road along the Russian River. Keep driving for a few miles and you'll come to the ivy-covered brick Korbel Winery, where an excellent tour of the champagne-making process is offered. The building is surrounded by lovely gardens, which are also open for tours.

Highway 128 north through the Alexander Valley is another scenic byway. Johnson's Alexander Valley Wines is a unique stop. This small family-run vineyard is perhaps the only winery anywhere with a pipe organ in the tasting room.

These same roads are excellent for bike tours, but if you want something a little more unusual, vineyard tours are available in an antique 1920s car, not a bad idea if you want to do some serious tasting.

Come Sunday, you might want to take advantage of the great outdoors around Healdsburg. Healdsburg Memorial Beach offers a warm swimming spot on the Russian River plus picnic grounds. Canoeing on the river is a favorite pastime.

About 11 miles northwest is Lake Sonoma. It was created when the Warm Springs Dam went up in 1982, turning part of the Dry Creek Valley into 2,700 acres of water. The lake is a popular place for fishing and boating, and there is a nice overlook with picnic tables. Adjoining the lake is a visitors' center and fish hatchery, where a self-guided tour shows you how salmon and steelhead spawn. The fish are tranquilized so that eggs and sperm can be removed; the eggs are artificially inseminated and incubated, and later the baby fish are released into the stream. Which part of the process you can see depends on the time of year, but the whole story is shown on video.

If all of that sounds too strenuous, there are more wineries to visit and more good food to be enjoyed. They are among the special pleasures that make a trip to Healdsburg a treat.

Area Code: 707

DRIVING DIRECTIONS   Healdsburg is off Highway 101, about 75 miles north of San Francisco, 105 miles from Sacramento.

ACCOMMODATIONS   _Belle de Jour Inn,_ 17276 Healdsburg Avenue, Healdsburg, 95448, 433-7892, E–EE, CP • _Camellia Inn,_ 211 North Street, Healdsburg, 95448, 433-8182, M–E, CP • _Grape Leaf Inn,_ 539 Johnson Street, Healdsburg, 95448, 433-8140, M–E, CP • _George Alexander House_, 423 Matheson Street, Healdsburg 95448, 433-1358, M–E, CP • _Healdsburg Inn on the Plaza,_ 116 Matheson Street, Healdsburg, 95448, 431-2153, EE, CP • _Madrona Manor Inn,_ 1001 Westside Road, Healdsburg, 95448, 433-4231, E–EE • _Campbell Ranch Inn,_ 1475 Canyon Road, Geyserville, 95441, 857-3476, E–EE, CP.

DINING   _Souverain Restaurant,_ Chateau Souverain Winery, 400 Souverain Road, Geyserville, 433-3141, Friday through Sunday, EE • _Madrona Manor Inn_ (see above), EE • _Tre Scalini,_ 241 Healdsburg Avenue, Healdsburg, 433-1722, M–E • _Samba Java,_ 109-A Plaza Street, Healdsburg, 433-5282, I–M • _Bistro Ralph_, 109 Plaza Street, Healdsburg, 433-1380, M.

SIGHTSEEING   _Healdsburg Museum,_ 221 Matheson Street, 431-3325. Hours: Tuesday to Sunday 11 A.M. to 4 P.M. Free • **Vintage auto vineyard tours:** _Belle de Jour Inn,_ 433-7892.

WINERY TOURS   _Simi Winery_, 16274 Healdsburg Avenue, Healdsburg, 433-6981. Tours: Daily 11 A.M., 1 P.M., and 3 P.M. • _Korbel Winery,_ 13250 River Road, Guerneville, 887-2294. Tours: May to September, daily 10 A.M. to 3:45 P.M., rest of year to 3 P.M. • _Ferrari-Carano Vineyards and Winery,_ 8761 Dry Creek Road, Healdsburg, 433-433-6700. Tours by appointment, tasting room daily 10 A.M. to 5 P.M., fee for tasting. Many other winery tours are available by appointment; most tasting rooms are open without appointment from 10 A.M. to 4 or 5 P.M. For a complete listing of area wineries, ask for the Russian River Wine Road map at your inn or at the Healdsburg Chamber of Commerce.

ACTIVITIES   **Canoe rentals:** _Trowbridge Canoe Trips,_ 20 Healdsburg Avenue, 433-7247 • _Bike rentals and tours: Spoke Folk Cyclery,_ 249 Center Street, 433-3919.

INFORMATION   _Healdsburg Area Chamber of Commerce,_ 217 Healdsburg Avenue, Healdsburg, CA 95448, 433-6935, in California (800) 648-9922.

On the Blossom Trail in Fresno

Is spring a little late in your neighborhood? Getting tired of clouds and chill? For a quick fix, head south to Fresno. Here in California's agricultural heart, springtime begins as early as February, when thousands upon thousands of fruit trees burst into bloom, transforming the landscape into clouds of pink and white. The pastel panorama lasts well into April.

This isn't a city normally thought of as a weekend getaway, but it's well worth an excursion just to follow the Fresno Blossom Tour, a 67-mile route that has been developed by the local visitors' bureau to make the most of this annual show. While you're here, you can explore a flower-filled, fast-growing city with a surprising number of attractions. Afterwards, take in some glorious mountain scenery at three national parks in the neighborhood. You might even try some exciting springtime rafting on the King River. Should you want to make this a romantic getaway, a posh chateau awaits, hidden away north of town in Oakhurst, on the way to Yosemite National Park.

Seeing the lush farmlands of the San Joaquin Valley, it's hard to believe that this area was once barren desert. A man named Moses Church developed the first canals providing irrigation, eventually transforming Fresno County from barren to bountiful. In his honor, the canals are widely known as "Church ditches."

He is one of many local legends, men like rancher Clovis Cole, who became known as the nation's wheat king, and Francis Eisen, founder of the area wine industry and the creator of the raisin industry (in 1875, some of his grapes were left out too long and dried on the vine). Theo Kearney, the prime mover of Fresno's raisin industry at the end of the century, became a millionaire, earning titles such as "Raisin King of California" and "Prince of Fresno." His ranch house mansion is one of the local attractions.

Today Fresno County leads the nation in agriculture, producing more than 200 commercial crops worth a whopping $2.6 billion per year. Simonian Farms, at the corner of Clovis and Jenson avenues, is a good place to get a sense of the wide variety of the area's bounty. The farm has been in the same family for three generations and has become a local tourist attraction for its labeled fields, vineyards, and orchards yielding 60 varieties of produce, from apples to kiwis to persimmons to ten kinds of peaches. There's a shop, too, for stocking up on nuts and dried fruit, including some of the plumpest, tastiest raisins around.

The farm is one of the stops on the Blossom Trail, a self-guided drive out of Fresno. Write or call ahead for a free copy of the Blossom

Trail brochure, or pick one up at your lodging. Almonds, apricots, and plums flower from mid-February to early March, peaches and nectarines later in March, and apples and citrus fruits remain for the latecomers who visit in April.

The brochure tells about the different trees along the way and points out other things to watch for. You'll learn a bit about how things are grown in California, passing "trellis trees" that make for easier picking; the Friant-Kern Canal, part of the Central Valley Project, which currently supplies water for agriculture; and fields using drip irrigation, a system developed to conserve that precious water. Stop for a while in Reedley to see some of the oldest homes in Fresno County, in a town founded by one of the area's wheat barons. The quaint downtown has some interesting shops. One is the Mennonite Quilting Center, where you can watch patchwork techniques demonstrated Monday to Saturday. A gift shop sells the colorful completed quilts, with proceeds aiding the Mennonite Relief Fund. An annual sale and auction is held in early April each year at Fresno Pacific College, featuring lots of crafts displays, quilting demonstrations, and food booths.

Fresno can occupy more than a day on its own. A premier attraction is the Chaffee Zoo in Roeding Park, a lovely green oasis in the city. The reptile house here is the only one in the world in which computers control the environment for individual residents. You can come eye-to-eye (against the glass) with boa constrictors, pythons, alligators, poison frogs, and other creepy creatures, some of them rare species in gorgeous Technicolor.

Another standout exhibit is the tropical rain forest, a 20,000-square-foot enclosure where visitors travel along a walkway to view 50 species of iguanas, monkeys, turtles, and brightly hued birds, roaming or flying free amid tropical foliage, enclosed only by netting.

Natural barriers rather than cages are the rule here, so you can visit a series of habitats such as an African plain, and visit with elephants, lions, tigers, a rhino, and a grizzly bear, who is often found enjoying a waterfall shower. The zoo includes 700 species of mammals, birds, and reptiles.

This is great diversion for families, and right next door is a playground. Then comes Storyland, a mini–amusement park offering little ones a castle to explore, a giant beanstalk to climb, and more small animals. In season, there are performances at Pinocchio's Theater, a children's playhouse. If spring showers spoil the family fun, there's year-round indoor ice skating at the Icelandia rink in town.

The Fresno Metropolitan Museum of Art, History and Science merits a look for its permanent collection of photos by former resident Ansel Adams, plus an Asian Gallery, Dutch old masters, and the Salzer collection of European and American still-life paintings. The museum also has changing exhibits, so check for the current shows.

Fresno boasts two fine historic homes, both on the National Register. The Kearney Mansion Museum, reached via a nine-mile palm-lined driveway, is the expansive, carefully restored ranch house of raisin king Theo Kearney. It is in a 225-acre park, amid what was once Kearney's 5,000-acre Fruit Vale Estate west of town. The estate was donated to the University of California on his death in 1906. The European furnishings are elegant, and the guided tour is filled with tales of Kearney's colorful career.

The Meux Home Museum is a Victorian beauty built in 1888 by a pioneer Fresno physician, and has been authentically furnished to reflect Fresno's earliest years.

For Victorian or any other kind of antiques, head for the Tower District, Fresno's art deco area, and the big Fulton's Folly mall on Oliver Street, a cooperative housing some 80 dealers. There are also some interesting bookstores and vintage-clothing stores in this neighborhood, so take time to browse.

The centerpiece of the area is the restored 1920s Tower Theater at 815 East Olive Street, a former movie theater that now features live entertainment. Nearby, there's deco dining at the Daily Planet, beer tasting at Butterfield's Brewery, and a scattering of clubs featuring jazz. Roger Rocka's Music Hall, across from the Tower, is a popular dinner theater presenting Broadway musicals.

The visitors' bureau will provide a walking tour of some of the 1920s and 1930s homes in nearby residential areas. If you don't want to walk, take a drive to admire the flowering shrubs that adorn almost every neighborhood in town. They are especially pretty if you head north toward Fig Garden Village, the upscale shopping center that houses the two best restaurants in town, Harlands for fine California cuisine and the Ripe Tomato for country French. A local specialty is Basque food, served up family style in big quantities at the Hotel Santa Fe or the Basque Hotel. George's in the downtown Galleria looks like a diner but serves authentic Armenian food that is a delicious bargain for lunch, and is one of the city's favorite spots for a hearty breakfast.

Fresno's Farmer's Market is another interesting stop, an enclosed mall at 2736 Divisadero, with produce stalls, a variety of shops, and lots of ethnic restaurants.

Fresno is surrounded by magnificent wilderness areas leading to its national park neighbors. Spring runoff means exciting white-water rafting on the nearby King River, amid the magnificent Sierra Nevadas. And as the snow melts, the waterfalls in the parks should be at their tumultuous best. It is a 55-mile drive east on Highway 180 to Kings Canyon and Sequoia, 92 miles north on Highway 41 to Yosemite.

Oakhurst is a little town about midway between Fresno and Yosemite, and it offers a hidden treasure for those in search of gourmet dining and luxurious lodging. In this unlikely spot, a motel-filled small town in the mountains, Austrian chef Erna Kubin-Clanin created a restaurant that would be at home in the south of France. The tile-roofed, white stucco Mediterranean-style retreat, filled with Old World ambience, opened in 1984 and proceeded to win rave reviews from *Gourmet* magazine and noted food writers countrywide, who continue to heap praises on Erna's prix fixe six-course dinners. The menu, which might be described as California-European, changes nightly, varying with the season to take advantage of fresh local produce. There's a special menu each year when the elderberry harvest comes in at the end of July.

In 1991, to accommodate many diners reluctant to face a long drive back after such a repast, Erna opened an appropriately lavish place for overnight guests, a veritable castle at the top of the hill. Dubbed Chateau du Sureau, it is sumptuous, with marble and stone walls and floors and French antiques, tapestries, and hand-painted tiles. For those who can afford the tab, it is the ultimate escape for a Blossom Trail weekend—or any time at all.

Area Code: 209

DRIVING DIRECTIONS   From north or south, Fresno is reached via Highway 99. Highway 41 runs west to the central coast area, and turns north into Yosemite National Park. Highway 180 East leads to Sequoia and Kings Canyon national parks. Fresno is 185 miles from San Francisco, 170 miles from Sacramento.

PUBLIC TRANSPORTATION Fresno is served by Delta, United Express, American, USAir, and Skywest airlines, as well as by Amtrak.

ACCOMMODATIONS   Fresno choices are all motels or hotels. *Piccadilly Inn,* 2305 West Shaw Avenue, Fresno, 93711, 226-3850, nice neighborhood, a best bet, M • *Centre Plaza Holiday Inn,* 2233 Ventura Street, Fresno, 93709, 268-1000 or (800) 465-4329, attractive hotel downtown, M • *Fresno Hilton,* 1055 Van Ness, Fresno, 93721, 485-9000, another center-city hotel, M • *San Joaquin Suites,* 1309 West Shaw, Fresno, 93711, 225-1309, all suites, M–E • *Sheraton Smugglers Inn,* 3737 N. Blackstone, Fresno, 93726, 226-2200 or (800) 742-1911, M • *Chateau du Sureau,* P.O. Box 577, Oakhurst, 93644, ultimate luxury, EE, CP.

DINING   *Ripe Tomato,* 5064 North Palm Avenue, 225-1850, French bistro, M–E • *Harlands,* 722 West Shaw, 225-7100, American nouvelle, M–E • *Daily Planet,* 1211 North Wishon, 266-4259, contemporary California, M–E • *Nicola's,* 3075 N. Maroa, 224-1660, popular Italian, M • *Santa Fe,* 935 Santa Fe Avenue, 266-2170, big Basque dinners, I–M • *Original Basque Hotel,* 1102 F Street, 233-2286, I–M •

George's Shish Kebab, Galleria, 2405 Capitol Street, 264-9433, Armenian, breakfast and lunch, I • *Erna's Elderberry House,* 48688 Victoria Lane, Oakhurst, 683-6800, widely praised, reservations essential, prix fixe multicourse dinner, EE. Also lunches, Wednesday to Friday, and Sunday brunch.

SIGHTSEEING *Chaffee Zoological Gardens,* Roeding Park, 894 West Belmont, Fresno, 498-2671. Hours: March to October, daily 9 A.M. to 5 P.M.; rest of year, 10 A.M. to 4 P.M. Adults, $4.50; ages 3 to 14, $2, parking fee, $1 • *Storyland,* Roeding Park near the zoo, 264-2235. Hours: May 1 to Labor Day, daily 10 A.M. to 5 P.M.; rest of year, weekends only. Closed in December. Adults, $2.75; ages 3 to 14, $1.75 • *Kearney Mansion Museum,* 7160 West Kearney Boulevard, Fresno, 441-0862. Hours: Friday to Sunday 1 P.M. to 4 P.M. Adults, $3; ages 13 to 17, $2; ages 3 to 12, $1 • *Meux Home Museum,* Tulare and R streets, Fresno, 233-8007. Hours: June to August, Thursday to Sunday noon to 3:30 P.M.; rest of year, Friday to Sunday noon to 3:30 P.M. Adults, $3; ages 13 to 17, $2; ages 5 to 12, $1 • *Metropolitan Museum of Art, History and Science,* 1555 Van Ness Avenue, 441-1444. Hours: Wednesday to Sunday 11 A.M. to 5 P.M., on Wednesday to 7 P.M. Adults, $4; children, $3; free first Wednesday each month • *Fresno Art Museum,* 2233 North First Street, 441-4220. Hours: Tuesday to Friday 10 A.M. to 5 P.M.; Saturday, Sunday noon to 5 P.M. Adults, $2; children, $1; free on Tuesday • **White-water rafting:** *Kings River Expeditions,* 233-4881, or *Spirit White Water Rafting,* (408) 373-3275 or (800) 400-RAFT • **Ice skating:** Icelandia Rink, 2455 N. Marks, 275-1119.

INFORMATION *Fresno Convention and Visitors' Bureau,* 808 M Street, Fresno, CA 93721, 233-0836 or (800) 788-0836.

Golden Daffodils in Gold Country

Forget about the calendar. It's the carpet of gold on Daffodil Hill that officially marks the arrival of spring in Amador County, with a six-acre show of bulbs in bloom that brings admirers from miles around.

Perhaps they're partial to gold around here because that's what these towns in the center of the mother lode were all about. The Kennedy Mine in Jackson was one of the richest in the state. Sutter Creek's Lincoln Mine made its own share of millionaires, and Sutter Creek has mellowed into one of the most attractive towns remaining from Gold Rush days.

As a bonus, this is scenic countryside, rising into the wooded High Sierra foothills. The region is also gaining note for its Zinfandel wines, and there are several small family-owned wineries that welcome visitors. Add the dazzle of daffodils and there's every good reason to plan a visit.

Sutter Creek is the recommended home base, with several inns. Three of the best are within walking distance of one another and the town's best restaurants.

For elegance, choose the Foxes, named for the fox decor throughout the 1857 home. Many rooms have fireplaces and old-fashioned tubs; all include breakfast in bed, served on a silver tray. The Sutter Creek Inn next door was a country estate in 1859 and still has country charm, with canopy beds, fireplaces, antiques, and rooms set around attractive lawns and gardens. The main house has a cozy living room that invites company with a piano, magazines, and games.

Right across Main Street is Ron and Nancy's Palace, a onetime saloon turned atmospheric restaurant with stained glass, old-fashioned lighting, and a long-sociable bar. Stepping inside is a return to the 1850s.

The Hanford House, just around the corner, looks more motel than inn from the outside, but there's nothing standard about the rooms. They are big and comfortable, and each has a distinct decor and personality, from country to Oriental. Next door is Perlargonium, an odd name for a pretty restaurant ensconced in a Victorian house.

Farther down Hanford Street is the Grey Gables Inn, which brings a touch of English decor to the area in rooms named for English poets.

A stroll beneath the wooden arcades along Sutter Creek's picturesque Main Street makes a fine start to the day. Ask your innkeeper for the local walking-tour map giving a rundown on the history of each building.

Captain John Sutter, a wealthy early Sacramento settler, lent his name to several towns that sprang up when he sent his men out into the Sierra foothills to search for timber. James Marshall, the first to discover gold, was the foreman of Sutter's Mill in Coloma, about an hour away. The stampede that followed became Sutter's downfall when all his employees took off to search for their own fortunes. Sutter tried his luck at mining, too, but he wasn't successful. He might take some small comfort from the plaque in his honor in front of the City Hall.

Far more fortunate was a merchant named Leland Stanford, who acquired a stake in the Lincoln Mine as settlement for a customer's debts. Stanford struck it rich, then sold his shares and used the proceeds for other investments, including railroads that would make him a multimillionaire and leading citizen, eventually governor and founder of a great university. The home Stanford occupied while tending to his mining business is near the corner of Spanish and Amelia streets.

Along Main Street are many fine homes dating from the 1860s or earlier, with architecture ranging from modest New England–style clapboard to Victorian gingerbread. The Methodist church at the southern end of town dates to 1862.

Behind many of the facades are shops, including Sutter Creek Antiques, combining wares of eight dealers, and Fine Eye, a high-quality gallery of crafts, jewelry, woodwork, and art. Creekside Unusual Shops and Antiques also brings several shops under one roof, and a detour onto Eureka Street leads to more antiques and browsing in a quaint setting.

Also on Eureka Street is the Knights Foundry, the only water-powered foundry in the United States, which has been operating since 1876. If you want to see the process, castings are usually poured on Friday afternoons, and you can watch from the door. Sparks fly madly when the furnace is opened. The red-hot molten iron flows into heavy pots, which are lifted by a crane and carefully emptied into molds.

When you are ready to see daffodils, head out on the Sutter Creek–Volcano Road, a lovely drive along the creek with a leafy canyon on either side. The creek is a popular spot for latter-day treasure seekers who want to try their luck at panning for gold.

The drive to Daffodil Hill could be done in about 30 minutes, but you'll no doubt want to stop for a while in the hamlet of Volcano, population 85. The name came from the town's location, in a mountain basin that reminded settlers of the crater of a volcano. In its best days Volcano was a lively place with two theaters, three breweries, and several dance halls. It boasts several California "firsts," including the first private law school, public library, and little theater group.

But Volcano's day in the sun was short. The gold ran out, and so did the residents, in search of better diggings. The handful of weathered buildings are untouched remains of the glory days, evoking a more powerful nostalgia for the past than do many elaborately restored towns. A general store remains, as do the old jail and the schoolhouse, now a private residence. And there is still a theater troupe, known as the Volcano Community Theater and housed in a former 1850s cigar emporium.

The most impressive spot is the St. George Hotel, which has been in operation since 1863. The bar is full of colorful artifacts, including a ceiling papered with dollar bills and calling cards. Dinner is served on weekends in the pleasant old-fashioned dining room. There is one seating, and one menu—whatever the lady of the house feels like cooking that night. It is dependably tasty, and very moderately priced, but note that advance reservations are essential. Planning ahead is a good idea also if you want to take in a show at the theater after dinner.

Volcano takes on an especially festive air in early April, when the annual Rites of Spring celebration lines the town's quaint lanes with booths offering art and handcrafts of every kind, from carved wooden animals to watercolors. The event is timed for what is usually the peak of the daffodil blooms. It's worth checking the dates before making your weekend plans.

Keep driving uphill from Volcano into the pine-scented high country, and follow the signs for three miles to Daffodil Hill. The hill is actually private property, a ranch that is opened to the public by the McLaughlin family, who generously share the pleasure of their colorful spring landscape. According to family legend, the first bulbs in this brilliant display were brought overland in the family's covered wagon. They were planted by the children as a memorial when their mother died in 1857. That began a tradition, with more bulbs planted each year, and eventually people began coming by to admire the spring show.

The bigger the crowds, the more bulbs the McLaughlins planted. There are now more than 400,000 daffodils and tulips of 200 varieties covering a six-acre hillside. On any day there may be as many as 2,500 people on hand, admiring the flowers as well as the historic farm buildings and the resident animals and birds, which include 14 peacocks.

It's all free and available to the public for four weeks, as soon as the blooms are out. That usually means mid-March to mid-April, but because the ranch is in high country, a lingering winter can delay things. It's best to phone the Amador County Chamber of Commerce to check before planning an early trip.

Another worthwhile detour is beyond Volcano on Route 88 to Pine Grove. The Indian Grinding Rock State Historic Park, an important Miwok Indian site, is one of the best-done Indian museums around. The star attraction is an enormous grindstone measuring 173 by 82 feet, covered with rock carvings known as petroglyphs. The rock was a well-used gathering place. The stone has more than a thousand holes or cups known as "chaw'ses," once used by tribal women to pulverize acorns and seeds. Besides an attractive museum, the park also boasts a re-created village including bark dwellings, a roundhouse, and an Indian ball field. If Indian history interests you, this is worth a trip. There is a choice inn in Pine Grove, as well, the Druid House, on a ridge with soaring views.

A Sunday excursion from Sutter Creek might also lead in other directions. One option is to acquaint yourself with some gold mine lore. The Amador County Museum in Jackson is an excellent place to learn how gold mining actually was done. The main building, a vintage 1859 home, is realistically furnished right down to the kitchen tools. Out back in the stable are working scale models of one of the area's largest mines, the Kennedy Mine, including a replica of its enormous Tailing Wheel No. 2. There's a short multimedia explanation of the mining operations plus a guide on hand to answer further questions. A stamp mill from the North Star Mine is also on display.

Two of the original Kennedy tailing wheels can be seen north of town on Jackson Gate Road. They are enormous, 58 feet in diameter, and moved as much as 850 tons of the residue known as tailings each day from the Kennedy and Argonaut mines. Kiosks tell the history of the wheels.

Across the highway, the frame of the Argonaut Mine is also visible. The worst tragedy in the gold era took place here in 1922, when a fire killed 47 miners.

Jackson itself is a commercial center, but there are still some traces of the past on Water Street, and it merits a short stroll. The National Hotel is the heart of the history, with a rowdy western saloon that is still very much in operation.

To complete your Gold Rush education, drive north on Highway 49 to Coloma and the 240-acre Marshall Gold Discovery State Park. It is an especially inviting destination in spring, when the poppies are in bloom.

The high point of the park is a realistic reproduction of the mill that stood near the American River, where Marshall found the flakes that changed California's destiny. Other exhibits include a restored miner's cabin, a Chinese general store, an old jailhouse, stagecoaches, a reconstruction of Marshall's cabin, assorted mining artifacts, and a gallery of art in the 1855 Friday House.

To get your bearings, start with the film at the Gold Museum explaining what happened at Sutter's Mill—and the stampede to California that followed. Exhibits at the museum include some of James Marshall's memorabilia.

Marshall is buried on the hill overlooking the mill. In 1890, the state honored him belatedly by erecting his statue over the grave.

A second outing from Sutter Creek has nothing to do with history. It is a visit to some of Amador County's wineries. There were nearly 20 at last count, all using a custom bottle embossed with the Amador Vintners logo. Most specialize in zingy Zinfandels. The Stonebridge Winery is in rural Sutter Creek. Many more wineries are clustered in the Shenandoah Valley near the town of Plymouth, north of Amador City. From Highway 49, take Shenandoah Road (E 16) and you'll find a number of vineyards along this road, Shenandoah School Road, and the connecting Steiner Road.

Most wineries offer tours and tastings on weekends, a pleasant way to wind up your visit. Several have scenic picnic grounds, and some have art galleries as well. Sobon Estate includes the Shenandoah Valley Wine Museum, tracing the history of farming and wine-making in the area. Since these are small operations, a call ahead is always a good idea. The Amador Vintners Association publishes a helpful free guide and map giving hours and phone numbers of all area wineries. It is available from the Amador County Chamber of Commerce.

Area Code: 209

DRIVING DIRECTIONS   Sutter Creek is on Highway 49, the main route following the mother lode through gold country. It is 140 miles from San Francisco, 45 miles from Sacramento.

ACCOMMODATIONS *The Foxes,* 77 Main Street, Sutter Creek, 95685, 267-5882, E–EE, CP • *Hanford House,* 61 Hanford Street, Sutter Creek, 95685, 267-0747, M–E, CP • *Sutter Creek Inn,* 75 Main Street, Sutter Creek, 95685, 267-5606; I–M weekdays, M–E Friday, Saturday, and holidays; CP • *Grey Gables Inn,* 161 Hanford Street, Sutter Creek, 95685, 267-1039, M–E, CP. **Other nearby options:** *The Heirloom,* 214 Shakeley, Ione, 95640, 274-4468, M, CP • *Druid House,* 13887 Druid Lane, Pine Grove 95665, 296-4156 or (800) 276-5781, M–E, CP • *Imperial Hotel,* P.O. Box 195, Amador City, 95601, 267-9172, I–M.

DINING *Ron & Nancy's Palace,* 76 Main Street, Sutter Creek, 267-9852, M • *Pelargonium,* 1 Hanford Street, Sutter Creek, 267-5008, M • *St. George Hotel,* Main Street, Volcano, 296-4458, M • *Imperial Hotel,* Amador City (see above), M.

SIGHTSEEING *Daffodil Hill,* Volcano, acres of daffodils and other bulbs, usually open for four weeks mid-March to mid-April; phone 296-7048 or contact Amador County Chamber of Commerce for current dates and exact driving directions. Donation • *Amador County Museum,* 225 Church Street, Jackson, 223-6386. Hours: Wednesday to Sunday 10 A.M. to 4 P.M. Donation. Mine model tours, Saturday and Sunday, $1 • *Volcano Community Theatre,* P.O. Box 88, Volcano, 95689, 223-HOME. Phone for current offerings • *Indian Grinding Rock State Historic Park,* 14881 Pine Grove—Volcano Road, Pine Grove, 296-7488. Hours: Museum open weekdays 11 A.M. to 3 P.M., weekends 10 A.M. to 4 P.M. Park open daily 8 A.M. to 5 P.M. Parking fee, $5.

WINERIES Phone to verify hours before making a trip. *Amador Foothill Winery,* 12500 Steiner Road, Plymouth, 245-6307. Hours: Tours and tastings, weekends noon to 5 P.M. Picnic tables • *Santino Winery,* Steiner and Upton roads, Plymouth, 245-6878, tastings and informal tours. Hours: Daily by appointment, noon to 5 P.M. • *Shenandoah Vineyards,* 12300 Steiner Road, Plymouth, 245-4455. Hours: Tastings daily 10 A.M. to 5 P.M. Contemporary art gallery • *Sobon Estate,* 14430 Shenandoah Road, Plymouth, 245-6554. Hours: Tasting room daily 10 A.M. to 5 P.M. Self-guided tours of museum and wine cellars, scenic picnic grounds • *Charles Spinetta Winery,* 12557 Steiner Road, Plymouth, 245-3384. Hours: Tastings daily 10 A.M. to 5 P.M. Wildlife art gallery • *Stoneridge,* 13862 Ridge Road East, 2.2 miles east of Highway 49, Sutter Creek, 223-1761. Hours: Tastings and tours Saturday and Sunday noon to 4 P.M.; other times by appointment.

INFORMATION *Amador County Chamber of Commerce,* P.O. Box 596, Jackson, CA 95642, 223-0350.

By the Bay in Monterey

Monterey has been attracting visitors for almost four centuries. The magnificent natural setting at the head of Monterey Bay was discovered early, and this town was thriving when San Francisco was only a village. It was a capital under Spanish and Mexican flags, and a favored home port for fishermen and whalers. In 1835, Richard Henry Dana in *Two Years Before the Mast* described Monterey as "decidedly the pleasantest and most civilized looking place in California." It was here that the state of California was born.

Thanks to one of the best preservation efforts on the West Coast, this rich history has been preserved. More than 40 structures built before 1850, including some prize adobe homes, remain in the midst of modern Monterey. Add matchless sea vistas and one of the country's top aquariums, and it's no wonder the town is often packed.

To avoid the crowds, a good time for a visit is early spring, before the summer fog and the annual deluge of tourists roll in. Time your visit for the first weekend in March and you can take in "Dixieland Monterey," an informal festival that brings lots of lively bands to town. Or come in April, "Adobe Month," for tours through privately owned historic homes.

One excellent plan for sightseeing is to work backward in time, taking in the best of the contemporary sights on Saturday and saving your history for Sunday.

Start early, before the crowds arrive on Fisherman's Wharf. Ignore the tacky souvenir stands and walk on to the end of the pier to concentrate on the glorious salty panorama—the forest of tall masts in the marinas near shore, the fishing fleet at the municipal wharf, the playful sea lions' croaking calls from below, and the endless Pacific beckoning in the distance. You'll begin to understand Monterey's eternal appeal.

Then come back to land and appreciate more beauty on the stroll along the Shoreline Park path leading to Cannery Row, the bawdy, brawling old sardine fishing and canning area made immortal by John Steinbeck. The former warehouses and canneries are now filled with restaurants, inns, and shops, but the architecture has been preserved, so there's still a lingering flavor of bygone days. Many shops are touristy and disappointing, but there are a few surprises, such as the turn-of-the-century carousel in the Edgewater Packing Company complex.

At the end of the Row is the Hovden Cannery, once the largest of them all. It now houses the town's biggest attraction, the Monterey Bay Aquarium, which averages 1.7 million visitors each year. The crowds are well deserved, but once again, it's best to get here early to avoid the worst of the crush. You can get your hand stamped, leave during the busiest part of the day, and return when the numbers thin. Allow plenty of time; you'll want to stay a while.

Built in 1984 with a $55 million gift from computer whiz David Packard, who was the cofounder of Hewlett Packard, the aquarium is an outstanding educational and research facility that is also just plain fun. It puts you up close to sharks, sea otters, and other denizens of Monterey Bay, more than 6,500 specimens representing 525 species of the fishes, mammals, and plants found in the surrounding waters.

The show-stopper exhibit is the three-story-high Kelp Forest, the tallest aquarium exhibit in the world. It gives a deep-sea diver's view of a dynamic underwater community with a host of fishes weaving among giant fronds of kelp. The big crowd pleaser, however, is the sea otter exhibit, a close-up look at these frisky, frolicking mammals from above as well as through windows.

There is excitement at both exhibits during feeding time, especially at the Kelp Forest, where divers descend to feed by hand. Otter feedings are at 10:30 A.M., 1:30 P.M., and 3:30 P.M., Kelp Forest feedings at 11:30 A.M. and 4 P.M.

There's so much more to see. Monterey Bay Habitats features sharks, bat rays, salmon, striped bass, and other ocean fishes in settings that re-create the bay's deep reefs, sandy sea floor, and shale reefs. The wharf area comes complete with actual 30-year-old pilings. The Great Tide Pool contains sea stars, anemones, crabs, and a variety of fishes; it opens into the Bay, so sea otters and harbor seals drop in occasionally to feed or rest. The pool also serves as a training ground for injured adult sea otters and orphaned pups, who can sometimes be seen swimming with the staff, being prepared to return to the ocean.

Hands-on activities let you touch bat rays and tide pool animals, steer video cameras, and peek into microscopes. Visitors can also share video images broadcast from a remote-controlled research submarine, views that take you 6,000 feet down into the canyon at the bottom of the Bay.

By the time you read this, there will likely be even more to see. A new aquarium wing, due to debut in two parts, in 1996 and 1998, will be devoted to the marine life in the deep water where Monterey Bay meets the Pacific Ocean. It will include a million-gallon exhibit of open ocean fishes, including seven-foot ocean sunfish, schooling tunas and bonita, green sea turtles, and barracuda. Another gallery will feature beautiful jellyfish species and seldom-seen fishes and other animals from deep in the Monterey submarine canyon. New learning activities are planned especially for families with younger children.

On Sunday, it's time for Old Monterey and the "Path of History," a winding tour through downtown created to link together the most important sites of Monterey's impressive past. The first stop is the State Park Visitor Center at the Stanton Center on Custom House Plaza, where you can join a guided walking tour or pick up a self-guiding tour brochure. A free short film here gives an overview of the town.

This is also headquarters for the Maritime Museum of Monterey, an overview of the explorers, conquerors, and fishermen who shaped the region's history. The historic Fresnel lens of Point Sur Lighthouse illuminates the museum. Standing almost two stories tall, its 1,000 prisms serve as a beacon to exhibit areas on two floors. The museum boasts an exceptional collection of ship models from early clipper ships to fishing boats to World War II vessels.

Monterey's story began with Spanish explorer Sebastian Vizcaino, who arrived in 1602 and claimed the land for his king. In 1770 the Presidio of Monterey was established, a fort that served as the first capitol of the area known as Alta California. It housed the Spanish governor and his generals and missionaries. Father Junipero Serra founded the first of the Franciscan missions here in 1770, though it was later moved to Carmel. Monterey remained the capital when the Mexicans declared their independence from Spain in 1822. The Stars and Stripes went up in 1846, when marines and sailors occupied Monterey and claimed California for the United States. The 1849 constitutional convention paving the way for statehood the next year was held here in Colton Hall.

The Path of History runs along Pacific Street to the water, back up Alvarado, and along several adjoining avenues, leading past the spot where the conquistadors landed, then along a stretch of whalebone sidewalk to the Royal Chapel, on to Colton Hall, and past many antique-filled adobe homes, some open for touring, some privately owned.

Several are of special note. The Royal Chapel, built in 1795, which makes it Monterey's oldest building, marks the site of the earliest presidio. The present structure was built of stone when the first chapel on this site was lost to a fire. Colton Hall has been restored upstairs as it was when the constitutional convention was held here. On the grounds is the Old Monterey Jail that Steinbeck wrote about in *Tortilla Flat*.

The 1822 Custom House, used by the Mexicans for collecting the port duties that helped support Alta California, is the oldest government building on the West Coast. It now displays items from a typical ship's cargo of the 1830s. The Larkin House is one of the best examples of the architectural mix of Spanish adobe and American woodwork and balconies that became known as the Monterey Colonial style. Interesting House and Garden Tours are offered on weekends by Monterey State Historic Park; check for current schedules.

Other buildings that may be toured include Casa del Oro, a restored general store; Pacific House, now a museum of California history; and two more interesting adobe homes, the 1820 Casa Soberanes and the 1829 Cooper-Molera Adobe. Another notable address is the Robert Louis Stevenson House, where the writer rented a room in 1879 while he gained inspiration for his novel *Treasure Island*. California's first theater is along the way, and still offers old-fashioned melodramas in the evening.

Many of the structures open to the public are part of the Monterey State Historic Park, and one ticket gains admittance to all.

When you've had an ample helping of history, there's more than enough left to do to fill any remaining time. The Monterey Peninsula Museum of Art is worth a stop for exhibits that include the art of California, Asia, and the Pacific Rim. Cyclers and walkers alike are welcome along Monterey's shoreline Recreation Trail, spanning the entire coastal boundary of the city and giving access to some of the most scenic coastline in the state. Bikes can be rented in several locations.

Families may want to visit the colorful playground in the Dennis the Menace Park near Lake El Estero. It was built by Dennis's creator, cartoonist Hank Ketchum, a local resident.

A variety of boats can take you out into the Bay for sailing or fishing excursions, naturalist cruises, or whale watching in season. If you want to view the Bay from the bottom up, you can take a trip on the *Nautilus,* an underwater viewing vessel that lets you come eye-to-eye with the sea creatures down below. Kayaks can be rented for a different view of the rugged coastline, and hang-gliding lessons are available near town for the adventuresome. There are many public golf courses in the area, including those famous links at Pebble Beach. Or you can visit Victorian Pacific Grove or take the fabled 17-Mile Drive. See page 129 for more details.

Monterey offers some choice lodging, though the best are on the pricey side. At the top of the scale, Old Monterey Inn is lovely, an English Tudor home set in lush gardens and beautifully furnished with antiques. The Spindrift is a surprise, a posh small hotel smack in the middle of Cannery Row, with many fireplaces and smashing ocean views. The Hotel Pacific in town is a striking blend of Spanish ambience and modern good taste, and the Jabberwock is a bed-and-breakfast charmer. Those watching the budget will find a host of motel choices with convenient locations and the very modest Del Monte Beach Inn, where a continental breakfast comes with the reasonable rates. If these don't please, Pacific Grove and Carmel are just a few minutes away, with dozens of additional possibilities.

Diners should be alerted that Café Fina is the one recommended oasis amid the hurly-burly of Fisherman's Wharf. And everyone should save for a splurge dinner at Fresh Cream, Monterey's culinary pride. It is not only the best in town; many put it among the best in the state.

Area Code: 408

DRIVING DIRECTIONS Monterey is located on the northern head of the Monterey Peninsula, about 125 miles south of San Francisco, 210 miles from Sacramento. From Highway 1 or Highway 101, take Route 68 west into town.

ACCOMMODATIONS *Old Monterey Inn,* 500 Martin Street, Monterey, 93940, 375-8284, EE, CP • *Spindrift Inn,* 652 Cannery Row, Monterey, 93940, 646-8900, in California (800) 841-1879, EE, CP • *Hotel Pacific,* 300 Pacific Street, Monterey, 93940, 373-5700, in California (800) 554-5542, EE, CP • *The Monterey Hotel,* 406 Alvarado Street, Monterey, 93940, (800) 727-0960, recently restored in-town hotel, M–E, CP • *Merritt House,* 386 Pacific Street, Monterey, 93940, 646-9686, E, CP • *The Jabberwock,* 598 Laine Street, Monterey, 93940, 372-4777, whimsical B&B home, E–EE, CP • *Sand Dollar Inn,* 755 Abrego Street, Monterey 93940, 372-7551, good choice in the long lineup of motels, I–M • *Del Monte Beach Inn,* 1110 Del Monte Avenue, Monterey, 93940, 649-4410, budget choice, I, CP. See also Pacific Grove, pages 127 to 131, and Carmel, pages 228 to 232.

DINING *Fresh Cream,* 100-C Heritage Harbor, 375-9798, nouvelle French, superb, E–EE • *Montrio,* 414 Calle Principal, 648-8880, newcomer in an old firehouse, rave reviews, M-E • *Café Fina,* 47 Fisherman's Wharf, 372-5200, seafood with an Italian accent, best on the wharf, M–E • *Cibo,* 301 Alvarado Street, 649-8151, Mediterranean look, Italian menu, I–M • *Spadaro's,* 650 Cannery Row, 372-8881, modern decor, striking water views, Italian, M • *Sardine Factory,* 701 Wave Street, 373-3775, longtime landmark, seafood and continental dishes, M–E • *Kiewels Café,* 100-A Heritage Harbor, 372-6950, views, outdoor dining, M • *Clock Garden,* 565 Abrego Street, good spot for lunch, I, or moderately priced dinners, I–M • *Tarpy's Roadhouse,* 2999 Monterey-Salinas Highway (Route 68), 647-1444, worth the drive for creative dishes served in a rustic stone house or on the patio, M • *Tutto Buono,* 469 Alvarado Street, 372-1880, good Italian deli, I • *Old Monterey Café,* 489 Alvarado Street, Monterey, 646-1021, recommended for breakfast. See also Pacific Grove, pages 127 to 131, and Carmel, pages 228 to 232.

SIGHTSEEING *Monterey Bay Aquarium,* 886 Cannery Row, Monterey, 648-4888. Hours: Daily 10 A.M. to 6 P.M. Adults, $11.25; ages 3 to 12, $5 • *Stanton Center—Maritime Museum and History Center,* Custom House Plaza, Monterey, 373-2469. Hours: Daily 10 A.M. to 5 P.M. Adults, $5; ages 6 to 12, $2 • *Path of History Walking Tour,* 44 sites, including Monterey State Historic Park Properties. *Colton Hall Museum,* Madison and Pacific streets, Monterey, 646-5640. Hours: Spring and summer, daily 10 A.M. to noon and 1 to 5 P.M.; rest of year to 4 P.M. Free • *Monterey State Historic Park,* 525 Polk Street, Monterey, 649-7118. Hours: Most sites March to October, daily 10 A.M. to 5 P.M.; rest of year to 4 P.M.; some properties may have different hours.

Walking tours leave at 10:15 A.M., 12:30 P.M., and 2:30 P.M. Homes open for touring: Pacific House and Custom House, free. Other sites: Adults, $5 for all; children, $3. Individual buildings: Adults, $2; children, $1 • *Monterey Peninsula Museum of Art,* 559 Pacific Street, Monterey, 372-7591. Hours: Tuesday to Saturday 10 A.M. to 4 P.M.; Sunday from 1 P.M. Suggested donation, $2 • *Nautilus,* Fisherman's Wharf, 647-1400. Underwater viewing vessel. Hours: Daily except Tuesday, 9 A.M. to 5 P.M., check for specific tour schedules. Adults, $24.95; children, $14.95 • *17-Mile Drive,* Pebble Beach, 625-8426. Hours: Daily sunrise to sunset. Per car, $6.

ACTIVITIES **Bike rentals:** *Adventures by the Sea,* 299 Cannery Row, 372-1807; *Aquarian Bicycles,* 444 Washington Street, 375-2144; *Bay Bikes,* 640 Wave Street, 646-9090 • **Water sports:** *Monterey Bay Kayaks,* 693 Del Monte Avenue, 373-KELP; *Adventures by the Sea,* 299 Cannery Row, 372-1807 • **Hang gliding:** *Western Hang Gliders,* Marina State Beach, Marina, 384-2622 • **Fishing:** *Monterey Sport Fishing,* 90 Fisherman's Wharf, 372-2203; *Randy's Fishing Trips,* 66 Fisherman's Wharf, 372-7440 • **Diving and snorkeling:** *Dive Monterey,* 598 Foam Street, 655-DIVE or (800) 348-4645. Check the Chamber of Commerce for more complete current listings.

INFORMATION *Monterey Peninsula Chamber of Commerce,* P.O. Box 1770, 380 Alvarado Street, Monterey, CA 93942, 649-1770.

High Marks for Palo Alto

Without its university, Palo Alto might be like any other affluent Peninsula community—a nice place to live but not one you would tend to visit. It is the presence of Stanford, one of America's foremost centers of learning, that makes this a West Coast destination equivalent to England's Oxford or Cambridge—or to that other Cambridge, across the country.

Like all great universities, this campus has many cultural attractions, including the Stanford Museum and its Rodin Sculpture Garden, and prize collections from minerals to Hemingway memorabilia. To add to the pleasure of a visit, Stanford is not only one of the leading universities in the West, but one of the most beautiful anywhere. And as a springtime bonus, the Filoli Estate, with one of the Bay Area's outstanding gardens, is just a few minutes' drive away.

Palo Alto itself is a pleasant community, with scores of bookstores and a very special upscale shopping center. There's a hidden mini-museum guaranteed to delight anyone who ever played with a Barbie doll. The Allied Arts Guild in neighboring Menlo Park adds to the weekend agenda with a group of art and crafts stores in a beautiful Spanish setting. Make the necessary advance reservations at Filoli and plan for a pleasant mix of books, browsing, and blossoms.

A good plan is to spend Saturday in Palo Alto and Menlo Park and head for Filoli on Sunday. And the first stop is Stanford.

Leland Stanford, who amassed a fortune as one of the founders of the Central Pacific Railroad, established the school with his wife, Jane, in 1885 as a memorial to their only child, Leland Junior, who had died of typhoid at age 15 a year earlier. Stanford was determined that it would be a significant memorial, the first great university in the West. Two years after the college opened in 1891, Stanford died, leaving the university an endowment of $25 million, a sum said at the time to be more than the endowments of Harvard and Columbia universities combined.

Stanford's visions of greatness were scoffed at in his day, but even he could not have foreseen some of the great innovations that would come from a school that is now an acclaimed educational center for science, engineering, and medicine. Birth control pills, gene splicing, heart transplants, the IQ test, the laser, the microprocessor, and music synthesizers all were born at Stanford, and the school was the spawning ground for the nearby high-tech Silicon Valley. In 1994, the 1,324 faculty members included ten Nobel laureates, five Pulitzer Prize winners, and 142 members of the American Academy of Arts and Sciences.

The campus was built on Stanford's 7,200-acre Palo Alto horse farm. He collaborated with Frederick Law Olmsted, the famous landscape architect best known for designing New York's Central Park, to create a monumental plan, but he was firm in wanting a distinctively California design. The original buildings show a Romanesque influence, but they are prime examples of the mission style, with sandstone walls, arches, and long low arcades lending all the serenity of a cloister. There is a sense of peace and order throughout the campus.

Palm Drive, the formal promenade leading to the school, is an impressive entry, lined with tall stately palms that set the campus off from the rest of the town. It leads to an outer Quadrangle, where there is parking. To the left as you face the campus, just down Serra Street, is the information center in the lobby of Memorial Hall, across the street from the Hoover Tower, a campus landmark. Free one-hour campus tours led by students leave from the center at 11 A.M. and 3:15 P.M., and they are highly recommended for giving a sense of student life and an idea of some of the exceptional prospective students who hope to continue the high Stanford standards. If you'd rather see things on your own, campus maps are available at the information center.

Arched gates lead to the Inner Quad, 12 original classroom buildings joined by arcades. The showplace at the far end is Memorial

Church. On its facade is a wonderful tile mosaic of the Sermon on the Mount. The vaulted interior is lit up by glowing stained glass. Behind the altar is a replica of the Sistine Chapel's *Last Supper,* re-created with special permission from the Vatican.

Beyond the Inner Quad are the campus center and the Tresidder Union Building, where you will find another information center on the bottom floor. Come on a sunny day and you can join the students enjoying outdoor barbecue for lunch in the center court. Stanford has more than 13,000 students today, almost equally divided between graduate and undergraduate.

Take the elevator to the top of the 285-foot Hoover Tower for an overall view of the campus, the quadrangles, the red-tiled roofs, and the surrounding landscape, stretching into the foothills of the Santa Cruz Mountains. The 35-bell carillon in the tower makes melodious music if you are lucky enough to be on hand when it is played.

The tower is also home to the Hoover Institution, the well-known conservative think tank and research center, named for a Stanford graduate, former president Herbert Hoover. The tower contains many historical documents, including Hoover's private collections, over 30 million documents.

Exhibits in the Leland Stanford, Jr., Museum span the ages, with art ranging from Renaissance paintings to California landscapes. The Asian art is notable, but the most famous exhibit is the golden spike that Leland Stanford drove to mark the completion of the transcontinental railroad. Unfortunately, the museum suffered extensive damage in the earthquake that hit the campus a few years ago, and is not expected to be open until 1996 or 1997.

Adjoining the museum is the Rodin Sculpture Garden, boasting 20 of Auguste Rodin's original bronze-cast sculptures, including *The Thinker.* It is one of the largest collections of the sculptor's work to be seen outside France.

More art awaits in the campus art gallery, and a stop at the Green Library is a must for Hemingway fans. The Charles D. Field Collection of Ernest Hemingway includes first editions, letters, and galley proofs. Some of the specialized collections, such as the minerals at the School of Earth Science, the Anthropology Museum exhibits showing current research, and the shell collection at the Geology Department, are open Monday to Friday only, but the Red Barn, the restored Victorian stable built by Leland Stanford more than a century ago, is always open to visitors.

There are many specialized tours of the campus by appointment, including campus sculpture, the Hoover Archives, the Jasper Ridge Biological Preserve, and, for high-tech enthusiasts, the Stanford Linear Accelerator Center, a research center operated by Stanford for the U.S. Department of Energy. The facility has a two-mile-long linear accelerator that generates high-energy electron beams.

When you've done the campus sights, go back to Palm Drive, which runs directly into University Avenue, the main street of Palo Alto. Book lovers will find lots to occupy them. The Stanford Bookstore, Staceys, Chimaera Books and Records, and Megabooks, a used-book store, are right on University. Printer's Ink on California Street is a café and bookstore in one—a good place for a break.

Not far off University on Waverly Avenue is the Barbie Doll Hall of Fame, showing examples of Barbie, Ken, and their friends from 1959 to 1989. This offbeat attraction is the private collection of Evelyn Burkhalter, who will likely be on hand to tell you about some of the rarest items. She claims to have more than 14,000 dolls, 99 percent of all the dolls and outfits manufactured during that 30-year period. The earliest dolls now sell for as much as $1,000 each. This is an irresistible stop, a nostalgic look at American fashion and hairdos accurately reflected in the costumes of Barbie and Ken.

The rest of the shops on shaded, brick-paved University Avenue are standard suburban, but the Stanford Shopping Center is something else again. Located not far from campus, it is the only shopping center in the world owned by a university and is interesting for its landscaping and artwork as well as its stores. There are six major department stores here, and a range of wares from gourmet foods at the Oakville Grocery to African antiquities at the Tribal Eye. Stop at Max's Opera Café for deli sandwiches served up by singing waiters and waitresses.

Menlo Park begins just a couple of blocks from University Avenue. It offers antiques shops and the very special Allied Arts Guild. The guild's Spanish-style buildings, courtyards, fountains, and murals create an Old World atmosphere for the artisans who demonstrate their crafts. A tasty lunch is served indoors and in the courtyard; it is prepared by volunteers, with proceeds going to the Lucille Salter Packard Children's Hospital. To reach the guild, turn north on El Camino Real and make a left on Cambridge Avenue to the intersection of Arbor Road.

On weekdays Menlo Park offers an added attraction in the headquarters of *Sunset* magazine. There are free guided tours of the offices and test kitchens, and anyone is welcome to enjoy a walk outside in the serene gardens.

Palo Alto and Menlo Park have plenty of motel and hotel lodgings to accommodate visitors. The cream are the classy Garden Court Hotel, downtown in Palo Alto, and Menlo Park's Stanford Park, near the university. The Victorian on Lytton is an elegant little bed-and-breakfast inn, while the Cowper Inn is a homey, less expensive alternative.

Restaurants in this sophisticated college town run the gamut from classic French to natural foods. Theatreworks, the local theater group, is an excellent repertory company. The opulently restored Stanford Theater shows film classics made before 1950. If you visit in May, you can take in the Palo Alto Film Festival, featuring the work of Bay Area moviemakers. To find out more about activities on campus, phone the Tresidder Student Union at 723-4311.

On Sunday head west to I-280, get off at Edgewood Road, and then go north on Canada Road to the Filoli Estate, a property of the National Trust for Historic Preservation. The 43-room Georgian-style mansion may look familiar: It is the home that was shown on TV's "Dynasty." It was built by William Bourn, heir to the Empire Mine fortune, in 1916. The Empire was the richest of all the California gold mines, as you can see by Bourn's opulent estate. The name, incidentally, is a contraction of Bourn's motto: "Fight, Love, Live." The most memorable room in the mansion is the ballroom, with 16-foot ceilings and columns gilded with gold from the mine.

Filoli's 16 acres of formal gardens are at their most glorious in April and May, when the daffodils and tulips are in bloom and the magnolias and other flowering trees provide a pastel canopy. There are 250 varieties of camellias and daphne. The gardens are laid out as separate "garden rooms" among parterres, terraces, lawns, and pools. The Walled Garden, the centerpiece of the grounds, is particularly lovely. It includes a Chartres Cathedral Garden representing a stained-glass window with boxwood borders, a precisely planted Dutch Garden, and a wonderful corner called the Wedding Place, with a fifteenth-century Venetian fountain. Remember that Friday is one of the few days that you can visit without an advance reservation.

Flower lovers headed back toward San Francisco may take a detour off I-280 at Hickey Boulevard and have a last taste of floral finery at Rod McLellan Company on El Camino Real, the nursery better known as "Acres of Orchids." This immense greenhouse and showroom is filled with exquisite orchids in a rainbow of colors. One-hour behind-the-scene tours are offered daily. It's a safe bet you won't be able to resist coming home with an orchid bouquet.

Area Code: 415

DRIVING DIRECTIONS   Palo Alto is 33 miles from San Francisco, 155 miles from Sacramento. Take Highway 101 to the Embarcadero Road exit or I-280 to the Sand Hill Road exit.

ACCOMMODATIONS   _Garden Court Hotel,_ 520 Cowper Street, Palo Alto, 94301, 322-9000 or (800) 824-9028, EE • _Best Western Creekside Inn,_ 3400 El Camino Real, Palo Alto, 94306, 493-2411, M • _The Victorian on Lytton,_ 555 Lytton Avenue, Palo Alto, 94301, 322-8555, M–E • _Cowper Inn,_ 705 Cowper Street, Palo Alto, 94301, 327-4475, I–E • _Stanford Park Hotel,_ 100 El Camino Real, Menlo Park, 94025, 322-1234, EE • _Adella Villa,_ 122 Atherton Avenue, Stanford,

94039, 321-5195, Tyrolean-style home north of Palo Alto, with heated pool, M, CP.

DINING *Chantilly Français,* 530 Ramona Street, Palo Alto, 321-4080, traditional French, E • *L'Amie Donia,* 530 Bryant Street, Palo Alto, 323-7614, popular French bistro, excellent chef, E • *Maddalena's,* 544 Emerson Street, Palo Alto, 326-6082, classic formal continental dining, E–EE; and *Café Fino,* same address and phone, informal Italian bistro next door, M • *Il Fornaio,* Garden Court Hotel (see above), 853-3888, popular Italian, I–M • *Blue Chalk Café,* 630 Ramona Street, Palo Alto, 326-1020, Southern home cooking, hush puppies, fried catfish, etc., M • *Nataraja Restaurant,* 117 University Avenue, Palo Alto, 321-6161, Indian specialties, I • *Osteria,* 247 Hamilton Avenue, Palo Alto, 328-5700, Italian, expect crowds, I–M • *MacArthur Park,* 27 University Avenue, Palo Alto, 321-9990, ribs, mesquite grill, California cuisine, M • *Max's Opera Café,* Stanford Shopping Center, Palo Alto, 323-6297, lunch, I; dinner, M • *Gordon Birsch Brewery,* 640 Emerson Street, Palo Alto, 323-7723, brew pub serving interesting ethnic dishes, M • *Dal Baffo,* 878 Santa Cruz Avenue, Menlo Park, 325-1588, classic continental menu, E; good choice for an elegant lunch, M • *Allied Arts Guild Restaurant,* 75 Arbor Road, Menlo Park, 324-2588, best bet for lunch, I • *Beau Séjour,* 170 State Street, Los Altos, 948-1388, nouvelle cuisine with an Oriental twist, highly rated, E.

SIGHTSEEING *Stanford University* (note that campus facilities may be closed during holidays, exam weeks, and breaks between sessions). **Information centers:** Memorial Hall: Daily 10 A.M. to 4 P.M., 723-2560. Hoover Tower Lobby: Daily 10 A.M. to 4 P.M., 723-2053. Tresidder Memorial Union: Weekdays 8 A.M. to 10 P.M., weekends 10 A.M. to 10 P.M., 723-4311 • *Hoover Tower Observation Platform,* 723-2560. Hours: Monday through Sunday 10 A.M. to 11:45 A.M., 1 P.M. to 4:30 P.M. Adults, $1; under 13, $.50 • *Stanford Museum,* 723-3469 (check to be sure it has reopened). Hours: Tuesday through Friday 10 A.M. to 5 P.M., weekends 1 P.M. to 4 P.M. Free • *Rodin Sculpture Garden,* always open • *Green Library Special Collections.* Hours: Monday to Friday 9 A.M. to 5 P.M., Saturday 9 A.M. to noon. Rare books exhibited in the Hoover Institution exhibit pavilion and Green Library lobby • *Stanford Linear Accelerator Center,* 926-2204, guided tours by appointment. Free • *Barbie Doll Hall of Fame,* 433 Waverly Avenue, 326-5841. Hours: Tuesday to Friday 1:30 P.M. to 4:30 P.M., Saturday 10 A.M. to 2 P.M. Admission, $4 • *Allied Arts Guild,* Cambridge Avenue and Arbor Road, 325-3259. Hours: Monday to Saturday 10 A.M. to 5 P.M. Free • *Sunset Magazine, Lane Publishing Company,* Willow and Middlefield roads, Menlo Park, 324-5479. Hours: Guided tours Monday to Friday 10:30 A.M. and 2:30 P.M. Gardens open Monday to Friday 9 A.M. to 4:30 P.M. Free • *Filoli Estate,* Canada Road, Woodside (off I-280, Edgewood Road exit to Canada Road), 364-2880. Hours: Mid-February to early November, guided tours of house and gardens by reservation only, Tuesday to Thursday 10 A.M. and 1 P.M. except April, May, and June 9:30 A.M., 11:30 A.M., and 1:30 P.M. Saturday tours are every half hour from 9:30 A.M. to 1:30 P.M. No reservations needed for self-guided tours on Friday and the first Saturday and second Sunday of each month. House and garden tour: Adults, $8; ages 2 to 12, $4. Docent-led 3-mile nature hike of the estate: Adults, $5; children, $1 • *Rod McLellan's Acres of Orchids,* 1450 El Camino Real, South San Francisco, 871-5655. Hours: Daily 9 A.M. to 6 P.M., tours 10:30 A.M. to 1:30 P.M. Free.

A Touch of Cape Cod in Mendocino

When the Hollywood producers of TV's "Murder, She Wrote" went searching for a perfect New England village, they didn't have to journey across the continent. They simply headed up the California coast to Mendocino.

This surprising charmer, perched high on a coastal headland, grew up during the Gold Rush, when surrounding redwood forests were supplying lumber for the booming Bay Area. It was built and populated by lumbermen from the East Coast, accounting for why their homes, featuring peaked roofs, picket fences, and clapboard facades, seem as much Cape Cod as California. The look is so unique in this part of the country that the entire town is on the National Register of Historic Places.

When the logging economy declined in this century, Mendocino was rediscovered by San Francisco artists. They moved here for low rents and scenic inspiration, and in 1959 founded the Mendocino Art Center, a place for classes and exhibits, which is still flourishing.

Next came the weekenders, to browse through the studios, walk the headlands for ocean views, and seek out the quaint homes that were rapidly turning into bed-and-breakfast inns. Today this tiny town of 1,000 is usually packed with strollers—and enough sophisticated inns, shops, and restaurants to accommodate them. Come before the summer high season for all the charm without the crowds.

Many of the artists have been priced out, but Mendocino still has the air of an escapist's haven, partly because of the number of long-bearded men seen around town.

Exploring the shops and galleries is the first order of the day. Don't expect bargains in this well-discovered art center, but do expect an endless variety of temptations. Main Street and parallel Albion and Ukiah streets, and the small lanes tucked in between, are filled with Victorian homes and Cape Cod cottages that have been transformed into galleries and shopping enclaves.

Look for the Mendocino Art Center Showcase, 560 Main Street, one of the best contemporary galleries, and Artists Co-op, 45270 Main Street, showing work by local painters, with artists in residence upstairs. In addition to art, the Highlight Gallery, at 45052 Main, specializes in handcrafted furniture. It's worth a detour to the Mendocino Art Center, 45200 Little Lake, for excellent changing exhibits of local and regional art and crafts.

As for the shops, their wares include Irish knits, handmade quilts, antiques, and novelties from seashells to toys. There are interesting selections of offbeat jewelry and clothing. In Mendocino, even the T-shirts are artistic.

When wallets are depleted, the place to learn a bit about the town's unusual history is the Kelley House Museum. This 1861 home is the headquarters of Mendocino Historical Research, Inc., and is filled with photos and the memorabilia of early residents. Fine gardens bordering the house include a pond and wildflower and camellia walks.

Deciding where to stay in Mendocino is a delightful dilemma. Inns located in town have an advantage. They are within walking distance of shops and restaurants, sparing the need to vie for parking spaces. A top choice is the John Dougherty House, which carries out the Cape Cod theme with country antiques in an 1867 home and cottages. The exterior of Blair House Inn will be familiar to fans of "Murder, She Wrote," where it appears as the home of Jessica Fletcher. Agate Cove Inn is a cottage colony set on a bluff with dramatic views; the Joshua Grindle Inn has old-time charm and some quarters in a picturesque water tower, while the Mendocino Hotel is a historic haven of Victoriana in the center of town with luxurious suites hidden in a garden just behind the inn.

Some of the sublime hideaways on the Coast Highway just below Mendocino are hard to resist, even if they do require a drive to town. Among the best are the posh contemporary Stanford Inn by the Sea and, in Little River, Glendeven and Heritage House. Heritage House, made famous as the setting for the 1978 movie *Same Time, Next Year,* is a luxurious cottage colony on 37 prime seaside acres. Glendeven is farther from the ocean but is romantic nevertheless, a secluded enclave of farmhouse and barns artistically decorated and with its own barn art gallery.

Two other luxury spots not to be overlooked are the Stevenswood Lodge, a striking, art-filled modern hideaway tucked into the redwoods, and the Albion River Inn, perched on a bluff with dazzling water views.

The most renowned of Mendocino's restaurants is Café Beaujolais, though the food surpasses the no-frills ambience. Breakfasts here are also legendary, though they are now served only on weekends. Other best dinner bets are the airy, arty 955 Ukiah or the warm Victorian MacCallum House. Dinner in front of the fire in the MacCallum bar is a cozy bargain.

Along the coast, the Little River Restaurant, Ledford House, and the Albion River Inn are highly recommended locally.

No trip to Mendocino is complete without walking its wild and beautiful coastline. Ford House, an interpretive center on Main Street, provides guides to Mendocino Headlands State Park. The park includes trails along the sandstone bluffs that enclose the town on three sides, plus a path down to a small beach along the mouth of Big River. The bluffs are the perfect spot to see a spectacular Mendocino sunset over the Pacific. This park is the favorite spot for whale watching in winter and is home to a summer concert series featuring members of the San Francisco Symphony.

Another popular local outdoor adventure is a canoe trip up the Big River. The placid water leads through a narrow forested canyon and into the habitat of harbor seals, great blue herons, ospreys, and wood ducks. Catch-a-Canoe at the Stanford Inn has all the equipment for an excursion.

South of town, Little River is the entranceway to Van Damme State Park and a hiking trail through the luxuriant growth of Fern Canyon, a lush trail meandering along a clear coastal stream between steep canyon walls. The Fern Canyon trail overlooks the Pygmy Forest in the park's southeastern section. Trees here are 50 to 100 years old, but have grown only a few feet tall and an inch in diameter, a quirk of nature caused by acidic soils and poor drainage. The Discovery Trail leads through the forest.

There are two worthwhile stops on Highway 1 north of Mendocino. At Jughandle State Reserve, five wave-cut terraces let you climb a "stairway" up the dunes and ridges that make up the region's unique landscape. On the highest and oldest level are one- to three-foot dwarf pine and cypress trees, one of several pygmy forests found in this area.

Mendocino Coast Botanical Gardens offers a delightful stroll along paths through a 47-acre seaside garden. Some of the outstanding displays are rhododendrons, azaleas, fuchsias, and heathers. As a bonus, the trails lead to a bluff with outstanding views of the rugged shoreline.

Luckily, the loggers did not fell all of the ancient redwood trees, so Mendocino also can be a home base for an excursion through the heart of the forest aboard the California Western Railroad, a string of old-fashioned coaches fondly known as the "Skunk Train." There are half-and whole-day excursions from the station in Ft. Bragg, ten miles north of Mendocino. A look at the redwoods will convince you that you are a long way from Cape Cod.

Area Code: 707

DRIVING DIRECTIONS Mendocino is located on Highway 1, the Pacific Coast Highway. The quickest route from the south is via Highway 101 north to Cloverdale, then west on Highway 128 to the coast. It is about 160 miles north from San Francisco, 200 miles from Sacramento. A slower, more scenic route is north along Highway 1, paralleling the roller-coaster coastline.

ACCOMMODATIONS *Agate Cove Inn,* 11201 Lansing Street, Box 1150, Mendocino, 95460, 937-0551 or (800) 527-3111, M–EE, CP • *Blair House,* 45110 Little Lake Street, Box 1608, Mendocino, 95460, 937-1800, M, CP • *John Dougherty House,* 571 Ukiah Street, Box 817, Mendocino, 95460, 937-5266, M–EE, CP • *Headlands Inn,* Howard and Albion streets, Box 132, Mendocino, 95460, 937-4431, E–EE, CP • *Joshua Grindle Inn,* 44800 Little Lake Road, Box 647, Mendocino 95460, 937-4143 or (800) GRINDLE, E–EE, CP • *Mendocino Hotel and Garden Suites,* 54080 Main Street, Box 587, Mendocino, 95460, 937-0511 or (800) 548-0513, I–EE • *Mendocino Village Inn,* 44960 Main Street, Box 626, Mendocino, 95460, 937-0246, M–E, CP • *Whitegate Inn,* 499 Howard Street, Box 150, Mendocino, 95460, 937-4892, E–EE, CP • *Stanford Inn by the Sea,* Highway 1, Box 487, Mendocino, 95460, 937-5615, E–EE, CP • *Glendeven,* 8221 N. Highway 1, Little River, 95456, 937-0083, E–EE, CP • *Heritage House,* 5200 N. Highway 1, Little River, 95456, 937-5585, EE, MAP • *Stevenswood Lodge,* 8211 N. Highway 1, Box 170, Little River, 95460, 937-2810 or (800) 421-2810, E–EE, CP • *Albion River Inn,* 3790 North Highway 1, Box 100, Albion, 937-1919, E–EE, CP • *Grey Whale Inn,* 615 N. Main Street, Ft. Bragg, 95437, 964-0640 or (800) 382-7244, M–E, CP • **More bed-and-breakfast inn lodgings:** Contact Mendocino Coast Innkeepers Association, P.O. Box 1141, Mendocino, 95460. For free reservations in homes, inns, or cottages, phone Mendocino Coast Reservations, (800) 262-7801.

DINING *Café Beaujolais,* 961 Ukiah Street, Mendocino, 937-5614, M–E • *955 Ukiah Street* (at that address), 937-1955, M • *MacCallum House* (see above), M • *Mendocino Hotel* (see above), M • *Little River Restaurant,* Coast Highway, Little River, 937-5942, M • *Ledford House,* Coast Highway, 937-0282, M–E • *Albion River Inn* (see above), M • *North Coast Brewing Company,* 444 N. Main Street, Ft.

Bragg, 964-BREW, congenial spot for informal fare and homemade brew, M.

SIGHTSEEING   *Kelley House Historical Museum,* 45007 Albion Street, 937-5791. Hours: Friday to Monday 1 P.M. to 4 P.M. Donation, $1 • *Ford House,* Main Street, 937-5804. Hours: Daily 10 A.M. to 4 P.M. Donation, $1 • *Mendocino Headlands State Park,* surrounds the town of Mendocino, information from Ford House (above) • *Van Damme State Park,* Highway 1, three miles south of Mendocino, information from Ford House (above). Parking fee, $5 • *Mendocino Coast Botanical Gardens,* Highway 1 south of Ft. Bragg, 964-4352. Hours: March to October, daily 9 A.M. to 5 P.M.; rest of year, 10 A.M. to 4 P.M. Adults, $5; ages 13 to 17, $3; under 12, free • *California Western Railroad* (Skunk Train), P.O. Box 907, Ft. Bragg, 964-6371, excursions to Willets leave mornings daily, half-day trips to Northspur morning and afternoon. Phone for current schedule. Day trip: Adults, $26; age 5 to 11, $12. Half-day trip: Adults, $21; children, $10.

INFORMATION   *Ft. Bragg–Mendocino Coast Chamber of Commerce,* P.O. Box 1141, Ft. Bragg, CA 95437, 961-6300 or (800) 726-2780.

Fun and Frills in Ferndale

Ferndale is a rare combination of nostalgia and wacky fun.

The village is a rainbow patchwork of prize Victorian homes surrounded by gardens and greenery. Main Street, listed on the National Register of Historic Places, could be a turn-of-the-century Hollywood set. In fact, it *was* the set for a recent movie called *Outbreak,* starring Dustin Hoffman.

But scenery is not all that sets this town apart; Ferndale's personality comes from the people who live here. Many of the colorful residents are artists, and some would do credit to a scriptwriter's fantasy. A case in point: Hobart Brown, the originator of the World Championship Kinetic Sculpture Race, a madcap three-day mega-event each Memorial Day weekend.

When you start with what many call California's best-preserved Victorian town and finish with one of the craziest races in all 50 states, a memorable time is guaranteed.

First comes a place to stay, and you'd better plan far ahead to reserve at Ferndale's much-photographed peach-and-gold Gingerbread

Mansion. No frill is too fancy here, from hand-dipped chocolates to a suite with his-and-hers claw-foot tubs for bubble baths in front of the fireplace.

If there's no room, all is not lost, for the Shaw House Inn is another vintage (1854) charmer, the town's oldest house, set in a tangled garden bordered by a white picket fence. And more small inns and motels are opening to accommodate the growing number of visitors.

All the same, Ferndale's lack of major touristy facilities is part of its appeal. The whole town covers just a square mile, and there are no modern intrusions such as streetlights and parking meters. They don't even have mail delivery—everyone just stops by the post office.

A good plan is to begin with a walk to admire the fine homes on the side streets off Main Street. If you're dying to get inside, the Gingerbread Mansion shows its downstairs parlors from noon to 2 P.M. daily, and an outlying residence, Fern Cottage, is open for tours by appointment.

The fanciest houses are often referred to as "butterfat palaces," since they belonged to rich dairy farmers who built them with proceeds from the herds that grazed on the plains of the nearby Eel River. The flourishing dairies gave the town the nickname "Cream City" in the 1800s. Descendants of those first immigrant farmers are still living in the area, some still tending herds on the land. The Danish and Portuguese halls on Main Street are evidence of their continuing influence. More town history can be gleaned at the little Ferndale Museum.

The beautifully preserved Main Street was inspired by one determined resident, Viola Russ McBride. In the early 1960s, when she heard local businessmen complaining about their aging buildings, McBride feared for the town's future and began to preserve the Victorian architecture by buying up property, which was cheap in those days. She offered it to artists for low rents, spawning the town's eclectic population.

Others hopped on the preservation bandwagon, and in 1962 the local newspaper editor called in a paint consultant and recruited store owners to join in a Main Street "paint up," rejuvenating downtown in one whirlwind weekend. Once peeling paint was replaced by vibrant Victorian hues, the beauty of the architecture suddenly was visible. Visitors began to appear, and civic pride grew. By the 1970s the town had passed a design-review ordinance to ensure that the charm would remain. Recently, when the transportation department wanted to replace the 75-year-old bridge across the Eel River, residents protested and saved the graceful arches of their bridge, the oldest reinforced concrete spandrel bridge in the world.

To appreciate the diverse residents who make this town unique, you need only step into the shops behind the bright facades. For example, the Swedish owners of the Gazebo at 475 Main Street not only sell Scandinavian crafts and folk art but are prime movers in the Midsummer Festival Association, which has sponsored an annual gala in mid-June for more than 40 years. The fun at the fairgrounds includes foods such as aebleskiver (Danish doughnuts), open-face sandwiches, Swedish meatballs, and Danish pastries, plus folk dancers in traditional costumes and many displays of Scandinavian crafts and culture.

Carlos Benemann says he won his store at 405 Main in the continuing poker game held in the back of Becker's, the café next door. He has filled the store with an extraordinary stock of out-of-print and rare books. Many of the volumes are worth thousands.

To get an idea of the whimsy of Joseph Koches, you need only look at the business card for his Blacksmith Shop at 455 Main. The card features drawings of Koches's cats Spotty, Gina, and Thumper, who are labeled "Owners." The human owner is a onetime orthopedic surgeon's assistant who was taken with Ferndale, took advantage of the low rent, and made a new career of forging wrought-iron gate latches and fire pokers. Like many of the artisans who came for the reasonable cost of living, he lives behind his shop.

As you stroll Main Street, notice the old movie house transformed into the Ferndale Repertory Theater, a mainstay in town for two decades and a worthwhile evening's entertainment.

Some local artists contribute to the work seen in the many galleries along Main; others welcome visitors to their studios. Stop into Stan Bennett's studio at 427 Main and the bearded sculptor will show off some of the fascinating whimsy of his intricate metal kinetic wonders, such as spinning planes, the *Magic Marble Machine,* and other moving wire sculptures that are displayed in galleries up and down the Pacific Coast.

At Hobart Galleries you can meet the exuberant Hobart Brown, who may show you his work or invite you upstairs to see his Victoriana-jammed living quarters, a veritable museum. He will certainly tell you all about the event he spawned back in 1969, when he raced his "pentacycle," fashioned from a child's tricycle, down Main Street in a contest against another metal sculptor, Jack Mays, who was driving a homemade tank. The next year dozens showed up to join them, racing weird creations made from discarded junk, and the Kinetic Sculpture Race was on.

These days more than 50 moving sculptures enter the annual World Championship Cross-Country Kinetic Sculpture Race. The contestant's vehicles must roll *and* float (no easy feat) in order to navigate the tricky 38-mile course across shifting sand dunes, the Eel River, Humboldt Bay, mudflats, and freeway traffic. There's hot competition to come up with the craziest-looking contraption, giving rise to entries in the shape of alligators, lady's slippers, and unidentifiable objects with names like

Quagmire Queen. The Kinetic Sculpture Race Museum at 580 Main displays many amusing and amazing past entries.

Following the course of the race affords the opportunity to visit neighboring towns, since the competition begins in the plaza in Arcata on noon Saturday and runs through Eureka before ending with a flourish in Ferndale on Memorial Day Monday.

After the contestants clear out, there's time to stroll Arcata's plaza and admire its artistic murals. The Chamber of Commerce offers walking and driving tours of mid-1800s architecture. If you want to stay awhile, this pleasant small coastal college town has much natural beauty to enjoy. Come to the Arcata Marsh and Wildlife Sanctuary for bay views and great bird watching. Docents from the local Audubon Society chapter lead walks every weekend.

The second day of racing starts at Eureka's Bayshore Mall at 9 A.M. and proceeds to the bay crossing. The town of Eureka is the commercial center for the North Coast. Owing to its location on sheltered Humboldt Bay, near the heart of the coastal redwoods, Eureka was an important seaport for the early loggers, as well as for the miners and fishermen. A legacy from those days is the magnificent Carson Mansion, said to be the most-photographed Victorian home in California. It was built in 1885 by lumber magnate William Carson, supposedly as a project to keep mill workers busy during the slow season.

Today Eureka boasts two showplace inns, An Elegant Victorian Mansion, a restored 1888 East Lake Victorian on a rise overlooking the city, and the Carter House, a handsome Victorian haven with an unusual history. Owner Mark Carter, using plans he found in an 1890 book, built the house from scratch, down to the 40,000 fish-scale shingles. For those who favor modern comforts such as whirlpool baths and TV sets, there's the 20-room Hotel Carter just across the street, with attractive country pine furnishings and a highly regarded dining room.

Eureka remains a major fishing port, with a fleet of more than 500 fishing boats bringing in rockfish, salmon, Dungeness crab, shrimp, and oysters. The bounty makes for some fine seafood dinners.

Downtown Eureka is sprucing up, with an attractive island marina blossoming just across a bridge from town and a revitalized shopping area in the historic section known as Old Town. Old Town's interesting shops and galleries for browsing are concentrated between First and Third streets, from D to H streets. The Clarke Museum is worth a stop for its regional history and a marvelous collection of Native American basketry.

Other popular pastimes in Eureka are tours on the Old Town Trolley, cruises on the bay, the local zoo in a setting of giant redwoods, and an all-you-can-eat meal served family-style at the long tables of the Samoa Cookhouse, the last of the old lumber mill cookhouses.

It's back to Ferndale's Main Street on Monday for the race finale somewhere around noon. The day actually begins at Camp Calistoga for what the program describes as a "slosh into slough" and the crossing of the Eel River before rolling into town. Hobart Brown suggests that the southernmost part of the Bay, at South Jetty, is one of the best vantage points.

Wherever you stand, it's an unforgettable sight. Don't forget the camera, and bring plenty of film.

Area Code: 707

DRIVING DIRECTIONS   Follow Highway 101 north to the Frenbridge/Ferndale exit, Highway 211, and drive 5 miles west into the village. Ferndale is about 260 miles from San Francisco, 167 miles from Redding, 280 miles from Sacramento.

PUBLIC TRANSPORTATION   Closest airport is Arcata-Eureka, 40 miles, served by United Express and American Eagle.

ACCOMMODATIONS   *The Gingerbread Mansion,* 400 Berding Street, Ferndale, 95536, 786-4000, E–EE, CP • *Shaw House Inn,* 703 Main Street, Ferndale, 95536, 786-9958, M–E, CP • *Grandmother's House,* 861 Howard, Ferndale, 95536, 786-9704, small B & B catering to families and children, M, CP • *Fern Motel,* 342 Ocean Street, Ferndale, 95536, 725-9511, basic motel, but several suites with kitchen facilities, I • *An Elegant Victorian Mansion,* 1406 C Street, Eureka, 95501, 444-3144, M–E, CP • *Carter House Inn,* 1033 Third Street, Eureka, 95501, 445-1390, E–EE, CP • *Hotel Carter,* 301 L Street, Eureka, 95501, 444-8062, M–EE • *Old Town Bed & Breakfast Inn,* 1521 Third Street, Eureka, 95501, 445-3951, modest Victorian, M–E, CP.

DINING   *Bibo and Bear,* 460 Main Street, Ferndale, 786-9484, most interesting menu in town, M • *Me and Dino's Pizza,* 607 Main Street, Ferndale, 786-4345, pizza and pasta, I • *Roman's,* 315 Main Street, Ferndale, 725-6358, Mexican-American, I • *Diane's,* 553 Main Street, Ferndale, 786-4950, good for breakfast and lunch, I • *Ramone's Restaurant,* 209 East Street, Eureka, 445-1642, bakery-café by day, gourmet's delight at night, M • *Hotel Carter* (see above), M • *Eureka Inn,* Seventh and F streets, landmark hotel, M–E • *Samoa Cookhouse,* Cookhouse Road, Eureka, 442-1659, eat-till-you-drop meals in one of the last authentic cookhouses, I.

SIGHTSEEING   *Ferndale Museum,* Third and Shaw streets, Ferndale, 786-4466. Hours: Wednesday to Saturday 11 A.M. to 4 P.M., Sunday 1 P.M. to 4 P.M. Adults, $1; ages 6 to 16, $.50 • *Fern Cottage,* 2121 Centerville Road, Ferndale, 786-4835. Hours: By appointment. Phone for hours and rates • *Clarke Museum,* Third and E streets, 443-1947. Hours: Tuesday to Saturday noon to 4 P.M. Donation • *Humboldt Bay Maritime Museum,* 1410 Second Street, 444-9440. Hours: Daily 11 A.M. to 4 P.M. Donation • *Humboldt Bay Harbor Cruise,* Humboldt Bay Maritime Museum, 75-minute cruises, Sunday brunch cruises. Phone 444-9440 for current information • *Carson Mansion,* 143 M Street, Eureka. Lookers and photographers welcome, but house is privately owned, not open to visitors • *Sequoia Park and Zoo,* Glatt and W streets, Eureka, 442-6552. Hours: 10 A.M. to 5 P.M., in summer to dusk. Free.

INFORMATION *Ferndale Chamber of Commerce,* P.O. Box 325, Ferndale, CA 95536, 786-4477; *Eureka/Humboldt County Convention & Visitors Bureau,* 1034 Second Street, Eureka, CA 95501, 346-3482 or in California (800) 338-7352.

Clear Sailing in Lake County

When you grow weary of the same old places and the same old inflated prices, it's time to get acquainted with Lake County.

Though it boasts Clear Lake, California's largest natural freshwater lake, and is located just above the Napa Valley—only three hours from San Francisco—this unpretentious area is still unexplored territory for many people. The exception up to now has been owners of RVs, since many of the resorts seen on the main highway are designed for recreational vehicles and trailers. They are places that are down-to-earth, no frills, maybe even a little frumpy.

But that's not the whole Lake County story. Look a little harder and you discover pockets of interest and lodging places to please even the pickiest weekender. They offer the chance to enjoy the lake and breathe some of the air that the California Air Resources Board declared number one in the state for quality. Besides prize fishing and water sports on a lake with more than 100 miles of shoreline, there are two interesting state parks to visit, one with an exceptional nature museum. Both parks abound with natural beauty and bird life.

Some local wineries and a cluster of antiques shops offer more worldly diversions. In spring the landscape is aglow with pear blossoms, for Lake County ranks second in the nation for its Bartlett pears, boasting well over a thousand orchards. Walnut trees, vivid spring redbuds, and wildflowers add to the seasonal show. Come on up now to explore before everybody gets hooked on Lake County's lures.

Lakeport, a pretty little town of 5,000 directly on the lakeshore, is the regional center and one of two recommended bases for a Lake County stay. The county seat since 1861, the town has some fine old buildings, including a Carnegie library. The 1871 County Courthouse is a state historic landmark. The Historical Museum is surprising, small but of genuine interest for its displays of American Indian baskets and ceremonial clothing, period rooms of the late 1800s, and a gem and mineral collection.

Library Park runs along the waterfront and makes the most of the setting with green lawns, picnic tables, and playgrounds for the kids. In small-town fashion, there's a gazebo in the park, with free concerts in summer.

Lakeport is a popular retirement haven, and also has its share of artists. It is headquarters for the Lake County Arts Council, and also boasts a co-op gallery, known as the Upstairs Gallery, at 325 North Main.

The Forbestown Inn, a small bed-and-breakfast home in town, offers attractively furnished rooms, a beautiful pool out back, and lavish breakfasts. The most pleasant dining in town is at Park Place, where pastas are interesting and the upstairs deck offers lake views.

Kelseyville, although just a little country hamlet, is another winning spot, boasting one of the area's best attractions, Clear Lake State Park, as well as Lake County's best-known winery. There's a good deli in town, and the Oak Barrel, one of the region's best restaurants. Two golf clubs in this region also have dining rooms open to the public and are also well recommended.

Kelseyville's Soda Bay area is home to two excellent lodgings. Konocti Harbor is a busy full-scale resort with a beautiful lakeside location, nicely landscaped grounds, and every kind of recreation— two swimming pools, wading pools, a marina full of boats for rent, tennis, an elaborate spa, miniature golf, even a paddlewheeler offering cruises on the lake. And there are four golf courses nearby. The resort presents big-name entertainment by the lake. The rooms in lodges around the grounds are motel standard but spacious, and the prices are surprisingly low for all these facilities.

If something quieter is more to your taste, try the Bell Haven Resort, a complex of eight very private rustic cabins with kitchens and every modern comfort, all in a shady wooded setting. There's a big lawn leading to the lake, a private beach, and a pier for fishing and swimming.

Clear Lake State Park is located along Soda Bay Road on the southwestern shore of the lake, with prime views of 4,300-foot Mt. Konocti. It is classified as an active volcano, but not to worry—there hasn't been any sign of life for the last 10,000 years. The park offers picnic grounds, a swimming beach, good fishing, and many miles of hiking trails through oak woodland, with nice vistas along the way. Walkers may spot deer, bobcats, raccoons, wild turkeys, and other inhabitants of the park. This is also a great place for seeing wildflowers and brilliant redbuds in spring. Both woodlands and tule marshes are good territory for bird-watchers, with 150 species having been spotted.

The nice surprise here is the visitors' center, built entirely by staff and volunteers with the help of the California Conservation Corps, a project that took more than three years. The result is the very model of a nature museum, a great place for kids because it is small enough to allow visitors to easily take in the wealth of information. An 800-gallon aquarium shows the fish that inhabit Clear Lake in a realistic environment made by using castings of the shoreline. A replica of one of the park's mazes of caves is complete with such typical residents as bats, ringtail cats, snakes, mountain lions, and mice. There are even re-creations of the Indian etchings found by archaeologists in 1989 on the floor of one of the natural caves.

There's still more to see—all in a compact space—including a diorama giving a prehistoric view of the lake at sunrise, an exhibit of Pomo Indian life, a woodland habitat similar to the upper reaches of the park, and a "touch corner" for hands-on learning about the environment.

This is a fine place to learn more about the lake, including some of its problems. Clear Lake is unique for its age, estimated at 450,000 years, making it one of the oldest in the United States. Lake Tahoe, at 5,000 years, is a baby in comparison. And Clear Lake is superproductive, rich in algae that make it a paradise for fish and fisherman. The water is teeming with bass, crappie, bluegill, carp, and catfish. The lake is known as the "Bass Capital of the West."

If there is a heavy blooming season, however, the algae that the fish relish can be trapped at the water's surface in confined areas such as lagoons or coves, where the sun's rays kill it, producing pea soup–like slicks and an unwelcome aroma—and sometimes resulting in dead fish along the lakeshore, not a pleasant sight. A resource management committee is trying to counter the algae problem by using high-pressure hoses to break up the trapped algae before they die.

This problem does not occur every year, nor does it cover the entire lake. The timing is unpredictable; you might want to call for a report before you go. The condition is often at its worst in late summer. With luck, you'll find a beautiful blue lake in the early spring, when the water is at its deepest. There are many places to rent boats to make the most of it.

Circling the entire lake by car is not a priority, since much of the road is built up and does not offer prime lake views. Pick specific destinations instead, starting with Kelseyville's Konocti Winery, a grower's cooperative, best known for its Cabernet Sauvignons and Sauvignon Blancs.

Antiquers may want to visit Upper Lake, a rather down-at-the-heels village that has managed to collect most of the area's antiques shops.

There were eight in and around town at last count. Beyond Upper Lake begins Mendocino National Forest, 900,000 acres with lots of wilderness hiking possibilities.

At the southern end of the lake near the town of Clearlake, Anderson Marsh State Historic Park offers a chance to visit the restored 130-year-old Anderson Ranch complex as well as some American Indian archaeological sites and an almost reconstructed Pomo Indian village. The 540-acre Anderson Marsh National Preserve within the park protects a large part of the marshy tule habitats on Clear Lake. Trails lead around the marsh and to the McVicar Wildlife Preserve, owned by the Audubon Society. From fall through early spring hikers may see bald eagles nesting in the trees surrounding the marsh, soaring above, or swooping down to hunt for fish. White pelicans have been spotted lately as well. The Redbud Audubon Society hosts a guided nature walk on the first Saturday of each month, meeting at 9 A.M. at the Anderson Ranch house. A club pamphlet with a map showing the best birding areas around the lake is available at the visitors' information center in Lakeport.

A regular spring event is the Native American Cultural Day, held at the roundhouse at the Pomo village site and featuring native dancing, demonstrations of American Indian skills, and some indigenous foods. It's a special chance to see volunteers from the local Native American community show the techniques used by their ancestors to make tools for daily living.

Even farther south is the Guenoc Winery in Middletown. It is of interest because fabled entertainer Lillie Langtry once lived here in the graceful balconied Victorian house. The shaded picnic area has nice pond views, and visitors are welcome at the tasting room. Mark it down as a likely detour if you are heading south on the way home.

Area Code: 707

DRIVING DIRECTIONS Lake County is north of the Napa Valley. Take Highway 29 north, bear left on Route 175 at Middletown, and stay on until the road rejoins Highway 29, continuing north to Kelseyville and Lakeport. From Highway 101, take Route 175 east from Hopland to Highway 29. Lakeport is about 132 miles from San Francisco, 96 miles from Sacramento.

PUBLIC TRANSPORTATION Greyhound Bus service is available to Lakeport and Clear Lake.

ACCOMMODATIONS *Konocti Harbor Resort and Spa,* 8727 Soda Bay Road, Kelseyville, 95451, 279-4281 or (800) 660-LAKE,

I–M • *Bell Haven Resort,* 3415 White Oak Way, Kelseyville, 95451, 279-4329, I–M • *Forbestown Inn,* 825 N. Forbes Street, Lakeport, 95453, 263-7858, M–E, CP • *Featherbed Railroad Company,* 2870 Lakeshore Boulevard, Nice, 95464, 274-8378 or (800) 966-6322, a novelty—nicely furnished rooms in restored railroad cars, M–E, CP.

DINING *Park Place,* 50 Third Street, Lakeport, 263-0444, steaks, seafood, and creative pastas, lake-view deck, best in the area, I–M • *Oak Barrel,* 6445 Soda Bay Road, Kelseyville, 279-0101, seafood specialties, M • *Tee Room Restaurant,* Buckingham Golf & Country Club, 2855 Eastlake Drive, Kelseyville, 279-1140, excellent chef: lamb specialties, I–M • *The Riviera Restaurant,* Clear Lake Riviera Yacht & Golf Club, 10200 Fairway Drive, off Soda Bay Road, Kelseyville, 277-7575, extensive menu, M • *Lyn-Deli's,* 4015-B Main Street, Kelseyville, 279-2213, tasty lunches and takeout, I • *Boar's Breath Restaurant,* 21159 Calistoga Street, Middletown, 987-9491, varied menu, I–M.

SIGHTSEEING *Clear Lake State Park,* 5300 Soda Bay Road, Kelseyville, 279-4293. Open 24 hours year-round. Per car, $5. Visitors' center hours: Mid-June to Labor Day, Wednesday to Sunday 10 A.M. to 4 P.M.; rest of year, Saturday only. Free • *Anderson Marsh State Historic Park,* Highway 53, Lower Lake, 994-0688. Hours: Wednesday to Sunday 10 A.M. to 5 P.M., docent tours on Saturday. Per car, $5 • *Lake County Historical Museum,* 255 Main Street, Lakeport, 263-4555. Hours: Wednesday to Saturday 11 A.M. to 4 P.M. Donation • *Konocti Winery,* Highway 29 at Thomas Drive, between Kelseyville and Lakeport, 279-8861. Hours: Tasting room Monday to Saturday 10 A.M. to 5 P.M., Sunday from 11 A.M. • *Guenoc Winery,* 21000 Butts Canyon Road, 6 miles east off Highway 29, Middletown, 987-2385. Hours: Thursday to Sunday 10 A.M. to 4:30 P.M.

ACTIVITIES **Boat rentals:** *On the Waterfront,* 60 Third Street, Lakeport, 263-6789; *Will-O-Point Water Sports,* 1 First Street, Lakeport, 263-0969; *Jim's Soda Bay Resort,* 6380 Soda Bay Road, Kelseyville, 279-4837; *Konocti Harbor Resort Marina,* 8727 Soda Bay Road, Kelseyville, 279-1808 • Complete updated list available from information center.

INFORMATION *Lake County Visitor Information Center,* 875 Lakeport Boulevard, Lakeport, CA 95453, 263-9544 or (800) 525-3743.

Big Scenery at Big Sur

The original name was *El Pais Grande del Sur*, "the big country of the South." It was given by Spanish settlers to the unexplored wilderness south of Monterey, where the Santa Lucia mountains edge the rocky Pacific shoreline in one of nature's most stupendous meetings of land and sea.

To many people today, Big Sur means the 90-mile stretch of Highway 1 skirting that coast from south of Carmel to San Simeon, a dipping and soaring parade of hairpin curves around the cliffs with vistas of crashing surf around almost every bend. This road built by Chinese workers and prison laborers was an engineering feat that took 15 years to complete. It meant blasting through rock and constructing 29 bridges to span the mountain peaks. The road was opened in 1937 and later named California's first scenic highway. It remains one of America's most remarkable drives, with plenty of lookouts where you can stand on a high precipice, hear the sea lions call in the distance, watch the hawks soar, and look down to incomparable views of the restless sea.

Big Sur is a destination as well as a drive, but there is no sign or town to tell you that you have arrived. It is as much a state of mind as a location. Its remoteness has long made the area a counterculture haven, a shelter for bohemian writers like Henry Miller and Beat generation idols like Jack Kerouac, for artists, and in recent years for the New Age teachings and encounter groups of the Esalen Institute. Despite the legions of tourists who drive through on the highway, there are still only 1,400 or so permanent residents, many of them determined escapists living in harmony with nature and Big Sur's mellow, laid-back lifestyle.

The wilderness has been preserved in national forests and state parks. A local land trust has helped by buying up private land to stave off development. No neon signs, shopping malls, golf courses, or movies have been allowed to intrude. The closest thing to a town is the string of general stores, eateries, gas stations, and one or two modest gift shops on the stretch where Highway 1 comes inland. The only nightlife is music in a couple of cafés.

So why come? Because Big Sur, offering rich wildlife, prime hiking, and access to hidden beaches, is a supreme getaway for those who love nature and serenity. And there are some wonderful places to stay and to dine, tranquil retreats where you can sit back and ponder the quixotic moods of the sun and sea, the clouds and mist. Come in spring, after the winter rains, when wildflowers are in full bloom. April and May are the best times, before the summer fog descends.

Lodgings range from comfortable cabins in the woods of Pfeiffer

Big Sur State Park to luxury in one of California's most famous and fabulous retreats, Ventana, tucked into the woods on a clifftop with vast ocean vistas. If you can't stay at Ventana, do not miss coming for a meal or a drink. (For more on Ventana, see pages 242 to 243.)

Across the road is a newer luxury hideaway, the Post Ranch, a cluster of futuristic glass-walled redwood lodgings on a high precipice towering over the Pacific. Triangular tree houses float on poles among the oaks and redwoods, other houses are bunkered into the hillside with sod for roofs. All of the 30 rooms have a fireplace, a balcony made of rusting industrial steel, and a massage table under the bed. Some people absolutely love Post Ranch, others find it sterile, but no one can quibble about the dazzling views.

Deetjen's Big Sur Inn, another local legend and a historic landmark, is a collection of snug, rustic redwood cabins in a shady grove, built by hand in the 1930s, with their original charm still carefully preserved. Several other cabin colonies are also available, including Gorda-by-the-Sea, an excellent spot for whale watching and spotting elephant seals.

For those who want to experience the Esalen Institute, there are introductory workshops and weekend seminars with such titles as "Using Risk to Effect Change" and "Self-Acceptance Training." When the spartan double rooms are not filled by workshop participants, they are available to overnight guests, and include vegetarian meals, plus soaks in the hot springs on the property and wonderful massages. Be aware that many guests don't feel compelled to don bathing suits to swim in the cliffside pool.

The major activity center for nature lovers is Pfeiffer Big Sur State Park, which lies inland, in the protected Big Sur Valley, and gives access to the area's three environments: beaches, forests of coastal redwoods, and backcountry. The park was named in honor of the proprietors of Pfeiffer's Ranch Resort, which opened in 1884 on the site of today's Big Sur Lodge. Many of the fine rustic buildings and the amphitheater where summer programs are held were constructed by the Civilian Conservation Corps during the Depression in the 1930s.

A variety of scenic hikes show the diversity of the landscape. Head to the top of Pfeiffer Ridge for panoramic views of the Pacific and the mountains. An hour's stroll through coastal redwoods leads to Pfeiffer Falls, a 60-foot cascade at the end of the trail. A cutoff on the Falls Trail comes out at the Valley View overlook, a point for taking in much of Big Sur Valley, Point Sur, and the coast.

The Oak Grove Trail is the best way to appreciate the contrasts of the park's terrain, which weaves through dim redwood groves to open oak woodland to hot dry chaparral on the arid south-facing slopes, where manzanita and yucca grow. The chaparral is good territory for bird-watchers. Red-tailed hawks, golden eagles, owls, flickers, kingfishers, and stellar and scrub jays are among the residents.

The redwoods tend to grow in the cool fern-filled canyons. The oldest growth is the Proboscis Grove near the ranger station, where the trees date back 800 to 1,200 years. The largest redwood is the "Colonial Tree" near the softball field, with a circumference of 27 feet.

About a mile south of the park on the ocean side of the road, watch for unmarked Sycamore Canyon Road, an almost-hidden turnoff for Pfeiffer Beach. Jiggle along the bumpy road until you come to the parking lot, then walk through a clearing in the wind-carved cypress trees to a generous curve of powder sand and a view of surf spuming in and out of blowholes in massive boulders in the sea. This was the romantic backdrop for the Elizabeth Taylor–Richard Burton film *The Sandpiper.* The water is rough for swimming, but it's hard to imagine a more magical setting for picnicking and sunning. Just be sure to pick a calm day for your outing. When the wind picks up, this is not a pleasant place to be.

Pfeiffer Big Sur also serves as official headquarters for smaller preserves nearby. Andrew Molera State Park to the north provides more ocean access. A one-mile trail through the trees along the Big Sur River ends at a two-mile beach. The beach is strollable only at low tide, but the level Bluffs Trail alongside is always open. Take the tougher Panorama Trail up the ridge for views that explain the name.

Just before the river mouth is the easier Headlands Trail, for beach views and a chance to see otters, seals, and seabirds nesting on the rocks. Molera is in the middle of a sea otter refuge area, and this trail gives you a chance to look for the otters eating, resting, and grooming while floating on rafts of kelp in the quiet lagoons. Harbor seals and California sea lions are often out sunning on the rocks or swimming in the waves. Molera Trail Rides lets you take in all this fine scenery on horseback.

Julia Pfeiffer Burns State Park lies farther south, with 4,000 acres straddling the highway. Here you may hike into Los Padres National Forest, picnic in the redwoods beside McWay Creek, or take a short walk along the creek through the tunnel under the road to Saddle Rock and the cliffs above Waterfall Cove for an unusual sight, a waterfall that plunges into the sea. Below the cliffs, otters and seals are at play, as they are all along the coast. In winter this is a choice spot for whale watching, as is the Point Sur Lighthouse. Both have whale-watching programs; check Pfeiffer Big Sur State Park for schedules.

The 1899 lighthouse is worth a look, whales or not. It is maintained by the Coast Guard, and tours are sometimes offered.

Hardy hikers and backpackers will want to head for the Ventana Wilderness, the untamed part of Los Padres National Forest, which comprises a 2-million-acre sprawl of peaks and valleys laced with canyons and streams and crisscrossed by 2,000 miles of trails.

Big Sur does not offer sightseers much beyond its natural resources, nor is it a place for shopping, but there are a few stops of special interest. The Henry Miller Memorial Library formerly was the modest home of the author's best friend and fellow artist, the late Emil White, who created a quirky shrine filled with a clutter of Miller memorabilia, including drawings, photos, and first editions. The library is open by chance or by appointment, so check before making a special trip.

The Coast Gallery, constructed of old redwood water tanks, is the long-standing showcase for Big Sur artists and coastal craftsmen. It is a must stop for fine art and crafts of all kinds, including paintings, prints, posters, and sculpture. On weekends in season, artists can be seen at work. There's an upstairs café with an expansive deck offering ocean views.

Finally, Nepenthe is a veritable symbol of Big Sur, a multilevel open wooden structure high on a cliff that is part restaurant, part gift shop, and part heavenly perch 800 feet above the Pacific. It is named for an ancient Egyptian drug that was used to induce forgetfulness of suffering. Orson Welles and Rita Hayworth are said to have spent their honeymoon here. There is a restaurant upstairs with a deck for drinks and sunset watching. The Café Kevah just below offers tasty light fare and another deck. Unfortunately, Nepenthe is too well known. It can be crowded with tourists, and the food is not as good as the views. Come by, but if lines are long, admire the view and settle for a sandwich at the Café, a walk around the grounds, and a look into the Phoenix Shop for jewelry, wind chimes, crystals, and books about Big Sur.

Area Code: 408

DRIVING DIRECTIONS   The Big Sur coastline runs along Highway 1 beginning south of Carmel; the central portion near Pfeiffer Big Sur State Park is about 159 miles from San Francisco, 225 miles from Sacramento.

PUBLIC TRANSPORTATION   Closest air service is Monterey Peninsula Airport, about 35 miles. Summer bus service from Carmel to Nepenthe parking lot via Monterey Peninsula Transit, 372-4494.

ACCOMMODATIONS   (Mileage noted here and below is measured driving south from the Carmel River Bridge) • *Ventana,* Highway 1, mile 28.1S, Big Sur, 93920, 667-2331 or (800) 628-6500, heavenly, EE • *Post Ranch Inn,* Big Sur, 93920, (800) 527-2200, spectacular site, EE, CP • *Big Sur Lodge,* Pfeiffer Big Sur State Park, Highway 1, mile 26S, Big Sur, 93920, 667-2171, rustic cottages with motel-type furnishings, M; with fireplace and/or kitchen, E • *Deetjen's Big Sur Inn,* Highway 1, mile 30.2S, Big Sur, 93920, 667-2377, cozy cabins, rustic landmark, I–E • *Gorda-by-the-Sea,* Highway 1, mile 62S, Big Sur 93920, 927-3918, ocean-view cottages, EE • *Ripplewood Resort,*

Highway 1, mile 25S, Big Sur 93920, 667-2242, cabin colony, ask for cabins 1 to 9 along the Big Sur River; avoid lodgings near the road, I–M • *Esalen Institute,* Highway 1, mile 41S, Big Sur, 93920, 667-3000, weekend and five-day programs year-round, phone for current offerings and rates; rooms without programs, M–E, MAP if available.

DINING   *Nepenthe,* Highway 1, mile 28.8S, 667-2345, rustic hide-away with great views—and crowds, I–M • *Ventana* (see above), highly recommended for dinner, E; and for lunch, when you can appreciate the view, I–M • *Sierra Mar,* Post Ranch Inn (see above), intimate café, excellent reviews, EE • *Deetjen's Restaurant* (see above), M–E • *Whale Watcher Café,* Gorda-by-the-Sea (see above), seaside patio for informal dining, live music on weekends, I–M • *Rocky Point Restaurant,* Highway 1, mile 11S, 624-2933, steak and seafood, great surf views, M • *Coast Gallery Café,* Highway 1, mile 33S, 667-2301, indoor and outdoor lunches, I.

SIGHTSEEING   **State parks,** all reached at 667-2315: *Pfeiffer Big Sur State Park,* Highway 1, mile 26S. Hours: Daily 8 A.M. to 10 P.M., office hours 8 A.M. to 6 P.M. Per car, $6. *Andrew Molera State Park,* Highway 1, mile 21S. Parking, $4; *Julia Pfeiffer Burns Park,* Highway 1, mile 38S. Parking, $6 • *Molera Trail Rides,* 625-8664 for information, rates • *Henry Miller Memorial Library,* Highway 1, mile 29.4S, 667-2574. Hours: Daily, erratic hours, phone ahead. Free • *Coast Gallery,* Highway 1, mile 33S, 667-2301. Hours: Daily 9 A.M. to 5:30 P.M. Free.

INFORMATION   *Big Sur Chamber of Commerce,* P.O. Box 87, Big Sur, CA 93920, 667-2100.

A Capital Trip to Sacramento

You say you've never seen the State Capitol? Waste no more time. Head for Sacramento, where the fine government complex is only the start of the attractions. Once considered a dull backwater town, Sacramento has revived its romantic past while moving into a promising future.

Besides touring the splendid Capitol building you can stroll the state's largest collection of Gold Rush–era buildings in Old Sacramento, visit one of the nation's best railroad museums, take a ride on a steam train or a riverboat—and even spend the night on the *Delta King,* the historic paddlewheeler now permanently moored on Sacramento's rapidly reviving riverfront.

If you come in March you'll enjoy a bonus, the chance to see neighborhoods bedecked with more than a million camellia bushes in bloom. Or wait for Memorial Day weekend and the annual Jazz Festival, when Dixieland bands and jazz groups of all kinds fill the air with music.

While Sacramento retains its small-town ease, it is also one of the ten fastest-growing regions in the United States and has gained city amenities that were missing a decade ago. It now boasts fine and trendy dining and plenty of nightlife. Much of the activity is centered in Old Sacramento—roughly three blocks between I and L streets near the river—which boasts 30 restaurants and 100 shops and attracts 5 million visitors each year.

Sacramento grew up and prospered during the Gold Rush, when a fortunate location at the confluence of the Sacramento and American rivers turned it into the gateway to the mother lode—and one of the nation's busiest ports.

It was the rivers that prompted John Sutter to build a fort here in 1839, intending to create a trading post and a haven for European immigrants. The original fort, with living quarters and cooper's and blacksmith's shops, a prison, and other carefully restored areas, is open to visitors. Nearby is the small but interesting California State Indian Museum, with exhibits of the work of even earlier residents, including a fine collection of baskets.

Sutter hadn't considered the possibility that one of his foremen would strike gold. His employees disappeared to try their luck in the gold fields, and the fort was overrun by wild-eyed newcomers who trampled the crops and slaughtered the livestock. Dejected and in debt, Sutter turned his holdings over to his son, who subdivided the land and had the streets surveyed, christening the settlement Sacramento.

The heart of the new city moved about two miles from the fort to the Sacramento River, where 800 ships docked in 1849. Some of the passengers were hoping to strike it rich in the mother lode; others planned to make their fortune supplying prospectors with food and equipment. The merchants built shops, hotels, and saloons for the miners, and were soon able to build mansions for themselves.

The city's future was ensured when it was made the state capital in 1854, but the riverside, always subject to periodic flooding, began a steady decline in the 1870s, after the completion of the transcontinental railroad put an end to the riverboat era. By the 1950s it was a skid row, hidden from the rest of the city by a concrete floodwall.

The first sign of life began in the early 1960s with one building, Sacramento Engine Company No. 3, an 1853 firehouse that was rehabilitated and turned into the very successful Firehouse restaurant. Serious renovation of the area began a few years later. The floodwall that stood between the city and its Gold Rush past was removed, and one by one buildings were restored. Now the area is spiffy, with cobblestone streets, wooden sidewalks, and old-fashioned streetlights, and the old arcaded buildings are full of antiques, crafts, clothes, and gew-gaws designed to tempt tourists to part with their money. Some of the area is undeniably commercial, but it has added new vitality to Sacramento and revived the river, which now has parkways and bicycle paths along its banks.

An exciting development was the arrival of the *Delta King.* Like its twin, the *Delta Queen,* the five-deck riverboat once took passengers from Sacramento to San Francisco. But after World War II, while the *Delta Queen* got a new lease on life on the Mississippi River, the *King* was allowed to rust away, and finally sank in San Francisco Bay. It was hauled out in the 1980s by entrepreneurs who restored the glamor and created a floating hotel and restaurant. The rooms are small compared to hotel quarters, but the ambience is unbeatable. If you don't stay here, at least come for a tour and a meal at the Pilothouse Restaurant, or for a drink in the Paddlewheel Saloon or the Delta Lounge. There's also a theater onboard, with old-fashioned offerings such as performances by a Mark Twain impersonator.

The best way to see Old Sacramento is simply to take a walk, guided by a map available at the information center located in the old Steam Navigation Company Depot near K and Front streets, the former embarkation point for steamboat passengers.

The printed tour identifies many of the buildings and tells a bit about their colorful history. The B. F. Hastings Building at the corner of Second and J streets was the western terminus of the Pony Express. It now houses a Communications Museum and a reconstruction of the California Supreme Court chambers. The Brannan Building on J Street, which was a general store with supplies for miners, turned owner Sam Brannan into California's first millionaire. The Huntington-Hopkins hardware store in the Big Four Building on I Street was owned by two of Sacramento's earliest settlers, Collis Huntington and Mark Hopkins, who formed a partnership with residents Leland Stanford and Charles Crocker to form the Central Pacific Railroad, the first transcontinental line.

The story of the "Big Four" of railroading—all of whom became major figures in California history—along with the drama of the railroad's construction, is vividly told at the California State Railroad Museum on I Street at the end of Old Sacramento. You don't have to be a rail buff to gasp with awe when an introductory movie ends and a back curtain rises to reveal an amazing collection of early trains. There are 21 giant locomotives and long trains of vintage stock, all polished and shined up better than new. The Central Pacific's first locomotive is displayed in a diorama showing the construction of the railroad. Many of the engines still run, and you can take a short ride from the period depot next door. This is the largest railroad museum in North America, and it's hard to imagine a better one.

More Sacramento history awaits at the nearby Discovery Museum, a compact look at the city's development from Indian days to the present in a building that is a replica of the first city hall and waterworks. On display is a cool one million dollars in gold specimens. The museum includes hands-on exhibits, changing special exhibits, and science and craft demonstrations.

Down the river at Front and V streets is another of Sacramento's nostalgic treasures, the Towe Ford Museum. Around 200 antique Ford autos are on display, almost every model produced between 1903 and 1953, and some newer cars as well. Together, the cars form a fascinating chronological view of America's auto history.

Head to the center of town and you can't miss the most important building in California, the Capitol, set in its own landscaped 40-acre park, its gold dome glistening in the sunlight. A major restoration has returned the building's turn-of-the-century grandeur and applied the latest technology to protect it against earthquakes, ensuring that it will still be standing in the next century. With its soaring rotunda, hand-carved staircases, massive chandeliers, and the original 1906 marble mosaic floors, the building is undeniably impressive, and more interesting than most government buildings because the rooms are re-creations of the past.

Visitors are invited to take a guided tour or walk through on their own to see historic museum rooms on the first floor and the legislative chambers on the third. Free tours are offered on the hour, with tickets available a half hour before in Room B-27 on the basement level. A short film and a small museum acquaint you with the building and its restoration while you wait.

On the first floor are re-creations of offices as they would have appeared in the early 1900s, including the quarters of the attorney general, the secretary of state, and the governor. The state treasurer's office is shown as it was in 1906 and again as it looked in 1933, during the Great Depression. When the legislature is in session, the doors to the galleries are kept open so that anyone can come in and see the state government in action. Current offices of the governor and legislators are in the East Annex of the building.

Along the Capitol's corridors are portraits of the state's governors. Most are formal full-length studies of men in dark suits, but nonconformist Jerry Brown chose to have his portrait done by an abstract artist, who portrayed Brown's face in a wild palette of colors.

You'll hear more about ex-Governor Brown if you visit the Old Governor's Mansion, a handsome 15-room Victorian with 14-foot ceilings and fine furnishings. It housed all of the state's governors until 1967, when Ronald Reagan was elected and decided that the building was no longer suitable. A more elaborate home was constructed for more than $1 million, too late for the Reagans to move in, and their spartan successor, Jerry Brown, refused to live there. Eventually the house was sold, and California remains one of the few states without an official residence for its governor.

The shopping center of Sacramento, located near the Capitol, has been transformed into a modern plaza of shops, eating places, a complex of colorful clubs known as "America Live," and the River City Brewery.

Head the other way and the town is filled with more fine Victorian homes, mementos of its early prosperity. They can be seen from 7th to 16th streets, and from E to I streets. Leland Stanford's home at 800 N Street is of special note. The 135-year-old Stanford home is due for restoration as a house museum, to be completed, it is hoped, by the end of the decade. Meanwhile, the state parks department invites visitors in free to see what a historic home is like *before* the restorers go to work and to learn how archaeologists work to ensure an authentic re-creation.

Another of the most impressive Victorian houses is now the Crocker Art Museum, which boasts of being the oldest public art museum in the West. It was founded in 1873 by E. B. Crocker, the brother of the railroad magnate, to house his collection of European art, but it has grown to specialize in California paintings, Asian art, photography, and changing exhibits of contemporary art. The mansion itself is a work of art, with curving staircases, ornate woodwork and painted plaster, and inlaid floors.

The Crocker includes a Discovery Gallery with special children's workshops. If children are along, you may also want to add a visit to the Sacramento Zoo, where you can pay your respects to some 340 kinds of exotic animals.

Kids and parents alike enjoy river cruises, which are currently offered by several operators; boats include the *Spirit of Sacramento* from Old Sacramento and the *River City Queen* from Riverbank Marina, a developing area to the north that also has restaurants with dockside dining. If your taste runs to something more active, the Riverfront Park bike trail in Old Sacramento crosses the American River to join the Jedediah Smith Memorial Bicycle Trail winding through the American River Parkway for 23 miles to Folsom Lake, a state park that is one of the area's main recreational facilities. There are many pleasant picnic areas along the river. Miller Park, south of Old Sacramento, has more picnic tables and a two-mile bike path along the levee. Bikes can be rented in Old Sacramento.

If you happen to be in town on a weekday, it's worth noting that the tour of the Blue Diamond almond complex gives new awareness of the importance of one of California's top crops. It's fun to see how the almonds are sorted and packed, and there are free samples to boot.

The *Delta King* is by far the most interesting place to stay in Sacramento, though a number of nice small bed-and-breakfast inns have sprung up, like the Amber House and Vizcaya. Among the hotels within walking distance of the Capitol are the Holiday Inn Capitol Plaza and the big, posh Hyatt Regency. The Sterling is a notable smaller contemporary luxury hotel, and you might also consider driving a few miles out of town for the Radisson Hotel, nicely located on a private lake.

There's fine dining in Old Sacramento at the Firehouse, and excellent reasonable fare in pleasant surroundings at Fat City. The same Fat family also owns California Fats, a slightly more expensive place next door, and the very elegant Frank Fat Chinese restaurant, a longtime downtown favorite of the politicos. Other places where you're likely to see bigwigs are Biba, which is the current trendy favorite in town, Chanterelle, the Capitol Grill, and Paragary's. Chevy's and Woody's are among a lineup of informal spots with pleasant riverside decks on the Sacramento River off Garden Highway.

By the time you've done the sights and sampled some of the newer restaurants in town, you'll likely agree that Sacramento today has all the ingredients for a capital weekend.

Area Code: 916

DRIVING DIRECTIONS   From the Bay Area and other points east or west, Sacramento can be reached via I-80 or Route 50; from north and south, it is located on I-5 and Highway 99. It is 88 miles east of San Francisco.

PUBLIC TRANSPORTATION   American, United, Delta, TWA, and America West airlines fly into Sacramento Metro Airport. Amtrak's *California Zephyr* offers direct service from the Bay Area. Boat cruises are also available between Sacramento and San Francisco; for information, contact Delta Travel, 372-3690.

ACCOMMODATIONS   *Delta King,* 1000 Front Street, Old Sacramento, 95814, 444-KING, E, CP • *Sterling Hotel,* 1300 H Street, Sacramento, 95814, 448-1300, E–EE • *Abigail's Bed & Breakfast,* 2120 G Street, Sacramento, 95816, 441-5007, M–EE, CP • *Vizcaya,* 2019 21st Street, Sacramento, 95818, 455-5243, M–EE, CP • *Amber House,* 1315 22nd Street, Sacramento, 95816, 444-8085, M–EE, CP • *Hyatt Regency,* Capitol at 12th and L streets, Sacramento, 95814, 443-1234, EE, M–E most weekends • *Holiday Inn Capitol Plaza,* 300 J Street, Sacramento, 95814, 446-0100, M • *Radisson Hotel Sacramento,* 500 Leisure Lane, Sacramento, 95815, 922-2020, M.

DINING   *Biba,* 2801 Capitol Avenue, 455-2422, current favorite, rave reviews, E • *Chanterelle,* Sterling Hotel (see above), 442-0451, French country, elegant, M–E • *Capitol Grill,* 28th and N streets, 736-

0744, creative American, M • *Paragary's Bar & Oven,* 28th and N streets, 457-5737, California cuisine, M • *Firehouse,* 1112 2nd Street, Old Sacramento, 442-4772, continental, great ambience, E • *Lemon Grass,* 601 Monroe Street, 486-4891, interesting Viet-Thai cuisine, I–M • *Harlow's,* 2714 J Street, 441-4693, local favorite for Italian, M • *California Fats,* 1015 Front Street, Old Sacramento, 441-7966, E • *Fat City,* 1001 Front Street, Old Sacramento, 446-6768, M • *Frank Fat,* 8th and L streets, 442-7092, elegant Chinese, I–M • *Food for Thought Cafe,* 2416 K Street, 441-3200, creative regional and ethnic cuisine, good for lunch, I, or dinner, M • *Chevy's Mexican Restaurant,* 1369 Garden Highway, 649-0390, riverfront-deck dining, I–M • *Woody's,* 1379 Garden Highway, 924-3434, informal, more river views, I–M.

SIGHTSEEING   *State Capitol,* 10th and Capitol Mall, 324-0333. Hours: Daily 9 A.M. to 5 P.M., fall and winter weekends from 10 A.M.; tours begin on the hour. Free • *California State Railroad Museum,* Second and I streets, Old Sacramento, 448-4466. Hours: Daily 10 A.M. to 5 P.M. Adults, $5; children, $2 • *Train rides from Central Pacific Depot.* Hours: April through Labor Day, weekends 10 A.M. to 5 P.M.; October to December, first weekend of each month, noon to 3 P.M. Train ride without museum visit: Adults, $5; ages 6 to 12, $2 • *Crocker Art Museum,* 3rd and O streets, 264-5423. Hours: Wednesday to Sunday 10 A.M. to 5 P.M., Thursday until 9 P.M. Adults, $3; ages 7 to 17, $1.50 • *Old Governor's Mansion State Historic Park,* 16th and H streets, 324-0539. Hours: Daily 10 A.M. to 4 P.M., tours begin on the hour. Adults, $2; ages 6 to 17, $1 • *Discovery Museum,* 101 I Street, Old Sacramento, 264-7057. Hours: Tuesday to Sunday 10 A.M. to 5 P.M.; winter hours, Wednesday to Friday noon to 5 P.M., weekends 10 A.M. to 5 P.M. Adults, $3.50; ages 6 to 17, $2 • *Sutter's Fort State Historic Park,* 27th and L streets, 445-4422. Hours: Daily 10 A.M. to 5 P.M., last tour 4:15 P.M. Adults $2; ages 6 to 17, $1 • *California State Indian Museum,* 2618 K Street, 324-0971. Hours: Daily 10 A.M. to 5 P.M. Adults, $2; ages 6 to 17, $1. • *Towe Ford Museum,* 2200 Front Street, 442-6802. Hours: Daily 10 A.M. to 6 P.M. Adults, $5; ages 14 to 18, $2.50; ages 5 to 13, $1 • *Blue Diamond Growers Visitors Center,* 1701 C Street, 446-8439. Hours: Tours Monday to Friday 10 A.M. and 1 P.M. Free • **Riverboat cruises** (check for current schedules and rates): *Spirit of Sacramento,* Old Sacramento waterfront, 552-2933; *River City Queen,* 1401 Garden Highway, 921-1111 • **Bicycle rentals:** *Cycle Depot,* 918 Second Street, Old Sacramento, 441-4143.

INFORMATION   *Sacramento Convention and Visitors Bureau,* 1421 K Street, Sacramento, CA 95814, 264-7777; weekends and holidays, 442-7644.

Standing Tall amid the Redwoods

Majestic. Inspiring. Regal. None of the usual adjectives do full justice to the titans of Redwood National Park. The redwood trees are a miracle that can be appreciated only when you actually see them here as nature intended, safe from saw blades and bulldozers, left to grow unhampered in thick groves near the sea, where mist and heavy winter rains nurture them to soaring heights.

The distant branches form a canopy that keeps the forest floor hushed and dim. Rays of sun glimmer through openings like celestial rays in a cathedral that seems to reach to the very heavens. In the mist, the scene takes on a dreamlike quality. Whether in dreamy mist or radiant sunlight, it is a sight that leaves even the most jaded visitors in awe.

Redwoods grow for about 500 miles in a narrow strip along the central and northern California coast, but they are at their grandest along this north coast, where the rainfall averages more than six feet each year. The grandest of the groves are in Redwood National Park and to the south in Humboldt Redwoods State Park. Many of these ancient trees stand over 300 feet, taller than a football field set on end. Also in the national park is the tallest tree in the world, measuring 367.8 feet. The sign nearby gives its approximate age as 600 years.

This national park grows more important with each passing year. It has been estimated that commercial logging has taken 85 percent of the old-growth redwoods—and that virtually all of the old-growth forest outside the parks may be gone by the end of the 1990s.

Highway 101 goes directly through the park, and you could easily cover the 40 miles between Orick, the southern entrance, to the Crescent City end in one hour, admiring trees along the way. But you could also spend days exploring the many attractions in between. Forty miles of rugged coastline, herds of Roosevelt elk, 125 miles of hiking trails, the wild and scenic Smith River, the waters of Redwood Creek, and the tallest groves are just a few of the pleasures awaiting beyond the initial stands of trees along the highway. Late June, when the rhododendrons are in bloom but the summer crowds are not yet in full flower, is a fine time for a visit.

Approaching from the south, stop at the Redwood Information Center in Orick to check the schedule of ranger-guided activities and pick up a map and a useful sheet with tips on how to see the park. The center also has audiovisual programs about the park and its resources, and a relief map to give you the lay of the land. Outside, there is a spectacular ocean view and a boardwalk leading to the Redwood Creek estuary.

As you'll see from the map, the park is narrow, no more than seven miles at its widest point, so you don't have to go far to reach most sights. Among the many groves of trees, three are not to be missed. In season, shuttle buses operate from the Center to the Tall Trees trailhead; off season, you can get a pass to drive down yourself. Either way, it is a 2½-mile round-trip walk from the trailhead to see the tallest tree and its almost equally lofty neighbors—and it is worth every step. The nutrients deposited in the soil by adjoining Redwood Creek are the reason this grove is so lofty.

Mother Nature also helps the redwoods live to a ripe old age by giving them the ability to store water inside, providing protection against forest fire. Some of the giants can hold thousands of gallons.

Some other interesting sights of the old-growth forest are large erect dead trees, called snags, which may stand for as long as 200 years, and the fallen trees that sometimes lie on the forest floor in a slow state of decay for centuries. The fallen trees show the enormous length of the redwoods even more dramatically than some of the giants whose tops are beyond sight.

Another important stop, three miles north of Orick, is the Lady Bird Johnson Grove, named for the conservation-minded former First Lady. Reached via Bald Hill Road, the grove offers an easy one-mile round-trip walk through old-growth trees to the 1969 park dedication site.

The third important redwood grove is at the northern end of the park. Just before Crescent City, go right on Elk Valley Road to Howland Hill Road and take the slow unpaved eight-mile drive to reach one of the most magnificent stands in the park, Stout Grove. If you can see only one grove, this is my choice. It is hushed, lush with ferns and moss, and contains many magnificent trees, including one of the biggest in the park, the Stout Tree, 340 feet tall and 18 feet in diameter.

Once you see these mighty trees close up, you understand better why people have fought so hard to preserve them. Redwoods have existed since the days of the dinosaur. It was only after the Gold Rush brought hosts of newcomers to California, creating a building boom, that commercial logging began to take its toll. The same durability and resistance to disease and fire that enable redwoods to grow for hundreds of years make them prize building material, and soon the rush was on for this new "red gold."

The state was quick to see the danger, and established parks to save the trees as early as 1902. In 1908 President Theodore Roosevelt set aside the Muir Woods National Monument near San Francisco, and in 1918 the Save-the-Redwoods League was organized to raise funds to buy up redwood land and gain support for preservation. The league encouraged citizens to get involved and has established more than 280 memorial groves named for their benefactors, a practice that continues today.

But timber interests are strong, and the virgin forests were disappearing with alarming speed when the national park was established in 1968. Even then, only 58,000 acres were designated for the park, half of this in three state parks that were already protected. The three parks, Prairie Creek Redwoods State Park, Del Norte Coast Redwoods State Park, and Jedediah Smith Redwoods State Park, are still independent units operating within the national park.

When logging outside the park continued to threaten the old trees, Congress finally responded in 1978 by almost doubling the original site, bringing the total to 106,000 acres and creating a 30,000-acre protection zone as well. Little of the new land contains old-growth redwoods, and much of it is in need of rehabilitation. This is a prime aim of the Park Service, which has replanted forests, blocking out unsightly logging roads. It is estimated that it will take centuries to repair the damage caused by careless cutting practices.

There are other prime detours off Highway 101, many of them leading to the coast and wonderful picnic spots. Like Stout Grove, some of the best spots are reached via unpaved roads, but they are well worth a bumpy journey.

One of these unpaved beauties is Davison Road, which leads along the water to Gold Bluffs Beach and Fern Canyon. The beach, dotted with agates and shells, is fine for beachcombing and is also home to one of the park's two herds of Roosevelt elk. The canyon offers a fabulous half-mile hike through a 30-foot-deep canyon made lush and green by thick walls and carpeting of ferns. This is an easy hike, but it traverses the creek, which can all but take over the canyon floor after heavy rain. Wear old sneakers or shoes that you don't mind getting wet.

Off Highway 101 in Prairie Creek Redwoods State Park is the Elk Prairie Visitor Center, with displays on the wildlife and pioneer history of the area. The park's elk preserve is another chance to see the Roosevelt elk. Their gigantic many-pronged antlers are truly a marvel of nature.

Requa Road, a paved drive along the Klamath River, winds to an overlook where the river meets the ocean, whose wild waves crash against the cliffs. On a clear day you'll see the seals; in the fog you'll hear their hoarse barking. Here is the start of the scenic, partially unpaved Coastal Drive and a trailhead for the Coastal Walking Trail, which can also be entered at Orick. This fabulous trail runs for 30 miles, but even a short portion is rewarding.

In the Klamath area, turn off Highway 101 to picnic on the beach or fish in the freshwater lagoon at Lagoon Creek. A self-guided nature trail here takes about an hour. Many other options are well marked on the park maps.

While the redwoods are the main attraction, there are a few other diversions on the north coast. Sport fishing in the Smith and Klamath rivers is a favorite activity, with guided trips available for beginners as well as pros. Innkeepers can suggest the best guides.

One easy way to enjoy some of the fishing bounty is by attending the annual Klamath Salmon Festival, held on the last Sunday in June. It features open-pit barbecued salmon, plus contests and entertainment for all.

A much-visited spot is the Battery Point Lighthouse in Crescent City, a chance for a guided tour through a working lighthouse. Drive farther north into Del Norte and Curry counties and you're in the area where more than 90 percent of the commercially produced lilies in the United States are grown. Colorful fields in bloom are visible from Highway 101 in late spring and summer.

Should you want to take the inevitable photo of your car coming through the middle of a redwood, there's a tour-through tree in Klamath. And if you want to take home redwood burl slabs or bowls as souvenirs, there are plenty of shops in Orick and Klamath that will be more than happy to supply them.

Incidentally, you needn't worry that trees have been cut down to create these handsome wooden pieces. Burls are warty growths that form on injured or damaged areas on the base as nature's way to counterbalance a tree's tendency to lean in one direction or another. They can be cut off without harming the tree, and the swirls of redwood growth create interesting patterns.

The best lodging for a visit to Redwood National Park is the Requa Inn, an old-fashioned family-run hostelry that has operated on the same site since 1885. It is conveniently located on Requa Road, across from the Klamath River and about midway through the park. There is also a popular AYH Redwood Hostel north of Klamath. Otherwise, the closest options are motels in Klamath or Crescent City.

Less convenient but far more appealing are the choices about 20 minutes south of Orick in Trinidad. You may gladly make the drive in order to stay at the fresh and pretty Lost Whale Inn, overlooking the ocean. Parents might note that this is one inn where the warm hosts particularly welcome families.

Trinidad also offers some of the area's best dining. In fact, everything about this tiny oceanside town is so appealing, you may well decide it deserves a weekend of its own.

Area Code: 707

DRIVING DIRECTIONS Redwood National Park runs along Highway 101, beginning 41 miles north of Eureka in Orick and running 40 miles to Crescent City. Orick is 301 miles from San Francisco, 182 miles from Redding, 335 miles from Sacramento.

PUBLIC TRANSPORTATION Air service to Eureka and limited air service to Klamath.

ACCOMMODATIONS *Requa Inn,* 451 Requa Road, Klamath, 95548, 482-8205, I–M, CP • *Motel Trees,* 15495 Highway 101, Klamath, 95548, 482-3152, I • *Camp Marigold Motel,* 1601 Highway 101, Klamath, 95548, 481-3585, housekeeping cottages, lodge, I • *Northwoods Inn,* 655 Highway 101 south, Crescent City, 95531, 464-9771, I–M • *Curly Redwood Lodge,* 701 Highway 101 south, Crescent City 95531, 464-2137, built from one redwood tree, I • *Ship Ashore Resort,* 12370 Highway 101 north, Smith River, 95567 (just north of Crescent City), 487-3141, pleasant motel on the river, good spot for fishermen, I–M • *The Lost Whale Inn,* 3452 Patrick's Point Drive, Trinidad, 95570, 677-3425, serene, secluded, M–EE, CP • *Trinidad Bed & Breakfast,* P.O. Box 849, Trinidad, 95570, 677-0840, Cape Cod–style home overlooking the Bay, E–EE, CP • *Bishop Pine Lodge,* 1481 Patrick's Point Drive, Trinidad, 95570, 677-3314, cottage colony in the pines, I–M • *AYH Redwood Hostel* (*DeMartin House*), 14480 Highway 101 at Wilson Creek Road, Klamath, 95548, 482-8265, busy, reserve well in advance, I.

DINING *Larrupin',* 1658 Patrick's Point Drive, Trinidad, 677-0223, M • *Seascape,* at the harbor, Trinidad, 677-3762, M • *Requa Inn,* Klamath (see above), I–M • *Rolf's Park Restaurant,* Highway 101 north of Orick, 488-3841, tiny gem for German-Swiss food and highly praised game specialties, M • *Ship Ashore Resort,* Smith River (see above), I–M • *Harbor View Grotto,* 155 Citizen's Dock Road, Crescent City, 464-3815, overlooking harbor, I–E • *Beachcomber,* 1400 Highway 101/ South Beach, Crescent City, 464-2205, seafood on the beach, M.

SIGHTSEEING *Redwood National Park,* information centers at the southern entrance, Orick, 488-2171, and northern entrance, Crescent City, 464-9533. Hours: Mid-June to Labor Day, 8 A.M. to 7 P.M.; rest of year, 9 A.M. to 5 P.M. Parking fee, $5. Written information from 1111 2nd Street, Crescent City, 95531, 464-6101• *Tour-Thru Tree,* 430 Highway 169 (off Highway 101), Klamath, 482-5971. Hours: Daylight hours. $2 • *Battery Point Lighthouse,* foot of A Street, Crescent City, 464-3089. Hours: April to September, Wednesday to Sunday 10 A.M. to 4 P.M. Adults, $2; children under 12, $.50.

INFORMATION *Crescent City–Del Norte County Chamber of Commerce,* 1001 Front Street, Crescent City, CA 95531, 464-3174 • *Klamath Chamber of Commerce,* P.O. Box 476, Klamath, CA 95548, 482-7165 • *Trinidad Chamber of Commerce,* P.O. Box 356, Trinidad, CA 95570, 677-3448 • *Redwood Empire Association,* 785 Market Street, 15th Floor, San Francisco, CA 94103, (415) 543-8334.

Back to the Past in Columbia

A Gold Rush prospector magically transported to the twentieth century would feel right at home in Columbia. This "Gem of the Southern Mines" is the best preserved of all the towns along the 120-mile ore-rich mother lode. The town is unique, truly a bit of living history, because the buildings of the historic area are in use. This is a real community, where museums and displays stand beside operating hotels, restaurants, banks, and shops.

It was 1850 when gold was first found nearby, lodes of yellow treasure whose value eventually totaled more than $1.5 billion in today's currency. Fortune seekers came running, erecting a tent city, then wooden buildings that included 30 saloons, 7 boardinghouses, 4 hotels, and many fine restaurants and theaters. The population zoomed to more than 5,000 in no time, making this one of California's largest cities.

When fire destroyed many of the hastily put up wooden structures in the late 1850s, they were rebuilt in fireproof brick with iron fire doors—and that's just the way they remain. In 1945 the state legislature created Columbia State Historic Park to ensure that a remarkable page from the past would be saved for us today.

For a real sense of the past, come early in June for Columbia Diggin's, when the town comes alive with a four-day program reenacting early life in the gold camps, including a re-creation of the first tent town.

Anytime you come, a walk around Columbia puts you in the spirit of those golden olden days. To add to the fun, you can ride an old stagecoach, pan for gold, watch artisans demonstrating old-fashioned skills like blacksmithing, and visit a period theater and saloon. Best of all, you can stay in one of two antiques-filled Gold Rush–era hotels and dine wonderfully well in a nostalgic Victorian setting.

If there's no room in Columbia's inns, there are fine alternatives nearby. Jamestown is picture-pretty, as many moviemakers will attest. Sonora is now a thriving modern town, but still offers some very pleasing places to stay and dine just minutes away from Columbia's historic lanes.

If you do stay elsewhere and drive into Columbia, look for the parking lots on Broadway, as no cars are allowed in the heart of town. The five blocks of Main Street offer most of the sights, a diverting slice of the past livened by shops behind some of the old facades. The William Cavalier Museum, once a general store, is the place to see a slide show on Columbia's early days, look at relics of the Gold Rush era, and pick up a walking-tour map. You can also join one of the frequent walking tours led by costumed docents. They'll tell you that Columbia has had its own share of camera fame, seen in films such as Clint Eastwood's *Pale Rider* and on TV's "Little House on the Prairie."

Watch carefully to be sure you don't miss some of the interesting touches in the old shops. The pioneer barbershop, for example, still has old miners' bathtubs at the rear, and the Chinese Herb Shop includes a small temple. There's still plenty of action at the blacksmith shop, and Columbia Mercantile continues to serve the community with groceries.

Some shops, however, now offer merchandise that is very different from the wares originally sold. Look into the 1899 Brady Building, once a general store, and you'll find the Prospector's Trading Post, filled with western gear and gifts. The 1854 Cheap Cash Store, a one-time clothing shop, offers antiques and clocks. The Matelot Gulch Mining Company Supply Store now sells gold jewelry and gems—but this is also a place to get pointers on panning for gold or arrange for a tour of the Hidden Treasure Gold Mine in town. At the 1858 Wells Fargo Building, the old scales on display once weighed out $55 million in gold.

Stop at the Columbia Stage Line Depot to find out how it feels to ride in a stagecoach. Afterward, if you want proof that you've stepped back to the nineteenth century, pose for a souvenir photo wearing old-fashioned garb. A. DeCosmos Daguerrean Studio will be glad to oblige.

When you are ready for refreshments, there are several choices. The Kruse Saloon has turned into the Columbia House restaurant, and an old home, the 1870 Siebert House, is now the El Sombrero Restaurant, serving Mexican food.

If you are thirsty, the Jack Douglass Saloon is still going strong in its original line of business. It also offers sandwiches and sarsaparilla. Another popular saloon in town is What Cheer, at the rear of the City Hotel.

This 1856 hotel was completely restored in 1974. Along with the Fallon Hotel, around the corner, it serves as a classroom for Hospitality Management students from Columbia Community College. These eager-to-please young people, many dressed in Victorian garb, add to the pleasures of a stay.

Though the City Hotel kitchen can be uneven, when the chef is on target the food here is notable, the subject of many rave reviews. The dining room is open for both lunch and dinner; reserve far in advance.

Walk around the corner from the end of Main to Washington Street to see the other hotel beauty in town, the Fallon, once one of the finest lodgings of the mother lode. It has also undergone a spiffy restoration, and offers a nice option for dessert—an old saloon transformed into an ice-cream parlor.

The 1885 Fallon House Theatre also is very much in business, with the Columbia Actors' Repertory in residence from fall through spring and students from the University of the Pacific taking over in June through August with a summer stock season. The Eagle Cottage, down the block, once a boardinghouse for miners, now serves as dormitory for the students.

The Columbia Gazette Book Shop on Washington was rebuilt by the California Newspaper Publishers Association. Downstairs, a Printing Museum displays nineteenth-century printing equipment and traces the progress of journalism in the state.

The list of notable places continues on State and Jackson streets. Displays include mining equipment, early wagons, an 1860 schoolhouse, the old jail, some fine private homes, and a historic rose garden. The town cemetery, still in use, supposedly was moved to Burial Hill after overeager miners started digging on the original site.

With 69 historic sites on the map, Columbia can easily fill a day if you do it in depth. But be sure to save time for some nearby attractions.

A prime stop is the town of Jamestown. Though it is more commercial, Jamestown's pastel Main Street, with its arcades and wooden sidewalks, is one of the prettiest relics of the Gold Rush. Movies filmed here include *High Noon, The Virginian, My Little Chickadee,* and *Back to the Future III.* Behind the old wooden false fronts is a host of tempting gift and antiques shops. The Jamestown Hotel, another nicely restored 1800s lodging, is a good choice for dinner or an overnight stay.

There's lots to do around this town. At Railtown 1897 State Historic Park, you can ride an old steam train and tour the roundhouse museum. At the old Livery Stable on Main Street, you can sign on for panning lessons or a gold-prospecting expedition or, for a change of pace, join a white-water rafting trip on the American River. Jamestown is a good place to try your luck at panning—they're still finding remnants of gold in the vicinity. It's a thrill to swish away the pebbles and sand and find even a trace of shiny stuff in the bottom of your pan.

For some nighttime action, try winning some gold at the high-stakes bingo games at the Chicken Ranch on the Miwok Indian reservation, about a mile west of Jamestown.

North of Columbia, mother lode towns like Angels Camp and Murphys have a more authentic, less tourist-conscious look. Angels Camp, first known for its rich quartz mining, became even more famous in 1864, when Mark Twain used it as the setting for his story "The Celebrated Jumping Frogs of Calaveras County." In 1928 someone came up with the notion of holding a live version of the fictional derby, and the Jumping Frog Jubilee leaped into action. The event continues to be staged every May at the local fairgrounds, known as Frogtown. It's a lighthearted affair, but the competition is real. They'll even rent you a frog to vie for the $1,500 in prizes.

There's some interesting frog memorabilia along with town history to be seen in the little Angels Camp Museum, and a shed full of old carriages out back. Jensen's Pick & Shovel Ranch presents another opportunity to go prospecting for gold, and the town is also headquarters for Outdoor Adventure River Specialists, offering a variety of white-water river raft trips nearby.

The shaded main street of quaint Murphys, east of Angels Camp, has a historic atmosphere but is free of frills. They've even buried their wiring to keep the old-time look. The little walking tour won't take long, but it will show you some interesting original buildings, including Murphys Hotel, in use since 1860. This is a good place for a meal, and the Dunbar House, a few blocks away, is a winning bed-and-breakfast inn.

Cave lovers should continue east from Murphys to Mercer Caverns, a maze of stalactites, stalagmites, and other eerie formations set off by dramatic lighting. Continue east and you'll come to Calaveras Big Trees State Park, comprising more than 6,000 acres of canyons, rivers, and groves of some most impressive giant sequoia trees. It's a shady retreat should you want to get away into the woods.

There's plenty of variety to fill a weekend here in southern gold country. A visit will likely send you home convinced that those were, indeed, golden days.

Area Code: 209

DRIVING DIRECTIONS Columbia is off Highway 49, north of Sonora, about 140 miles from San Francisco, 119 miles from Sacramento.

ACCOMMODATIONS _City Hotel,_ Main Street, Columbia, 95310, 532-1479, M, CP • _Fallon Hotel,_ Washington Street and Broadway, P.O. Box 1870, Columbia 95310, 532-1470, I–M, CP, ask about theater packages • _Barretta Gardens Inn,_ 700 South Barretta Street, Sonora, 95370, 532-6039, well furnished, nice hosts, M, CP • _Lulu Belle's,_ 85 Gold Street, Sonora, 95370, 533-3455, homey, M, CP • _Llamahall Guest Ranch,_ 18170 Wards Ferry Road, Sonora, 95370, 532-7264, country charmer on a creek, with llamas in residence, M–E, CP • _Jamestown Hotel,_ Main Street, Jamestown, 95327, 984-3902, I–E, CP • _Dunbar House,_ 271 Jones Street, Murphys, 95247, 728-2897, lots of frills, cozy wood stoves, E–EE, CP.

DINING _City Hotel,_ Columbia (see above), E prix fixe • _El Sombrero,_ 11256 State Street, Columbia, 533-9123, basic Mexican, I • _Jamestown Hotel_ (see above), M • _Smoke Café,_ 18191 Main Street, Jamestown, 984-3733, popular Mexican stop, I • _Michaelangelo's,_ 18228 Main Street, Jamestown, 984-4830, excellent Italian in a period setting, M • _Hemingway's,_ 362 S. Stewart Street, Sonora, 532-4900, California cuisine, one of area's best, M–EE • _Murphys Hotel,_ Main Street, Murphys, 728-3444, go mainly for the ambience, I–M.

SIGHTSEEING *Columbia State Historic Park,* Main Street, P.O. Box 151, Columbia, 95310, 532-0150; museum phone, 532-4301. Hours: Daily 8 A.M. to 5 P.M., May to October to 6 P.M. Free • *Columbia Diggin's Living History,* first weekend in June, phone Tuolumne County Visitors' Bureau for current schedule • *Hidden Treasure Gold Mine,* Main Street, Columbia, 532-9693. Hours: Office opens 9 A.M., tours begin 10:30 A.M., schedule varies with season • *Railtown 1897 State Historic Park,* Fifth Avenue, Jamestown, 984-3953. Hours: Tours March to November, daily 9:30 A.M. to 4:30 P.M. Adults, $2.50; ages 3 to 12, $1.50. Train rides Saturday, Sunday, and holidays: Adults, $9; children, $5 • *Angels Camp Museum,* 753 South Main Street, Angels Camp, 736-2963. Hours: Daily 10 A.M. to 3 P.M. Admission, $1; ages 6 to 12, $.25 • *Chicken Ranch Bingo,* Chicken Ranch Road off Route 108, Jamestown, 984-3000 or (800) 752-4646. Hours: Thursday to Saturday, warm-up games 7 P.M., regular games 7:30 P.M. • *Historic Fallon House Theatre,* Fallon Hotel, Columbia, 532-4644. Phone for current programs • *Calaveras Jumping Frog Jubilee,* part of Calaveras County Fair held in May; for dates phone 736-2561 or Calaveras County Visitor Center, 736-0049 • *Mercer Caverns,* Ebbetts Pass Highway off Highway 4, Murphys, 728-2101. Hours: Memorial Day to September, 9 A.M. to 5 P.M., October to May, weekends only 11 A.M. to 4 P.M. Adults, $5; children, $2.50 • *Calaveras Big Trees State Park,* Highway 4, Arnold, 795-2334. Hours: Daylight hours daily. Per car, $5.

ACTIVITIES **Stagecoach rides, horseback riding:** *Columbia Stage Line & Stables,* Main Street, 532-0663 • **Gold panning lessons or prospecting trips:** *Hidden Treasure Gold Mine,* Main Street, Columbia 532-9693; *Gold Mine Expeditions & Store,* 18170 Main Street, Jamestown, 984-4653; *Jensen's Pick & Shovel Ranch,* Highway 4, P.O. Box 1141, Angels Camp, 736-0287 • **River rafting:** *Ahwahnee Whitewater Expeditions,* Columbia, (800) 446-1333/ext. 400; *Sierra Mac River Trips, Inc.,* 19 Bradford Avenue, Suite B, P.O. Box 366, Sonora, 532-1327 or (800) 457-2580; *Outdoor Adventure River Specialists,* Box 67, Angels Camp, 736-4677.

INFORMATION *Tuolumne County Visitors' Bureau,* P.O. Box 4020, Sonora, CA 95370, 533-4420 or (800) 446-1333.

SUMMER

Overleaf: *Summer fun in the Eel River. Photo courtesy of Redwood Empire Association.*

On Top of the World at Mt. Shasta

The lonely grandeur of Mt. Shasta signifies mystery to some, majesty to all. This mighty, dormant volcano stands alone, 14,162 feet high, its peak of perpetual snow visible for more than 150 miles. It has inspired numerous legends, and cults of all kinds have been drawn here, finding spiritual sustenance in the mountain's power.

The Indians believed that it was the home of the Creator, an ancient place of origin and continuing renewal. Even today there are those who believe that the mountain is a home for the Lemurians, a race of tiny beings who escaped from the lost continent of Mu. People also claim to have spotted footprints of the legendary Big Foot in the area. You can read up on the spiritual side of things at the Golden Bough, a New Age bookshop, or at the "I AM" reading room in town.

But myths and mysteries are not the concern of most of the visitors to Mt. Shasta, the pretty little town at the base of the mountain. They have other pursuits in mind up here in the area known as the Shasta-Cascade Wonderland, things such as clean, cool mountain air; a bit of biking, hiking, or mountain climbing; rafting on the upper Sacramento River; water sports; or relaxing beside a clear lake. Golfers enjoy four golf courses in the area, all with striking mountain views.

Not the least of Mt. Shasta's lures is the lack of crowds up here in peaceful Northern California. The pace is slow, leaving lots of time for some serene gazing at the odd-shaped clouds that gather around the mountain and for admiring the alpenglow produced by the sun reflecting off the snowy peak.

Helped by the year-round business generated by the ski area on the mountain, the town of Mt. Shasta has spruced up in recent years, and the downtown has a pleasant, unpretentious Old West feel. Residents boast about their pure cold water, fed by a huge spring southeast of town.

A fine time for a visit is the Fourth of July, the occasion for an old-fashioned small-town celebration complete with bands, a parade, races, lots of food booths, and an evening fireworks display over Lake Siskiyou. If you come on Labor Day weekend, you can take in the Blackberry Bluegrass Festival in the City Park, listening to lively music while you feast on blackberry pie and ice cream.

There is a choice of lodgings. The newest is the Mount Shasta Resort, a complex of chalet-style cottages on the forested shore of Lake Siskiyou. The resort has its own 18-hole golf course. Mount Shasta Ranch, a onetime working horse ranch just outside town, has great appeal, offering spacious rooms and informal ambience. Ward's

Big Foot Ranch is a contemporary home on ten private acres a couple of miles from town, where you'll be welcomed by the resident llamas, ducks, and geese, and enjoy lawn games as well as a great view of Mt. Shasta. Or you can opt for the Dream Inn, a small bed-and-breakfast home right in town.

Two other interesting choices are in neighboring communities. The McCloud Guest House is both a fine restaurant and a country inn in a special little village that was once the epitome of the well-kept company town. McCloud's neat row houses and the old wooden sidewalks are still in place. The Guest House once was used by the president of the McCloud River Lumber Company for VIP visitors. Among them were many members of the Hearst family, who still have a vacation hideaway on the river. The inn's parlor has a pool table from the Hearst collection.

The most unusual option nearby is the Railroad Park Resort in Dunsmuir, where guests sleep and dine in elegantly restored railroad cars. It's a novelty for all, and a rail buff's dream come true. The location is appropriate, since Dunsmuir is an old railroading town whose major event each year is the Railroad Days celebration in late June.

Having settled on a lodging, your first order of business is to see the local scenery, starting with that mountain looming over the town. Naturalist John Muir, founder of the Sierra Club, was the first to climb Shasta, and he has been followed by intrepid climbers ever since, as many as 100 a day. For those who aren't quite that energetic, there are easier walking trails to enjoy, and the Everitt Memorial Highway ends at 7,800 feet, halfway up the side of the mountain, with some very impressive views. Among the timbered mountain's fascinations are its five glaciers, the sulfur hot spring near the summit, and the perpetual snowfields.

In town, the main sightseeing attraction is the State Fish Hatchery, where 5 to 10 million trout are produced each year to stock the streams of Northern California. The old main building has been converted into the Sisson Museum, offering changing exhibits of local history and Native American life.

Lake Siskiyou, three miles west of town, is where people head for such water sports as windsurfing, boating, and swimming. This is the place to be if you want to rent a boat or have a snack bar handy. For solitude, pack up a picnic and drive a little farther to pristine Castle Lake, an idyllic Alpine lake amid the pines.

Fishing spots are legion—the local brochure lists 21 lakes and 19 rivers and streams. Bass, catfish, and plentiful trout are the area specialties. Stop at one of the sporting goods stores or bait shops for advice on where they are biting at the moment.

There are two prime drives from Mt. Shasta. Stop at the Mt. Shasta Visitors' Bureau for maps. Head east on Highway 89 to McCloud to tour the picturesque town. Then continue on Highway 89 to McCloud

Falls. Watch for the sign to Fowlers Campground and Lower McCloud Falls; the road leads to the best vantage point for the Lower Falls. There is paved parking beyond the campground and easy access to the falls.

Go back to the four-way stop sign and turn east onto a dirt road for one mile to the rugged Middle Falls Trail and overlook. Look for a cleared parking area to the north of the road. The Upper Falls parking and overlook are about a third of a mile farther. Take the right fork of the road along the river. There is a five-mile loop road that takes in the Middle and Upper falls.

The McCloud River, known for great trout fishing, is also a scenic route for river rafting. The Upper Sacramento, another prime rafting route, is three miles from Mt. Shasta.

If you continue east on Highway 89, you'll come to McArthur Burney Falls Memorial State Park and the chance to see the impressive 129-foot falls that have cut their way through the rock layers into the Pit River. Some 200 million gallons of water a day tumble over the lip. Take the easy hiking trail that leads to the base of the falls, where rainbows often form in the perpetual mist. The attractive park is filled with tall pines and oaks and is a fine place for a picnic.

Another interesting excursion is the trip 12 miles south from Mt. Shasta on I-5 to Castle Crags State Park. The imposing needle-shaped spires, polished by ancient glaciers, are more than 170 million years old. In summer there are ranger-led walks, campfire programs, and other informal talks about the area's geology and plant and animal life. A scenic overlook here also gives a dramatic perspective on distant Mt. Shasta.

This park is a great spot for hiking. The Indian Creek Trail is an easy one-mile self-guided walk with fine views of the crags, along with a sampling of the types of plants that grow in the area. The more challenging 2¾-mile Crags Trail rises 2,250 feet to the base of Castle Dome for exceptional vistas. A cutoff leads to Indian Springs, where cool, clear water bubbles out of the ground. Seven miles of the Pacific Crest Trail also run through the park along the base of the crags, much of it gentle walking with excellent vistas.

Castle Crags Park also includes about two miles of the upper Sacramento River, said to be a prime spot for rainbow trout fishing.

While you are in the neighborhood, you may want to detour off I-5 for lunch and a look at the Railroad Park Resort. It's one-of-a-kind, and the distant views of the crags can't be beat.

Driving still farther south on I-5 toward Redding brings you to the turnoff for Shasta Dam and to the huge lake it created. Shasta Lake is a prime place for houseboating and water-skiing. Take a look at those boaters out enjoying the cool blue water and you may just decide to start planning a weekend cruise of your own.

Area Code: 916

DRIVING DIRECTIONS   Mt. Shasta is located on I-5, 60 miles north of Redding. It is 290 miles from San Francisco, 235 miles from Sacramento.

ACCOMMODATIONS   *Mount Shasta Resort,* 1000 Siskiyou Lake Boulevard, Mt. Shasta 96067, 926-3030, M–E • *Mount Shasta Ranch,* 1008 W. A. Barr Road, Mt. Shasta, 96067, 926-3870, I–M, CP • *Dream Inn,* 326 Chestnut Street, Mt. Shasta, 96067, 926-6948, I, CP • *Ward's Big Foot Ranch,* 1530 Hill Road, Mt. Shasta, 96067, 926-5170, I–M, CP • *McCloud Guest House,* 606 West Colombero Drive, McCloud, 96057, 964-3160, M, CP • *Railroad Park Resort,* off I-5, Dunsmuir, 96025, 235-4440, I–M • *Tree House Best Western,* I-5 and Lake Street, Mt. Shasta, 96067, 926-3101 or (800) 545-7164, best of the local motels, indoor pool, I–E.

DINING   *Bellissimo,* 204A West Lake Street, Mt. Shasta, 926-4461, imaginative menus, great desserts, best in town for lunch, I, or dinner, M • *Highland House,* Mount Shasta Resort (see above), fine California cuisine, M • *Lily's,* 1013 Mt. Shasta Boulevard, 926-3372, eclectic menu with an ethnic touch, well recommended locally, I–M • *Serge's Restaurant,* 531 Chestnut Street, Mt. Shasta, 926-1276, French cuisine, mountain views from the terrace, M • *Michael's,* 313 N. Mt. Shasta Boulevard, Mt. Shasta, 926-5288, casual, American menu, homemade pasta, I–M • *Tree House Restaurant,* Tree House Best Western, Mt. Shasta (see above), M • *McCloud Guest House,* McCloud (see above), pleasant ambience, M.

SIGHTSEEING   *Mount Shasta State Fish Hatchery and Sisson Museum,* Old Stage Road, Mt. Shasta, 926-2215. Hours: Hatchery open daily 8 A.M. to sunset. Spawning can be viewed on selected Tuesdays in fall and winter; phone to check. Museum hours: May to September, daily 10 A.M. to 5 P.M.; rest of year, noon to 4 P.M. Free • *Castle Crags State Park,* I-5 six miles south of Dunsmuir, 235-2684. Hours: Daylight hours. Parking, $4 • *McArthur Burney Falls Memorial State Park,* Highway 89, northeast of Burney, 335-2777. Hours: Daylight hours. Parking, $5. For current lists of white-water rafting companies, pack trip operators, and guides, check with the Visitors' Bureau at the address below.

INFORMATION   *Mt. Shasta Visitors' Bureau,* 300 Pine Street, Mt. Shasta, CA 96067, 926-4865 or in California (800) 926-4865.

Making the Most of Marin

It's positively uncanny. San Francisco may be shrouded in summer fog across the Bay, even Sausalito right next door may disappear into the mist, yet tiny Tiburon, an enchanted village of million-dollar homes terraced up steep hillsides, seems to remain in bright sunshine through it all, looking out smugly at heavenly water views.

Most visitors come to Tiburon on a ferry to share that good life for a day. Whether they choose breakfast on the deck of Sweden House, lunch and a beer at Sam's, or a creative Mexican dinner at Guaymas, they hang out on the waterfront, basking in the sun and enjoying the salty breeze, the calls of the gulls, and the views of sailboats gliding by.

But Tiburon is worth more than a day trip. Taken in combination with its inland neighbor, Mill Valley, it serves as a gateway to the best of Marin's many virtues—coastal pleasures, sophisticated dining, and easy access to scenic wilderness. Add a trip to Angel Island, just a ferry ride away, and there's every ingredient for a fun-filled quick getaway.

Tiburon was settled in 1884, when a branch line of the San Francisco and North Pacific Railroad established a connection to San Francisco here via ferryboat. The big ferries lasted until 1909, followed by smaller shuttles to the city via Sausalito. According to local lore, the town's isolation, single access road, and wide shoreline made it a perfect bootlegging center. In those days the waterfront was lined with rowdy taverns.

But the world eventually passed Tiburon by, and things fell into decline until after World War II, when the town was rediscovered as a place to live. The community determined to spruce up its faded Main Street, and there was a dramatic change on one memorable September weekend in 1955, when volunteers painted the fronts of 15 buildings. In 1962 Tiburon got its own ferry service, tourists began to arrive, and revival began in earnest.

Now the town's quaint Main Street and Ark Row are lined with art galleries and shops selling everything from music boxes to exotic teas. Some of the picturesque wooden buildings on Ark Row were once houseboats. One old wooden structure, a former rooming house, is now home to Tiburon Vintners, where free wine tastings are offered.

The Corinthian Yacht Club stands at the corner of Ark and Main. A gracious landmark, the 100-year-old wooden building on the water's edge overlooks masses of masts of the boats moored just beyond.

Downtown changed even more in the late 1970s, when the old railroad yards were developed into a condominium and shopping complex. A shoreline park also was installed, stretching from downtown to the Donahue Building, part of the old town depot that is now a landmark used by the local recreation department. The walkway extends out into the Bay to Elephant Rock, where an observation platform atop the rock is a favorite spot.

Another old railroad right-of-way now is part of a scenic path around Richardson Bay, where residents can be found almost any time of day enjoying a stroll, a jog, or a bike ride. Visitors are welcome to join the parade.

There are a couple of historic sights to see as well, though note that they are open only on Wednesday and Sunday afternoons. Old St. Hilary's Church dates to 1884 and is one of the few Carpenter's Gothic churches in California to survive in their original settings. Built of redwood and fir, the interior with its vaulted ceiling is well worth a look. In spring the acres surrounding the church are carpeted with wildflowers.

Drive down Beach Road onto neighboring Belvedere Island, one of Marin's most exclusive enclaves, to admire the lavish homes and visit China Cabin. Once the luxurious saloon on the SS *China,* the structure was saved and served as a residence until 1978. It is now a small but unique marine museum, also used for private functions.

For a sunny nature escape, head for the Richardson Bay Audubon Center, a bird and wildlife sanctuary on 11 acres fronting the bay. From October to March this is a resting place for thousands of waterfowl and shorebirds. In summer you can follow a self-guided nature trail.

Spend the morning in Tiburon, then drive inland past Highway 101, where Tiburon Boulevard becomes Blithdale Avenue, leading into Mill Valley. This woodsy village on the slopes of Mt. Tamalpais was originally a logging town, but in the 1890s it grew into a tourist attraction, with railroad tracks carrying visitors from downtown up Mt. Tamalpais on the popular Scenic Railroad. It was strictly a summer getaway until after the 1906 earthquake, when many city people decided to weatherize their cottages and stay year-round. Today the old station has been coverted into a town square, and the town has become a quintessential Marin County community, an attractive laid-back town with an active arts schedule that includes a resident theater company and a noted October Film Festival.

Although there are few day-trippers here, the town plaza is usually crowded with a mix of residents—long-haired, barefoot flower children and preppy suburbanites, happily sharing the afternoon sun. Join them at the adjoining Depot Bookstore or at the Sunnyside Café in the El Paseo shopping complex, a local favorite for breakfast and lunch. The Mill Valley Inn, a downtown inn with attractive rooms and balconies looking at the tall redwoods, adds to the town's appeal. Many of the inn's furnishings were created by local artisans.

Take a walk around the town to browse through the pleasant shops and galleries, then drive up steep Cascade Drive off Throckmorton Avenue to see the attractive weathered shingled homes stair-stepped up the hills on narrow lanes amid tall trees.

For the hardy, hiking trails connect from Cascade Drive to Mt. Tamalpais, fondly known to all simply as Mt. Tam. This 2,600-foot peak, Marin's most visible landmark, is part of a 6,400-acre state park with 30 miles of trails wandering through a diversity of environments from redwood canyons and grasslands to oak woodlands. The entire San Francisco Bay Area can be seen from the East Peak, truly a glorious sight.

You don't have to hike for these panoramic views. Take Miller Avenue from the village back to Highway 101, turn right, and watch for signs to Highway 1. Take the turnoff and then turn again onto Panoramic Highway. This aptly named road winds steeply up and around almost to the top of the mountain to the visitors' center of Mt. Tamalpais State Park. Ask here about guided walks each weekend morning, stargazing hikes, and spring programs held in the Mountain Theater, an outdoor arena carved out of stone.

On Panoramic Highway is one of Marin's most dramatically perched lodgings, the Mountain Home Inn, a triple-level rustic hideaway of redwood and cedar with balconies looking over the trees to the sea. Rooms vary in size, but all are filled with artwork and wildflowers. The most lavish come with whirlpools and huge fireplaces. The views from the restaurant decks are superb. Overnight guests have their own dining room and deck; the public uses the upstairs dining rooms. This is the perfect place for a leisurely lunch admiring the views.

Hiking trails surround the Mountain Home Inn, including one leading down to Muir Woods National Monument. You can also drive there by taking the turnoff from Panoramic Highway onto Muir Woods Road. One of Marin's most-visited treasures, Muir Woods boasts redwoods as large as 18 feet thick and 300 feet tall. The shady walks beneath these towering trees are inspiring. The only problem with Muir Woods is a small parking lot that seems always to be filled. If you are patient and cruise around for a while, you'll usually find someone pulling out.

The Pelican Inn, another very special place to stay or dine, is at the bottom of Muir Woods near Muir Beach. Though the setting is California shoreline, the decor is English Tudor, and the snug guest rooms are furnished with English antiques and draped half-canopy beds. The food is also hearty English, featuring bangers, cottage pie, mixed grill, and roast beef with Yorkshire pudding.

Not far away on Highway 1 is the Audubon Canyon Ranch, a nature education center and wildlife sanctuary known for its great blue heron and great egret nesting colony. The rookery overlook is open to the public on weekends from March to July 4. Special family programs are scheduled often at nearby Slide Ranch, a working farm with a variety of nature programs available by advance reservation.

Continue to Stinson Beach for yet another gem of an inn, the Casa del Mar, a Mediterranean-style home with a red tile roof, perched high on a hillside. Steps away is another entrance to Mt. Tamalpais State Park; two blocks down is the beach. The rooms are clean and contemporary, with colorful paintings and fabrics standing out against the white walls. The grounds are outstanding; the entire hillside is a lavishly landscaped garden.

To complete your tour of the area's sights, pick up a picnic lunch, head for the Tiburon ferry dock, and sail away to Angel Island State Park for sunning and swimming or hiking and biking. Ayala Cove is the most popular of the sheltered beach spots; it offers picnic areas, a snack bar, and rest rooms. This is also the location of the visitors' center, where a slide show tells some of the island's unique history. Take the five-mile trail circling the island rim or climb to the 281-foot summit of Mt. Livermore for fabulous views.

This car-free 740-acre retreat was not always so peaceful. It served as a military outpost from Civil War days to its establishment as a Nike missile station in 1962. It was also once the headquarters for arriving immigrants from Asia, and was known as the "Ellis Island of the West." During World War II it served as an internment camp for Japanese-Americans. All of this makes for some interesting exploring. Docents lead tours of the most interesting sites and there is a tour tram that traverses the island with a narrative that re-creates the sights and sounds of the past.

The officers' quarters, bakehouse, and parade ground of Camp Reynolds on the northwest side comprise one of the largest remaining collections of Civil War military structures. The cannons aimed out to sea were intended to prevent a supposed Confederate plot to invade the Bay and steal riches from the gold country to finance their cause. The guns were never needed then, but today visitors can become part of a crew helping to fire a 12-pound mountain howitzer.

Also open to visitors on the island's eastern side are the 1899 Chinese Immigration Center, where new arrivals were confined early in this century, and Ft. McDowell, an embarkation point for Pacific troops during World War II.

Ferries operate directly from Angel Island back to San Francisco, or you can return to the sunshine of Tiburon, Marin County's own Brigadoon.

Area Code: 415

DRIVING DIRECTIONS   Take Highway 101 north to the Tiburon Boulevard exit and turn right into town. Tiburon is just 18 miles north of San Francisco, 70 miles from Sacramento.

PUBLIC TRANSPORTATION   Golden Gate Transit and Ferry Company from San Francisco, 453-2100 for information.

ACCOMMODATIONS *Tiburon Lodge,* 1651 Tiburon Boulevard, Tiburon, 94920, 435-3133 or in California (800) TIBURON, motel, pool, E, CP • *Mill Valley Inn,* 165 Throckmorton Avenue, Mill Valley 94941, 389-6608 or (800) 595-2100, E–EE • *Mountain Home Inn,* 810 Panoramic Highway, Mill Valley, 94941, 381-9000, E–EE • *Pelican Inn,* Muir Beach, 94965, 383-6000, EE, CP • *Casa del Mar,* 37 Belvedere Avenue, Stinson Beach 94970, 868-2124, E–EE, CP • *Bed and Breakfast Exchange of Marin,* 45 Entrata, San Anselmo, 94960, 485-1971, for accommodations in local homes.

DINING *Guaymas,* 5 Main Street, Tiburon, 435-6300, excellent Mexican, enchanting waterfront setting, M • *Sweden House,* 35 Main Street, Tiburon, 435-9767, unbeatable views and goodies for breakfast and lunch, I • *Sam's Anchor Café,* 27 Main Street, Tiburon, 435-4527, more knockout views, but the food doesn't match—stick to hamburgers, I–M • *Cactus Café,* 393 Miller Avenue, Mill Valley, 388-8226, no-frills good Mexican, I • *Avenue Grill,* 44 E. Blithdale Avenue, Mill Valley, 388-6003, funky, home-style comfort food, hearty portions, M • *Piazza D'Angelo,* 22 Miller Avenue, 388-2000, popular Italian, M • *El Paseo,* 17 Throckmorton Avenue, 388-0741, romantic setting, continental menu, M • *Buckeye Roadhouse,* 15 Shoreline Highway, Mill Valley, 331-2600, trendy entry from the owners of San Francisco's Fog City Diner, M • *Jennie Low's Chinese Cuisine,* 38 Miller Avenue, Mill Valley, 388-8868, packed with fans of this cookbook author's cuisine, I–M • *Mountain Home Inn,* Mill Valley (see above), California cuisine, superb views, M • *Pelican Inn,* Muir Beach (see above), English pub ambience, M • *Lark Creek Inn,* 234 Magnolia Avenue, Larkspur, 924-7766, an easy drive, gourmet's first choice for creative American fare, M–E.

SIGHTSEEING *National Audubon Society/Richardson Bay Audubon Center,* 376 Greenwood Beach Road, Tiburon, 388-2524. Hours: Wednesday to Sunday 9 A.M. to 5 P.M. Lyford House hours: October to April, Sunday 1 P.M. to 4 P.M. Admission, $2 • *Old St. Hilary's Historic Preserve,* Esperanza and Mar West, Tiburon, 435-1853. Hours: April to October, Wednesday and Sunday 1 P.M. to 4 P.M. Free • *Angel Island State Park,* 435-1915. Hours: Ferry service from Tiburon leaves regularly weekends year-round, weekdays June through September. For schedules and information, phone 546-2896 in San Francisco, 435-2131 in Tiburon • *Mt. Tamalpais State Park,* 801 Panoramic Highway, Mill Valley, 388-2070. Visitors' center hours: Saturday, Sunday, and holidays 10 A.M. to 5 P.M. Guided hikes, Saturday and Sunday 9:30 A.M. Plays in open-air Mountain Theater May and June • *Muir Woods National Monument,* Muir Woods Road off Panoramic Highway, Mill Valley, 388-2595. Hours: Daily 9 A.M. to 6 P.M. Free • *Audubon Canyon Ranch,* 4900 Highway 1, 868-9244. Hours: Saturday,

Sunday, and holidays 10 A.M. to 4 P.M. Free • *Slide Ranch,* 2025 Shore-line Highway (Highway 1), Muir Beach, 381-6155. Many weekend family programs by reservation only; phone for information.

INFORMATION *Tiburon Peninsula Chamber of Commerce,* 96B Main Street, Tiburon, CA 94920, 435-5633 • *Mill Valley Chamber of Commerce,* 85 Throckmorton Avenue, Mill Valley, CA 94941, 388-9700. *Marin Chamber of Commerce,* 30 N. San Pedro Road, #150, San Raphael, CA 94903, 472-7470.

Superlative Summer at Lake Tahoe

They call the 72-mile loop around Lake Tahoe "The Most Beautiful Drive in America," and who's to argue? Set in a matchless crown of mountain peaks, North America's largest Alpine lake is a sapphire gem, with water so pure they claim you can spot a white dinner plate 75 feet below the surface.

The Washoe Indians named it *Ta-ho-e,* meaning "big water," and there's no argument there, either. So big and so deep is the lake, its 39.75 trillion gallons of water could cover the entire state of California to a depth of 14 inches. It has been estimated that it would take 300 years of drought to significantly drain the basin.

Tahoe is a paradise for sailing, boating, water-skiing, windsurfing, and swimming, and heaven-sent for hikers, bikers, and horseback riders, who can take in magnificent vistas while exploring the surrounding high Sierra. Summer hums, with festivals such as the season-long Valhalla Summer Festival of Arts and Music at the Tallac Historic Site, using restored mansions from Tahoe's grand early days, when it was a retreat for the wealthy. Tallac also hosts Native American, Renaissance, and Great Gatsby festivals. Music and Shakespeare festivals also take place at Sand Harbor, on the eastern Nevada side of the lake.

Come for the August Dragon Boat Festival to see the lake dotted with colorful craft, or for the Star-Spangled Fourth, when Harrah's Casino presents a huge fireworks display over the water. Whenever you come, you'll understand why this lake inspires superlatives.

The big casinos like Harrah's and Caesar's just across the state line in Nevada are a mixed blessing for Lake Tahoe. They add gambling excitement and world-class entertainment to the natural attractions of the area, but they also account for the buildup of tacky motels along

Highway 50 in the town of South Lake Tahoe. The current multi-million-dollar facelift to improve this stretch along the lake is good news, even though it calls for two big new hotels on the California side as part of the redevelopment program. One of them, Embassy Suites, is already in operation.

The most attractive places to stay in South Tahoe are low-key, low-rise hotels and condominium resorts on wooded grounds hugging the lakeshore. For a truly rustic getaway, Camp Richardson is unique. A family resort since the 1920s, it offers no-frills lodge rooms or cottages plus stables, a marina, and a private beach with beautiful lake vistas, all at modest prices. There's even a fine restaurant at the marina, with an outdoor deck in summer.

Seeing the lake is the first order of business, and there are many ways to do that. The best overview is 2,000 feet up via the Heavenly tram ride. There's a restaurant at the top of the tram lift, a great place for Sunday brunch with a view.

For a lake-level view of the mountains, take one of the glass-bottom sternwheeler cruiseboats, the MS *Dixie II* or the *Tahoe Queen.* Or rent your own boat at one of the many marinas. Sailboats, pedalboats, rafts, kayaks, and canoes are all available, along with water-skiing, parasailing, and scuba gear and lessons. Fishing boats and guides are also plentiful. Check with the Visitors' Authority for current listings.

The famous drive around the lake can take a couple of hours or a full day, depending on how many stops you make along the way. It's the best way to find the spots where you'll want to spend more time. The free pamphlet from the local Chamber of Commerce highlights the most important points, or you can borrow an auto tape from the U.S. Forest Service visitors' center on Highway 89. Another tape is available for a trip to Angora Lookout, for a view of the Tahoe Basin and Desolation Wilderness.

Going west from South Lake Tahoe, the intersection of Route 50 and Highway 89 isn't part of the scenic tour, but the factory outlets there may be of interest. Continuing on Highway 89 takes you away from the congestion and into national forest land and the Pope Baldwin Recreation Area, with beaches backed by tall pines. Stop for a look at Camp Richardson's marina and beach, then visit the Tallac Historic Site to see the Valhalla, Pope, and Baldwin estates, rustic mansions built more than 100 years ago, which are under restoration and are open to visitors.

The Tallac mansions tell of the time when this was the mountain hideaway for San Francisco high society, an era that is also celebrated by the National Forest Service with a Great Gatsby Festival each year in mid-August. Held at the Keys Marina and on the grounds of the Tallac site, the event includes hot-air balloon rides, Dixieland jazz, a display of classic cars and wooden boats, crafts demonstrations, children's games, and "living history" performances re-creating bygone days. One of the jazziest events is the costume party benefiting the Lake Tahoe Historical Society, which features a spirited Charleston competition.

The U.S. Forest Service visitors' center, located on Highway 89 just past the Fallen Leaf Lake turnoff, near the Tallac Historic Site, can supply you with details, plus schedules of guided walks and cruises and lots of information on the sights ahead. An underground viewing chamber here lets you observe trout and other aquatic life beneath the surface of a flowing mountain stream. It's particularly interesting in fall, when the Kokanee salmon swim upstream to spawn.

The visitors' center offers separate sheets detailing hikes on the south, west, and northeast shores of the lake, with something for every ability. Even some of the easy walks offer breathtaking views. Best of all are the vistas along the Tahoe Rim Trail. So far, volunteers have completed 45 miles of the trail. Merged with the 50 miles of the Pacific Crest Trail that pass through the Lake Tahoe area, they provide access to fantastic natural beauty.

The next important site is Emerald Bay, one of the most beautiful and most famous sections of the lake. This is a favorite hiking area, and the lookout just past Eagle Creek and Falls is the classic picture-taking spot. It will probably be crowded, but it shouldn't be missed. Divers should note that Emerald Bay recently became the site of California's first Underwater Shipwreck Park.

Take the one-mile hike down a dirt road off Highway 89 to visit Vikingsholm, a replica of a Viking castle built by a wealthy heiress, Mrs. Lora Josephine Moore Knight, in 1928 for the then-exorbitant cost of $500,000. Knight also put up the quaint teahouse on tiny Fannette Island in the Bay. The California Parks System now owns Vikingsholm and offers daily tours in summer for a small fee.

As you continue north, the wooded west shore of the lake offers a long stretch of parks and beaches with beautiful lake vistas. Prime stops are Rubicon Bay in D. H. Bliss State Park and Meeks Bay. Next comes Sugar Pine State Park, and the chance to visit another historic residence, the Ehrmann Mansion. Remember, there are parking fees for state parks.

A detour leads to Squaw Valley and another memorable view from atop the gondola.

Make a stop at Tahoe City for the Fanny Bridge across the Truckee River. The bridge was named for all the tourists leaning over to see the giant trout in the water below. For more about Tahoe City and North Tahoe, see pages 213 to 218.

From Tahoe City, Route 28 continues around the north end of the lake and across the Nevada border. The north shore is built up, the lakeside cluttered with a number of small resorts and restaurants. The road continues through Crystal Bay, Nevada, where there are a few low-key casinos, and onward for some wonderful lake vistas from the forested eastern Nevada shore. Detour into Incline Village to see one of the most luxurious lakeside residential developments.

Fans of TV's famous series "Bonanza" may also want to stop to see the place where it was filmed, the Ponderosa Ranch on Route 28. There's a guided tour of the Cartwright ranch house, plus a touristy western town to explore. Continue looping farther south to the Nevada Lake Tahoe State Park and one of the most beautiful beaches of them all.

Past the settlement of Glenbrook is Cave Rock, where the highway passes through 25 yards of solid stone. According to legend, the Washoe Indians considered this spot sacred. They buried their dead in the cold waters below the outcroppings.

Soon you're back to civilization, past Zephyr Cove's busy marina and on into Stateline, with its high-rise hotels and casinos, the last stop before completing the loop back to California and South Lake Tahoe.

Having staked out your favorite spots, you can now plan the rest of your weekend. Just don't let the casinos keep you up so late that you sleep the day away.

Area Code: 916

DRIVING DIRECTIONS   South Lake Tahoe is located on Highway 50 about 100 miles from Sacramento, 200 miles from San Francisco.

PUBLIC TRANSPORTATION   South Lake Tahoe has its own Tahoe Valley Airport as well as shuttle bus service from the Reno, Nevada, airport, 58 miles.

ACCOMMODATIONS   Rates listed are for summer and ski season; they are lower in spring and fall • *Richardson's Resort,* Highway 89 and Jameson Beach Road, South Lake Tahoe, 95731, 541-1801, rustic, secluded, great setting, like summer camp; lodge, I, beach motel, M, cabins, M–E • *Tahoe Beach and Ski Club,* 3601 Lake Tahoe Boulevard, South Lake Tahoe, 95705, 541-6220 or (800) 822-5962, M–EE • *Lakeland Village Beach and Ski Resort,* Box 705002, South Lake Tahoe, 95705, 541-7711 or (800) 822-5969, lakeside condo suites, fireplaces, pools, M–EE • *Inn by the Lake,* 3300 Lake Tahoe Boulevard, South Lake Tahoe, 96150, 542-0330 or (800) 877-1466, suite hotel, kitchens, pool, nice lakeside grounds, M–EE, CP • *Tahoe Seasons Resort,* Saddle Road at Keller, South Lake Tahoe, 95729, 541-6700, luxury hotel across from Heavenly ski area, M–EE • *Embassy Suites,* 4130 Lake Tahoe Boulevard, South Lake Tahoe,

96150, pricey but comfortable suites are ideal for families, EE. Motels galore; write for the list. For North Tahoe lodgings, see page 217.

DINING *Evan's American Gourmet Café,* 536 Highway 89, South Lake Tahoe, 542-1990; the name says it—one of the area's best, E • *Scusa!,* 1142 Ski Run Boulevard, South Lake Tahoe, 542-0100, attractive, airy setting, good Italian food, I–M • *Nephele's,* 1169 Ski Run Boulevard, South Lake Tahoe, 544-8130, long-time local favorite, California cuisine, M • *The Beacon,* Highway 89 and Jameson Beach Road, Camp Richardson, 541-0630, great water view, outside deck, M–E • *The Fresh Ketch,* 2435 E. Venice, Tahoe Keys Marina, South Lake Tahoe, 541-5683, seafood and another great view, M–E • *Samurai,* 2588 Highway 50, South Lake Tahoe, 542-0300, Japanese dishes and sushi bar, M • *The Seasons,* Tahoe Seasons Resort (see above), M–E, lavish Sunday brunch, M • *Swiss Chalet,* 2540 Lake Tahoe Boulevard, 544-3304, Swiss decor, veal specialties, M–E. Most Nevada casino hotels offer buffets for breakfast, lunch, and dinner, meals that are not memorable but are quite reasonable; bigger hotels like Caesar's, Harrah's, and Harvey's have excellent, posh, and expensive dining rooms.

SIGHTSEEING *Tallac Historic Site,* Highway 89 north of Camp Richardson, 541-4975. Hours: Memorial Day to Labor Day, site open daily dawn to dusk, visitor center open Monday to Friday 9 A.M. to 6 P.M. Call for information about numerous special events, including *Valhalla Festival of Art & Music,* summer-long concerts and exhibits • *Music at Sand Harbor* and *Shakespeare at Sand Harbor,* Sand Harbor State Park, Nevada, (702) 583-9048; outdoor lakeside concerts; annual summer events in lakeside amphitheater; phone for current schedules • *Ponderosa Ranch,* Route 28, Incline Village, Nevada, (702) 831-0691. Hours: May to October, daily 9:30 A.M. to 5 P.M. Adults, $7.50; ages 5 to 11, $5.50.

ACTIVITIES **Lake cruises:** *Tahoe Queen,* 970 Ski Run Boulevard, South Lake Tahoe, 541-3364 or (800) 23-TAHOE; MS *Dixie,* 760 Highway 50, Zephyr Cove, Nevada, (702) 588-3508 • **Boat rentals and parasailing:** *Camp Richardson's Ski Run Marina,* Highway 89, South Lake Tahoe, 541-7272. For more complete current list of rentals and fishing boats, contact Visitors' Authority • **Hiking information:** *U.S. Forest Service,* 870 Emerald Bay Road (Highway 89), South Lake Tahoe, 573-2600.

INFORMATION *Lake Tahoe Visitors' Authority,* 1156 Ski Run Boulevard, South Lake Tahoe, CA 96150, 544-5050 or (800) AT-TAHOE.

Blowing Off Steam at Lassen

Lassen Volcanic National Park is proof of the awesome power of nature. Lassen Peak, at 10,457 feet considered the world's largest plug dome volcano, was long thought to be extinct. That was a small misconception. The volcano suddenly erupted in 1914, beginning a long series of outbursts. The high point quite literally came in 1915, when the cone blew a huge mushroom cloud seven miles high. The discharge of lava from the eruptions dramatically altered the landscape for miles around.

The area was declared a national park in 1916 to preserve these changes for all to see, a living laboratory of volcanic phenomena. Today it also serves as a record of how the earth slowly but surely heals from even the most devastating damage.

The park also includes an area of geothermal activity, a bubbling and steaming indication that something is still brewing underground. Seeing the result of the volcano's fury, as well as exploring the park's interplay of geologic features—Alpine meadows, jagged mountains, deep forest, and steamy thermal basin—makes for a memorable visit.

This untamed section of Northern California, a wilderness of clean rivers, woods, and mighty peaks, is also just the place for letting off a little steam yourself—hiking, fishing, and generally unwinding city tensions.

You have two choices of headquarters when you plan your trip. For a totally back-to-nature weekend, there are cabin colonies or rustic ranch resorts in woodsy settings. Drakesbad Guest Ranch, nestled in a serene and scenic mountain valley within the boundaries of the park, is the most picturesque and secluded. It is more than 100 years old and remains determinedly primitive. They purposely don't have electricity in the cabins—kerosene lanterns are a lot more like the old days. The ranch offers hiking, fishing, swimming in a pool fed by hot springs, and horseback riding, including daily guided rides into Lassen Park. Guests get three ample meals, which include sack lunches if you want to go off for the day. For a small sampling of the ranch, guests are welcome for dinner, but by reservation only.

If you prefer a few citified comforts, the recommended place is Red Bluff, a little-heralded gem of a town. And there are a couple of nice bed-and-breakfast inns in Chester, a bit closer to the park.

Wherever you stay, reserve at least one complete day for Lassen Volcanic National Park. Though the main scenic loop can be driven in an hour, it passes trails, lakes, volcanoes, hot springs, and bubbling mud pots that can be appreciated fully only at close range. Names like Fantastic Lava Beds and Chaos Jumbles give you an idea of the scenery. Some of the devastated areas, once completely denuded, have slowly come back to life, first with herbs and grasses, then shrubs followed by pine trees.

In summer there are many ranger-guided hikes that give interesting insight into the area, some with whimsical names like "Ooze and Aaahs." There are also evening programs in the Summit Lake and Manzanita Lake amphitheaters, and "Night Prowls" in twilight and darkness. Two programs for youngsters, "Junior Rangers" for 7- to 12-year-olds and "Senior Rangers" for teens, offer special projects of fun and discovery.

For those who can handle the climb, the walk to the top of Lassen Peak is worth tackling. It is 2,000 feet uphill, but once you reach the top the walk is easy and interesting. It traces the volcanic eruptions and includes sites swept clean by the mudflow.

There are rewarding shorter hikes as well. The Trail to Paradise is a three-mile round-trip to a beautiful glacier-carved meadow of wildflowers. King Creek Falls, also three miles round-trip, follows a mountain stream through open meadow and forest and descends to a 30-foot waterfall. The easiest walk is the one-mile Lily Pond Nature Trail along the lakeshore and forest edge.

The eeriest path goes through the Bumpass Hell area, one of the park's geothermal regions, full of hissing steam vents, gurgling mud pots, and steaming hot springs. Boardwalks allow you to traverse the area safely.

Serious hikers can proceed to Lassen's backcountry for 150 miles of hiking trails, including 17 miles of the Pacific Crest Trail.

If you want to combine Lassen with some small-town pleasures, plan to stay in Red Bluff. Named for its location on a high vertical bluff at the bend of the upper Sacramento River, Red Bluff is small and isn't a tourist mecca at all, which makes it all the nicer. The main shopping street and shady residential blocks date back more than 100 years, to when the town was the stopping place for pack trains from points as far away as Oregon and Idaho. Later, for more than a century, it was the head of navigation on the Sacramento River.

There are enough classic Victorian buildings in town to warrant a printed-map tour. The old mercantile stores and livery stables fronting on Main, Walnut, and Oak streets still boast facades from the town's heyday, from 1860 to 1890, though inside the stores are thoroughly modern. The finest homes are along the streets named for presidents—Washington, Jefferson, Madison, Monroe, Jackson, and Lincoln—or for some of the towering old trees that canopy the streets—Oak, Elm, Ash, Pine, and many more.

One handsome residence, the 1880 Kelly Griggs House, is now elegantly restored and open to visitors. A few other homes have been converted to attractive Victorian bed-and-breakfast inns. The Jeter Victorian is especially appealing.

One of the earliest settlers in Red Bluff was Peter Lassen, whose name now graces a national park, a county, a volcano, and a highway. Another was William B. Ide, commander of the settlers who revolted against Mexican rule in Sonoma in 1846, proclaiming the Republic of California. Ide was "President of the Republic" from June 10 to July 8, when word came that California had been claimed by the United States. His modest pueblo home has been reconstructed on a scenic spot on a riverbank north of town. It is now part of the state park system and a shady, pleasant stop for a picnic and a brief tour.

If you are more interested in shopping, the printed guide to antiques stores in the area can keep you happily occupied. In Red Bluff, Washington Street Antiques & Uniques is the most impressive, with 4,000 square feet of quality furniture and collectibles. And don't miss a look at the antique carousel figures being restored at the little nameless shop just behind the Snack Box restaurant.

Outdoor activities galore can also be found nearby—two golf courses, a hot-air balloon company, and rafting on the Sacramento River north of town. Red Bluff calls itself the "Inland Salmon Fishing Capital of the West," and the Chamber of Commerce has a long list of fishing guides.

Even if you don't want to catch fish, you might want to have a look at the salmon from the viewing plaza at Diversion Dam on the Sacramento. Underwater TV cameras monitor the fish ladders as the salmon swim upstream to spawn; if you hit the right day, you can see the giant fish trapped for examination. The best viewing times are September and October.

Red Bluff seems to have a lot going on for a peaceful small town, but the pace is slow. It's just the place to sit back and enjoy the old-fashioned ambience—a nice counterpoint to the wildness of Lassen Park.

Area Code: 916

DRIVING DIRECTIONS   Lassen Park has five entrances; the most easily accessible are Manzanita Lake, 48 miles east of Redding via State Highway 44, and the Southwest Entrance, 50 miles east of Red Bluff via Highways 36 and 89. Red Bluff is on I-5, 30 miles south of Redding, 195 miles from San Francisco, 125 miles from Sacramento.

ACCOMMODATIONS   _The Faulkner House Bed & Breakfast,_ 1029 Jefferson Street, Red Bluff, 96080, 529-0520, I–M, CP • _The Jeter Victorian Inn,_ 1107 Jefferson, Red Bluff, 96080, 527-7574, I–EE, CP • _The Jarvis Mansion,_ 1313 Jackson Street, Red Bluff, 96080, 527-6901, I–M, CP • _Drakesbad Guest Ranch,_ Chester, 96020, within Lassen National

Park, 47 miles from park entrance, lodge and cabin bedrooms, bungalows, duplexes, EE, AP. Phone c/o Susanville Operator—ask for Drakesbad 2. Open early June to early October. Off season, contact California Guest Services, Inc., Abode Plaza, 2150 Main Street, Suite 5, Red Bluff, 96080, 529-1512 • *Bidwell House,* One Main Street, Chester, 96020, 258-3338, attractively furnished inn overlooking a lake, about 27 miles east of the southwest Lassen entrance, I–E, CP • *The Cinnamon Teal,* 227 Feather River Drive, Chester, 96020, 258-3993, homey ambience, I–M, CP • *Lassen Mineral Lodge,* P.O. Box 160, Mineral, 96963, 595-4422, motel 9 miles from southeast park entrance, pool, tennis, restaurant, I • *Lassen Lodge Cabins,* 35350 Highway 36E, Paynes Creek, 96075, 597-2952, cabins with wood stoves, 13 miles from southwest park entrance, I • *McGoverns' Vacation Chalets,* reservations c/o 563 McClay Road, Novato, 94947, (415) 897-8377, located 9 miles west of southwest park entrance, E. Write to the park for additional listings of motels, campgrounds, and cabin resorts in the area.

DINING   *Green Barn,* 5 Chestnut Street, Red Bluff, 527-7390, modest local favorite, I • *Marie's Family Restaurant,* 604 Main Street, Red Bluff, 529-6571, basic menus, I • *Golden Corral,* 250 Antelope Boulevard, Red Bluff, 527-3950, potato and salad bar, I • *Countryside Deli,* 1007 Main Street, Red Bluff, 529-3869, home cooking, soups a specialty, I • *Wild Bill's Rib Steakhouse,* 500 Riverside Way, Red Bluff, 529-9453, on the river, outside dining, I–M • *Snack Box,* 257 Main Street, Red Bluff, 529-0227, hearty breakfasts, I • **Near Lassen:** *Drakesbad Guest Ranch* (see above), M • *Chester Saloon and Italian Restaurant,* 159 Main Street, Chester, 258-2887, excellent pasta, live music on weekends, I–M • *Blackforest Lodge,* I-5, Box 5000, Highway 36, 10 miles west of Chester, 258-2941, noted for German food and fresh trout, I–M.

SIGHTSEEING   *Lassen Volcanic National Park,* P.O. Box 100, Mineral, 96063, 595-4444. Admission, $5 per car for a one-week permit • *Kelly Griggs House Museum,* 311 Washington Street, Red Bluff, 527-1129. Hours: Guided tours daily 2 P.M. to 5 P.M. Donation • *William B. Ide Adobe State Historic Park,* Adobe Road, Red Bluff, 527-5927. Hours: Daily 8 A.M. to dusk. $3 • *Salmon Viewing Plaza,* Diversion Dam, Sale Lane (off Highway 36, east of I-5), Red Bluff. Hours: Daily 8 A.M. to 8 P.M. Free. For current fishing, jet boat excursions, ballooning, and golf information, check the Red Bluff Chamber of Commerce.

INFORMATION   *Red Bluff–Tehama County Chamber of Commerce,* 100 Main Street, Red Bluff, CA 96080, 527-6220 • *Lassen County Chamber of Commerce,* P.O. Box 338, Susanville, CA 96130, 257-4323.

Glorious Garlic in Gilroy

The scent gets to you miles before you arrive. It is the unmistakable and irresistible aroma of garlic, an aphrodisiac that each year draws food lovers by the thousands to Gilroy, a little town in the Santa Clara Valley that proclaims itself "Garlic Capital of the World."

Close to 150,000 people come for the three-day Garlic Festival in Gilroy's Christmas Hill Park, an orgy of eating, entertainment, and good fun that is well worth the trip. Gilroy is just 20 miles from San Juan Bautista, a restored town combining history and charm with some choice antiquing, so there's good reason to stay and make a weekend of it.

The Garlic Festival was founded in 1979, inspired by a similar event in France. After all, California produces 90 percent of the garlic grown in the United States (a $54 million industry), and most of it comes from within 90 miles of Gilroy, so what better way to put the town on the map? And the festival has done just that as the event grows more popular every year. Some 4,000 volunteers do the work, sharing the proceeds with nonprofit groups in the area.

If you come during festival hours, avoid some of the traffic coming in off Highway 101 by getting off before Gilroy at San Martin Avenue. Head west and turn south again on Santa Teresa Boulevard, curving past town and making a left onto Miller Avenue. Park on one of the shady residential streets in this area, within walking distance of the festival grounds.

The big festival draw is Gourmet Alley, an alfresco kitchen where local culinary wizards toss giant skillets full of fabulous food—calamari, scampi in lobster butter, fifty bushels of fresh vegetables from nearby fields. Huge slabs of sirloin are basted with rosemary mops dunked in garlic marinade. Thousands of giant stuffed mushrooms are also served, and mountains of garlic bread. More than a ton of minced garlic goes into the making of dishes that are amazingly delicious, considering the huge quantities that must be prepared. The lines are long, but they do move fast, and no one complains after tasting the food.

There are other food booths for those who prefer to settle for more ordinary fare, plus several other sections to fill out the day. Art Alley is the place to browse for arts and crafts, which include nice things with garlic motifs, including pottery garlic holders that look great in the kitchen back home. And there are stalls selling garlic everything— giant elephant garlic cloves; garlic braids, buckles, necklaces, and headbands; garlic ice cream, wine, candy, and jelly; and, of course, garlic-motif T-shirts.

In the Garlic Grove you can watch contestants topping and braiding, with prizes going to the winners. And on Saturday the finalists in the

Great Garlic Recipe Contest and Cook-Off prepare dishes, hoping for first prize. The contest usually is judged by a celebrity chef.

Meanwhile, four stages offer continuous entertainment, from country to big-band music, and there is a special section for the kids, with games, face painting, puppeteers, and clowns.

It's truly a festive festival, and Gilroy itself turns out to hold some pleasant surprises to fill out your day. Buffered by mountain ranges east and west, it offers breezy temperate evenings even when the days are warm. You can enjoy those breezes at Country Rose Inn in San Martin on the Gilroy border, a nearby shady retreat in the middle of the fields, with attractive rooms and lavish breakfasts.

Antiquers will find shops on Monterey Street and the Monterey Highway, and festival or no, there are shops with names like Garlic Grocery and Garlic World selling garlic cloves, garlic-flavored foods, and garlic-motif everything.

A major Gilroy attraction near Highway 101 at Leavesley Road is the growing Pacific West Outlet Center—over 140 stores including lots of big names such as Liz Claiborne, Capezio, and Anne Klein. The town's motels are clustered nearby.

The most important central building is the 1905 Old City Hall at the corner of Sixth Street, now converted to a restaurant. A Historic District tour guide available from the visitors' bureau points out some other interesting buildings in the modest commercial district, a blend of twentieth-century period revivals, 1920s art deco, and 1940s Moderne styles. On Fifth Street are two National Register buildings and the Gilroy Historical Museum, housed in the town's Carnegie Library.

For a scenic drive, take the Hecker Pass Highway—Route 152— leading to the coast, a roller-coaster beauty that climbs and dips past 37 acres of colorful flower beds cultivated by Goldsmith Seeds, the second-largest flower-seed producer in the world. Along this road are located many Santa Clara County wineries, small, no-frills operations where the owner is likely to be filling your glass. Thomas Kruse, probably the best-known name, makes Gilroy White and Red and a bubbly champagne. Live Oaks has wine vinegar as well as hearty red Burgundies. The tasting room is in an underground cellar, and there is a gallery displaying more than 500 celebrity photos.

At the summit of the Pass—1,800 feet up—is Mt. Madonna Park, a quiet retreat with impressive views and resident deer tame enough to eat from your hand. The Mt. Madonna restaurant near the park entrance has a full wall of windows overlooking the same pretty panorama; on a clear day you can see Monterey Bay. A family theme park is due to open at Hecker Pass in 1996.

The Gilroy area is also prime growing country, and summer is the time of year for fresh-picked corn, peaches, plums, strawberries, and vegetables. "Country Crossroads," the free Santa Clara County farm trails map, will lead you to many farm stands in the area. Close at hand are LJB Farms, 585 Fitzgerald Avenue in San Martin, and Garlic World, 4800 Monterey Highway, selling produce as well as more fresh garlic. The latter is owned by the Christopher and Tognetti family, owners of one of the biggest area farms, with marked fields in evidence all around Gilroy. The family also owns Harvest Time, the closest thing to fine dining in town, and a good place to try roasted garlic bulbs.

Come Sunday, drive south on Highway 101 past more flower fields and turn east on Route 156 to San Juan Bautista. As district headquarters for the northern half of Alta California in the nineteenth century, it was the rallying point for two revolutions and the site of many colorful events.

Founded in 1797, San Juan Bautista for its first 25 years was a frontier mission under Spanish rule, where area Indians were taught the Christian religion, the Spanish language, and a useful trade. The mellowed stone church, surrounded by a lush garden, was begun in 1803 and, despite damage from several earthquakes, has been in continuous use since 1812. (Earthquakes are a constant threat here, since the San Andreas fault runs along the base of the hill below the cemetery beside the northeast wall of the church.)

The church is one of the loveliest of the old Spanish missions. It was grand for its day, with three naves that made it the widest of all the mission churches. The much-photographed three mission bells are all that remain of the original set of twelve. The main altar and reredos were painted by Thomas Doak, a sailor who jumped ship at Monterey and is said to have been the first U.S. citizen to settle in Spanish California. He did the work in exchange for room and board. The present museum rooms were once the padre's living quarters; the lush gardens were the center of mission activity, where Indians learned skills such as carpentry, tanning, and weaving. As many as 1,200 Indians lived and worked here at a time; more than 4,300 of them are buried in the old cemetery.

The rest of the buildings set around the town plaza comprise the state historic park, and can be visited on a self-guided tour. They tell a lot of California history, including the clashes between José Maria Castro, prefect of the Spanish district, and John C. Frémont, who used San Juan Bautista as a gathering place for his U.S. Army during the Mexican War in 1846. Later, the town was a major stagecoach stop for this part of the state.

The tile-roofed, balconied Castro House looks much as it did when it was built in the 1840s, but the interior is furnished in the style of the Breen family, who lived here in the 1870s. The Plaza Hotel, built in 1858, was a busy stage stopover, and its stables were filled with traffic. Behind the stable is a blacksmith's shop with tools of the trade. Plaza Hall was a residence downstairs and a public hall above, where dances, meetings, and traveling shows were held.

Much of the rest of the town of San Juan Bautista is equally venerable, and many of its privately owned adobe buildings have been beautifully restored. A number of them now house shops and restaurants, most located on Third Street. Pick up a walking-tour guide at the Chamber of Commerce and take a stroll. Allow plenty of time for shopping in half a dozen antiques shops and at several other stops, such as Reyna's Galleries, featuring Native American art and jewelry, and a Christmas shop. Then end your day with a meal in a properly historic setting.

If you are one of the many who fall in love with San Juan Bautista, make it your weekend headquarters with a stay at the San Juan Inn, a particularly pleasant motel.

Area Code: 408

DRIVING DIRECTIONS   Gilroy is off Highway 101, 30 miles south of San Jose, 66 miles from San Francisco, 144 miles from Sacramento.

ACCOMMODATIONS   *Country Rose Inn,* 455 Fitzgerald Avenue #E, San Martin, 95046, 842-0441, M–E, CP • *Forest Park Inn,* 375 Leavesley Road, Gilroy, 95020, 848-5144, motel, I • *Best Western Inn,* 360 Leavesley Road, Gilroy, 95020, 848-1467, motel, I • *San Juan Inn,* Route 156 and the Alameda, San Juan Bautista, 95045, 623-4380, motel on attractive grounds, I.

DINING   *Harvest Time,* 7397 Monterey Street, Gilroy, 842-7575, garlic-flavored everything, best in town, M • *Joe's Ristorante Italiano,* 1360-B First Street, Hecker Pass Plaza, Gilroy, 842-1446, modest, popular, I • *The Golden Oak,* 16695 Condit Road, Morgan Hill, 779-8085, varied menu, M • *Mt. Madonna Inn,* Hecker Pass Highway, Gilroy, 724-2275, varied menu, exceptional views, M • *Cademartori's,* First and San Juan streets, San Juan Bautista, 623-4511, Italian in historic surroundings, patio, valley views, M • *Felipe's Mexican and Salvadorean Cuisine,* 313 Third Street, San Juan Bautista, 623-2161, unusual dishes, I. *La Casa Rosa,* 107 Third Street, San Juan Bautista, 623-4666, delicious lunch casseroles, I • *Faultline,* 11 Franklin Street, 623-2117, valley views, continental, most ambitious menu in town, M–E • *Jardines de San Juan,* 115 Third Street, San Juan Bautista, 623-4466, Mexican in a flower-filled courtyard, I • *The Donkey Deli & German Restaurant,* 322 Third Street, 623-4521, great for lunch, beergarden ambience and music, make your own sandwiches and pay by the ounce, I; full-service restaurant at night, I–M.

SIGHTSEEING   *Gilroy Garlic Festival,* 7473 Monterey Street, Gilroy, 842-1625. Three days, the last weekend in July. Check for current date and admissions • *Gilroy Historical Museum,* 195 Fifth Street, Gilroy, 848-0470. Hours: Monday to Friday 9 A.M. to 5 P.M., some Saturdays 11 A.M. to 3 p.m; phone to check. Free • *San Juan Bautista State Historical Park,* 200 Second Street, San Juan Bautista, 623-4881. Hours: Grounds open daily 8:30 A.M. to 7 P.M. in summer, 7:30 A.M. to 5 P.M. rest of year; buildings 10 A.M. to 4:30 P.M. Admission, $2 for all buildings except the mission; children, $1 • *Mission San Juan Bautista,* 623-4528. Hours: Daily 9:30 A.M. to 4:30 P.M. Donation.

WINERIES   *Thomas Kruse Winery,* 4390 Hecker Pass Highway, Gilroy, 842-7016, tastings, picnic grounds. Hours: Daily noon to 5 P.M. • *Fortino Winery,* 4525 Hecker Pass Highway, 842-3305, tastings, tours. Hours: Daily 10 A.M. to 5 P.M. • *Live Oaks Winery,* 3875 Hecker Pass Highway, 842-2401, tastings, picnic grounds. Hours: Daily 10 A.M. to 5 P.M. • *Hecker Pass Winery,* 4605 Hecker Pass Highway, 842-8755, tastings. Hours: Daily 10 A.M. to 5 P.M.

INFORMATION   *Gilroy Visitors' Bureau,* 7780 Monterey Street, Gilroy, CA 95020, 842-6436 • *San Juan Bautista Chamber of Commerce,* 402A Third Street, San Juan Bautista, CA 95045, 623-2454 • "Country Crossroads," Santa Clara and Santa Cruz counties farm trails map, available at the Gilroy Visitors' Bureau or by mail with stamped self-addressed envelope from Santa Clara County Farm Bureau, 1368 North Fourth Street, San Jose, CA 95112.

Giant Steps in the Sequoias

The giant sequoias of the Sierra Nevada wield a powerful impact. "One naturally walked softly and awestricken among them," wrote John Muir when he saw these trees, earth's largest living things. Muir was one of those responsible for preserving the greatest of these wonders way back in 1890, as part of our second-oldest national park.

Thanks to those far-sighted conservationists, we can still step through the sequoias, standing silent and marveling at nature's largesse. In 1940 Kings Canyon National Park was set aside, adjoining and enlarging the original boundaries, providing an added panorama of deep canyons, waterfalls, and towering peaks that makes these twin parks a thrilling place to visit.

The surprising thing is that more people don't come. Sequoia and Kings Canyon national parks draw just more than a million visitors to their sprawling acres each year, less than a third of the number who throng to Yosemite National Park, just 80 miles to the north. That's too bad, but it's good news for those who do make the trip. Even in the comparatively busy midsummer, the crowds don't get in the way of appreciating the special treasures found here in great abundance.

The biggest attraction remains the trees that John Muir first saw in the area he named the "Giant Forest." Four of the world's largest trees stand here. Sequoias differ from their coastal cousins, the redwoods, in that they grow shorter, thicker, and to an older age. They are found only on the west slope of the Sierra Nevada mountains, usually at an elevation of 5,000 to 7,000 feet. Only 75 groves remain, and the two greatest of them are here.

In the Giant Forest area alone are 40 miles of paths leading to stands of magnificent trees and wildflower-filled meadows. You can see them on your own or on a number of informative ranger-led walks.

The most mammoth tree of all is the General Sherman, said to be the largest living thing on earth. Pegged at somewhere between 2,300 and 2,700 years of age, it stands 275 feet tall with a ground circumference of 103 feet. Think about that—bigger around than a third of a football field. There are taller trees and older ones, but nothing equals this for total volume. The largest branch is seven feet in diameter, larger than many a good-size tree trunk. An adult could lie on top of the limb and not be seen from the ground. Admirers lined up to take photos in front of the General Sherman look like pinpoints in contrast to the massive trunk.

Amazingly, the tree is still growing, adding about 500 board feet in girth each year. That's roughly equal to a tree growing 50 feet from the ground and a foot in diameter yearly.

Beyond this phenomenon, the easy two-mile Congress Trail beckons with more mighty giants, most notably the President and the Washington and Lincoln trees. Two marvelous groves here were named in honor of the House and the Senate. Buy the inexpensive trail guide and learn why the sequoias live so long and grow so big. One of the reasons is their natural resistance to fire and disease. You see many trunks with fire scars, but the hearts of the trees remain undamaged. The bark, which can be as much as two feet thick, contains no resin, the substance that makes other trees burn, so it protects the sequoia. Fire actually helps when it takes surrounding sugar pine and fir trees, opening the forest canopy to let in more light. It also prepares a rich ashy seedbed and provides the heat needed to open the fragile sequoia seeds.

The thing that usually fells a sequoia is simply its own size. The root system is shallow, and eventually the weight of the tree may cause it to topple. Visitors are asked not to walk too close to the trees so as not to damage the roots lying not far underground.

Even fallen sequoias remain decay-resistant, serving for years as a nursery bed for other kinds of vegetation and a home for forest creatures great and small.

During the summer, wildflowers and ferns add to the beauty of the forest floor. The best place for spotting wildflowers is along the short trail circling flower-filled Crescent Meadow.

The most exciting vista in this park is from the top of Moro Rock, a dome-shaped granite monolith much like those found in Yosemite. It is a short, steep climb of 300 vertical feet to the top for a 360-degree panorama. To the west are the foothills and the San Joaquin Valley below. To the south and down more than 5,000 feet, the middle fork of the Kaweah River can be seen snaking through a rugged canyon. To the east are the snowcapped peaks of the Great Western Divide and the Kaweah peaks, the highest of which is Mt. Kaweah at 13,802 feet. Just out of sight is Mt. Whitney, at 14,494 feet the nation's highest peak. Signs help identify the peaks of the Great Western Divide. The high ridges are part of one of our largest remaining wilderness areas.

The Giant Forest contains the major lodging area in Sequoia National Park, providing rustic cabins and motel rooms for visitors amid the fabulous trees. The attractive dining room behind the main reception area, about a mile away from the lodgings, has a wall of glass to reveal giant sentinels just outside. The trees are lit by spotlights at night, a magical sight as you dine. This is the one formal place to eat in either park, and it can get crowded, so consider dining early.

Other points of interest in Sequoia National Park are the Lodgepole area, for a major information center and more hiking trails, and Crystal Cave, located below the Giant Forest.

Though it is easy to spend a rewarding weekend or even a week within this one park, Kings Canyon beckons with its own grove of mammoth trees and some truly spectacular mountain scenery and vistas within one of the deepest canyons in the United States. Here, too, are many ranger-led activities. Bus tours are offered, taking in the major sites in both parks.

The main Kings Canyon lodging area is the Grant Grove section, not far from the park entrance at Highway 180. Though it is not quite as scenic a setting as the Giant Forest, this is actually a more central location, putting you midway on the Generals Highway, which connects the two parks. There are other smaller lodgings off the highway, open in summer only.

Along the drive from Giant Forest to Grant Grove, a pull-off affords distant views of Redwood Mountain, an even larger sequoia growing area than Giant Forest, but you can reach it only by hiking. This grove is younger; the trees won't attain their full height and heft for another thousand years or so.

Possibly, one or two will grow to rival Kings Canyon's General Grant tree, the third largest in the world, with a base diameter even slightly bigger than that of the General Sherman. It is as tall as a 27-story building, wider at the base than a three-lane freeway. President

Calvin Coolidge proclaimed this tree "The Nation's Christmas Tree," and in 1956 President Eisenhower designated it as a living national shrine in memory of Americans who died in war.

The tree is in the Grant Grove, which can be seen along a self-guided trail of just one third of a mile. Another giant here is the Robert E. Lee tree, named for the Confederate commander. Other trees in this area are named for our country's states. Several trails lead beyond the busy central area into the quiet of the forest. A quarter-mile hike from the parking area takes you to Panoramic Point for a vista of valleys and high mountain peaks.

Beyond Grant Grove, the General's Highway becomes Kings Canyon Highway and the deep canyon views become ever more superb as you head toward the mountains. The road ends past Cedar Grove; the remaining terrain is high-country wilderness, reserved for backpackers and serious hikers. At road's end you are standing on a flat, glacial valley gazing up at canyon walls rising nearly a mile above the Kings River basin. There are some easy trails from Cedar Grove that lead to great sights, such as the impressive Roaring River Falls, which fits its name, and the expanses of Zumwalt Meadow.

This is the quietest end of the park and one of the most spectacular, a place to follow the good advice of John Muir: "Climb the mountains and get their good tidings. Nature's peace will flow into you as sunshine flows into trees."

Area Code: 209

DRIVING DIRECTIONS   Take Highway 99 to Fresno, then Highway 180 for 84 miles east to Kings Canyon and Sequoia national parks. The parks are about 280 miles from San Francisco, a six-hour drive. If driving in November to May, carry tire chains. In winter Giant Forest is accessible only via Route 198 from Visalia, a tortuous corkscrew ascent. The General's Highway within the park connecting it with Grant Grove may be closed due to snow.

ACCOMMODATIONS   National Park accommodations: *Giant Forest:* Open May through October; motel, M; cabins, I–M; cabins with fireplace, E • *Grant Grove:* year-round, cabins, I–M • *Cedar Grove and Stony Creek:* Summer only, motel, M. Reserve for all through guest services as listed below • *Montecito-Sequoia Lodge,* P.O. Box 858, Grant Grove, 93633, 565-3388, rustic lodge and cabins 10 miles south of Grant Grove, heated pool, lighted tennis courts, games, dining room, year-round, M–E.

DINING   Park dining: *Giant Forest:* Dining room, mid-May to mid-October, breakfast and dinner, I–M • *Village Cafeteria,* May to

October, three meals, I • *Stony Creek:* Three meals, late May to September, I • *Grant Grove:* Coffee shop, year-round, three meals, I • *Cedar Grove:* Counter service, three meals, mid-May to September • *Lodgepole Center: The Deli:* sandwiches, meals to go, I; *The Ice Cream Shop.* Food markets with lunch supplies are located at Lodgepole Center and Grant Grove • *Montecito-Sequoia Lodge* (see above), M.

SIGHTSEEING AND INFORMATION *Sequoia and Kings Canyon National Parks,* Guest Services, P.O. Box 789, Three Rivers, CA; 93271, information line, 561-3134; reservations line, 561-3314. Entrance fee, $5 per car • *Lodgepole Visitor Center,* 565-3782. Hours: Daily 8 A.M. to 5 P.M., in winter from 9 A.M. • *Grant Grove Visitor Center,* 335-2856. Hours: Daily 8 A.M. to 5 P.M. • *Ash Mountain Visitor Center,* park entrance on Route 198, 565-3135. Hours: Daily 8 A.M. to 5 P.M. Bus tours, guided horseback rides: Check information centers for current schedules and fees. Ranger-led activities are detailed in the park newspaper, *The Sequoia Bark.*

Digging for Treasure in Benicia

Trinkets, trunks, teddy bears, and teapots. Victorian sofas and vintage postcards. Name your treasure and likely you'll find it at the Peddler's Fair in Benicia. On the second Saturday of August each year, Benicia's sidewalks overflow with dealers, transforming this tiny town into flea market paradise.

It's appropriate that mementos of the past are a specialty here, for Benicia boasts an impressive history, even serving for a short time as the capital of the state. Back in the 1850s, this waterfront community was an important military outpost and rivaled San Francisco as a port, with many ships sailing through the Carquinez Straits into the Bay. But while Benicia's port had the distinct advantage of being out of the fog belt, its day in the sun was short. Business moved elsewhere, and the tiny community was left to drowse, its vintage buildings unchanged with time.

As often happens in picturesque places, it was antiques shop owners and artists who first realized Benicia's possibilities. First Street now is lined with shops overflowing with "collectibles" year-round, and the town's old factories house a thriving art glass industry. More artists are moving in all the time, along with other residents who recognize the exceptional opportunities for recreation and boating in the area. Come for the Peddler's Fair and stay on to discover a town that grows more appealing by the year.

A short walking tour is in order to discover some of Benicia's claims to historic fame. (Benicia and Monterey were the first cities to be incorporated under the constitution of California.) Start at the ferry sites at the foot of First Street, where in 1847 the town's founder, Robert Semple, began transporting passengers and freight between Benicia and Martinez. The ferry was the first public utility to operate on San Francisco Bay.

The ferry site subsequently was moved to Fifth Street, where service continued off and on until 1962. Pony Express riders used the boats to make their way to Oakland and San Francisco. The original Transcontinental Railroad Depot at the foot of First Street went up in 1879; the present replacement was built in 1900. The two largest train ferries ever built operated between Benicia and Port Costa, until they were replaced by a railroad bridge in 1930.

Take a look at some of the buildings that served as thriving hotels, saloons, and brothels in those bustling early days. Jack London's favorite watering hole was Jurgensen's Saloon at First and A streets. Now quite run-down, the building is part of the Historic Triangle Project being considered for restoration near the waterfront.

Fate has been kinder to other structures. The Alamo Rooms on First Street, a brothel where hunters used to shoot mallards and canvasbacks from the bedroom windows, is now the Nantucket Fish Company restaurant. The 1882 Union Hotel at First and D streets remains busy, with a popular dining room and simple rooms upstairs furnished in quaint Victoriana. The hotel is a fine alternative if you can't get into the other delightful Benicia lodgings, Captain Dillingham's Inn on D Street, the charming 1800s home of a prosperous ship captain, and the beautifully furnished Captain Walsh House, in one of the prize historic homes in town.

When you get to H Street West, step into the lounge of the old Brewery to see seven colorful murals depicting the town's history. The project by California artist Les Vadre took two years to complete.

Benicia's most-visited site is the small 1852 Greek Revival City Hall, which became the State Capitol in 1853, an honor that lasted just 13 months, until Sacramento was chosen as a permanent home. The Senate Chamber is re-created on the first floor, the Assembly on the second. They remain just as they were in those glory days, right down to papers and top hats still in place on the desks. The site is now a state historical park, with rangers on hand to share the history. Weekend tours include the adjoining state-owned Fischer-Hanlon House, a Federal-style home with original furnishings from the 1850s.

Though the walking tour covers only a relatively few blocks, there's much to see. The 1920s Majestic Theatre at 701 First Street has been reborn as a live performing arts venue, with events on many weekends.

St. Paul's, the oldest Episcopal church in California, is at First and East J streets. It was built in 1859 by shipwrights, who created a unique interior of redwood with an arched ceiling that gives the illusion of an inverted ship's hull. To see it, you must come during the hours of services on Sunday or Wednesday, the only time the church is open.

The rectory next door also has an interesting history. It is a typical New England house, built in 1790, dismantled in Connecticut in 1868, and shipped around the Cape of Good Hope to Benicia, where it was reassembled.

The town's oldest home, the 1850 Frisbie-Walsh House at L and Third streets, now the Captain Walsh House, has a similar history. It is one of three identical homes shipped around the Horn from Boston. The second is General Vallejo's home in Sonoma; the third was burned in the 1906 San Francisco fire.

Fire buffs should make an appointment to see another Benicia first, the Benicia Fire Museum. Among its antique fire equipment is California's first fire engine, an 1820 model that was brought from New York to Benicia in 1846.

More history is told in the museums in the Camel Barns, sandstone warehouses named for the camels the U.S. Army kept there after an unsuccessful attempt to use them to transport supplies in the Southwest desert. The camels were auctioned off in 1864.

The Barns were part of the military installations that were an important presence in Benicia for more than 100 years, until they were phased out in 1964. The Arsenal, established in 1851, furnished arms and materials for survey parties as well as the Civil and Spanish-American wars. It was Pacific Coast Ordnance Headquarters during World Wars I and II and the Korean War. Some of the remaining buildings facing the Carquinez Strait, such as the Clock Tower Fortress and the Powder Magazine, are impressive examples of nineteenth-century military architecture. The Commandant's 1860 home is a gracious 20-room mansion. The 1856 Post Hospital was the first military hospital in the West.

Some of the old Arsenal buildings now house studios for painters and artists working in media such as ceramics, neon, and stained glass. Still more artists can be found in the Yuba Manufacturing Complex, a former industrial park on East H Street. The best-known occupant is the Yuba Arts Group, prominent makers of art glass, with a showroom at 675-701 East H Street. You will see glassblowers at work during showroom hours or at the annual open houses held the first weekends of May and December. Other art glass showrooms across the street are open most Saturdays year-round.

When you are weary of sights, pick up a picnic and head for Benicia's shoreline. West of town off I-780 is Benicia State Recreation Area, 400 acres of marshes and estuaries that are home to dozens of species of birds, small animals, and plants. It's a perfect place for hiking, biking, fishing, bird-watching, or just relaxing. From Dillon Point you can watch the waters of the Sacramento and San Joaquin rivers rushing through Carquinez Strait toward the sea. The east entrance to the park can be reached via the Waterfront Pathway System, a bike and walking path running from the town marina to West 14th Street.

Surprising little Benicia can easily fill your weekend, but one site across the bridge in Martinez is worth a visit. The John Muir National Historic Site is the 1882 Victorian home where the pioneering conservationist lived the last 24 years of his life and did much of his wonderful writing on nature. A short film and a self-guided tour of the 17-room house give a fresh sense of how much we owe to the man who was a prime mover in establishing five national parks and the U.S. Forest Service. Muir was a founder of the Sierra Club in 1892 and its president until his death in 1914. A special exhibit room is devoted to the club and its early outings.

Though the Muir home is now surrounded by development, some of the rich orchards that he established remain, producing apples, grapes, pears, plums, peaches, cherries, walnuts, and almonds. Muir's great skill as a farmer was overshadowed by his conservation work, but it was his ability as an orchardist and astute businessman that gave him the financial independence to devote himself to preserving America's natural resources.

The Martinez Adobe, a two-story adobe home built in 1849, is also on the grounds and is part of the tour. It was the home of Muir's daughter Wanda and her family, and Muir often came here to play with his grandchildren.

Area Code: 707

DRIVING DIRECTIONS Benicia is just across the Benicia-Martinez Bridge on I-780, reached via I-80 near Vallejo or I-680 from the East Bay. It is 37 miles northeast of San Francisco, 58 miles from Sacramento.

ACCOMMODATIONS _Captain Walsh House,_ 235 East L Street, Benicia 94510, 747-5653, E, CP • _Captain Dillingham's Inn,_ 145 East D Street, Benicia, 94510, 746-7164 or in California (800) 544-2278, M–E, CP • _Union Hotel,_ 401 First Street, Benicia, 94510, 746-0100, M–E, CP.

DINING _Union Hotel_ (see above), continental, M • _Captain Blyther's,_ 123 First Street, 745-1233, seafood, water view, outside dining, I–M • _Mabel's,_ 635 First Street, 746-7068, fifties diner ambience, good food, homemade soups, I–M • _First Street Café,_ 440 First Street,

745-4404, light meals, lunches to go, I • *Tia Theresa at the Brewery,* 120 East H Street, 745-2535, Mexican food amid murals, I.

SIGHTSEEING *Benicia State Capitol,* First and West G streets, 745-3385. Hours: Daily 10 A.M. to 5 P.M. Adults, $2; ages 6 to 13, $1. Weekend tours include Fischer Hanlon House, 745-3385. Hours: Saturday and Sunday noon to 3:30 P.M. • *Camel Barn Museum,* 2060 Camel Road, 745-5435. Hours: Wednesday to Sunday 1 P.M. to 4 P.M. Donation • *Benicia Fire Museum,* 16 Military West, 745-1688. Hours: Open by appointment • *Benicia State Recreation Park,* I-780 and Columbus Parkway, 746-4285. Parking, $5 • *Yuba Arts Glass Studios,* 675 and 701 East H Street, 745-5710. Hours: Monday to Saturday 10 A.M. to 4 P.M. • *John Muir National Historic Site,* 4202 Alhambra Avenue, Martinez, (510) 228-8860. Hours: Wednesday to Sunday 10 A.M. to 4:30 P.M. Adults, $1; under age 17, free.

INFORMATION *Benicia Chamber of Commerce,* 601 First Street, Benicia, CA 94510, 745-2120 or (800) 559-7377.

Southern Comfort at Yosemite

The southern side of Yosemite National Park is one that many visitors miss. True, it is not as dramatic as the sculptured walls and waterfalls of the valley, but this part of the park and the Sierra foothills beyond have their own personality and their own definite pleasures.

Here, amid tall pines and giant sequoias, you can drive, hike, or horseback ride through wonderful wilderness, enjoy a mountain lake, board an old-fashioned steam train, play a scenic golf course, find out about the park's beginnings, discover some Indian lore, and enjoy some very special lodgings. Since the main valley is only 35 miles away, it's easy to see the sights one day and then come back home, away from cafeteria lines and congestion. Even in midsummer, when park attendance is at its peak, this area is never uncomfortably crowded.

You will have to plan ahead, however, if you want to snag a room at the choicest lodging in the park's southern region, the Wawona Hotel. This rambling white wooden beauty with gingerbread balconies dates to 1876 and is a national historic landmark. It makes for an old-fashioned retreat, with modest rooms and prices to match. The welcoming lobby is warm with Victoriana, and the dining room is known for its buffet lunches. The sunset views from the porch are also widely admired, making advance reservations essential for dinner.

Wawona's nine-hole golf course opened in 1918 as the first mountain course in California. It remains one of the most scenic, especially late in the day, when the deer come out.

It's a short stroll from the hotel to the Pioneer Yosemite History Center, a collection of park buildings from the 1800s and early 1900s. Guides in period costumes lead tours here, bringing to life the park's early days. The stable next door offers two-hour rides for adults along the meadow or on longer trips to Chilnualna Falls or Deer Camp. The Center is the site of a special Fourth of July celebration each year, with a barn dance, a barbecue dinner, and a parade.

About halfway between Wawona and the valley is the road to Glacier Point, a perch 3,242 feet high. Stand on the rim and marvel at one of the world's great views, the wonders of Yosemite spread out below.

The biggest attraction at the lower end of the park is the Mariposa Grove of Big Trees, located a few miles south of Wawona. There are some 250 awe-inspiring giant sequoias here, several more than 200 feet high and 15 feet in diameter. The Grizzly Giant, more than 100 feet in circumference, is 2,800 years old, the oldest known giant sequoia.

No cars are allowed in the grove, but tram tours regularly make their way on a six-mile loop through the woods. To really appreciate the trees, it's even better to take a walking tour, especially one of those guided by a knowledgeable ranger. When the ranger asks the group to join hands to circle a tree and it takes more than 20 people to do so, you realize just how enormous these trees are.

Another way to see the big trees is on horseback on a guided ride with Yosemite Trails, outfitters in nearby Fish Camp. They lead a variety of trips from one hour to all day, including an evening ride and steak cookout, plus overnight pack trips.

An additional lodging option within the gates of the park is to rent a room, studio, or apartment from Yosemite's Four Seasons or a cabin from Redwoods Cottages. The little town of Fish Camp, only about two miles below the southern park entrance, also has its own special places to stay. One of the nicest is the Narrow Gauge Inn, a cozy mountain lodge surrounded by cedar and pine forests. Rooms are furnished with a mix of Old West and Victoriana, and offer wonderful wooded views, especially the lower row of rooms running along Spring Creek. There's a pool in a garden setting, a cozy rustic dining room with fieldstone fireplaces and redwood paneling, and an old-fashioned Victorian saloon.

The inn adjoins one of the area's favorite attractions, the Yosemite Mt. Sugar Pine Railroad, home of *The Logger*. This vintage steam train takes guests aboard open logging cars for a 45-minute excursion into the Sierra wilderness along tracks that were used by logging trains at the turn of the century. A shorter trip uses the quaint, small "Model A" powered railcars known as the Jennys. Both trips offer a narration that points out the scenery and describes some of the colorful history of logging days. Some passengers bring a picnic and get off at Shady Slab Creek, catching a later train back. Bring along a sweater—it gets cool in the deep woods.

Modest but quite inviting is Fish Camp's Apple Tree Inn, a cluster of six nicely furnished cottages among the trees, with cozy fireplaces for cool mountain evenings. Bed-and-breakfast fans will enjoy Karen's, a small contemporary bed-and-breakfast home in a secluded location. Those in search of a resort will find that Marriott's Tenaya Lodge has all the right amenities and activities, even though the motel-type architecture seems out of place in these surroundings. Rooms are well furnished, there are pools indoors and out, and parents may appreciate a summer day camp for kids ages 5 to 12.

The luxury winner in this area comes ten miles farther south in the unlikely town of Oakhurst. A block off motel-lined Highway 41 is the Chateau du Sureau, a lavish antiques-filled hideaway befitting the European castle that was its inspiration. It isn't cheap, but then castles never are. The Chateau stands just above Erna's Elderberry House, a handsome restaurant that has earned kudos from critics nationwide. Erna's is also expensive, but worth a visit. If you can't manage the dinner tab, come for lunch or brunch.

A very different kind of evening can be spent at Oakhurst's Golden Chain Theatre, where audiences love booing the villain in old-fashioned melodramas from Gold Rush days. Or you can visit Sierraland, a theme park opened by the New Christy Minstrels, the folksinging group best remembered for their popularity in the 1960s. Now organized into a new group called "A Gathering of Minstrels," they perform twice daily in a tentlike structure seating 1,000. Sierraland also includes a crafts village, a gold-panning exhibit, and on weekends, Wild West shows and line-dancing lessons.

Oakhurst offers some moderately priced motel accommodations for families, such as the Yosemite Gateway Best Western, with indoor and outdoor pools to keep the kids happy. If you choose to stay in town, you'll find a number of galleries and antiques shops for browsing.

More beautiful scenery and sequoias can be found in these Sierra foothills below Yosemite. Stop at the U.S. Forest Service headquarters in Oakhurst for information on the many hiking trails in the Sierra National Forest and a driving map of the Sierra Vista Scenic Byway, a 100-mile loop through the Sierra Nevada that climbs from 3,000 to more than 7,000 feet. *Sunset* magazine called this "the most spectacular little-known drive in California."

The Byway can easily be a full day's tour if you make all the sightseeing stops, especially since some sections of the road are unpaved. There are several fabulous viewpoints, the best being Mile High Vista, overlooking the Ansel Adams, John Muir, and Kaiser wilderness areas.

Redinger Overlook is another beauty spot for viewing the San Joaquin River and Redinger Lake, and there are several interesting rock formations along the way, such as Arch Rock and Fresno Dome.

To get to the Scenic Byway, head north from Oakhurst on Highway 41 and take Road 222 eastbound connecting to Road 274 and the Ranger Station at North Fork, the official start of the Byway. The Sierra Mono Indian Museum and the Mono Wind Nature Trail and Flower Farm invite a stop here. North Fork is the cultural center of the Mono people, a tribe known for its fine basketry, and the museum has an impressive collection of baskets and other crafts. Another part of the display is devoted to exhibits of California wildlife, including an eight-foot grizzly bear. Indian Fair Days early in August are a chance to see authentic dancing and crafts demonstrations and taste special Indian foods.

The nature trail and garden are the handiwork of Gaylen Lee, a Mono Indian, created as a tribute to Galen's grandparents. The self-guided one-mile trail identifies plants used by the Mono tribe for food and medicine, and passes by cedar bark houses typical of those once lived in by the Monos. The flower garden offers more than 100 varieties of colorful blooms that last from spring through the first frost. Visitors are welcome weekdays year-round, but a phone call is appreciated before dropping in on weekends.

If you are interested in Indian culture, you will also want to see the Wassama Roundhouse in Ahwahnee, one of the few surviving ceremonial Indian Roundhouses in the state. Maintained by members of local Miwok Indian tribes under sponsorship of the California State Park System, the oak-shaded site also includes picnic areas, old grinding stones and other Indian artifacts. Tribal ceremonies are still held at the Roundhouse to observe births and harvests, and to reach the spirits and mourn the dead.

Back to the Byway, for the best of the overlooks, continue from North Fork on Minarets Road, the eastern edge of the loop. At Clover Meadow Station the road's name changes to Beasore Road and leads to Cold Springs Summit, at 7,308 feet the high point. Continue south on Beasore and you are just 20 minutes from Bass Lake, a fine spot for fishing, boating, or a scenic lunch at Ducey's, a stylish lodge overlooking the lake. It is only another few minutes' drive on to Highway 41.

If you choose the long way from Cold Springs Summit you will have another two hours' drive on Sky Ranch Road, some of it unpaved. The incentive to do this is one of the major attractions in the Sierra National Forest, the Nelder Grove, where a short trail leads to the Bull Buck giant sequoia tree, one of the biggest in the world. Another one-mile self-guided national recreation trail, called Shadow of the Giants, runs along Nelder Creek past more big sequoias, including the ones called Granddad and the Grandkids, where one towering tree shelters a small forest of smaller sequoias under its out-stretched arms.

This grove is only five miles south of Yosemite's Mariposa Grove, yet it is dense forest without paved roads and with few visitors to disturb the serenity. It's a great place for a quiet picnic. If you don't want to take the byway drive, the shorter way in is by turning east on the lower portion of the Sky Ranch Road from Highway 41 and taking the paved portion of the road leading north to the turnoff to Nelder Grove.

Oakhurst also offers another small attraction, Fresno Flats Histori-cal Park, a chance to step back and see how pioneer settlers in this area lived and worked. Fresno Flats was the community's original name. The complex consists of an 1868 log cabin and cookhouse, an 1870s farmhouse, a museum of memorabilia, an old schoolhouse, a gazebo and wishing well, and a collection of old stagecoaches, farm wagons, and buggies.

But if you are here on a short visit, chances are you'll never get around to some of the history—not when you are surrounded by the serene natural beauty of the mountains and forests south of Yosemite, and when all the wonders of the park are waiting just up the road.

Area Code: 209

DRIVING DIRECTIONS   From the Bay Area, southern Yosemite is best reached via Highway 99 south to Merced, Highway 140 east to Mariposa, then Highway 49 south to Oakhurst. At Oakhurst, turn north on Highway 41 for 13 miles to Fish Camp and the park entrance just beyond leading to Wawona. It can also be approached via Highway 41 north from Fresno. Wawona is about 35 miles from the Yosemite Val-ley. Yosemite is 210 miles from San Francisco, 176 miles from Sacra-mento, 89 from Fresno, and 81 miles from Merced.

PUBLIC TRANSPORTATION   See page 198.

ACCOMMODATIONS   *Wawona Hotel,* Yosemite National Park, 375-6556, reserve through Central Reservations, Yosemite Concession Services Corp. 5410 East Home, Fresno, 93727, 252-4848, I–M • *Nar-row Gauge Inn,* 48571 Highway 41, Fish Camp, 93623, 683-7720, M–E • *Apple Tree Inn,* Highway 41, Fish Camp, 93623, 683-5111, M–E, CP • *Marriott's Tenaya Lodge,* 1122 Highway 41, Fish Camp, 93623, 283-6555 or (800) 635-5807, EE • *Karen's Bed & Breakfast,* 1144 Railroad Avenue, Fish Camp, 93623, 683-4550 or (800) 346-1443, M, CP • *Ducey's on the Lake,* P.O. Box 109, Bass Lake, 93604, (800) 350-7463, EE • *Chateau du Sureau,* P.O. Box 577, Oakhurst, 93644, 683-6860, EE, CP • *Yosemite Gateway Best Western,* 40530 Highway 41, Oakhurst, 93644, 683-2378 or (800) 528-1234, indoor

and outdoor pools, I–M • **Cottage and cabin accommodations:**
Yosemite Four Seasons Vacation Rentals, 7519 Henness Circle,
Yosemite National Park, 95389, 372-9000; rooms, I–M, studios, M,
apartments, E, homes, EE • *Redwoods Cottages,* furnished housekeeping cabins near Wawona, 375-6666, M–EE.

DINING *Wawona Hotel,* Yosemite National Park, serves three
meals, reservations required for dinner, 375-6556, M • *Narrow Gauge
Inn,* Fish Camp (see above), 683-6446, warm decor, M • *Ducey's on
the Lake,* Bass Lake (see above), M–E • *Erna's Elderberry House,*
48688 Victoria Lane, Oakhurst, 683-6800, California cuisine with a
European touch, rave reviews, prix fixe, EE; lunch on Wednesday,
Thursday, Friday, M; Sunday brunch, E • *Crystal Falls Inn,* 42424
Road 22, Oakhurst, 683-4242, creekside setting for California cuisine,
M • *Yosemite Forks Mountain Restaurant,* 42515 Highway 41, 683-
5191, informal family restaurant, three meals, I–M. For additional
Yosemite dining and lodging, see pages 198 to 199.

SIGHTSEEING *Yosemite National Park,* general park information,
372-0200. Admission, $5. Southern park activities include: *Wawona:*
Camera walks, Pioneer Yosemite History Center tours, stage rides,
campfire programs, horseback rides • *Mariposa Grove:* Tram rides,
ranger walks. *Glacier Point:* Guided walks, campfires, stargazing. For
complete schedules consult the weekly *Yosemite Guide* newspaper
given at each entry gate • *Yosemite Trails Pack Station,* P.O. Box 100,
Fish Camp, 683-7611. Guided rides and pack trips. Phone for details,
fees • *Yosemite Mt. Sugar Pine Railroad,* 56001 Highway 41, Fish
Camp, 683-7273, 4-mile steam train excursions into Sierra National
Forest. Phone for schedules. Steam train: Adults, $9.75; ages 3 to 12,
$4.95 • *Jenny Railcar:* Adults, $6.25; children, $3.25 • *U.S. Forest
Service,* Sierra National Forest Mariposa Ranger District, 43060 High-
way 41, Oakhurst, 683-4665; stop or write for hiking trails, map of
Sierra Vista Scenic Byway • *Fresno Flats Historical Park,* School
Road, Route 427, Oakhurst, 683-6570. Hours: Wednesday to Saturday
1 P.M. to 3 P.M., Sunday to 4 P.M. Adults, $2; children, $.75 • *Sierra
Mono Museum,* Roads 274 and 225, North Fork, 877-2115. Hours:
Monday to Friday 9 A.M. to 4 P.M. Adults, $2; students, $1; children,
$.75 • *Mono Wind Nature Trail,* 877-2710, phone to arrange a visit and
get exact driving directions • *Wassama Roundhouse State Historical
Park,* P.O. Box 328, Ahwahnee, 683-3631. Hours: Daily 11 A.M. to
4 P.M. Adults, $.75; under 12, free • *Sierraland,* Highway 49,
Oakhurst, 658-7001. Hours: Daily 10 A.M. to 10 P.M. Shows at 3 P.M.
and 7:30 P.M. Adults, $14.95; age 10 and under, $8.95 • *Golden Chain
Theatre,* Highway 41, Oakhurst, 683-7112. Old-time melodramas
April through October. General admission, $8; children, $6. Phone for
current schedule and any rate changes.

INFORMATION   *Southern Yosemite Visitors' Bureau,* 49074 Civic Circle, Oakhurst, CA 93644, 683-INFO • *Yosemite National Park,* National Park Service, P.O. Box 577, Yosemite National Park, CA 95389, 372-0265.

A Bite of Sebastopol's Big Apple

Aficionados will tell you that Gravenstein apples are the best in the world. They are just sweet enough, just tart enough, perfect for cooking, and absolutely delicious eaten fresh off the tree.

Sebastopol in western Sonoma County is the heart of Gravenstein country. The crop is so important here that Route 116 running through orchard country is known as the Gravenstein Highway. So it's not surprising that the harvest is cause for celebration, and since this is the earliest apple crop, the annual Gravenstein Apple Fair comes along in mid-August, just in time for a gala late-summer outing. Apple adventures combined with a day along the Russian River make for a great weekend.

The fair, sponsored by Sonoma County Farm Trails, is nothing huge or fancy but a small-town event, full of old-fashioned fun. At the start in the early 1900s, it was no more than neighbors gathering to share homemade food and listen to friends showing off on the banjo or guitar. The present organized fair began in 1973 and now may draw as many as 10,000 people, but the original flavor remains. Everything sold is handmade and farm-oriented, the music has a country twang, and exhibits range from antique farm equipment to demonstrations of fur spinning by a lady in calico with an angora rabbit nestled in her lap. Of course, there is an annual apple pie–baking contest.

Fairgoers entering the grounds at Ragle Park walk past a lineup of farm stands selling Gravensteins by the apple or by the bushel, along with all kinds of fresh-picked produce. Some of the stands offer another local specialty, bountiful bouquets of dried flowers.

Food stalls tempt with pies, dumplings, fritters, crêpes, turnovers, cider, caramel apples, and other apple treats. Shady benches and tables under the oaks are provided for enjoying refreshments accompanied by rotating entertainment that varies from barbershop quartets, bagpipers, and country cloggers to bands playing bluegrass, swing, and country-rock.

"Life on the Farm" is one of the most interesting sections of the grounds, the place to see demonstrations of ox teams, beekeeping, spinning, and sheep shearing. Some of the farm animals on display are so endearing they might have stepped from the pages of Mother Goose. The tiny pygmy goats are especially appealing.

A separate section for the kids features storytellers, clowns, jugglers, and puppeteers. Food stands around the grounds supplement the apple goodies with a variety of foods from ethnic fare to sandwiches and sausages made with locally grown smoked turkey.

Among the many crafts booths you'll find demonstrations and exhibits by the Sonoma County Woodcarvers Association and displays of apple dolls, a popular souvenir.

The closest thing to trendy is a corner where top area chefs show how to prepare some of today's fine Sonoma County cuisine. Some use local mustards and cheeses; others demonstrate and give out recipes for dishes such as apple trifle and Gravenstein chutney.

Proceeds from the fair help fund the printing of the annual "Sonoma County Farm Trails Map," a treasure that you can use any weekend as a guide to apple orchards and to farms of all kinds, from fruit trees to exotic fowl. Many of the farms have stands at the fair, or you can take off afterward to visit their home grounds.

Kozlowski Farm on Route 116, for example, is known for its no-sugar-added fruit conserves, while Pet-A-Llama Ranch sells handmade llama-wool garments and blankets as well as the fleece. Flowers both fresh and dried can be found in abundance at places like Devoto Gardens. This is also a great area to visit during the holiday season for wreaths and cut-your-own Christmas trees. Pelikan Spring Farm even offers wreath-making classes.

Sebastopol itself is a pleasant small town, with a couple of craft shops worth a stop. Antiquers should head directly to Route 116 south of town, a road lined with treasure troves such as the Antique Society, a collective of 90 dealers in a former factory building at number 2661, or School Bell Antiques at number 3655, where 24 dealers conduct business in a vintage schoolhouse. A surprise along the way, at number 1200, is the Enmanji Buddhist Temple, which was originally brought from Japan for the Chicago World's Fair.

Sebastopol has a range of restaurants, from fine French cuisine to old-fashioned apple pie hot from the oven at Mom's Apple Pie on Route 116 north. They disprove the age-old advice to avoid places called "Mom's."

The Gravenstein Inn, an 1872 Victorian farmhouse surrounded by apple orchards, is the best local lodging, but there are many choice possibilities nearby, as well. One of the best is the Inn at Occidental in a town that is about a ten-mile drive, via 116 north to Occidental Road west. This light and airy remodeled Victorian stands on a hill just above town. Rooms are tastefully furnished in antique pine, with cozy down comforters on the beds. A welcoming parlor invites you to relax in front of the fireplace when there is a nip in the air, and there is a garden terrace where breakfast is served on pleasant days.

The whole town of Occidental is about three blocks long, but it is beautifully set in a wooded valley and is known far and wide for two restaurants offering huge family-style Italian meals at minuscule prices. There's a bit of browsing to be done in any of the local antiques shops but the main diversion is a drive or bike ride into the surrounding countryside.

The Bohemian Highway leading to the Sonoma coast at Bodega Bay is the most scenic route, but almost any direction takes you into tranquil hills, past ranches, vineyards, and orchards. Two interesting nurseries are in the neighborhood on Harrison Grade Road. Occidental Nursery specializes in flowering plants that thrive in the shade, and the Miniature Plant Kingdom next door has miniature roses, dwarf conifers, Japanese maples, and bonsai plants.

Another possibility for fun and lodging is to follow Route 116 for 15 miles north of Sebastopol as it passes through Forestville and becomes the River Road west to Guerneville. This is the bustling center of activity for the Russian River, and you can easily fill a Sunday here with happy diversions. Rent a canoe, or join the fishermen, swimmers, and sun worshipers. Golfers will find a nine-hole course nearby in the redwoods, and Armstrong Redwoods State Reserve provides picnic and hiking areas through the tall trees. One way to enjoy the scenery is on a horseback trail ride with the Armstrong Woods Pack Station.

Wineries add to the area attractions. Korbel is an excellent choice for a lesson in how champagne is made, and Topolos at Russian River Vineyards offers dining in a woodland setting, a perfect sylvan retreat for a leisurely lunch. If you would like a romantic winery tour via old-fashioned horse and carriage, Wine Country Carriages in Sebastopol will oblige.

A local activity that intrigues many guests is soaking in the Osmosis Enzyme Baths in the town of Freestone. This is a Japanese treatment much like a mud bath, but using cedar fibers, which produce enzyme-generated heat, which supposedly cleanses and energizes. Some people swear by it.

Accommodations in the popular Guerneville region run the gamut from gracious rooms at Applewood, a top inn known for its fine dining room, to comfortable cottages at the Fern Grove Inn. Huckleberry Springs Country Inn offers five very private cottages on 56 acres of towering redwoods, plus a delicious option, gourmet meals available for guests only. Cazanoma Lodge is an old standby in a secluded rustic setting, with a German-American restaurant. Or you might continue on the River Road a few miles farther west—with a detour for the shopping complex at Duncans Mill—winding up in Jenner, where you can choose a room or a dining place overlooking the dramatic spot where the Russian River meets the sea.

Area Code: 707

DRIVING DIRECTIONS Sebastopol is at the intersection of Routes 12 and 116. From the Bay Area, take Highway 101 north past Petaluma and turn west on Route 116. It is 60 miles from San Francisco, 160 miles from Sacramento.

ACCOMMODATIONS *Gravenstein Inn,* 3160 Hicks Road, Sebastopol, 95472, 829-0493, in-town historic home, pool, M–E, CP • *Inn at Occidental,* 3657 Church Street, Occidental, 95465, 874-1047 or (800) 522-6324, tasteful, special, E–EE, CP • *Applewood,* 13555 Route 116, Pocket Canyon, 95446 (just south of Guerneville), 869-9093, cream of the Russian River lodgings, E–EE, CP • *Fern Grove Inn,* 16650 River Road, Guerneville, 95446, 869-9083, comfortable cottages in a redwood grove, some fireplaces, kitchens, pool; rooms, M, suites, E, villas with kitchen, EE, CP • *Huckleberry Springs Country Inn,* 8105 Old Beedle Road, Monte Rio, 95462, 865-2683 or (800) 822-2683, seclusion in the redwoods, pool and hot tub, EE • *Ridenhour Ranch House Inn,* 12850 River Road, Guerneville, 95446, 887-1033, rustic, appealing, M–E, CP • *Cazanoma Lodge,* 1000 Kidd Creek Road, off Cazadero Road, Cazadero, 95421, 632-5255, lodge and cabins on 147 acres in rustic setting, pool, waterfall, M, CP • *Murphy's Jenner Inn,* 10400 Highway 1, Jenner, 95450, 865-2377, modest inn rooms, cottages overlooking sea; rooms, I–M; cottages, E–EE; CP • *River's End,* Highway 1, P.O. Box 1800, Jenner, 95450, 865-2484, motel-type rooms terraced into the hillside with prize sea views, M.

DINING *Chez Peyo,* 2295 Route 116 south, Sebastopol, 823-9959, country French, M • *Sebastopol Grill,* 7531 Healdsburg Avenue, Sebastopol, 823-4418; New American, M, light menu, I • *Sapphire Mynx,* 101 South Main Street, Sebastopol, 829-3212, in old bank building, M • *Mom's Apple Pie,* 4550 Route 116 north, Sebastopol, 823-8330, lunch, dinner, and great apple pie, I • *Applewood* (see above), four-course prix fixe gourmet dinners, EE • *Ridenhour Ranch House Inn,* Guerneville (see above), dinner by prior reservation only, phone before 11 A.M., prix fixe, EE • *Sweet's River Grill,* 16251 Main Street, Guerneville, 869-3383, informal, pleasant café, I–M • *Union Hotel,* Main Street, Occidental, 874-3555; big, big portions of Italian food served family-style, M • *Bohemian Café,* 3688 Bohemian Highway, Occidental, 874-3931; big breakfasts and lunches, I, interesting dinner menus, M • *Topolos Russian River Vineyards Restaurant,* 5700 Route 116 north, Forestville, 887-1562, Greek and continental, lovely wooded setting for lunch, I, or dinner, M • *Cazanoma Lodge,* Cazadero (see above), German-American menu, overlooking trout pond and waterfall, M • *River's End,* Jenner (see above), tops for food and view, M–EE.

SIGHTSEEING *Gravenstein Apple Fair,* Ragle Park, Sebastopol, 829-GRAV, two days, usually second weekend in August; for current dates and admission, contact Sonoma County Farm Trails, P.O. Box 6032, Santa Rosa, 95406, 996-2154. Send self-addressed envelope with two stamps for free copy of this year's "Farm Trails" guide • *Armstrong Redwoods State Reserve,* Armstrong Woods Road, two miles north of Guerneville, 869-2015. Parking, $5 • *Armstrong Woods Pack Station,* Armstrong Woods State Reserve, Box 970, Guerneville, 887-2939. Phone for schedules, rates • *Korbel Champagne Cellars,* 13250 River Road, Guerneville, 887-2294. Hours: May to September, tasting room daily 9 A.M. to 5 P.M., free tours 10 A.M. to 3:45 P.M.; rest of year, tasting ends 4:30 P.M., tours end 3 P.M. • *Burke's Canoe Trips,* 8600 River Road, Forestville, 887-1222 • *Northwood Golf Course,* 19400 Route 116, Monte Rio, 865-1116, public nine-hole course in the redwoods. Phone for fees • *Osmosis Enzyme Bath,* 209 Bohemian Highway, Freestone, 823-8231, by appointment only. Phone for information.

INFORMATION *Sebastopol Area Chamber of Commerce,* 265 South Main Street, P.O. Box 178, Sebastopol, CA 95473, 823-3032 • *Russian River Region Visitor Center,* 14034 Armstrong Woods Road, Guerneville, CA 95446, 869-9212 or (800) 253-8800.

Mega-Fun at Mammoth Lakes

What a bonanza. Here in the glorious heart of the Sierra Nevadas is a town surrounded by soaring mountains and blessed with a chain of lovely lakes, sparkling rivers, and natural wonders such as Devil's Postpile National Monument and Rainbow Falls. Best of all, this is a ski town in winter, so while it is in beautiful wilderness, it is loaded with lodgings and restaurants. It wouldn't be a surprise to find Mammoth Lakes crammed with nature lovers in summer, but no — the inns are half empty, and the prices are a fraction of their winter highs. For a family excursion or a back-to-nature weekend, Mammoth is hard to match.

The reason for lack of congestion is the location, 250 miles from any big city. You can't get here from points to the north without crossing the Sierras. In winter, when the passes are closed, that means driving past Lake Tahoe, then proceeding much farther south, a long haul few Northern California skiers are willing to undertake. So the ski slopes are packed with Southern Californians, who can approach from the other side, and they are far more likely to return in warm weather, since the area is already familiar.

But come summer, Mammoth becomes a fine destination for a long weekend for Northern Californians. It can be approached by crossing the mountains on Route 120, Tioga Pass, through Yosemite National Park, a thrilling superscenic route that sets the stage for the pleasures to come.

Arrive in July and you can enjoy the annual Mammoth Lakes Jazz Festival, three days of fun with 15 bands performing. In August, the Sierra Summer Festival brings a three-week cornucopia of music from Broadway shows to bluegrass to rock, with something for every taste.

When you get into this friendly, informal ski town, the mountains are in sight in all directions. Since summer rates are so moderate, it's easy to splurge for the top of the line, the Mammoth Mountain Inn, at the base of the slopes. Or you can opt to be within walking distance of town restaurants by staying at the modest Snow Goose, an inn that serves up tasty breakfasts and wine and cheese at day's end.

An additional alternative is a stay at the very attractive rustic Tamarack Lodge on Twin Lakes, lovely oases of blue ringed by mountains. Yet another possibility is a stay in a condominium home, a good choice for families. There are scores of these in scenic locations. They serve skiers in winter, become bargains after the snow melts. Reservation services handle a variety of properties and can help zero in on one that is right for your needs and budget.

Having found a home base, the first order of business is to head for the Ski Area, park in the Mammoth Mountain Inn lot, and board a shuttle bus for the dizzying trip on a narrow road high into the mountains to the area's most famous sights. The bus makes the trip every half hour, stopping at several locations when it gets into mountains, so you can ride to one of the next stops or hike and catch up with the bus farther on.

First stop for most riders is Devil's Postpile National Monument, 800 acres of wilderness set 7,600 feet high on the slopes of the Sierra Nevadas, along the Middle Fork of the San Joaquin River. The intriguing feature here is a formation of basalt columns that might have been carved by a celestial sculptor. Some 100,000 years ago basalt lava erupted from the mountain, filling the valley below to a depth of 400 feet. Cracks formed on the surface of the lava as it cooled and shrank, eventually deepening to create a set of columns 60 feet high and amazingly uniform in shape.

They were discovered eventually when moving glaciers quarried away one side of the formation, revealing a steep wall of columns that some unknown explorer named "Devil's Postpile." The glacial movement also polished the ends to a smooth sheen. A steep but short hike to the top of the Postpile reveals what looks for all the world like a polished floor of perfect hexagonal tiles. There is nothing else like it in this country; the closest similar formations are Giant's Causeway in Ireland and Fingal's Cave in Scotland.

From the Postpile, a pleasant wooded hike leads to Rainbow Falls, a wide cascade formed at a point where the San Joaquin River drops 101 feet over a cliff. The falls was named for the rainbows that form in the mist as the water spumes into the river. A stairway leads to the bottom of the falls for a close-up view, but the rainbows are visible only from on high. If you want a shorter walk, begin the Rainbow Falls hike at Reds Meadow, the next bus stop; the distance from here is only one mile.

The longer hike, from the Postpile, also ends at Reds Meadow, where there is a rustic little café for lunch or refreshments. Those who want to stay in a glorious wilderness setting can rent a no-frills cabin here.

Back at the ski area base lodge, the gondola ride 11,038 feet up to the windblown summit of Mammoth Mountain affords a 360-degree view that bears testimony to why the mountain was so named. Hardy mountain bikers can be seen at the summit getting ready to take a run straight down on trails with names like Kamikaze, a prospect to strike terror in the hearts of the less adventuresome. In summer the whole face of the mountain becomes a Mountain Bike Park, utilizing the ski trails. A variety of activities is offered, including lessons for beginners and guided tours for all levels. Taking the gondola to the top makes it easy to ride down without the work of pedaling up.

A final outing from the lodge is a short drive following the bus route as far as Minaret Summit, where there's a four-star view of the Minarets, Mt. Ritter, and Mt. Banner. Turn right just before the entrance station to the main road to the mountains and drive one-quarter mile to the viewpoint. It's a great sight anytime, but it is magical at sunset.

A second day at Mammoth might lead in many directions. Follow Highway 203 past the Minaret Road intersection for Lake Mary Road, leading to the Lakes Basin and a series of Alpine lakes. There are 13 lakes in all, including 5 major ones, ideal for fishing, sailing, canoeing, or just admiring from easy flat walking trails. Lake Mary is the biggest, Twin Lakes is the most scenic, and Horseshoe Lake offers a small swimming beach. From the road you will also see the cascades of Twin Falls and mountain formations such as Mammoth Crest and Panorama Dome.

A road off the main Lake Mary loop road heads up Coldwater Canyon to the site of Mammoth Consolidated Mine, a onetime gold mine. It's only a short hike from the parking lot along Coldwater Creek to the crystal water of Emerald Lake.

Or you might take another direction altogether. Head south on I-395 for about 15 miles to the Rock Creek Lake turnoff at Tom's Place, and drive up a steep Sierra canyon to an even more spectacular lake, set in an ancient basin surrounded by 13,000-foot peaks.

Back on I-395, turn left and continue north to the airport exit. Then go right and follow the signs to Hot Creek Fish Hatchery, where you can see trout being bred in outdoor ponds. Another two miles east leads to Hot Creek Geologic Site, whose bubbling hot springs and steaming fumaroles are evidence that this is an active geologic area.

If you'd rather sightsee on a guided walk or bike tour, check the busy schedule of the Mammoth Ranger District. Their interpretive programs cover all of these sites, from forest to lakes, and include a tour of the Mammoth Mine. There are special programs just for junior rangers, ages 6 to 12, no adults allowed.

Amateur anglers can join a ranger fishing guide at Lake Mary to learn some of the tricks of the trade. There couldn't be a better area to try your luck. The San Joaquin River and the region's lakes are all happy hunting grounds for fishermen. Twin Lakes and Lakes Mary, George, and Mamie are also noted fishing spots; Hot Creek is said to be California's most popular catch-and-release wild trout stream; and manmade Crowley Lake is another prime place for trout.

To learn more about the history of the area or to pick up more fishing and hiking trips, drop in on some of the programs held on weekend afternoons at the Hayden Cabin, headquarters of the Mammoth Historical Museum. Further outdoor adventures beckon if you sign up for a one-day or longer horseback trip, or board a hot-air balloon for a sky-high view of the scenery.

A single weekend just isn't enough time for the mammoth delights of Mammoth Lakes.

Area Code: 619

DRIVING DIRECTIONS   Mammoth Lakes is off I-395. From the Bay Area, take Route 120 to I-395 and continue south to Mammoth Lakes exit, Highway 203. It is 319 miles from San Francisco, 242 miles from Sacramento.

ACCOMMODATIONS   All rates are lowest in summer. *Mammoth Mountain Inn,* Box 353, Mammoth Lakes, 934-2581 or (800) 228-4947, summer, M–EE. Ask about mountain bike and other special packages • *Snow Goose Inn,* 57 Forest Trail, Mammoth Lakes, 934-

2660 or (800) 874-7368, I–EE, CP • *Tamarack Lodge Resort*, Twin Lakes, P.O. Box 69, Mammoth Lakes, 934-2442 or (800) 237-6879, lodge rooms, cabins, I–EE • *Royal Pines Resort*, Viewpoint Road, Mammoth Lakes, 934-2306, moderate-price motel in scenic spot, some kitchen suites, I–M • *Shilo Inn,* Route 203, Mammoth Lakes, 934-7594, rooms with microwave and refrigerator, indoor pool, I–E. All zip codes are 93546 • *Condominium reservation services: Mammoth Reservation Bureau,* (800) 527-6273, in California (800) 462-5571; *Mammoth Sierra Reservations,* (800) 654-1143, in California (800) 325-8415.

DINING *Lakefront,* Tamarack Lodge, Twin Lakes, 934-3534, cozy rustic charm overlooking Twin Lakes, E–EE • *Anything Goes Café,* 645 Old Mammoth Road, Mammoth Lakes, 934-2424, bakery café with creative California-Mediterranean dinner menu, M • *Natalie's,* Old Mammoth Road in Sherwin Plaza III, Mammoth Lakes, 934-3902, intimate café serving country French fare, M • *The Mogul,* Tavern Road, 934-3039, long-established favorite for steak, prime ribs, salad bar, M–E • *Whiskey Creek,* Main Street at Minaret, 934-2555, varied menu, good reputation, M • *Slocum's Italian & American Grill,* Main Street, 934-7647, Victorian ambience, lively bar, good food, M • *Ocean Harvest,* Old Mammoth Road at Sierra Nevada Road, 934-8539, seafood, attractive, M • *Mountainside Grill,* Mammoth Mountain Inn, 934-0601, varied menu, Alpine setting, I–E.

SIGHTSEEING *Mammoth Adventure Connection,* P.O. Box 353 or c/o Mammoth Mountain Inn, 934-0606 or (800) 228-4947. Contact for current information about all of the following: *Bus shuttle to Devil's Postpile National Monument and Red's Meadow,* Mammoth Mountain Inn parking lot, Highway 203 at Minaret Road, 4 miles west of town. Hours: Daily on the half hour from 7:30 A.M.; last return bus from Red's Meadow, 5:30 P.M. Adults, $7; ages 5 to 12, $4 • *Mammoth Mountain Gondola ride,* Main Lodge, Mammoth Mountain. Hours: Daily, wind and weather permitting, 9 A.M. to 3:30 P.M. Adults, $10; ages 5 to 12, $5 • *Mammoth Mountain Bike Park,* Mammoth Mountain Ski Area, guided tours including park-use fees and gondola ride up: Adults, $20; under age 12, $12. Trail access pass without gondola: Adults, $10; under age 12, $6; bike rentals, $25 for half day • *Mammoth Ranger District Interpretive Programs,* U.S. Forest Service Visitor Center, Main Street, 924-5500. Check for current schedule of summer guided hikes, bike trips, gold mine tour, evening programs. Free • *Mammoth Lakes Jazz Jubilee,* P.O. Box 8540, 934-2478. Three days in mid-July. Check for current dates, rates • *Sierra Summer Festival,* P.O. Box 7710, Mammoth Lakes, 934-2409. Three weeks of concerts beginning in early August. Check for current schedules, rates • *Mammoth Historical Museum,* Hayden Cabin, P.O.

Box 65, Mammoth Lakes, 934-9918. Early June to Labor Day, daily 10 A.M. to 5 P.M.

ACTIVITIES **Ballooning:** *High Sierra Ballooning Company*, 934-7188 • **Bike rentals:** *Footloose*, 934-2400; *Mammoth Sporting Goods*, 934-3239 • **Horsepack trips:** *Mammoth Lakes Pack Outfit and Red's Meadow Resort & Pack Station*, Box 61, Mammoth Lakes, 934-2434; *McGee Creek Pack Station*, Highway 1, Box 162, Mammoth Lakes, 935-4324; *Agnew Meadows Pack Station*, Box 395, Mammoth Lakes, 934-2345 • **Fishing guides and equipment rental:** *Kittridge Sports*, 934-7566 or (800) 441-3331; *The Trout Fly*, 934-2517 • **Boat and canoe rentals:** *Twin Lakes Store*, 934-6974; *Tamarack Lodge,* Twin Lakes, 934-2442.

INFORMATION *Mammoth Lakes Visitors' Bureau*, 3399 Main Street, P.O. Box 48, Mammoth Lakes, CA 93546, 934-8006 or (800) 367-6572.

Tasting Time in the Sonoma Valley

Northern California winemaking was born in the Sonoma Valley back in 1824, when a Mexican padre planted grapevines to supply sacramental wines for his mission.

Today the lush 17-mile valley is home to more than 30 wineries, many of them world-renowned—yet wine tasting is only one of the good reasons to pay a visit. This is also the place for a taste of early California history, for sampling the beauty in the hills and meadows cradling the valley, and for enjoying fine cuisine inspired by the fresh produce that grows in profusion in this region's rich soil and temperate climate.

At the heart of the Valley is its earliest settlement, the picturesque town of Sonoma. This was the site of the last and northernmost of California's 21 missions, as well as the first (and only) capital of the independent republic of California. Much of this history has been preserved in the shady eight-acre plaza in the center of town, a national landmark and the state's largest town square. Many fiestas and historical events are celebrated here.

On one side of the plaza, the Mission San Francisco Solano is open to the public, as are the Sonoma Barracks, built to house Mexican army troops, and the restored wood-frame house known as Casa Grande, the home of the Mexican commander General Mariano Vallejo.

The original humble mission was founded and dedicated in 1824 by Padre Jose Altimira, the man who planted those first Sonoma grapes. When the Mexican army took over, it was rebuilt in its present form in 1840 by Vallejo. The stucco structure fell into sad disrepair in later years, until it became state property and restoration began in 1911. Archaeological digs as late as 1955 contributed additional authentic touches such as tile walkways, foundations of adobe walls along the east side of the church, and remnants of the earliest mission.

The Mexicans lost Sonoma in the famous 1846 Golden Bear uprising. Angered by Mexican law prohibiting them from owning land, a group of settlers led by John C. Frémont rode into town, arrested General Vallejo, and, without firing a shot, raised the Bear flag and declared California an independent republic. (A large rock topped with a bronze figure holding a replica of the flag now marks the site.) That status lasted exactly 25 days, until U.S. troops claimed the area as American territory and the Bear was replaced by the Stars and Stripes. In 1911 the Bear flag became the inspiration for the official flag of the new state of California.

When he was ousted by the Americans, the resourceful Vallejo found a second career. He became California's first commercial winemaker, planting new grapevines behind the barracks and on the north side of the plaza. His cellar, presses, and shop were housed in the barracks. The wines were sold in San Francisco under the name Lachryma Montis, or "tear of the mountain," the same name Vallejo gave to the redwood home he built on lavish grounds in 1856. The house, now a state landmark, is located about half a mile from the mission. It has been restored with many original furnishings.

Other interesting historical sights around the plaza include the 1840 Blue Wing Inn built by Vallejo, the 1886 Toscano Hotel, and the Swiss Hotel, which was built by the general's brother Salvador Vallejo as a home in the late 1830s and converted to a hotel in the late nineteenth century. Salvador Vallejo's second home, at 411 First Street West, was built in the early 1840s.

Besides this look into the past, the plaza and its environs offer a sampling of some of Sonoma's present-day claims to fame—galleries showing work by local artists, a well-stocked wine shop, and regional specialties at such shops as the Sausage Company and the Sonoma Cheese Factory. The latter is a good place to watch the making of Sonoma Jack cheese. This is also a good place to pick up a lunch for picnicking at the vineyards, one of the special pleasures of the wine country.

One place to enjoy that lunch is the picnic grounds at the venerable

Buena Vista winery. In 1856 a competitor to General Vallejo appeared in the person of a Hungarian count, Agoston Haraszthy, who founded Buena Vista. The two winemakers ended their rivalry with a pair of mergers in 1863, the marriage of Vallejo's daughters to Haraszthy's sons. The original stone cellar at Buena Vista is now a state landmark open to the public. It includes a wine museum and the aging caves dug by Chinese laborers in 1862.

Sebastiani Vineyard, another Sonoma old-timer, is still owned by the founding family. It is very popular for its excellent guided tours of the winemaking process and its collection of hand-carved redwood casks. Tours end with free tastings.

The Gloria Ferrer Champagne Caves south of town is a handsome winery opened by Freisenet of Spain in 1986. The Spanish-style building is beautiful, set on a knoll with vintage vineyard views. The setting and views come free, as do tours of the *méthode champenoise* process, but there is a charge for the tasting.

There are many dining choices in and around the town of Sonoma, but a long-time star for a splurge is the Grille at the Sonoma Mission Inn in nearby Boyes Hot Springs, with interesting continental dishes. Since Sonoma Mission Inn is well known as a spa as well as a luxury retreat, the Grille also features tasty low-calorie dishes.

In town, the El Dorado has been taken over by the owners of the Napa Valley's noted Auberge du Soleil and given an airy Mediterranean feel. The Sonoma Hotel, a venerable landmark more than a century old, has been restored with lots of turn-of-the-century memorabilia. The third-floor rooms with shared baths are good buys for those on a budget.

Sonoma also offers some appealing bed-and-breakfast choices just a stroll from the plaza. Victorian Garden Inn has pretty antique-filled rooms, some with private entrances around a delightful garden. The Thistle Dew Inn is furnished with collector-quality Mission Oak pieces by craftsmen like Gustav Stickley, master of the Arts and Crafts Movement.

On Sunday, you might enjoy a leisurely breakfast, then head to the hills for a closer look at the Sonoma scenery. The 750-acre Jack London State Park in Glen Ellen is highly recommended. Author Jack London named this estate his "Beauty Ranch," and it's easy to see why. The 1,400 acres of canyons, forest, and meadows sit high on a ridge approaching the 2,463-foot summit of Sonoma Mountain, with wonderful views of the landscape that London called the "Valley of the Moon," taken from the Indian word *sonoma,* which means "many moons." It is also the title of one of London's novels and is a name that is still often used for the Sonoma Valley.

The swashbuckling London gave up most of his wandering at the end of his life to put down roots here, raising livestock and farming his property. He used a onetime winery built in 1884 as a carriage house and guest house, and many of its adjacent stone buildings as barn and storage facilities. A cottage on the property was transformed into his own sanctuary, where he wrote many of his later stories and novels.

All of these buildings, now intriguing ruins, can be seen on a walking tour, or you can opt for a horseback tour offered by Sonoma Cattle Company in Glen Ellen. Most interesting of all is the short trail through forests of oak, fir, and redwoods leading to the stone walls that remain of the Wolf House, the stone-and-timber mansion London built at great expense for himself and his wife, Charmian. The house was lost in a tragic fire in 1913, before they ever moved in. The origin of the fire remains a mystery. The "House of Happy Walls" that Charmian London built after her husband's death in 1916 is now a small museum filled with photos and memorabilia of London's many adventures as sailor, outdoorsman, and world traveler, as well as author. His grave is on the property, marked by a large boulder.

For another view of Sonoma scenery, take the magnificent drive up Sonoma Mountain Road out of Glen Ellen, a road scaling the mountain and running through hilly farmland and groves of stately redwoods. Jack London was out in his horse and buggy when he discovered one of the loveliest pockets of this road at Cooper's Grove, an area he wrote about in *The Valley of the Moon*. It is a perfect spot for a picnic beneath the redwoods.

In the picturesque little hamlet of Glen Ellen, the Jack London Bookstore on Arnold Drive offers new and used copies of the author's works. Amedeo, in the little shopping complex across the road, is a restored mill turned restaurant, a scenic stop for lunch.

Or you might choose the inviting shady picnic grounds at Glen Ellen Winery, just at the base of the road to Jack London Park. The Benziger family bought and restored this century-old winery in the 1980s, and the original blue-shuttered wooden building and the steep terraced hillside vineyards make a pretty picture. At the least, stop to admire the vista and perhaps to visit the tasting room.

Little Glen Ellen also offers its own inviting lodgings. Beltane Ranch on Route 12 is a real charmer, a pale yellow house set off on a hillside. With its wraparound veranda, it looks a bit like a southern mansion. The place was once a working ranch, but today's crops are grapes, vegetables, and pretty flowers. Breakfast comes with home-made jams and goodies like fresh-picked berries. Each of the four guest rooms has a private entrance off the balcony and its own share of veranda sitting space with a view.

The Glenelly Inn is a lodge-style building in town with verandas and attractive country furnishings, while Gaige House is a vintage village Victorian with a deck overlooking a creek and, a welcome amenity in summer, a swimming pool. And then there is the Stone Tree Ranch, just one cabin complete with kitchen and its own hot tub with valley views.

Continuing north on Route 12 to Kenwood brings you to more

notable wining and dining. Kenwood and Chateau St. Jean are both highly regarded wineries. The latter, a handsome Mediterranean-style building with a tower and colonnade, offers an interesting self-guided tour of the process that produces sparkling wines. Fans of the Smothers Brothers may want to stop at their tasting room on Route 12; the vineyards are elsewhere in the area.

The Kenwood Restaurant is a sophisticated bistro offering yet another delicious taste of the Sonoma Valley, and the Kenwood Inn is a very posh and attractive hideaway, with the look of an Italian villa and a spa to pamper you.

Finally, for a last ridgetop view of the valley, continue on Route 12 north of Kenwood and turn off on Adobe Canyon Road to Sugarloaf Ridge State Park in the Mayacamas Mountains. The 2,700-acre park has 25 miles of trails to be covered on foot or horseback. The park reaches an elevation of 2,729 feet, a Sonoma Valley high.

Area Code: 707

DRIVING DIRECTIONS   Sonoma is located on Route 12, about 48 miles north of San Francisco, 68 miles from Sacramento. From the Bay Area, follow Highway 101 north to Route 116 east, then Route 12 north. From I-80, take 29 north to 121/12 west, then branch off at Route 12 north.

ACCOMMODATIONS   *El Dorado Hotel,* 405 First Street West, Sonoma, 95476, 996-3030, M–EE • *Sonoma Hotel,* 110 West Spain Street, Sonoma, 95476, 996-2996, E, M with shared bath • *Victorian Garden Inn,* 316 East Napa Street, Sonoma, 95476, 996-5339, M–E, CP • *Thistle Dew Inn,* 171 West Spain Street, Sonoma, 95476, 938-2909, E–EE, CP • *Sonoma Chalet,* 18935 Fifth Street West, Sonoma, 95476, 938-3129, M–E, CP • *Kenwood Inn,* 10400 Sonoma Highway, Kenwood, 95452, 833-1293, EE, CP • *Sonoma Mission Inn & Spa,* 18140 Sonoma Highway (Route 12 at Boyes Boulevard), Boyes Hot Springs; mailing address P.O. Box 1447, Sonoma, 95476, 938-9000 or (800) 862-4945, EE • *Beltane Ranch,* 11775 Sonoma Highway (Route 12), Glen Ellen, 95442, 996-6501, M–E, CP • *Gaige House,* 13540 Arnold Drive, Glen Ellen, 95442, 935-0237, E–EE, CP • *Glenelly Inn,* 5131 Warm Springs Road, Glen Ellen, 95442, 996-6720, M–E, CP.

DINING   *Eastside Oyster Bar & Grille,* 133 East Napa Street, Sonoma, 939-1266, creative chef, cozy bistro ambience, M • *Babette's,* 464 First Street East, Sonoma, 939-8921, California with a French accent, M • *Piatti,* El Dorado Hotel, Sonoma (see above), imaginative Italian, I–M • *Sonoma Hotel* (see above), old-fashioned decor, courtyard in warm weather, M • *The General's Daughter,* 400 West Spain Street, 938-4004, varied menu, historic landmark home, I–M • *The Grille,* Sonoma Mission Inn & Spa (see page 114), continental, widely praised, M–E • *Amedeo,* 14301 Arnold Drive, Glen Ellen, 996-3077, Italian, great setting, I–M • *Kenwood Restaurant,* 9900 Route 12, Kenwood, 833-6326, California cuisine, M.

SIGHTSEEING *Sonoma State Historic Park,* Sonoma Plaza, 938-1519. Buildings include Sonoma Mission, Sonoma Barracks, Vallejo Home, Blue Wing Inn, and Toscano Hotel. Hours: Daily 10 A.M. to 5 P.M. Adults, $2; ages 6 to 12, $1 • *Jack London State Historic Park,* Glen Ellen, 938-5216. Hours: Daily 10 A.M. to 7 P.M., museum to 5 P.M. Per car, $5 • *Sugarloaf Ridge State Park,* 2605 Adobe Canyon Road, Kenwood, 833-5712. Daylight hours. Per car, $5 • *Sonoma Cattle Company,* P.O. Box 877, London Ranch Road, Glen Ellen, 996-8566, guided horseback rides in Jack London and Sugarloaf Ridge state parks. Phone for current rates.

WINERIES (Free unless noted) *Buena Vista Winery,* Old Winery Road, Sonoma, 938-1266, self-guided tours, wine museum. Hours: Daily 10:30 A.M. to 4:30 P.M. • *Sebastiani Vineyards,* 349 Fourth Street East, Sonoma, 938-5532. Hours: Daily 10 A.M. to 5 P.M., guided tours 10:30 A.M. to 4 P.M. • *Gloria Ferrer Champagne Cellars,* 2355 Route 121, Sonoma, 996-7256. Hours: Daily guided tours 11 A.M. to 4 P.M., tastings 10:30 A.M. to 5:30 P.M. Fee for tasting • *Glen Ellen Winery,* 1883 London Ranch Road, Glen Ellen, 996-1066. Hours: Daily tastings 10 A.M. to 4 P.M. • *Kenwood Vineyards,* 9592 Sonoma Highway, Kenwood, 833-5891. Tours by appointment. Tasting hours: Daily 10 A.M. to 4:30 P.M. • *Chateau St. Jean,* 8555 Sonoma Highway, Kenwood, 833-4134, self-guided tours. Hours: 10 A.M. to 4 P.M., tastings to 4:30 P.M.

INFORMATION *Sonoma Valley Visitors' Bureau,* 453 First Street East, Sonoma, CA 95476, 996-1090. *Sonoma County Convention & Visitors Bureau,* 5000 Roberts Lake Road, Rohnert Park, CA 94928, 586-8100 or (800) 326-7666.

Photo Finish at Mono Lake

Mark Twain called Mono Lake a "solemn, silent sailless sea" and labeled its fantastic tufa towers "one of the strangest freaks of nature to be found in any land."

Some things have changed a great deal since Twain described California's own salt lake in *Roughing It* in 1872, but Mono Lake remains a moonscape wonder that never fails to fascinate. Photographers go bonkers at the sight of the lake's strange tufa towers, and never seem to tire of taking pictures.

Equally beguiling is Bodie, the eerie Gold Rush ghost town less than an hour's drive away, in a photo-finish tie with Mono for camera buffs' favorite location. And since Mono Lake lies near the town of Lee Vining, at the entrance to Tioga Pass and Yosemite's eastern high country, this can be a remarkably scenic weekend in one of the most photogenic areas in this or any other state. The intense colors of late summer make ideal backdrops.

The mysterious Mono Lake Basin is like no other on earth. The deep-blue 100-square-mile circular lake, said to be 700,000 years old, is a still inland sea in an incomparable setting—weathered ancient hills to the north and east, gray volcanic craters to the south, and snow-capped Sierra peaks to the west.

At first the glassy water seems devoid of life, but actually the high saline and mineral content makes it a perfect breeding ground for brine shrimp. They are visible farther out, trillions of them, drifting like leaves in the buoyant water, providing a rich food supply for ducks, gulls, and other waterbirds. The lake's islands are oases for millions of nesting birds, the source of 95 percent of the California gull population.

A good place to begin your visit is the Mono Basin Scenic Area just off Highway 395 north of Lee Vining, which includes exhibits about the natural and human history of the Mono Basin.

Some of Mono's most remarkable vistas are at the easily accessible South Tufa area, which protects 57,000 acres of lakeshore. The parking lot is on Route 120 to Benton, five miles east of I-395.

The dense, saline water makes for fun swimming along Navy Beach on the south shore. The water is so buoyant you can almost sit up and read a newspaper as you float.

But it is the tall tufa in surreal shapes in and around the lake that is the amazing main attraction here, a magical scene that changes from hour to hour as the sun's patterns of light change. Sunsets are wondrous, and can easily inspire you through a whole roll of film.

The towers begin to form when underground springs containing calcium come up through the bottom of the lake. The calcium combines with the carbonate lake water to form calcium carbonate, the coarse-grained whitish material known as tufa. It looks like stone but is actually quite fragile. Signs at South Tufa invite you to touch—but very carefully. The one-mile Mark Twain trail, a self-guided walk with signs explaining the formations, uses Twain's well-chosen words to marvel at nature's creations.

Tufa towers now found high and dry nearly a mile from Mono's shore are the reason why Mono supporters have been waging a long, hard battle against the Los Angeles Department of Water and Power. Since 1941, when they began diverting lake water to supply the L.A. area, the lake has lost an average of 18 inches a year. By 1990 the loss measured 40 vertical feet, which doubled the salinity of the remaining water. Trout fisheries in the streams have been devastated. Caustic dust from the exposed lakeshore is polluting the pristine air of the eastern Sierra. If the situation were allowed to continue, the increasing salinity would poison the lake's ecosystem, kill the shrimp, and deprive the birds of food.

California moved to help the lake by creating a state reserve in 1981, and national recognition came in 1984 through the establishment of the Mono Basin National Forest Scenic Area, identifying the water level needed to protect the lake. After resisting for many years, in 1994 the California State Water Resources Control Board finally ordered that the lake be allowed to rise about 17 feet from current levels, and also plans extensive restoration of the lake and its streams. Over 4,000 citizens wrote and testified in favor of this action.

The Mono Lake Committee, the local group that has raised funds, labored, and litigated long and hard to save the lake, will continue to lobby to see that these orders are carried out. The Committee has 20,000 supporters from all over America who have visited, then given donations and written letters supporting their efforts. When you see the rare beauty of the lake, you may well join the cause. Visit their Information Center and Bookstore in Lee Vining for information on the current status of the restoration.

One of the best ways to see the tufa formations is on a canoe tour sponsored by the Mono Lake Foundation, another organization dedicated to the preservation of the area's ecosystem. Canoes let you glide among the spires, dip your paddle into the swarms of brine shrimp, and float right next to diving birds.

Rangers lead walks at the lake, explaining the area's unusual geology, and the Mono Lake Committee also sponsors a tour. Schedules are available at the visitors' center. Wear a hat and bring sunscreen and drinking water on these trips; the sun gets strong here. Binoculars will also be welcome for close-up views.

Come back on a Tuesday or Friday night for stargazing and folklore at Navy Beach; bring your own chair or blanket, and a warm jacket.

The lake is the most unusual attraction but far from the only thing to see in the Mono Basin. Rangers will take you on a Volcano Tour of the eastern High Sierra, exploring a dozen craters resulting from the most recent volcanic action in the state.

A slightly more rigorous trip to Black Point on the north shore features fissures from 30 to 50 feet wide that were left by an Ice Age volcano. Black Point also affords the best vistas in the Basin. For an easier walk, choose the lovely Lee Vining Creek Trail, built in 1993 by Lee Vining residents with the help of the U.S. Forest Service, the Los Angeles Department of Water and Power, and the Mono Lake Committee. Pick up a guide at either town information center. The trail begins 50 yards south of the Best Western Motel on the east side of Highway 395.

There is also a scenic route around June Lake and the historic town of Bennettville. An auto tour of the Mono Craters covers eight scenic stops and requires no walking at all, and there are some tours designed especially for the kids.

If you want to learn even more, sign on for a weekend workshop cosponsored by the Mono Lake Foundation and the Committee. Topics include birds, volcanoes, wildflowers, mammals, geology, and photography.

Of course, you may prefer to explore on your own, and you'll certainly want to take in the Alpine sights on the spectacular road from Lee Vining to Yosemite National Park. In just 12 miles Route 120 climbs to 9,945-foot Tioga Pass, the highest road in California, and continues past fabulous high-country scenery leading into the heart of the valley. You may spot California bighorn sheep grazing not too far from the road. The road is usually open from Memorial Day through November.

One of the first attractions near the junction of Route 120 and Tioga Pass at Crane Flat is the Tuolumne Grove of giant sequoias. You can park at the grove and walk a short distance into the giants.

Other wonderful stops off the road are Tenaya Lake, one of the loveliest in the Sierras, and Tuolumne Meadows, the largest sub-Alpine meadow in the mountains and a mass of color when wildflowers are in season. The Tuolumne Meadows Lodge is a summer headquarters for picking up trail maps and has a small restaurant.

Five dormitory-style tent camps offer lodgings in the High Sierra in summer, surely among the most beautiful places to stay if you're willing to rough it a bit, but you'll have to plan far ahead. Otherwise, there are nonscenic motels in Lee Vining, though some do offer views of the lake and mountains. There are also motel-cottage complexes with views on June Lake, a turnoff about 11 miles south of Lee Vining that will have special appeal for fishermen, boaters, and hikers. An 18-mile loop around the lake includes some splendid canyon views. Silver Lake, midcanyon with Carson Peak towering in the background, is a photographer's favorite.

It is 25 miles south from Lee Vining to the far more appealing town

of Mammoth Lakes, and about 18 miles north to more motels and one
historic inn in Bridgeport, not a bad stopping place if you plan to drive
the next day to Bodie. This is not gourmet territory, though you may be
content to feast on the scenery.

Bodie State Historic Park is another place that will inspire you to
swing your camera into instant action. When an already deserted road
turns to gravel, you have an inkling of what is ahead. Instead of trying
to restore or re-create, the state parks department has wisely left this a
genuine gold-mining ghost town, carefully maintained in a state of
"arrested decay." The weathered buildings whisper a story of the past
far better than would false fronts and Victorian froufrou.

You can see the Standard Mine and Mill standing off on the west
slope of Bodie Bluff. In its heyday it yielded nearly $15 million over
25 years, causing the 1878 rush to Bodie, when the population grew
from 20 to an estimated 10,000. The town soon boasted 65 saloons, a
reputation for bad men and bad whiskey, and the worst climate in the
West. According to the park guidebook, one little girl on her way to the
remote, infamous town wrote in her diary, "Goodbye God, I'm going
to Bodie," and the phrase was soon known far and wide. Killings, rob-
beries, and street fights were everyday occurrences, and the fire bell
tolling the ages of the deceased was a familiar sound.

Then the gold was gone, and soon so were the settlers. By the 1930s
no one was left. Bodie is quiet now, and the only thing that remains
wicked is the weather. Though it gets hot in summer, this is the best
time to come, because it is the only season when the weather is pre-
dictable. Only about 5 percent of the buildings from the 1880s heyday
remain, but they are enough for some fascinating wandering, peeking
into windows of homes and shops left just as they were when the gold
and the people ran out.

Pick up the inexpensive park brochure for a map identifying who
lived where, who married whom, and where people worked, shopped,
went to school, had their horses shod, picked up mail, and landed in
jail. The old Methodist church still stands, though no services have
been held since 1932. The Cain residence at Green and Park streets
was one of Bodie's showplaces, owned by the town's principal property owner; Cain and his partner supposedly took $90,000 in gold from
the mine in 90 days. The Donnelly House was the only place in town
with a garden; the hops Donnelly grew were said to be the only green
plants that could survive in Bodie.

Each shaky structure has its own tale, and if you follow the trail
winding past the once-grand hotel, the few remains of Chinatown, and
the town cemetery, you'll be in a time warp, caught in Bodie's spell.
Just hope that the silence that is so much a part of the Bodie experience is not broken by a mining company, which has bought land on
Bodie Bluff and is test drilling to see if anything of value remains.
Bodie, as it stands, is already as rare as gold.

Area Code: 619

DRIVING DIRECTIONS   Lee Vining is located on I-395, near the intersection of Route 120. From I-5, I-395 can be reached via routes 50, 108, or 120, the latter being spectacular, steep up-and-down mountain drives. Mileages vary according to the route, all of which are about six hours' driving time from San Francisco, five hours from Sacramento.

ACCOMMODATIONS   *Best Western Lake View Lodge,* I-395, Lee Vining, 93541, 647-6543, the best of the motels, I–M • *Gateway Motel,* I-395, Lee Vining, 93541, 647-6467, I–M • *Murphey's Motel,* I-395, Lee Vining, 93541, 647-6467, I–M • *Cain House,* 11 Main Street, Bridgeport, 93517, 932-7040, historic local home, M–E, CP • *Best Western Ruby Inn,* I-395, Bridgeport, 93517, 932-7241, I–M • *Walker River Lodge,* I-395, Bridgeport, 93517, 932-7021, motel on the river, M • *Boulder Lodge,* Route 158, June Lake, 93529, 648-7533, lakefront motel and cottages, indoor pool, I–M • *Whispering Pines,* Route 158, June Lake, 93529, 648-7762, motel and A-frame cottages, mountain views, I–E.

DINING   *Nicely's Restaurant,* I-395, Lee Vining, 647-6446, all three meals, I–M • *Mono Inn,* I-395 north of Lee Vining, 647-6581, I–M • *Yosemite Trails Inn,* I-395, 647-6369, I–M • *Yosemite Trading Company & Deli,* I-395, Lee Vining, 647-6369, for deli lunches, I • *Carson Peak Inn,* Route 158, June Lake, 648-7575, scenic setting, M–E • *Sierra Inn,* Route 158, 648-7774, overlooks June Lake, 648-7774, M.

SIGHTSEEING   *Mono Basin National Forest Service Scenic Area Visitor Center,* I-395 just north of Lee Vining, 647-3044. Hours: Daily in summer, rest of year, weekends, 9:30 A.M. to 4:30 P.M. Information on all area activities, including ranger tours • *Mono Lake Committee Information Center and Bookstore,* I-395, 647-6595. Hours: Summer, daily 9 A.M. to 9 P.M.; rest of year, to 5 P.M. Information on the lake, tours, and reservations for canoe tours • *Mono Lake Tufa State Reservation,* Route 120 east of I-395, 5 miles south of Lee Vining, 647-6331. Hours: Area open 24 hours • *Mono Lake Field Workshops,* P.O. Box 153, Lee Vining, 93541, 647-6496. Two-day workshops held June to August. Check for current offerings • *Bodie State Historic Park,* Route 270 east turnoff, south of Bridgeport, 647-6445. Hours: Summer, daily 9 A.M. to 7 P.M.; rest of year, to 4 P.M. After summer, check the Mono County Sheriff's Office in Bridgeport for road and weather conditions before making the trip. Parking fee, $5.

INFORMATION   *Lee Vining Chamber of Commerce,* P.O. Box 130, Lee Vining, CA 93541, 647-6629.

FALL

Overleaf: *Victorian gingerbread in Ferndale. Photo courtesy of Eleanor Berman.*

Secret Summer at Bodega Bay

Between summer fogs and winter rains, there is a perfect lull on the Sonoma Coast, a time when the mist gives way to skies of blue and balmy days are made to order for biking, beachcombing, tidepooling, or just sitting back and basking in the sun. The natives at Bogeda Bay call this period their "secret summer."

Ironically, these glorious days come in September and October, soon after the real summer tourists have gone home. For those in the know, this is the prime time to visit.

Don't come to Bodega Bay expecting manicured beaches or fancy shops. Though word of the area's attractions is spreading, this remains first and foremost a fisherman's town, with a fleet of 300 boats that make it the major fishing port between San Francisco and Ft. Bragg.

The beaches of Sonoma County run wild and beautiful from Bogeda Bay along the Pacific for 13 miles to Jenner. Many are along sheltered coves beneath dramatic cliffs linked by blufftop trails that make for spectacular strolling. The dunes and bluffs give a bird's-eye view of the many offshore rock formations that loom out of the sea, capped with foam from the breaking waves.

Some of those waves are not to be taken lightly. At Death Rock, an offshore rock island, the currents form peculiar patterns, giving rise to "sleeper" waves that seem to come from out of nowhere in a calm sea, overwhelming the island and anything else in their path. It's not safe to turn your back on the ocean here. Every year a few who ignore the warnings are drowned.

Maybe it was the danger of the waves that inspired Alfred Hitchcock to choose Bodega Bay and its inland near neighbor, Bodega, as the backdrop for his classic thriller *The Birds*. These days the birds are benign. In fact, the area is nirvana for bird-watchers. Some 200 species have been spotted along the mudflats and the salt marshes, including great blue herons, white and brown pelicans, cormorants, ospreys, sandpipers, and gulls. In fall, bigger raptors such as the peregrine falcon often stop by on their migration south.

Bodega Bay got its name from a Spanish explorer, Don Juan Francisco de la Bodega, who anchored here in 1775. It was the Russians, however, who established the first permanent settlement in 1812, a base for farming and hunting sea otters. The natural harbor served nicely to house the boats they used to carry back their valuable collections of sea otter pelts. By 1841, with the otters and the farmland both depleted, the Russians had left and American settlers came in, using the port to ship milk, butter, and potatoes from local farms.

Eventually fishing established itself as the town's main industry. Turn off Highway 1 to any of the marinas in the late afternoon and you'll see the boats unloading their catch. The biggest fleet is found at the Spud Point Marina. In the fall, crab pot buoys and bait jars add color to the docks as they are set out to be repaired, repainted, and readied for action during the Dungeness crab season, from mid-November through June. Later in the winter comes herring season, and in spring and early summer the salmon run. All this delicious bounty from the sea can be sampled at informal marina restaurants like Lucas Wharf and the Tides Wharf, where you can watch the fishing fleet in action while enjoying the fruits of their labors.

Return in the spring for one of the area's big events, the blessing of the fleet, featuring a parade of boats bedecked with flowers and finery.

These waters are also happy hunting grounds for sport fishermen. Several outfitters offer daily charter trips for fishing for rock cod and ling cod year-round and for salmon in season.

Most of Bodega Bay's accommodations are of the resort-motel variety, but they offer a special advantage—wonderful ocean views. The pick of the pack is Bodega Bay Lodge, located in the dunes with both bay and ocean vistas. The wicker and oak furnishings are tasteful, and every room has a private waterfront balcony. Some rooms come with private whirlpools and fireplaces. This is an ideal choice for golfers, as it is next door to one of Bodega Bay's prides, the Bodega Harbour Golf Links, an 18-hole Robert Trent Jones II course overlooking the Pacific. The lodge offers special golf packages. Other facilities include a glass-walled hot whirlpool, a sauna, an exercise room, and an outdoor pool. Rooms are more modest at the Holiday Inn, but the water views are equally fine.

The Inn at the Tides is across the road from the shore, but it is nevertheless an attractive choice, with individual lodges set on six acres. Many rooms have bay views and fireplaces, and there is an indoor-outdoor pool as well as a sauna and whirlpool.

The most elegant inn is not on the sea. The Sonoma Coast Villa, south of town, is a very private Mediterranean-style stucco complex with red-tile roofs. The six rooms at this hideaway are big, with beamed ceilings, fireplaces, and handsome furnishings.

Budget watchers will find more moderate rates at both the rustic Chanslor Guest Ranch and the Bodega Harbor Inn, a cluster of houses on a sloping lawn across the road from the water. Bed-and-breakfast fans will enjoy Bay Hill Mansion, a new home in Queen Anne Victorian style, high on a hill with a sweeping view.

You hardly need an itinerary for Bodega Bay, since this is the ideal place to forget about schedules and just hang out on the beaches. The water is too cold and rough for swimming on the ocean side, but the long strands of sand are unbeatable for beachcombing for shells and driftwood. At low tide a favorite sport is tide pooling, poking into the world of kelp and sea creatures that dwell in the shallow water. Digging for clams and picking mussels is another popular pastime.

Each beach has its own attractions. South of the harbor, Doran Park forms a buffer between ocean and bay. The ocean beach is a sheltered spot for swimming, and the bay side is a popular spot for clamming and admiring the host of birds attracted to the salt marsh.

Take the kids to Campbell Cove, a small, safe bay beach with lots of space for building castles in the sand. At the top of the cove is the "Hole in the Head," a 12-story-deep hole left by a power company when protests stopped its plan to build a nuclear reactor. Now it serves as a pond for the birds.

At Bodega Head, the rocky bluffs that guard the harbor are separated from the dunes by the infamous San Andreas Fault. The Head offers a view for miles out to sea, making this a favorite winter spot for whale watching. The University of California Marine Lab is nearby and is open to visitors on Fridays between 2 and 4 P.M.

Some of the best hiking trails branch out from the Bodega Head parking lot to the rim of the cliffs. One trail following the ridge overlooks Horseshoe Cove and the Marine Lab and continues on to Salmon Creek.

North of Bodega Head, most of the Pacific beaches are part of Sonoma Coast State Park. At Salmon Creek/Bodega Dunes Beach, the long cluster of dunes leads to the creek and to Salmon Creek, a small community set beside the stream. Wright's Beach looks out at Death Rock and those ominous sleeper waves. Goat Rock at Goat Rock Beach in Jenner looks as if it would be fun to climb, but don't be tempted. It is another formation that attracts those dangerous sleepers.

The Russian River runs into the sea at Goat Rock Beach, making for one of the most fascinating spots along the coast. A long, sandy arm called Penny Island divides the two bodies of water, creating tide pools ripe for exploring. And this is the place for a close-up look at harbor seals. They gather at the mouth of the river to harvest the steelhead and salmon struggling to make their way upstream. At night the beach inspires romantics, who find it a favored spot for moon watching.

Along the river, the tiny hamlet of Jenner spills down the hillside, offering fine dining as well as lodgings with a view. The Jenner Inn has ten reasonably priced rooms and several cottages, some overlooking the water. River's End, one of the best restaurants in the area, has greenhouse windows right over the spot where the river meets the sea. A few lodgings tucked into the hillside are simple but offer that same fascinating view.

About five miles north of Jenner is another possibility, the Timber Cove Inn, a 47-room timbered complex located on a rocky promontory with smashing views of crashing waves. The views are more outstanding than the accommodations, but you may be so taken with the sea that you never notice. About half of the rooms have fireplaces, some with sunken, tiled tubs or showers with sea views. This inn has an unusual welcoming committee, a group of tame raccoons who hang out in front of the entrance.

What to do when you're not on the beach or gazing out to sea? If you are up to it, bring your bike and take off along the scenic rolling hills leading inland. Or sign up for a horseback ride along the dunes. From Jenner, take Route 116 inland; it becomes the River Road to the handsome Korbel Winery and an interesting tour showing how sparkling wines are made.

Bodega Bay isn't a shopper's heaven, but there are a few small shops, including a kite store along Highway 1. The wild scenery attracts artists, some of whose work can be seen at local galleries. Branscomb's features works by West Coast artists, and the Ren Brown Collection carries work by Japanese printmakers as well as paintings and ceramics by regional painters.

A drive inland to tiny Bodega gives you a look at the schoolhouse made famous in *The Birds,* as well as the white-spired St. Teresa's Church, an 1861 structure that has been named a historic landmark. Bodega also has a couple of shops offering antiques and arts. All the shops are small, relaxed, and low-key, like Bodega Bay itself.

When you want to get away from hassle and pressure and enjoy an unspoiled and uncrowded coastline, this is the place—and the secret summer is the time.

Area Code: 707

DRIVING DIRECTIONS   Bodega Bay is on coastal Highway 1, 68 miles north of San Francisco, 100 miles from Sacramento. Take Highway 101 north, take the East Washington Street–Petaluma exit, and follow the signs 30 miles west.

ACCOMMODATIONS   *Bodega Bay Lodge,* 103 Highway 1, Bodega Bay, 94923, 875-3525 or (800) 368-2468, E–EE, CP • *Holiday Inn,* 521 Highway 1, Bodega Bay, 94923, 875-2217 or (800) 346-6999, E–EE • *Inn at the Tides,* 800 Highway 1, Bodega Bay, 94923, 875-2751 or (800) 541-7788, E–EE • *Sonoma Coast Villa,* 16072 Highway 1, Bodega, 94922, 876-9818, E, CP • *Bodega Harbor Inn,* P.O. Box 161, Bodega Bay, 94923, 875-3594; inn rooms, I, CP; cottages, M–E • *Chanslor Guest Ranch,* 2660 Highway 1, Bodega Bay, 94923, 875-2721, I–E, CP • *Bay Hill Mansion B & B,* 3919 Bay Hill Road, Bodega Bay, 94923, 875-3577, M–EE, CP • *Jenner Inn,* 10400 Highway 1, Jenner, 95450, 865-2377; rooms, I–M; cottages, M–EE, CP • *River's End,* Highway 1, P.O. Box 1800, Jenner, 95450, 865-2484, M • *Timber Cove Inn,* 21780 Highway 1, Jenner, 95450, 847-3231, E–EE.

DINING *Lucas Wharf,* 595 Highway 1, Bodega Bay, 875-3522, informal, seafood overlooking the harbor, M • *The Tide Wharf and Restaurant,* 835 Highway 1, Bodega Bay, 875-3652, also overlooks a fishing harbor, I–M • *Ristorante di Mare,* 2001 Highway 1, Bodega Bay, 875-3333, Italian, I–M • *The Bayview Room,* Inn at the Tides (see page 126), M–E • *Sushi Osaka,* 2001 Highway 1, Bodega Bay, 875-2550, change of pace, I • *Sonoma Coast Villa* (see page 126), varied menu, M • *River's End,* Jenner (see page 126), top food and view, M.

ACTIVITIES **Golf:** *Bodega Harbour Golf Links,* off Highway 1, 875-3538 • **Sport fishing:** *Challenger Sportfishing,* 1785 Highway 1, 875-2474; *New Sea Angler & Jaws Sportfishing,* The Boat House, 1445 Highway 1, 875-3495 • **Horseback riding:** *Chanslor Stables,* 2660 Highway 1, 875-2721.

INFORMATION *Bodega Bay Area Chamber of Commerce,* 850 Coast Highway 1, P.O. Box 146, 555 Highway 1, Bodega Bay, CA 94923, 875-3422.

Fall Flutter in Pacific Grove

In October each year, a parade is held in Pacific Grove. The purpose: to welcome back some highly treasured visitors, the majestic orange-and-black monarch butterflies, who choose this as their winter shelter each year from fall to early March. Join the fun to see the marching bands and the local children charmingly costumed as butterflies. At the same time, you will discover a town that has emerged from its own prim cocoon as a singularly lovely destination on the Monterey Peninsula.

Despite a wealth of Victorian charm and a prime location on the rocky shore between Monterey and Pebble Beach, Pacific Grove took a while to blossom because of a history that is quite different from its neighbors.

It was founded by Methodists in 1875 as a religious retreat; understandably, they found the views inspiring. Land was donated for a tent campground on the condition that there be no gambling or drinking of alcohol on the property. To further keep things on the straight and narrow, the camp was enclosed by a high wooden fence, and strict rules were imposed, including a 9 P.M. curfew. The tents were stored away at the end of the season.

In 1879 the Methodists added the first Chautauqua Assembly in the western United States, a summer gathering of educational classes and concerts that continued annually until the outbreak of World War I. During these years tents gave way to gingerbread-trim cottages and spacious Victorian boardinghouses to take care of visitors, lodgings that were prime candidates for transformation into inns. The no-liquor laws remained in effect, however, discouraging the opening of restaurants and lodgings in town until they were repealed in 1969. It is since then that the town has really come into its own as a resort. Now it is gaining an increasing reputation as a culinary center.

Pacific Grove is still quieter than neighboring Monterey or Carmel, which is just why many people like it so much. This is a place for a peaceful stroll, a bike ride, or a drive to enjoy the homes and appreciate the sea. The three-mile scenic stretch along Ocean View Boulevard, rimming the northern tip of the Peninsula, has some prime vantage points along the way. One of the nicest is Lovers Point Beach. Don't be misled—the full title is Lovers of Jesus Point—but there is romance here nevertheless, the thrill of watching waves crash against the craggy shore, spotting sea otters, or, in winter, spying a passing whale. All the shoreline is prime for sunset watching.

The Marine Gardens Park, an offshore aquatic park, is known for its brilliantly hued seaweed. All these shore areas are happy hunting grounds for tidepoolers. So rich is the marine life that Stanford University chose this area for its research facility, the Hopkins Marine Station at China Point.

Continuing west along the water, you can admire the granite Point Pinos Lighthouse, the state's oldest working lighthouse, in service since 1855. The Coast Guard offers tours on weekends.

Continue past the lighthouse as the road changes its name to Sunset Drive to reach Asilomar State Beach, a particularly attractive shore area, backed by dunes and forest. At the end of the beach is the Asilomar Conference Center, a wonderful wooded setting of cypress and pines that was once a YWCA retreat and is now a nonprofit meeting facility run by the state. Stop to see the handsome original shingle-and-stone buildings, many of them historic landmarks, designed by Julia Morgan, who was also the architect of Hearst Castle. Rooms are available here at very reasonable rates, but you'll have to reserve far in advance. Andril Fireplace Cottages in this area is also exceptional value for simple cottages in the pines, all with fireplaces and full kitchens.

As you might expect, there's a wonderful choice of Victorian inns in town. Green Gables, an 1888 Queen Anne mansion by the sea, has great charm and fabulous water views from the front rooms. The same owners also run Gosby House, a more modest and modestly priced establishment. The Gatehouse Inn, an 1884 charmer, has been renovated with a fresh, light, and airy look, and the Martine Inn is a veritable mansion overlooking the Bay. Seven Gables is even more elaborate, a period home filled with formal European antiques.

Though Pacific Grove is a small town, there's no shortage of things to do. One local home of special note is the John Steinbeck Memorial Museum, housed in a small Victorian that belonged to the author's grandparents. The house contains memorabilia, souvenirs, and photos of the youthful Steinbeck. He built and lived in the cottage next door in the 1930s during the Depression and it still contains his desk and typewriter.

To learn more about the area's natural wonders, visit the Pacific Grove Museum of Natural History, marked by the gray whale sculpture out front. Founded by the Chautauqua Assembly in 1881, it is a particularly fine small museum of its kind, featuring a diorama of local marine life and exhibits of various seabirds, plus native plants and insects. There are Native American artifacts as well, and a facsimile butterfly tree. A video shows the life cycle of the monarch butterfly.

For the real thing, just look in the trees near the Butterfly Grove Inn, 1073 Lighthouse Avenue, or in Washington Park. Thousands of butterflies come back each year to the central coast of California to enjoy the temperate weather, and Pacific Grove is one of their favorite resting spots. They find shelter in the foliage of the pine and eucalyptus trees, hanging together in dense clusters that look almost like dead leaves—until the sun comes out. Then they spread their velvety wings and fly out in search of food, a glorious sight.

Pacific Grove has no major shopping complexes, but browsers will find a variety of pleasant small shops on Lighthouse Avenue and a couple of galleries on Grand Avenue. Bargain hunters can try their luck at the American Tin Cannery on Ocean View Boulevard, near the Monterey Bay Aquarium.

The aquarium is one of two well-known attractions that lie just past the border of Pacific Grove in Monterey. In the other direction is the 17-Mile Drive, the famous dramatic route along the coastline leading to Carmel. Turnouts allow for lingering at points of interest, such as the aptly named Seal Rock, Bird Rock, Cypress Point, and then that famous solitary Lone Cypress clinging to a cliff over the water, one of the best-known symbols of the Monterey Peninsula. There are gorgeous private homes to admire along the way, as well as the Pebble Beach resort area, nirvana for golfers, with seven championship courses. If you can't afford a stay at the Inn at Spanish Bay or the Lodge at Pebble Beach, you're welcome to stop in for a look and a lunch or tea.

Pacific Grove has its own public golf course, near the lighthouse, with a fee that is a fraction of the fees at the more illustrious links. And that is typical of this unassuming town. Make your forays and then come back to enjoy the tranquility and the unsurpassed vistas of this late bloomer, a Victorian village that proudly calls itself "Butterfly Town, USA."

Area Code: 408

DRIVING DIRECTIONS   Pacific Grove is on the coast just below Monterey, about 125 miles from San Francisco, 215 miles from Sacramento. From Highway 1, take the Pacific Grove/Pebble Beach exit, Route 68 west, and follow the signs to Pacific Grove. From Monterey, follow Cannery Row west until it becomes Oceanview Boulevard, leading into Pacific Grove.

PUBLIC TRANSPORTATION   Air service into Monterey Peninsula Airport, three miles east of Monterey. Airport limousines, hotel shuttles, taxis, and car rentals are available. Greyhound buses also stop at Monterey.

ACCOMMODATIONS   _Green Gables Inn,_ 104 5th Street, Pacific Grove, 93950, 375-2095, E–EE, CP • _The Martine Inn,_ 255 Oceanview Boulevard, Pacific Grove, 93950, 373-3388, E–EE, CP • _Gosby House Inn,_ 643 Lighthouse Avenue, Pacific Grove, 93950, 375-1287, M–EE, CP • _Gatehouse Inn,_ 225 Central Avenue, Pacific Grove, 93950, 649-1881, E–EE, CP • _Seven Gables Inn,_ 555 Ocean View Boulevard, Pacific Grove, 93950, 372-4341, E–EE, CP • _Andril Fireplace Cottages,_ 569 Asilomar Boulevard, Pacific Grove, 93950, 375-0994, excellent budget choice, M–E; in winter, some rooms I • _Pacific Gardens Inn,_ 701 Asilomar Boulevard, 93950, 646-9414 or (800) 262-1566, another less pricey choice, pleasant motel, M • _Asilomar Conference Center,_ 800 Asilomar Boulevard, Pacific Grove, 93950, 372-8016; rooms, I–M; cottages and suites, E, MAP • _Lodge at Pebble Beach,_ 17-Mile Drive, P.O. Box 1128, Pebble Beach, 93953, 624-3811, EE • _Inn at Spanish Bay,_ 17-Mile Drive, Pebble Beach, 93953, 647-7500, EE.

DINING   _Old Bath House,_ 620 Ocean View Boulevard, 375-5195, continental, ocean views, E • _Fandango,_ 223 17th Street, 372-3456, Mediterranean menu and setting, M • _Central 159,_ 529 Central Avenue, 655-4280, acclaimed "new American" chef, M • _Pasta Mia Trattoria,_ 481 Lighthouse Avenue, 373-8523, appealing café with excellent Italian food, I–M • _Melac's,_ 663 Lighthouse Avenue, 375-1743, charming slice of France, M–E • _Gernot's Victoria House Restaurant,_ 649 Lighthouse Avenue, 646-1477, Austrian dishes, game, served in a Victorian mansion, M–E • _Peppers Mexicali Café,_ 170 Forest Avenue, 373-6892, popular Mexican, I • _Taste Café and Bistro,_ 1199 Forest Avenue, 655-0324, informal, quality French and Italian country cooking at reasonable prices, M • _The Fish Wife,_ at Asilomar Beach, 1996 Sunset Drive, 375-7107, local favorite for seafood, I–M.

SIGHTSEEING   _Pacific Grove Museum of Natural History,_ 165 Forest Avenue, 648-3116. Hours: Tuesday to Sunday 10 A.M. to 5 P.M.

Free • *John Steinbeck Memorial Museum,* 222 Central Avenue, 373-6976. Hours: Daily 10 A.M. to 4 P.M. Donation, $3 • *17-Mile Drive,* 625-8426. Per car, $6 • *Point Pinos Lighthouse,* Ocean View Boulevard, 648-3661. Hours: Saturday and Sunday 1 P.M. to 4 P.M. For more sightseeing and sports activities in the area, see Monterey, starting on page 17.

INFORMATION *Pacific Grove Chamber of Commerce,* Forest and Central avenues, P.O. Box 167, Pacific Grove, CA 93950, 373-3304 • *Monterey Peninsula Chamber of Commerce,* 380 Alvarado Avenue, P.O. Box 1770, Monterey, CA 93942, 649-1770.

Bubbles and Brew near Hopland

Mention Mendocino County and most people think of the quaint coastal town of Mendocino. But the county's inland portion offers its own pleasures. The beautiful Anderson Valley between the coast and Highway 101 is tranquil apple tree, sheep farm, and grapevine country, a great place for a drive in the fall. Highway 101 itself holds some nice surprises between Hopland and Ukiah, wine and brew, a most remarkable culinary learning center, and the chance to soak away your cares at Vichy Springs, a resort built around one of the state's oldest and best-known mineral springs.

Vichy Springs Resort is such a pleasant, unpretentious place you might want to make it your headquarters. You could, in fact, have a tranquil weekend if you never left the grounds. The original resort was founded in 1854 and flourished at the turn of the century, noted for the crystal-clear, naturally carbonated hot spring water, which was said to have magic curative powers. Mark Twain stayed here, as did Jack London, Robert Louis Stevenson, and three U.S. presidents—Grant, Harrison, and Theodore Roosevelt.

The resort waned, but the water did not. It still bubbles up from a depth of 15,000 to 25,000 feet at the rate of 65 gallons a minute, enough to provide sparkling mineral water for bottling, plus enough to fill a swimming pool and hot tub, as well as be on tap at the individual stone baths where guests can lie back and be soothed by the warm bubbles. To fill the tub, you lift a long, metal stopper at one end, allowing the water to gush forth naturally; the stopper fits into the drain at the other end. Any doubt about the relaxing properties disappears the first time you feel the magic effect of those bubbles on your body. You'll understand why they were known as "Champagne Baths." And Mother Nature's water temperature is perfect.

New owners have restored the long 12-room wooden lodge to modest but attractive quarters with private baths. The long porch in front faces an expansive lawn, and there's a great sense of quiet and tranquility, especially in the two 1854 cottages that have been restored at the top of the lawn. The resort sits on 700 acres abounding in woods, meadows, streams, and hills, great territory for walkers.

Ukiah-area vineyards welcome visitors, and while Ukiah itself is a lumber town and hardly a tourists' mecca, it does hold one special treasure. The Grace Hudson Museum and the Sun House are dedicated to artist Grace Hudson, known for her sensitive portraits of the native Pomo Indians, and her husband, ethnologist Dr. John Hudson, a noted scholar and collector of Native American artifacts. Her paintings and his collections are displayed, including some rare examples of Pomo pottery. Paintings by contemporary artists of Mendocino County are also shown in changing exhibits. A museum visit includes a guided tour of the Hudsons' exceptional redwood Craftsman-style bungalow, standing near the museum site. The Hopi sun symbol at the entrance explains the name "Sun House."

Another happy possibility is a stay in Hopland. This tiny town is truly hopping with visitors, due to its two prime attractions, one dedicated to wine, the other to beer. The town was named for the large amount of hops that grew in the valley, an important ingredient in the brewing of beer. Maybe it was prophetic, for though plant disease and a shrinking market ended the commercial growth in the 1940s, the Mendocino Brewing Company arrived in 1982 to open the first brewery in California since Prohibition. Their Red Tail Ale was a huge success, and their pub, known as the Hopland Brewery, is always packed with customers sampling ale as well as other brews such as traditional porters and stouts. The brewery restaurant serves up spicy sausages, hamburgers, chili, and daily specials to go with the beer.

The brewery is housed in a 100-year-old building that was once called the Hop Vine Saloon, with stamped-tin walls and a handcrafted early California–style oak-and-brass bar. Guests can see the brewing process through windows in the adjoining brewhouse, which has a dart room and a stage where live music and entertainment are featured every Saturday night. There's also an adjoining beer garden for fine days. The wildest time to visit is during the annual Oktoberfest, highlighted by a keg-toss competition.

You can also do some wine tasting in Hopland, at the McDowell Valley Vineyards tasting room and at the elaborate Fetzer Vineyards quarters in the former town high school. The building includes a tasting room, a gourmet food shop, and a local artisans' gallery.

Far more interesting and unusual is Fetzer's Valley Oaks Food &

Wine Center, just east of town on Route 175. Established in 1985 as a culinary research center, this is a place dedicated to learning and teaching about the growing and preparation of food and wine. The grounds include vineyards and a remarkable seven-acre organic garden with over 1,000 varieties of fruits, vegetables, herbs, and edible flowers.

An ongoing Lifestyle Series under the direction of Fetzer's Culinary Director, the noted chef John Ash, brings some of the nation's brightest and most influential chefs, instructors, and authors to Hopland to teach both consumers and professionals. Topics have ranged from making herbal medicines to organic cooking. Classes have learned how to prepare Ahi tuna; how to cook with grains, beans, and legumes; and how to match wine with food. Sessions vary from a half to a full day, and most include lunch. They are good reasons for a visit to Hopland, and you can stay right on the property in a very pleasant nine-room inn with a swimming pool. While it offers special rates to Lifestyle participants, the inn is open to the general public when rooms are available.

If Valley Oaks is full, an alternative in town is the restored Thatcher Inn, an 1890 Victorian.

For a Sunday excursion, turn west on Highway 128 and head for Boonville, one of the quaintest of the area's towns. If the language sounds odd, you are hearing Boontling, a local dialect that is a mix of English, Spanish, French, and Pomo. It's a reminder of how isolated this area was until wineries came and brought new people. You can see a sample of Boontling on names of local shops like the Rookie-To Gallery, a good place to shop for intriguing handcrafts.

This is a surprising town, only a dot on the map, yet the Boonville Hotel is known far and wide for its dining room, and the simple rooms are furnished with beautiful furniture created by local artisans. The Buckhorn Saloon, right across the street, is an informal eatery above, a brew pub below, housing the Anderson Valley Brewing Company and serving some highly regarded local brew. If you prefer a picnic lunch at a vineyard, stop at the Boont Berry Farm market on Highway 128 for good local produce and deli fare.

If you come in late September, note that Boonville is the home of the annual Mendocino County Fair and Apple Show.

Some top wineries can be found a few miles farther on Highway 128 around Philo, including respected names like Husch and Roederer. Scharffenberger Cellars in Philo makes some of California's best sparkling wines. Kendall-Jackson has a Wine Country Store in Philo serving wines from all over the state. The facility offers a picnic area and lovely views.

If you want to settle in for some tasting, the Philo Pottery Inn is the place, a lodging built entirely of redwood in 1888, and once a stagecoach stop on the way to the north coast. Rooms are simple country style, but the breakfasts are memorable.

A different kind of outing might take you north of Ukiah to scenic Lake Mendocino, where there are 14 miles of walking trails. At the north end of the lake is the Pomo Visitors' Center, in a round shape modeled after the Pomo ceremonial dance house. Built by the U.S. Army Corps of Engineers and operated by a local Native American council, it displays Pomo crafts and jewelry, as well as dispensing information to broaden your appreciation of the beauty of inland Mendocino County.

Area Code: 707

DRIVING DIRECTIONS Hopland is on Highway 101, 90 miles north of San Francisco, 132 miles from Sacramento. To reach Vichy Springs, continue north on Highway 101 to the Perkins Street–Vichy Springs Road exit in Ukiah, make a right turn at the end of the ramp to Vichy Springs Road, and follow the signs for three miles.

ACCOMMODATIONS *Vichy Springs Resort,* 2605 Vichy Springs Road, Ukiah, 95482, E; cottages, EE; CP • *Fetzer Valley Oaks Inn,* P.O. Box 611, Hopland, 95449, (800) 959-4035; April–October, E–EE, November to March, M–E, CP • *Thatcher Inn,* Highway 101, Hopland 95449, 744-1890, M–EE, CP • *Boonville Hotel,* Highway 128, Boonville, 95415, 895-2210, M–E, CP • *Philo Pottery Inn,* 8550 Highway 128, Philo, 95466, 895-3069, M, CP.

DINING *Hopland Brewery,* 13351 South Highway 101, Hopland, 744-1361, I • *Thatcher Inn,* Hopland (see above), I–M • *Angelo's Italian Restaurant,* 1639 State Street, Ukiah, 462-0448, best in a limited town, I–M • *North State Café,* 801 North State Street, Ukiah, 462-3726, brick-oven pizza, I–M. *Boonville Hotel,* Boonville (see above), I–M • *Buckhorn Saloon,* Boonville, 895-2337, downstairs in Anderson Valley Brewing Company, I–M.

SIGHTSEEING *Grace Hudson Museum and the Sun House,* 431 South Main Street, Ukiah, 462-3370. Hours: Wednesday to Saturday 10 A.M. to 4:30 P.M., Sunday from noon. Donation • *Fetzer Valley Oaks Food and Wine Center,* 13601 Eastside Road (Highway 175), Hopland, 744-1250 or (800) 959-4035; ask for a Lifestyle Series schedule • *Pomo Visitors' Center,* 1160 Lake Mendocino Drive, Ukiah, c/o Corps of Engineers, 462-7581. Hours: April to September, Wednesday to Sunday 9 A.M. to 5 P.M., October to November 15, weekends 1 P.M. to 5 P.M. Free.

WINERIES **Hopland area:** *Fetzer Wine Tasting & Gourmet Food,* 13500 South Highway 101, Hopland, 744-1737. Hours: Daily 10 A.M.

to 5 P.M. • *McDowell Valley Vineyards,* 3811 Route 175, Hopland, 744-1053, Winery by appointment only. Tasting room in Hopland, 13441 Highway 101, 744-1516. Open daily 10 A.M. to 5 P.M. • *Mendocino Vineyards,* 13450 South Highway 101, Hopland, 744-1730, tasting room. Hours: Daily 10 A.M. to 5 P.M. • *Milano Winery,* 14594 South Highway 101, Hopland, 744-1396. Hours: Daily 10 A.M. to 5 P.M. • **Anderson Valley area:** *Husch Vineyards,* 4400 Route 1128, Philo, 895-3216, tastings, picnic area, self-guided vineyard tour. Hours: Daily 10 A.M. to 6 P.M. • *Scharffenberger Cellars,* 7000 Highway 128, Philo, 895-2065 or (800) 824-7754, tastings, tours by appointment. Hours: 11 A.M. to 5 P.M. • *Navarro Vineyards,* 5601 Highway 128, Philo, 895-3686, tastings, picnic grounds. Hours: 10 A.M. to 6 P.M. • *Roederer U.S. Inc.,* 4501 Highway 128, Philo, 895-3688. Hours: Thursday to Monday 11 A.M. to 5 P.M. **Ukiah area:** *Dunnewood Vineyards,* 2399 North State Street, Ukiah, 462-2987. Hours: Daily 10 A.M. to 5 P.M. • *Jepson Vineyards,* 10400 South Highway 101, Ukiah, 468-8936, tastings. Hours: Daily 10 A.M. to 5 P.M. • *Parducci Wine Cellars,* 501 Parducci Road, Ukiah, 462-3828, tours, tastings. Hours: 9 A.M. to 5 P.M., tours 10 A.M. to 3 P.M.

INFORMATION *Greater Ukiah Chamber of Commerce,* 495-E East Perkins Street, Ukiah, CA 95482, 462-4705.

Boning Up on Berkeley

Mention Berkeley to half a dozen people and you'll get half a dozen reactions, depending on their age, affluence, and inclinations.

For some it is primarily the home of a great university—one of the state's most prestigious seats of higher learning—and a town blessed with the cultural opportunities that abound in a fine college community. Others see it as the last outpost of the 1960s, a haven for overage hippies and the homeless, a hotbed of protesters who are always on the march for the latest cause. For food fanatics, it is the culinary Berkeley that stands out, for this is where "California cuisine" was born and still flourishes. Still others see a community with beautiful residential areas, a wealth of parks and woodland, and lots of interesting places to shop.

The thing is, they're all right. There is no one Berkeley. This is a fascinating, multifaceted town. You'll be hard-pressed to see it all in a weekend.

The first and most important stop is the beautiful wooded campus of the University of California. Rising into the Berkeley hills, it seems a perfect, tranquil California setting, the stately buildings blended with shady groves of giant oak, redwood, and eucalyptus. The campus originally designed by Frederick Law Olmsted and Calvert Vaux in 1865 radiated from the Campanile, the landmark bell tower modeled after the Campanile in Venice.

The campus was redesigned after Mrs. Phoebe Apperson Hearst decided to found a School of Mining in memory of her husband and in 1899 sponsored an international competition for a new plan. When the winning Paris architect refused to come to America to oversee the project, his beaux arts designs were turned over to a New York architect, John Galen Howard, who was responsible for many of the fine white granite buildings at the heart of the campus.

Guided tours are offered regularly on Monday, Wednesday, and Friday, but only occasionally on Saturday; phone ahead to check the dates. If you are touring on your own, stop at the information desk in the Student Union Building for a map that shows you the most important sites.

If you don't know already, you'll learn from the guide or the college literature that Berkeley is one of our most esteemed public universities, renowned for its research and a faculty that boasts nine Nobel laureates. California included provisions for a state university in its first constitution, and this was the second site for the "College of California" when it was dedicated in 1860. The statistics it has compiled are impressive. The library system boasts more than 8 million volumes and is the fourth largest academic library in the country. The current enrollment of 31,000 students, one third of them graduate students, can choose from 7,000 courses and 100 majors—and look forward to excellent instruction. More of its graduates go on to complete doctorates than do graduates of any other university. Berkeley also awards more doctoral degrees—and more to women and minorities—than any other American university.

The most visible symbol of the campus remains the Campanile, the slim bell tower at the center that is officially called Sather Tower. It chimes on the hour and provides a melodious free carillon concert on weekdays at 7:45 A.M., noon, and 6 P.M., and on Saturday at noon, 6 P.M., and 10 P.M. On Sunday, there is a recital from 2 P.M. to 2:45 P.M. An elevator leads to the observation platform for a bird's-eye view of the campus.

There are several museums of interest on campus. The University Art Museum features a sculpture garden, a gallery of paintings by Hans Hoffman donated by the artist, and five other galleries exhibiting works from early modern art to twentieth-century painting and sculpture. The museum also houses the renowned Pacific Film archive and holds regular evening showings of both classic and new avant-garde films.

The Hearst Museum of Anthropology in Kroeber Hall is a major research facility in the field and has changing exhibits on the peoples of the world. Recent shows have ranged from archaeological finds to different types of money to photos of children at play.

The Paleontology Museum in the Earth Sciences Building offers a variety of collections, from rocks to maps.

The Bancroft Library offers changing exhibits of rare books and manuscripts, as well as paintings of early California and the first nugget found in the 1849 Gold Rush.

Off campus but worth a stop is the Judah L. Magnes Museum, the Jewish Museum of the West, said to be the third largest such collection in the Western Hemisphere, with over 10,000 objects of Jewish ceremonial art, folk art, and fine art from around the world.

Perhaps the most impressive Berkeley museum is the Lawrence Hall of Science, a fascinating world of hands-on exhibits, computer games, and a variety of participatory learning programs. Lectures, films, and planetarium shows are also offered.

The steep approach to the Lawrence via Centennial Drive is magnificent, the road zigzagging through the campus to the top of the hill, where the views of the university, Berkeley, and the Bay beyond are breathtaking.

On the way up you can turn off for the Botanical Garden in Strawberry Canyon, outstanding for its variety of 8,000 plants. A redwood grove, a Chinese medicinal herb garden, and a pygmy garden are among the many attractions.

Another interesting garden awaits if you follow Centennial beyond the Lawrence Hall of Science into Tilden Regional Park. The Botanical Garden here shows plants from every part of the state—from seacoast bluff to arid desert—condensing 160,000 square miles of California into an easily strollable ten-acre plot.

This is only the start of the activities available in this wonderful local park, which includes a scenic 18-hole public golf course, a lake with a swimming beach, and a children's area that offers excursions on a miniature train, pony rides, and the chance to mount a steed on an antique merry-go-round. A nature area features a small farm with domestic animals and nature trails around Jewel Lake.

Tilden has many picnic areas and a myriad trails that provide solitude. The Nimitz Way, open for hiking, biking, and horseback riding, is part of the scenic 31-mile East Bay Skyline National Trail, which continues into the wilder and more rugged adjoining Wildcat Canyon Regional Park. If the weather is right, you may want to come back here on Sunday, armed with a picnic lunch, and spend the day. Drive back via Marin Avenue to experience Berkeley's steepest street, then turn left on Grizzly Peak Boulevard and right at Canyon Drive to enter the park.

These Berkeley hills are lovely, lined with rustic wood-shingled homes nestled into the hillside, many dating to the early part of this century. Stop to enjoy the Berkeley Rose Garden, a tranquil oasis at the intersection of Euclid Avenue and Eunice Street, where more than 150 varieties of roses bloom.

Back down to Earth, check out the action at Sproul Plaza, the Student Union complex. In the 1960s this was the heart of the student protests; today it is the best spot on campus for people-watching. Cross the street to stroll colorful Telegraph Avenue, where sidewalk vendors hold sway, including holdovers from the 1960s who are still hawking tie-dyed everything. This area abounds in interesting bookstores, such as Moe's, Shakespeare and Co., and the famous Cody's, where poetry readings and talks by noted authors are scheduled regularly.

Take a break at the Caffe Mediterraneum, one of the many coffee-houses favored by students. Other favorite haunts are Café Strada and Café Milano.

Telegraph is a little less fun than it used to be, as students now share it with the homeless and a smattering of drug dealers. The famous People's Park on Haste just off Telegraph was the site of vehement protests when the university tried to remove the homeless people who had taken up residence in favor of volleyball courts for students. The park remains.

At dinnertime, Berkeley offers everything from inexpensive ethnic, the students' favorites, to the "Gourmet Ghetto," which has spread far beyond its original boundaries on Shattuck between Rose and Virginia. It all began with Alice Waters and her Chez Panisse, credited with creating the first menus that are now known everywhere as California cuisine. Waters has spawned a generation of disciples who have become famous on their own, and Berkeley has remained a magnet for creative chefs.

Chez Panisse has an informal and slightly less expensive café upstairs for those who can't manage the prices below. Waters's latest adventure is even less formal, a takeout stand called Café Fanny that sells sandwiches by day and Mexican fare at night.

When it comes to shopping, Berkeley has something for every taste. The neighborhood around Chez Panisse on and around Shattuck has many shops dedicated to the love of food. You can buy freshly baked bread and a whole world of cheeses at the Cheese Board, 1504 Shattuck, and join the regulars sipping and buying the huge variety of coffees and teas at Peet's Coffee & Tea, a block off Shattuck on Vine. You can also sip an espresso at the French Hotel, the best place to stay if you want to be in the middle of the food action.

Berkeley has many interesting art galleries, some of them located along Shattuck Avenue. Another important art venue is the Berkeley Art Center on Walnut Street in Live Oak Park, presenting significant contemporary work in changing shows. It is open to the public Thursday through Sunday from noon to 5 P.M.

Antiquers will want to head to the small southside pocket around Ashby and Adeline, where more than 20 shops are clustered.

A neighborhood highly recommended for both dining and shopping is Fourth Street, farther south near the Bay. Fortify yourself with a breakfast at Bette's Ocean View Diner, which is always packed with customers for its huge and highly creative dishes, and browse through a collection of unique shops spaced along an easy-to-cover three-block area, most of them selling articles relating to the home, from stained glass and lamps to some wonderful collections of furniture. Among them is the Builders Booksource, an amazing store with books about everything you ever wanted to know about construction—even boat-building—or home maintenance. Also in this blooming neighborhood are outlet stores, including Sweet Potatoes, which carries Merrimekko clothing for children.

Plan to stay around for dinner, for two top Oriental restaurants are on this block, O Chame for Japanese with a French twist, and Ginger Island for a variety of Asian cuisines.

To find out what's going on in the evening in Berkeley, pick up a copy of the *Berkeleyan* or the *Daily Californian,* campus papers that are readily available, or phone the Chamber of Commerce hot line. On campus, events may include drama at the Durham Studio Theatre, plays or concerts at the Zellerbach Playhouse, or films at the Archives. Off campus, the Berkeley Repertory Theater presents many fine productions, and there's a local opera, ballet, and symphony. If you visit in season, the California Shakespeare Theater is in action not far away in the Lt. G. H. Bruns III Memorial Amphitheatre in Orinda.

One of the busiest places around Berkeley at night is the Triple Rock Brewery, with a roof garden and lots of local brews. A newer rival is the Bison Brewing Company, with unusual offerings such as honey-basil ale and chocolate stout. By day you might want to check out Takara, the local sake factory, with a tasting room and a slide show about this popular Japanese rice wine.

If you haven't checked into the charming little French Hotel, other choices include Gramma's Rose Garden Inn, a set of two Victorians in gardens near the campus, and standard hotel lodging at the Hotel Durant, just off campus. More unusual are two smaller properties that are both historic landmarks, the Bancroft Club Hotel, an Arts and Crafts–era building across the street from campus, and the Berkeley City Club, with an indoor pool for guests. There's a Marriott on the Marina at the foot of University Avenue, overlooking the San Francisco skyline and Golden Gate Bridge; it also provides an indoor pool as well as good weekend package rates. Or you might opt for one of California's grandes dames, the imposing Claremont Resort, high on a hill on the Berkeley–Oakland border, where you can enjoy pools, tennis, and a full spa.

But if you want more sightseeing, take Route 24 across to I-680 for the 20-minute ride to Danville. Take the Sycamore Valley Road exit and drive 4½ miles east to Blackhawk Plaza, an upscale shopping center where UC-Berkeley has joined in an unlikely partnership.

It all began when Kenneth Behring, a real-estate tycoon who developed the Blackhawk community, spent $12 million for a stunning structure of glass, granite, and marble facing a waterfall, built to house his $100 million collection of vintage cars. About 100 of the 250 cars in the collection are displayed at one time, and they are beauties— Packards, Rolls-Royces, the short-lived Tucker, a 1924 Hispano-Suiza racer, Rudolph Valentino's 1926 Isotta Fraschini, and Clark Gable's 1935 Duesenberg convertible, to name just a few.

Behring planned this as the first part of a cultural center in conjunction with UC-Berkeley. The college now has its own Museum of Art, Science and Culture connected to the Auto Museum. There are changing exhibits from university collections as well as traveling shows, and a schedule of lectures and workshops.

While you are in Danville, if time allows take Diablo Road for the quite spectacular driving tour through Mt. Diablo State Park. It's hard to think of a more scenic end to the weekend.

Area Code: 510

DRIVING DIRECTIONS   Berkeley is in the East Bay off I-80, across the Oakland Bay Bridge from San Francisco. It is about 12 miles from San Francisco, 75 miles from Sacramento. From I-80, take the University Avenue exit to the UC-Berkeley campus.

PUBLIC TRANSPORTATION   BART service is available from San Francisco.

ACCOMMODATIONS   *Hotel Durant,* 2600 Durant Avenue, Berkeley, 94704, 845-8981, M–E • *French Hotel,* 1538 Shattuck Avenue, Berkeley, 94709, 548-9930, M–E, CP • *Bancroft Club Hotel,* 2680 Bancroft Way, 94704, 549-1000 or (800) 549-1002, M–E • *Berkeley City Club,* 1325 Durant Avenue, 94704, 848-7800, M, CP • *Gramma's Rose Garden Inn,* 2740 Telegraph Avenue, Berkeley, 94704, 549-2145, M–EE • *Claremont Resort and Spa,* Ashby and Domingo avenues, Oakland, 94623, 843-3000 or (800) 551-7266, EE • *Marriott Berkeley Marina,* 200 Marina Boulevard, 94710, 548-7920, E–EE • *Golden Bear Motel,* 1620 San Pablo Avenue, Berkeley, 94702, 525-6770, I.

DINING   *Chez Panisse,* 1517 Shattuck Avenue, 548-5525, Alice Waters's culinary landmark, prix fixe menus are less on weekdays, least expensive on Monday, EE • *Café at Chez Panisse* (same address as above, upstairs), 548-5049, California-Italian, M–E • *Café Fanny,* 1603 San Pablo Avenue, 524-5447, Waters's latest, takeout, sandwiches for lunch, Mexican for dinner, I • *Ginger Island,* 1820 Fourth Street, 644-0444, creative Asian menus, M • *O Chame,* 1830 Fourth

Street, 841-8783, excellent Japanese, M • *Trudy's,* 1585 University Avenue, 649-1230, eclectic with some all-American favorites, M–E • *Rivoli's* 1539 Solano Avenue, 526-2542, more inventive California cuisine, M • *Caffe Venezia,* 1799 University Avenue, 849-4681, reliable Italian, I–M • *Santa Fe Bar and Grill,* 1310 University Avenue, 841-4740, California-Southwest, M • *Lalime's,* 1329 Gilman Street, 527-9838, innovative Mediterranean, M • *Kirala,* 2100 Ward Street at Shattuck Avenue, 549-3486, Japanese, sushi and robata-grilled specials, I–M • Two contenders for top Thai: *Plearn,* 1050 University Avenue, 841-2148, I–M; and *Siam,* 1181 University Avenue, 548-3278, I–M • *Bette's Ocean View Diner,* 1807A Fourth Street, 644-3230, funky, enormous, delicious breakfasts, long line but free coffee while you wait, I • *Fat Apples,* 1346 Martin Luther King Boulevard, 526-2260, another breakfast winner, I • *Bridge's Restaurant,* 44 Church Street, Danville, 820-7200, California-Mediterranean menu, good reviews, M • *Blackhawk Grille,* Blackhawk Plaza Circle, Danville, 736-4295, classic car decor, wood-fired pizzas, pastas, steak, M–E • **Coffeehouses:** *Caffe Mediterraneum,* 2475 Telegraph Avenue, 841-5634; *Café Milano,* 2522 Bancroft Way, 644-3100; *Peet's Coffee & Tea,* 2124 Vine Street, 841-0564 • **Breweries:** *Triple Rock Brewery,* 1920 Shattuck Avenue, 843-2739; *Bison Brewing Company,* 2598 Telegraph Avenue, 841-7734. **For takeout lunches:** *Made to Order,* Hopkins Avenue, Berkeley, 524-7552.

SIGHTSEEING *University of California at Berkeley: Visitor Center,* 101 University Hall, 2200 University Avenue at Oxford Street, 642-5215. Free campus tours Monday, Wednesday, and Friday at 10 A.M. and 1 P.M., and some Saturdays; phone to check dates • *Information Center,* Student Union Lobby, northeast corner, Bancroft Way and Telegraph Avenue, 642-INFO. Hours: Weekdays 8 A.M. to 5 P.M., Saturday 10 A.M. to 4 P.M. • *University Art Museum/Pacific Film Archive,* 2625 Durant Avenue, entrances at 2621 Durant Avenue and 2626 Durant Way, 642-1207; 24-hour line, 642-0808; film archive, 642-1412. Hours: Wednesday to Sunday 11 A.M. to 5 P.M., Thursday to 9 P.M. Adults, $6; ages 12 to 17, $4. Free on Thursday 11 A.M. to noon and 5 P.M. to 9 P.M. Film admissions: Adults, $5.50; children under 12, $3.50 • *Botanical Garden,* Strawberry Canyon, 642-3343. Hours: Daily 9:30 A.M. to 4:45 P.M., guided tours on Saturday and Sunday at 1:30 P.M. Free • *Bancroft Library,* 643-9999. Hours: Monday to Thursday 8 A.M. to 9 P.M., Friday 8 A.M. to 5 P.M., Saturday and Sunday 1 P.M. to 5 P.M. Free • *Phoebe Apperson Hearst Museum of Anthropology,* 103 Knoeber Hall, Bancroft Way at College Avenue, 643-7648. Hours: Monday to Friday 10 A.M. to 4:30 P.M., Thursday to 9 P.M., Saturday and Sunday noon to 4:30 P.M. Adults, $2; children, $.50; free on Thursday • *Museum of Paleontology,* 1101 Valley Life Science Building, near Oxford and University avenues, 642-1821. Hours: Monday to

Sunday 8 A.M. to 5 P.M. Free • *Lawrence Hall of Science,* 642-5132. Hours: Daily 10 A.M. to 5 P.M. Adults, $5; ages 7 to 14, $4; ages 3 to 6, $2. Planetarium shows: $1.50; under 6, not admitted • *Campanile* (officially Sather Tower). Hours: Monday to Saturday (except school holidays) 10 A.M. to 3:30 P.M., Sunday 10 A.M. to 1:45 P.M. Elevator to observation platform, $.50 • *Judah L. Magnes Museum,* 2911 Russell Street, 549-6950. Hours: Sunday to Thursday 10 A.M. to 4 P.M. Donation • *Takara Sake USA Inc.,* 708 Addison Street, 540-8250. Hours: Daily noon to 6 P.M. Free • *UC-Berkeley Museum of Art, Science and Culture* and *Behring Auto Museum,* Blackhawk Plaza, Danville, 736-2277. Hours: Tuesday to Sunday 10 A.M. to 5 P.M., Wednesday and Saturday to 9 P.M. UC museum: Adults, $3; under age 18, $2. Auto museum: Adults, $5; under age 18, $3 • *California Shakespeare Theater,* Lt. G. H. Bruns III Memorial Amphitheatre, Gateway Boulevard, Orinda, 254-2395. Performances late June to mid-September; phone for current information • *Tilden Regional Park,* Berkeley, 562-PARK. Call for seasonal hours, information on activities • *Mt. Diablo State Park,* Diablo Road, 5 miles east of I-680, P.O. Box 250, Diablo, 837-2525. Hours: Daylight hours. Per car, $5.

INFORMATION *Berkeley Chamber of Commerce,* 1834 University Avenue, Berkeley, CA 94703, 549-7040 or (800) 847-4823; visitor hot line for special events and sightseeing and lodging information, 549-8710.

Fair Forecast in Santa Rosa

Horticulturist Luther Burbank called California's Sonoma County "the chosen spot of all the earth as far as nature is concerned." Burbank arrived in 1875, settled in Santa Rosa, and never left, an option that tempts many first-time visitors today.

To be sure, the city that is now the commercial center of the county has grown beyond Burbank's wildest dreams, but it is a pleasant small city, and you need not go far to find the farms and wineries that continue to flourish. An excellent time to get acquainted is around Halloween, when Santa Rosa is host to the annual Sonoma County Harvest Fair, celebrating the rich agricultural heritage that goes back to Burbank's day.

In many ways, this is a good old country fair, with buildings showing off prize poultry and livestock, milking demonstrations, sheep dog trials, and nonstop entertainment. Irresistible animals such as pygmy goats, miniature potbellied pigs, and llamas are among the crowd favorites.

But this is the heart of vineyard country and a gourmet's haven, so it stands to reason that food and wine are big parts of the show. The annual grape-stomping contest is a big attraction, as is the tasting gazebo, where the area's best products can be sampled, from herbs to breads to chocolates. Many varieties of apples are also on hand for tasting.

In the Showcase Restaurant, wine- and food-tasting seminars go on all day, and there are cooking demonstrations by the area's best chefs. Fairgoers can also sample the winners of the wine-judging competition in the Hall of Flowers, where "wine by the ounce" is offered for a small fee.

Children have their own "Stomping Grounds," with a haunted house and a clown theater, a "Barnyard Scramble" where they can participate in egg hunts and sack races and tackle an obstacle course, and their own competitions, from grape stomping to pumpkin carving to mummy wrapping.

It's a full day of fun, and when it's over Santa Rosa has enough interesting shops, sights, and good restaurants to occupy you happily for the rest of your weekend.

Santa Rosa's modern look is only partly intentional. Much of the town was lost to the 1906 earthquake. The most picturesque portion remaining is the area known as Railroad Square, where buildings of locally quarried stone, such as the old railroad station and the Hotel La Rose, survived the quake. Some date back to 1870, when the first Santa Rosa and North Pacific train arrived.

There are several antiques shops in this restored neighborhood, plus a handful of specialty and clothing stores and some excellent restaurants.

Santa Rosa's other major sights center on its most prominent residents, past and present. The Luther Burbank Home and Gardens is where the famous horticulturist lived and did much of his work, introducing more than 800 new varieties of plants and flowers. Guided tours tell a bit about the man and take you through his greenhouse and his home, still with its original furnishings. The gardens have been restored to show the amazing number of plant varieties Burbank propagated, some 800 in all, everything from 200 types of fruit trees to the shasta daisy and the Burbank potato to 13 kinds of raspberries, thornless blackberries, and spineless cactus. Californians celebrate Luther Burbank's birthday on March 7 each year as Arbor Day, planting trees in his memory. His hometown also salutes Burbank with a Rose Festival and Parade in mid-May.

Just a block from the Burbank Home is the Robert L. Ripley Memorial Museum, devoted to the man who made the phrase "Believe it or not" a household phrase. Ripley was born in Santa Rosa and is buried here. The man who spent a lifetime reporting oddities would no doubt approve of the location of his museum, in a church built of wood entirely from one giant redwood tree. Lots of colorful memorabilia, original cartoons, and photos of Ripley with a gallery of famous personalities are here, along with an eerily lifelike wax figure of Ripley in the Oriental robe and slippers he liked to wear while he worked.

Charles Schulz, creator of the "Peanuts" comic strip, is very much a part of today's Santa Rosa. He built the Redwood Empire Ice Arena for public skating in 1969, and can often be seen dining at the coffee shop. The building has stained-glass windows featuring that noted champion skater Snoopy. Snoopy's Gallery, on the grounds, claims to have the largest selection of Snoopy merchandise in the world. Upstairs is a museum of Schulz's awards, original drawings, and personal photos. The rink is open to the public for skating year-round.

The chalet-style Redwood Arena also can be converted into an auditorium seating 3,000, and many top entertainers have played here. More entertainment, from opera to ballet to folk music, is offered at the Luther Burbank Center for the Arts. Check the current schedules. The center also houses the California Museum of Art, with changing exhibits.

A bit of local history can be learned at the Sonoma County Museum, a former post office building that now holds changing exhibits.

Or you might prefer to spend some time visiting the many vineyards in the area. By far the best place for an introduction is the Sonoma County Wine & Visitors' Center, just off Highway 101 in neighboring Rohnert Park. Supported by all of the area's wineries, this elaborate center has a demonstration vineyard with 500 Chardonnay vines and a model winery. It is designed to teach about the winemaking process, even how corks are made. Visitors enjoy free tastings of a changing menu of regional wines at the Tasting Bar, and can watch a video of the area's highlights in order to plan an itinerary. The County Visitor Center is adjoining, with piles of pamphlets and maps.

One small Sonoma winery not to be overlooked is in the hills just outside Santa Rosa. Matanzas Creek is worth the visit if only for the setting amid acres of lovely lavender and landscaping with a magnificent variety of grasses. The winery is also known for its fine Chardonnays. Then it is only a few minutes' drive to Sonoma or to the Russian River wineries. The free "Russian River Wine Road" map available at the Visitors' Center lists 54 wineries. If you head in that direction, Topolos Russian River Vineyards is a delightful spot for lunch or dinner in a wooded setting.

If you'd rather enjoy the out-of-doors on a fine crisp October day, Santa Rosa boasts parkland and wilderness galore right next door on the eastern edge of town. Annadel State Park comprises 5,000 acres where you can walk in cool shaded forest, along meadow and lakeshore. One hiking trail leads to Spring Lake, a 320-acre county park with picnic sites, more trails, and a 72-acre lake for fishing, boating, and swimming. A bike path goes from Spring Lake to Howarth Park, a town park with a lake for rowing and swimming, an animal farm, and a mini–amusement park for the kids.

Santa Rosa offers a variety of appealing lodgings and restaurants.

The Hotel La Rose, just opposite Railroad Square, has been attractively restored and decorated with vintage charm. Vintners Inn, at the north end of town, is at the busy intersection of Highway 101 and the River Road, but you'd never know it inside this Mediterranean-style complex, a group of small buildings surrounded by vineyards and clustered around a courtyard complete with splashing fountains. Spacious rooms have beamed ceilings, posh country pine furnishings, and patios or balconies; many come with attractive vineyard views. Not the least of the inn's attractions is the adjacent restaurant, the highly regarded John Ash & Company Mixx, an informal bistro in the historic district, the choice for creative cooking at moderate prices.

Two unusually attractive hotels are the Doubletree, with big, comfortable rooms in a cluster of low buildings terraced around a pool, and the striking modern Fountain Grove Inn, also with a pool. For inn lovers, the place is the Gables, a nicely restored stately Victorian with 12-foot ceilings and marble mantels.

Area Code: 707

DRIVING DIRECTIONS   From the Bay Area, take Highway 101 north directly to Santa Rosa. It is about 58 miles from San Francisco, 80 miles from Sacramento.

ACCOMMODATIONS   *Hotel La Rose,* 308 Wilson Street, Santa Rosa, 95401, 579-3200, M, CP on weekends • *Vintners Inn,* 4350 Barnes Road, Santa Rosa, 95403, 575-7350 or (800) 421-2584, E–EE, CP • *Doubletree Hotel,* 3555 Round Barn Boulevard, Santa Rosa, 95403, 523-7555 or (800) 654-2000, ask about special weekend packages, M–E • *Fountain Grove Inn,* 101 Fountaingrove Parkway, Santa Rosa 95403, 578-6101 or (800) 222-6101, M–EE, CP • *The Gables,* 4257 Petaluma Hill Road, Santa Rosa, 95404, 585-7777, M–E, CP. Fairgoing families on a budget might consider the *Sandman Motel,* 3421 Cleveland Avenue, Santa Rosa 95403, 544-8570, I; or *Best Western Hillside Inn,* 2901 Fourth Street, 95409, 546-9353, I; both allowing children under 12 free in parents' rooms.

DINING   *John Ash & Company,* Vintners Inn (see above), 527-7687, noted chef, sophisticated menu, M–E; café menu, I • *Mixx,* 135 Fourth Street, 573-1344, eclectic, delicious, I–M • *La Gare,* 208 Wilson Street at Railroad Square, 528-4355, French, M–E • *Siena Ristorante,* 1229 North Dutton Avenue, 578-4511, Italian, outdoor patio pleasant for brunch, I–M • *Lisa Hemenways,* 714 Village Court, Montgomery Village, Farmers Lane at Sonoma Avenue, 526-5111, highly rated California cuisine, M–E • *Omelette Express,* 112 Fourth Street, 525-1690, funky favorite for breakfast, I.

SIGHTSEEING   *Luther Burbank Home and Gardens,* Santa Rosa and Sonoma avenues, 524-5445. Hours: April to mid-October, Wednesday to Sunday 10 A.M. to 3:30 P.M. Adults, $2; under age 12, free with adult. Garden, April to October, daily 8 A.M. to 7 P.M., rest of year to 5 P.M. Free • *Redwood Empire Ice Arena,* 1667 West Steele Lane, 546-7147. Call for current skating schedule and rates • *Robert L. Ripley Museum/Church of One Tree,* 492 Sonoma Avenue, 524-5233. Hours: April to October, Wednesday to Sunday 10 A.M. to 3:30 P.M. Adults, $1.50; ages 7 to 18, $.75 • *California Museum of Art,* Luther Burbank Center for the Arts, 50 Mark West Springs Road, 527-0297. Hours: Wednesday to Sunday 11 A.M. to 4 P.M. Donation • *Sonoma County Museum,* 425 Seventh Street, 579-1500. Hours: Wednesday to Sunday 11 A.M. to 4 P.M. Adults, $2; ages 12 to 18, $1 • *Luther Burbank Center for the Arts,* 50 Mark West Springs Road, 546-3600. Phone for schedule of events • *Sonoma County Wine & Visitors' Center,* 5000 Roberts Lake Road, Rohnert Park (Golf Course Drive exit off Highway 101 northbound, watch for signs), 586-3795. Hours: Daily 10 A.M. to 5 P.M. • *Matanzas Creek Winery,* 6097 Bennett Valley Road, Santa Rosa, 528-6464. Hours: Monday to Saturday 10 A.M. to 4 P.M., Sunday noon to 4 P.M. • *Parks* (all open daylight hours): *Howarth Memorial Park,* Summerfield Road, Santa Rosa, 543-3292 • *Spring Lake County Park,* Summerfield Road and Newanga Avenue, Santa Rosa, 539-8092 • *Annadel State Park,* 6201 Channel Drive, Santa Rosa, 539-3911.

INFORMATION   *Sonoma County Convention and Visitors' Bureau,* 5000 Roberts Lake Road, Rohnert Park, CA 94928, 586-8100 or (800) 326-7666.

Autumn in the Trinity Alps

Who says you have to trek to New England to see autumn foliage? There's color right here in California in the forested northern mountains known as the Trinity Alps. From east or west, Route 299 into Weaverville winds into the woodlands with a procession of scenic overlooks. And that's only a preview of even more spectacular scenery to come on the Trinity Heritage National Scenic Byway, an auto tour through the Shasta-Trinity national forests.

Along the way you'll discover some delightful little towns, clear lakes and rivers for fishing and boating, wilderness hiking, and your choice of rustic cabins by the water or a wonderful country inn. Dams constructed by the Central Valley Project created two of the major lakes, Lewiston and Trinity.

Best of all, this serene area offers complete escape from crowds and congestion. Though the lakes have existed for well over a decade, they still are not widely known. And while Trinity County is bigger in size than either Rhode Island or Delaware, its total population is under 14,000. The region is wonderfully undeveloped, especially in the half-million-acre Trinity Alps Wilderness Area. There's not a freeway or a traffic light in sight.

Weaverville, the county seat, is the first happy surprise. It's a picture-book nineteenth-century town sandwiched between mountains, with a bandstand, a picturesque old courthouse, and a Main Street of arcaded sidewalks, wooden spiral staircases, and storefronts straight out of the Old West. The whole town is on the National Register of Historic Places, and preservation remains a local priority. The splendid 1901 bandstand was restored as the county's official bicentennial project.

A pleasant few hours of exploring can be done here. The town walking tour map available at the Chamber of Commerce office tells the history of more than 100 buildings, most dating from the 1850s to the 1880s. Many of the earliest wooden structures were lost to fire, and brick replacements went up in the 1850s. The courthouse, built in 1856–57, is the second oldest courthouse in California and holds all records from the county's beginnings. The Pacific Brewery Building, now a restaurant, also has been in use ever since it was rebuilt in 1856. The Weaverville Drug Store, the state's oldest, has been in operation since 1862 and displays bottles and medicines from the early years.

Since frontage on Main Street was at a premium, many buildings had space for businesses upstairs as well as down, with outside spiral staircases for easy access. Three of these staircases remain. Behind many of the old storefronts are some very appealing little shops and galleries.

Weaverville's most exciting days came during the Gold Rush. The Joss House, the town's prime historic site, was built in the early 1850s as a house of worship by the more than 2,000 Chinese who had come here to seek their fortune. The original temple was destroyed by fire and rebuilt in 1873. It is now part of the state park system but is still used for worship, the oldest continuously used Chinese temple in California. The brightly painted interior includes ornately carved wooden canopies and a nineteenth-century altar.

Ranger-guided tours of the Joss House explain a bit about Chinese religion and also bring to life the time when Weaverville had a thriving Chinatown. One of the legends concerns the war between two rival tongs in 1854, fought with pitchforks while raucous miners cheered on both sides. A marker on Highway 3 by the elementary school commemorates the battle. Most of the rest of Chinatown was lost to fire.

At the J. J. (Jake) Jackson Memorial Museum and Trinity County Historical Park, the history of the town is traced from the days of the Indians to the time of gold fever, with photos and displays of how the early settlers lived. Artifacts include old firearms, baskets, quilts, and clothing. In the jail cells moved here from the old county courthouse, the walls still bear the drawings done by prisoners whiling away their time. The museum also boasts a complete blacksmith's shop and numerous displays of fossils and minerals.

Displays outside include an authentic miner's cabin and a steam-powered gold ore mining stamp mill. The mill operates periodically to demonstrate how rock was crushed and quicksilver used to release the gold.

Just across the street, in a pioneer residence built in 1893, the Highland Art Center serves as a showcase for local artists.

Weaverville is the start of the National Scenic Byway auto tour mapped out by the U.S. Forest Service. The entire 111-mile drive extends above Mt. Shasta, a bit far for a weekend outing, but the Trinity County portion provides plenty of sights and scenery. Signs mark the route as you travel.

The first stop north on Route 103 is tiny Lewiston. Also once a boom town, Lewiston fell on hard times, but its 1860s buildings are slowly coming back to life as antiques and gift shops, and the 1862 hotel has been reborn as a funky restaurant. The hamlet gained its own historic landmark status in 1988.

From Lewiston center, follow the road north past the hotel to the intersection with Highway 105, Trinity Dam Boulevard. Across the highway a road leads to the Trinity River Hatchery, where visitors are welcome. It is an artificial spawning facility built to replace the natural salmon and steelhead spawning grounds lost when Lewiston Dam was constructed. The dam is directly above the hatchery.

The fish begin their annual upstream migration at the beginning of September, ascending the fish ladder and entering the holding ponds. Eggs are taken from the females and fertilized with milt from the males. Young salmon and steelhead hatch after 50 to 60 days in the incubator and are fed until they are big enough to be released. The timetable corresponds with natural downstream migrations. The best time to visit the hatchery is late afternoon, when the young fish are fed.

The stretch of the Trinity River between Lewiston Dam and the old bridge is considered "blue ribbon" water and attracts fly-fishing aficionados from miles around.

Go back to Highway 105, turn right for about a mile, and stop at Lewiston Vista for a view of the waters created by the dam. Lewiston Lake, drawn from Trinity Lake, has a surface area of 750 acres. The water is kept at a constant level, which makes it a favored habitat for eastern brook, rainbow, and brown trout. The Vista is also a fine place to spot bald eagles and ospreys diving for their dinner, a sight most common in early evening.

Another seven miles to the north is the Trinity Dam Vista. The dam, completed in 1961, is one of the highest earth-fill dams in the world. The generators in the building at the base can produce enough electricity to supply a small city.

Two miles farther north, at the Trinity Vista, you can see the lake created by the dam, California's third-largest manmade lake. Beyond are the peaks of the Trinity Alps Wilderness Area, 513,000 acres of rugged peaks, Alpine meadows, and thick forests.

As you continue west toward Highway 3, the result of past timbering can be seen along the road. The land is being replanted by the Forest Service.

Turn right at Highway 3 and continue for four miles over Montgomery Ridge and down along Slate Creek for a closer view of Trinity Lake, officially named Clair Engle Lake, for the senator responsible for the damming of the river. Those whose land was flooded by the project bitterly refuse to recognize this name.

Trinity Lake's forested shoreline has many hidden coves, ideal for fishing, swimming, water-skiing, houseboating, or camping. The western side of the lake offers rustic resorts, restaurants, marinas, picnic areas, and beaches; the eastern side is more primitive, the place for campers seeking solitude.

Highway 3 continues north to Trinity Center. The original site of this town, along with neighboring farms, ranches, and other small towns, is now under Trinity Lake. Before the site was flooded, a few of the buildings were moved to this location, as a link to the past.

Farther north along the lake, mounds of bare rock and gravel can be seen, evidence of the gold dredging that occurred here at the turn of the century.

Lodgings in the area are limited but do offer variety. Weaverville provides a pair of small bed-and-breakfast homes, and there is a tiny inn in Lewiston. Many rustic cabins and cottages can be found in Trinity Center or in Coffee Creek, north of Carrville. Or you might opt for a houseboat on the lake or the western ambience of the Coffee Creek Guest Ranch, where activities include riding, fishing, hiking, and panning for gold. Ranch rates are by the week, though shorter stays are possible off-season. While the ranch is an ideal spot for families, several weeks also are earmarked for adults only.

Serious fishermen may want to head for the no-frills motel and cabins at the Elkhorn Lodge, right on the Trinity River, a prime waterway for steelheads. The Elkhorn also sponsors fly-fishing seminars. Wherever you stay, guide service is available to help you find the best fishing spots. You can also sign on for overnight pack trips, water-ski rentals and lessons, canoe rentals, or a guided canoe trip.

There are several favorite day hikes in the area. The Stuarts Fork Hike at Bridge Camp just past the Trinity Alps Resort offers views of mountain ridges and rushing waters. Bowerman/Long Canyon trail leads through high-country meadows, dividing to tougher terrain in Long Canyon and a gentler walk in Bowerman. Eleanor/Shimmey Lake Trail is a moderate trail that begins at the end of Lake Eleanor Road, off Swift Creek Road. A half-mile walk brings you to Lake Eleanor, a picturesque mountain lake. About three miles farther is Shimmey Lake, with views of towering Ycatapom Peak. Those in good hiking form can tackle the steep Granite Peak Trail, reached via Granite Peak Road off Highway 3 just before the Mule Creek guard station.

Whether you get out on the lake or into the autumn woods, or just admire the scenery from your car windows, the Trinity Alps are hard to beat for beauty—especially when they are wearing their autumn cloaks of many colors.

Area Code: 916

DRIVING DIRECTIONS   Weaverville is reached via Route 299, from Eureka to the west, 100 miles, or Redding to the east, 45 miles. It is 278 miles from San Francisco, 212 miles from Sacramento.

ACCOMMODATIONS   *Old Lewiston Inn,* P.O. Box 688, Lewiston, 96052, 778-3385, I, CP • *The Old Yellow House,* P.O. Box 2595, Weaverville, 96093, 623-2274, I, CP • *Granny's House,* P.O. Box 31, Weaverville, 96093, 623-2756, I, CP • *Weaverville Victorian Inn,* 1790 Main Street, Weaverville, 96093, 623-4432, motel, I • **Cabin resorts:** *Bonanza King Resort,* Route 2, Box 4790, Trinity Center, 96091, 266-3305, cabins along the creek, I • *Coffee Creek Chalet,* Star Route 2, Box 3969, Trinity Center, 96091, 266-3235, a single chalet in the woods, I • *Ripple Creek Cabins,* Star Route 2, Box 3899, Trinity Center, 96091, 266-3505, I • *Coffee Creek Guest Ranch,* HC 2, Box 4940, Trinity Center, 96091, 266-3343, EE, AP • *The Elkhorn,* Route 299 West, P.O. Box 51, Helena, 96048, 623-6318, very modest motel and cabins, recommended only for fishermen, I • **Houseboats** (phone for current rates): *Trinity Alps Marina,* P.O. Box 670, Lewiston, 96052, 286-2282 • *Cedar Stock Resort and Marina,* Star Route 510, Lewiston, 96052, 286-2225.

DINING   *The Brewery,* 402 Main Street, Weaverville, 623-3000, I–M • *Marino's Italian Restaurant,* Nugget Lane, Weaverville, 623-2696, I • *The Nugget,* 602 Main Street, Weaverville, 623-6749, I • *Allan's Oak Pit Bar-B-Q,* 1234 Nugget Lane, Weaverville, 623-2182, I

• *Lewiston Hotel,* Deadwood Road, Lewiston, 778-3823, I–M •
Mama's Place, Trinity Dam Boulevard, Lewiston, 778-3177, I • *Airporter Inn,* Airport Road, Trinity Center, 266-3223, I–M • *Trinity Alps Resort,* Stuarts Fork, 288-2205, I–M • *The Mustard Seed,* 252 Main Street, Weaverville, 623-2922, good for lunch, noted for their pies, I.

SIGHTSEEING   *Weaverville Joss House State Historic Park,* P.O. Drawer W, Weaverville, 623-5284. Hours: May to September, daily 10 A.M. to 5 P.M.; rest of year, Thursday to Monday. Tours hourly, 10 A.M. to 4 P.M. Adults, $1; ages 6 to 17, $.50 • *J. J. (Jake) Jackson Memorial Museum and Trinity County Historical Park,* Box 333, Weaverville, 623-5211. Hours: May 1 to October 31, daily 10 A.M. to 5 P.M.; April and November, daily noon to 4 P.M. Free, but donations appreciated • **Boating and fishing:** Check with Chamber of Commerce for current listings for boat rentals, river trips, and fishing guide services.

INFORMATION   *Trinity County Chamber of Commerce,* 317 Main Street, P.O. Box 517, Weaverville, CA 96093, 623-6101.

Vintage Days in the Napa Valley

California's Napa Valley ranks high among the great wine-growing regions of the world. The beauty of the vineyards hugging the hillsides and the chance to taste the fine wines they produce draws 3 million visitors each year—a number that is a mixed blessing. The popularity of the area accounts for the fine lodgings and dining that can make a Napa visit sublime, but it also makes for quite a traffic jam on weekends, given a 35-mile valley with only two roads running the entire length.

The congestion is worse when the grapes are being crushed—during harvest time in early autumn—but, nevertheless, Napa really should be experienced at least once during this peak season. There's nothing to match the sight of the vineyards lush with ruby grapes ripe for picking. And this is the only time you can see the whole process of winemaking taking place, from vine to vats.

So make your reservations early and come prepared to join the lines for the most popular winery tours. You won't be sorry you made the trip to the Napa Valley.

While there are 32,000 acres of vineyards in the valley and more than 250 wineries, most of the better-known labels are concentrated in a ten-mile area between Yountville and St. Helena known as "Wine Alley," making these two towns the most popular places to stay.

Yountville, small and quaint, is a tidy village of historic stone buildings that has gone upscale chic. Shopaholics will be happy here. One of the most atmospheric old structures, an 1870 winery, is now a posh complex known as Vintage 1870, with boutiques, galleries, shops, and restaurants. There are more galleries and interesting stops in town, and another major shopping area is just outside town on Highway 29.

Yountville lodgings are also a mix of old and new. Rooms at the Vintage Inn in town are modern and luxurious, with wood-burning fireplaces, whirlpool baths, and patio or balcony. The cozy Burgundy House, an old distillery built of local fieldstone, is more than 100 years old and would seem right at home in the French countryside. The restored Maison Fleurie, built in 1873, is now a Victorian haven with a garden and a choice of rooms in the hotel or in the more luxurious Old Bakery and Carriage House buildings, where you can have canopy beds and fireplaces.

Perched high above the highway just north of Yountville is a very special small inn, the Sybron House, with a homelike feeling, tasteful decor, and magnificent views of the valley.

Drive farther north on Highway 29 through Oakville and Rutherford and you can't miss St. Helena, since the highway runs right through the heart of town. While it is a pleasant town with old-fashioned streetlights and some period buildings, the highway means there is more traffic and less sense of a cohesive community.

St. Helena has some interesting shops and galleries along Main Street, but the main sightseeing stop in town is more literary and is, in fact, part of the Public Library Center. The Silverado Museum is a building wing devoted to the life and works of Robert Louis Stevenson, who wrote about the area. Exhibits include Stevenson manuscripts, letters, first editions, and artwork.

Bargain hunters will want to take note of the Village Outlets at 3111 North Highway 19, where upscale labels like Donna Karan, Coach, and Brooks Brothers can be found at considerable savings.

There are some very nice lodgings just off Highway 29 as well, including two larger properties. The Wine Country Inn has country decor, attractive grounds, and a pool, and the Harvest Inn, despite motel decor, offers big rooms in individual Tudor-style cottage units, beautiful grounds, and its own pool. The old St. Helena Hotel has been nicely restored with a Victorian look, though the rooms seem small for the price.

Creekside Inn and Chestelson House are two small, modest in-town bed-and-breakfast inns with somewhat more moderate rates. The guest suites at the Prager Winery are unique, mini-apartments that put you in the heart of the vineyards, and Villa St. Helena is worth seeking out if you want luxurious quarters in a lavish, secluded, Mediterranean-style villa on a hilltop.

Escapists might head for the hills off the Silverado Trail, the alternate, less-crowded country route running the length of the valley to the east, parallel to Highway 29. One prize lodging in this area is Bartels Ranch, a comfortable informal home with a pool, set on 100 acres of rolling meadows. The delightful hostess serves wine, cheese, and locally grown fruit each afternoon. She has drawn up her own map to make sure guests don't miss anything worthwhile in the area.

Two of the best luxury resorts in wine country are also in this general area, both members of the prestigious Relais & Chateaux group. Auberge du Soleil in Rutherford is widely known as an elegant escape with posh rooms in individual casitas hidden in hillside greenery. Meadowood in St. Helena is less formal in feel, less expensive, and hard to beat for lovely country lodgings, beautiful woodsy grounds, and activities from golf, tennis, and swimming to croquet.

Having settled in, most Napa visitors want to head straight for the wineries. A good plan for a first-time visit is to start with a tour that stresses area history, then select an informative tour on winemaking. Afterward, if you are up for more sampling, you can visit tasting rooms at a variety of wineries.

On your arrival at the larger facilities, first ask for tickets for the next available tour, then, depending on the length of the wait, either browse in the tasting room or head off for sightseeing. It isn't necessary to tour in order to sample a certain number of wines gratis in the tasting rooms, but tours usually get preference. Understandably, most vintners charge if you want to taste their most prestigious wines.

One of most venerable of the wineries, the stately stone Greystone Cellars that used to house the Christian Brothers Winery, is now home to a West Coast campus of the prestigious training school for chefs, the Culinary Institute of America. Its graduates will no doubt add to the area's already much-lauded restaurant scene. There were plans at press time for a student-staffed restaurant serving Mediterranean cuisine; check to see if it is in operation and you can get an early taste of the talents of soon-to-be-great chefs.

Beringer, the oldest continuously operating winery in the Napa Valley, is a top choice for a tour that tells a lot about the area's history. You'll also see the aging caves that were dug into the hillside back in the 1880s. The original nineteenth-century mansion is now a visitors' center.

For an introduction to the art of making wine, it's hard to match Mondavi, where the tour starts with the vineyards, then proceeds to grape crushing and the aging and bottling of different varieties of wine. Groups get a private tasting in a shady arbor. Mondavi is deservedly crowded, so come early. The lush grounds of this lovely winery are worth a visit, tour or not.

Across the highway is one of the most dramatic wineries in the valley, Opus One, a joint venture of Mondavi and the Rothschild family of France. It is definitely worth making the advance appointment necessary for a tour of this striking structure of limestone and redwood, burrowed into a hill amid 75 acres of vineyards. The inside, with its hand detailing, lavish furnishings, and circular stair, is lavish, and the winemaking process is state-of-the-art. A taste of the super-expensive Opus One wines comes with a tour, or you can come without an appointment for a high-priced sampling in the tasting room.

Another informative tour, though in less remarkable surroundings, is at Beaulieu Vineyards, south of St. Helena in Rutherford. The tour at the striking modern complex of Domaine Chandon is different because it demonstrates the traditional French *méthode champenoise* used to produce champagne and sparkling wines. There is a charge here to taste, but as the wine is served with a small snack on the terrace, you may decide it's worth it to sit back and take in the superb vineyard view.

Connoisseurs may want to stop at some of the more prestigious smaller wineries, such as Grgich Hills in Rutherford, or Trefethen in Napa. And there are dozens of small, specialized vineyards to be visited, such as Prager, one of the few in California producing fine port.

Those who want to escape Highway 29 traffic can swing over to the Silverado Trail, where they can find respected names such as Stag's Leap and Mumm Napa Valley, as well as smaller spots such as Chateau Boswell, Rutherford Hill, Conn Creek, and Silverado. These smaller wineries tend to be less crowded and more personal, places where you are likely to actually meet the owner. Though they welcome visitors, many small wineries prefer to operate by appointment, so phone ahead.

A popular pleasure on a lovely day in the Napa Valley is a picnic at grounds provided by several vineyards. Once again, Domaine Chandon stands out. Rutherford Hill, Chateau Boswell, and Folie A Deux in St. Helena also provide pleasant picnic areas. If you really want to escape, head north to Bothe–Napa Valley State Park. The top place to stock up for your picnic is the Oakville Grocery on Highway 29 in Oakville.

Another way to escape the crowds is by taking a balloon ride over the vineyards, a favorite Napa diversion that affords a fabulous perspective on the autumn scene.

Or you can take a ride on the controversial Napa Valley Wine Train. Some of the locals hate the idea of a train bringing still more people into their valley, but the trip from Napa to St. Helena aboard the restored 1915 vintage cars is a relaxing way to enjoy the scenery without worrying about traffic, and the meals and wine served, while pricey, are first rate.

But then, the whole Napa Valley is known for its fine dining. Again, Yountville and St. Helena are among the cream of the restaurant crop.

St. Helena's Terra serves exquisite food with a touch of the Orient supplied by the Japanese chef-owner. Tra Vigne offers top northern Italian food in a dramatic setting, and Trilogy is another recommended blend of French and California cuisines.

Oakville's new culinary star is the Stars Oakville Café, an informal spot with fine food; celebrity chef Jeremiah Tower is part owner.

In Yountville, the favorites include the cheerful Italian Piatti and the French Laundry, a romantic hideaway in a garden setting. Yountville's gourmet standout is Domaine Chandon, open for lunch and dinner. Like the sparkling wines made here, the food is a delicious blend of California-French.

One of the most popular spots in town is the local diner. It is packed for breakfast and a good bet for an inexpensive lunch or early dinner, when Mexican specialties are added to the American menu. On Highway 29 outside town is Mustard's Grill, a casual bistro with an always lively atmosphere and reliably tasty food.

Below Yountville, at the northern edge of Napa, is the bright and cheerful Bistro Don Giovanni, with excellent pastas and eclectic main courses at very reasonable prices. There's another prime lodging choice, La Residence, within walking distance of the Bistro. Though it seems uncomfortably close to the road, this is a beautifully furnished inn with attractive grounds, and effective soundproofing means you are not disturbed by the whirr of traffic.

Whatever your choice, make your dinner reservations as early as your inn arrangements; the places are small and the demand is great.

Having endured the height of the season in wine country, you deserve a return trip when the crowds are gone, perhaps in late autumn, after the grapes have been picked but before the colorful leaves have fallen from the vines. Early spring is another prime time, when the hillsides are at their greenest and mustard plants carpet the vineyards with gold. Winters are mild and are the best time for tasting, without too much competition for space at the bar.

Area Code: 707

DRIVING DIRECTIONS   From Highway 101, take Route 37 east above San Rafael, then Highway 29 north to Napa, Yountville, and St. Helena. From I-80, take Route 12 west to Highway 29 north. Yountville is about 58 miles from San Francisco, 60 miles from Sacramento. St. Helena is about 10 miles farther north. To avoid traffic, take the turnoff from Highway 29 to the Silverado Trail north in Napa and cross over to 29 via the Yountville Cross Road or Deer Park Road in St. Helena.

ACCOMMODATIONS *Maison Fleurie,* 6529 Yount Street, Yountville, 94599, 944-2056, E–EE, CP • *Burgundy House,* 6711 Washington Street, Yountville, 94599, 944-0889, E, CP • *Vintage Inn,* 6541 Washington Street, Yountville, 94599, 944-1112, EE, CP • *Bartels Ranch & Country Inn,* 1200 Conn Valley Road, St. Helena 94574, 963-4001, EE, CP • *Villa St. Helena,* 2727 Sulphur Springs Avenue, St. Helena, 94574, 963-2514, EE, CP • *Harvest Inn,* 1 Main Street, St. Helena, 94574, 963-9463 or (800) 950-8466, E–EE, CP • *Chestelson House,* 1417 Kearney Street, St. Helena, 94574, 963-2238, M, CP • *Creekside Inn,* 945 Main Street, St. Helena, 94574, 963-7244, M, CP • *Prager Guest House,* Prager Winery & Port Works, 281 Llewelling Lane, St. Helena, 94574, 963-3720, E • *Sybron House,* 7400 St. Helena Highway (Highway 29), Napa, 94558, 944-2785, E–EE, CP • *La Residence,* 4066 St. Helena Highway (Highway 29), Napa, 94558, 253-0337, EE, CP • *Oak Knoll Inn,* 2200 E. Oak Knoll Avenue, Napa, 94558, 255-2200, secluded location in the vineyards south of Yountville, huge elegant rooms, EE, CP • **Resorts:** *Auberge du Soleil,* 180 Rutherford Hill Road, Rutherford, 94573, 963-1211, EE • *Meadowood,* 900 Meadowood Lane, St. Helena, 94574, 963-3646, EE. No room at the inns? There are many motels in Napa; get a listing from the Chamber of Commerce at the address below.

DINING *Domaine Chandon,* California Drive (off Highway 29), Yountville, 944-2892, EE • *French Laundry,* 6640 Washington Street, Yountville, 944-2380, EE • *Mustard's Grill,* 7399 St. Helena Highway, Yountville, 944-2424, M • *Piatti,* 6480 Washington Street, Yountville, 944-2070, M–E • *The Diner,* 6476 Washington Street, Yountville, 944-2626, I • *Stars Oakville Café,* 7848 St. Helena Highway, Oakville, 944-8905, E • *Terra,* 1345 Railroad Avenue, St. Helena, 963-8931, M–E • *Tra Vigne,* 1050 Charter Oak Avenue (off Highway 29), St. Helena, 963-8888, M; cantinetta, light fare, I • *Trilogy,* 1234 Main Street at Hunt, St. Helena, 963-5507, M–E • *Brava Terrace,* 3010 St. Helena Highway north, St. Helena, 963-9300, French-American bistro, M • *Showley's at Miramonte,* 1327 Railroad Avenue, St. Helena, 963-1200, restored 1907 hotel, imaginative French menu, M • *Bistro Don Giovanni,* 4110 St. Helena Highway, Napa, 224-3300, excellent value, M • *Auberge du Soleil,* Rutherford (see above), EE • *Napa Valley Wine Train,* 1275 McKinstry Street, Napa, 253-2111 or (800) 522-4142, brunch, lunch, or dinner aboard vintage trains, advance reservations required, EE.

SIGHTSEEING *Silverado Museum,* St. Helena Public Library Center, 1490 Library Lane, 963-3757. Hours: Tuesday to Sunday noon to 4 P.M. Free • *Napa Valley Wine Train,* 1275 McKinstry Street, Napa, 253-2111 or (800) 522-4142, two-hour round-trip ride from Napa to

St. Helena, phone for current rates • **Balloon rides:** *Napa Valley Balloons,* P.O. Box 2860, Yountville, 253-2224 or in California (800) 253-2224; *Balloons Above the Valley,* P.O. Box 3838, Napa, 253-2222; *Balloon Aviation of Napa Valley,* 2299 Third Street, Napa, 252-7067 or (800) 367-6272.

WINERIES *Beaulieu Vineyard,* 1960 St. Helena Highway (Highway 29), Rutherford, 963-2411. Hours: Daily tours 10 A.M. to 3 P.M., tasting room to 4 P.M. • *Beringer Vineyards,* 2000 Main Street, St. Helena, 963-4812. Hours: Tours and tastings daily 9:30 A.M. to 5 P.M. • *Chateau Boswell,* 3468 Silverado Trail, St. Helena, 963-5472. Hours: Friday to Sunday 10 A.M. to 5 P.M. • *Conn Creek Winery,* 8711 Silverado Trail, St. Helena, 963-9100 • Hours: Daily 10 A.M. to 4 P.M. • *Domaine Chandon,* California Road (off Highway 29), Yountville, 944-2280. Hours: Daily May to October, tours 11 A.M. to 6 P.M.; rest of year, Wednesday to Sunday • *Grgich Hills Cellar,* 1829 St. Helena Highway, Rutherford, 963-2784. Hours: Daily tastings 9:30 A.M. to 4:30 P.M., tours by appointment • *Inglenook Winery,* 1991 St. Helena Highway, Rutherford, 967-3355. Hours: Tastings daily 10 A.M. to 5 P.M., tours from 11 A.M. Wine museum, goblet collection • *Louis Martini,* 254 St. Helena Highway, St. Helena, 963-2736. Hours: Daily tastings and tours 10 A.M. to 4:30 P.M. • *Robert Mondavi Winery,* 7801 St. Helena Highway, Oakville, 963-2736. Hours: Tasting room daily 9 A.M. to 5:30 P.M. May to October, to 4:30 P.M. rest of year. One-hour tours offered frequently all day. Three-hour in-depth tours by reservation only are offered Sunday and Monday at 10 A.M. May to October • *Mumm Napa Valley,* 8445 Silverado Train, Rutherford, 942-3434. Hours: April to October, daily 10:30 A.M. to 6 P.M., free public tours hourly 11 A.M. to 4 P.M.; rest of year, 10 A.M. to 5 P.M., tours 11 A.M. to 3 P.M. • *Opus One,* St. Helena Highway, Oakville (across from Mondavi), 963-1979. Tours by appointment; best to call at least one week in advance. Tasting room hours vary, so phone also to check • *Prager Winery & Port Works,* 281 Llewelling Lane, St. Helena, 963-3720. Hours: Daily sales 10:30 A.M. to 4:30 P.M., tours and tastings by appointment • *Rutherford Hill Winery,* 200 Rutherford Hill Road, Rutherford, 963-7194. Hours: Tasting and tours 10 A.M. to 4:30 P.M. • *Silverado Vineyards,* 6121 Silverado Trail, Napa, 257-1770. Hours: Sales only, 11 A.M. to 4:30 P.M. • *Stag's Leap Wine Cellars,* 5766 Silverado Trail, Napa, 944-2020. Hours: Daily tastings 10 A.M. to 4:30 P.M., tours by appointment.

INFORMATION *St. Helena Chamber of Commerce,* P.O. Box 124, St. Helena, CA 94574, 962-4456 • *Napa Valley Visitors' Bureau,* 1310 Napa Town Center, Napa, CA 94559, 226-7459; Information Center off Highway 29 at the entrance to the Inglenook Winery in Rutherford.

Striking Gold in Nevada City

If ever there were a beauty contest for prettiest town in gold country, Nevada City, the "Queen City of the Northern Mines," would surely vie for the crown.

Part of it has to do with the setting—buildings terraced up steep forested hillsides, Victorian cupolas, and white church spires set against maples and pines. All of it is at its loveliest in fall, when the leaves of the sugar maples turn to scarlet.

This is another California town with more than a hint of New England. It is, in fact, early gold seekers from New England who are credited with bringing their native trees, as well as giving the town a solid foundation that kept it prosperous while other boom towns disappeared. The fine buildings built by the gold-rich settlers have been carefully preserved, and even the unfortunate intrusion of a modern highway hasn't spoiled the town's charm.

As a weekend destination, Nevada City is pure gold, with prize inns and dining, lively culture and nightlife, and two of the most fascinating bits of history along the 120-mile mother lode—Malakoff Diggins State Park and the Empire Mine in neighboring Grass Valley. The past comes alive most dramatically during Living History Days at the Empire Mine, where you can share life as it was in the boom days. The Days are held in spring and in fall. Come on up and strike it rich.

Rich was definitely the word for Nevada City. Back in 1849, they were pulling a pound of gold a day from the waters of Deer Creek. The unusual pattern of the streets, resembling spokes of a wheel, follows the first mule trails used by miners to travel home from the plaza at Deer Creek.

After a harsh first winter, the first gold seekers, 1,000 would-be millionaires, had a meeting and named their town Nevada, meaning snow-covered. The word *City* was added only after the state next door stole their name.

The town kept growing, as lumbering joined gold in bringing prosperity. Among the fine buildings that have been preserved are the 1856 National Hotel and the 1865 Nevada Theater. The hotel is still very much in business, and the restored theater is now home to the Foothill Theater Company, a local repertory group.

You can see these and other interesting sites via old-fashioned horse and carriage, or by picking up a walking tour at the Chamber of Commerce office in the South Yuba Canal Building on Main Street.

Another Main Street spot with a bit of history is the Assay Office, where the silver find at Nevada's Comstock Lode was first confirmed, setting off a rush across the Sierra.

Many of the town's oldest buildings can be found along Broad

Street, the gas-lit heart of the historic district. The hotel and theater are here, as well as a picturesque section of arcaded sidewalk. The original J. J. Jackson store dates from 1853. Firehouse No. 2 went up in 1861. A host of tempting shops beckon behind some of these old facades.

The local Historical Society houses a small museum of mining memorabilia up the hill in Firehouse No. 1, also an 1861 structure. Among its relics are a complete altar from a Chinese joss house and clothing, furnishings, and photos of early settlers.

Another part of local history is the Miners Foundry Cultural Center, an enormous 1865 building where the first Pelton wheel was manufactured in 1878. The huge wheel, 30 feet in diameter, was an important link between the waterwheel and the modern generator. One can be seen at the Mining Museum in Grass Valley. The foundry building now serves as a local cultural center, site of many concerts and special events year-round, including the International Teddy Bear Convention in April, when thousands of lovable bears come to town. The building also houses a small museum of Victoriana, a kind of attic grab bag of assorted treasures.

The loveliest of the local inns, Grandmere's Inn, holds yet another tidbit of town lore. The beautifully restored 1856 home was the residence of U.S. Senator A. A. Sargent, who introduced the legislation that eventually led to women's suffrage. Tasteful rooms here are spacious, with attractive floral fabrics and big sitting areas.

Another well-known lodging, the Red Castle, is a four-story 1860 Gothic Revival mansion clinging to a wooded hill above town. Also unique is Flume's Inn, an 1863 Victorian that perches on a hillside sloping down to a waterfall and Gold Run Creek. These three accommodations are the top choices, but there's no shortage of other pleasant nineteenth-century homes welcoming guests in Nevada City.

When you've done the town, take a drive north on Highway 49 to see the moonscape at Malakoff Diggins State Historic Park. Here you will learn a bit about the not-so-pretty side effects of gold mining fever. From the 1850s to the 1880s this was the site of the world's largest hydraulic gold mine, where giant nozzles were used to blast water against the cliffs, thereby washing the soil down into sluices, where gold could be easily collected. Needless to say, this did little for the land, and the muddy runoff killed life in the rivers and ruined farmland downstream. The sediment eventually even clogged San Francisco Bay. Outrage was universal, resulting in hydraulic mining's being outlawed in 1883, one of the country's first important environmental decisions.

The eroded cliffs left at Malakoff Diggins have been softened by a century of weather and today offer a fantasy of multicolored layers rimmed with dark green firs. The area has been compared to South Dakota's Badlands, Utah's Bryce Canyon—and to the moon. Walking the Rim Trail affords a good view of the mining site. It's spectacular at sunset, with the cliffs reflected in the tailing ponds.

Within the park is North Bloomfield, a preserved village that once was home to 2,000 people. Now it's a museum town. Among the old structures open to visitors are the livery stable, blacksmith shop, drugstore, general store, and church. The machine shop, where nuggets were melted and molded into gold bars, also remains. One of the exhibits is a 500-pound block of simulated gold, representing the typical monthly yield from the sluices.

The museum on the grounds offers a film that explains the mining process and shows how the miners lived. In season, rangers lead tours at 1:30 P.M. each day.

When you return to Nevada City for dinner, you'll find a range of choices, from family-style Italian to continental, California cuisine to Cowboy Pizza.

You should find plenty to do after dinner, what with the Foothill Theater and live music at many clubs and cafés, including Friar Tuck's and the National Hotel. In a quieter vein, classical guitarists or singers usually can be found at Earth Song Health Foods and Café. Music in the Mountains, sponsor of a major summer event, also holds occasional concerts year-round in Grass Valley. Check the current schedule.

On Sunday, leave plenty of time for Grass Valley and the 784-acre Empire Mine State Historic Park. The Empire Mine, one of the most productive of all, was the first electrified mine. In its 107 years in operation it produced 5.8 million ounces of gold (try figuring that out at today's market price). It has been estimated that even more gold remains in the ground, but getting at it is too expensive to be practical. As it was, the maze of tunnels dug covered 367 miles.

During a living-history program, locals dressed as miners, bosses, and ladies of the town tell you just how it was: about mules that spent their lives working underground, about the Cornish workers who carried meat pies—called pasties—and tea in their tin lunch pails—along with candles to heat their meals. You can also watch the sparks fly as blacksmiths work iron at the forge.

At the park museum, exhibits and films tell you all you need to know about the hard-rock quartz mining that was done here. Then you can wander on your own or join a guided tour. Have a look at the Rowe Mine headframe, a contraption used as an elevator to carry men and minerals into the mine shafts. You can't go underground, as most of the shafts are now flooded, but you can go down the stairs partway into one open shaft.

Hikers will enjoy the Hardrock Trail, a 2½-mile walk past shafts, tailings, and relics of old mines.

Up the hill are the handsome "cottage," rose gardens, and fountain of mine owner William Bourn. The inside of the home boasts handsome redwood paneling and stained glass. The gardener's cottage, carriage house, and clubhouse for guests also remain.

Those who want to know still more about mining should make a stop at the North Star Mine Museum in Grass Valley to see the famous collection of mining equipment, including an 1896 Pelton wheel, the largest one in the world. There are models and displays featuring the progress of mining technology.

The town of Grass Valley merits a stroll. It was home to two fabled ladies of Gold Rush days, Lola Montez and Lotta Crabtree. Montez came here to retire from the stage. Her home is currently headquarters for the County Chamber of Commerce, and still contains a few of her original furnishings. Pick up a town walking-tour guide while you are visiting.

Montez is said to have coached Lotta Crabtree, a winsome six-year-old who lived two doors away at 238 Mill Street. She did her work well. Crabtree began her career by singing and dancing Irish songs and jigs on tours through mining camps with her mother. Later she went on the stage, and is said to be the first American entertainer to become a millionaire.

When you are ready for refreshments, there are a number of places that will serve you a Grass Valley specialty, those flaky pasties that were miners' favorites.

A more elegant choice is the Holbrooke Hotel, a restored 1862 beauty. The guest book includes the names of presidents Grant, Harrison, Garfield, and Cleveland, and writers Mark Twain and Bret Harte. There's a colorful saloon for libations, a good dining room, and a patio open in season.

The Holbrooke is also a fine place for an atmospheric overnight, in rooms named after Gold Rush personalities and famous mines. Another inviting choice in Grass Valley is Murphy's Inn, a gracious Victorian on a leafy side street. Be forewarned—Grass Valley just may persuade you to extend your weekend.

Area Code: 916

DRIVING DIRECTIONS   Follow I-80 to Highway 49 north into Nevada City. It's about 155 miles from San Francisco, 65 miles from Sacramento.

ACCOMMODATIONS   *Grandmere's Inn,* 449 Broad Street, Nevada City, 95959, 265-4660, E–EE, CP • *Red Castle Inn,* 109 Prospect Street, Nevada City, 95959, 265-5135, E, CP • *Marsh Christie House,* 254 Boulder Street, Nevada City 95959, handsome Victorian home, opened as a promising inn by owners of the Red Castle after press time; check for rates • *The Parsonage,* 427 Broad Street, Nevada City, 95959, 265-9478, M–E, CP • *Downey House,* 517 West

Broad Street, Nevada City, 95959, 265-2815, I–M, CP • *Flume's End,*
317 South Pine Street, Nevada City, 95959, 265-9665, M–E, CP • *The
Holbrooke Hotel,* 212 West Main Street, Grass Valley, 95945, 273-
1353, M–E, CP • *Murphy's Inn,* 449 Neal Street, Grass Valley, 95945,
273-6873, M–E, CP.

DINING *Friar Tuck's,* 111 North Pine Street, Nevada City, 265-
9093, bricks and beams, American-continental cuisine, wine bar, M–E
• *Cirino's,* 309 Broad Street, Nevada City, 265-2246, family-friendly
Italian, M • *Potager at Selaya's,* 320 Broad Street, Nevada City, 265-
5697, Gold Rush decor, California cuisine, M • *Country Rose Café,*
300 Commercial Street, Nevada City, 265-6248, Country French in an
1800s brick building, M • *Cowboy Pizza,* 315 Spring Street, Nevada
City, 265-2334, funky Old West decor and some very imaginative pizzas, I • *Earth Song Health Foods and Café,* 135-A Argall Way, Nevada
City, 265-9392, good vegetarian food, serving all three meals, I • *The
Holbrooke Hotel,* Grass Valley (see above), I–M • For breakfast or
lunch, try the charming little *Apple Fare,* 121 Neal Street, Grass Valley, or the vast menu at *Tofanelli's,* 302 West Main Street, Grass Valley,
273-9927 • **For pasties:** *Marshall's,* 103 Mill Street, Grass Valley, 272-
2844; or *Mrs. Dubblebee's,* 251 South Auburn Street, Grass Valley,
272-7700.

SIGHTSEEING *Firehouse Cultural Museum,* 214 Main Street,
Nevada City, 265-9941. Hours: April to October, daily 11 A.M. to 4
P.M.; winter hours vary, so phone. Donation • *Malakoff Diggins State
History Park,* 23579 North Bloomfield Road, Nevada City, 265-2740.
Hours: Daily sunrise to sunset. Museum open June to September,
daily 10 A.M. to 5 P.M., tours at 1:30 P.M. Admission per car, $5 •
Empire Mine State Historic Park, 10787 East Empire Street, Grass
Valley, 273-8522. Hours: Grounds and gardens open daily, January to
May and September to December 10 A.M. to 5 P.M., May to early June
9 A.M. to 5 P.M., June to early September to 6 P.M. Guided tours daily
in season, weekends rest of year. Living History Days held in May,
June, September, and October; check current dates. Adults, $2; ages 6
to 12, $1 • *North Star Mining Museum,* Allison Ranch Road, Grass
Valley, 273-4255. Hours: May to October, daily 10 A.M. to 4 P.M.
Donation • *Miners Foundry and Cultural Center,* 325 Spring Street,
Nevada City, 265-5040. Hours: Monday to Friday 9 A.M. to 5 P.M.
Donation • *Nevada City Carriage Company,* 265-5348, horse-drawn
carriage tours, phone for schedule and rates • *Foothill Theater Com-
pany,* Nevada Theater, Broad Street, Nevada City, 265-9320. Check
for current productions • *Music in the Mountains,* c/o St. Joseph's
Hall, Grass Valley, 265-6124 or (800) 218-2188. Check for current
calendar.

INFORMATION *Grass Valley/Nevada County Chamber of Commerce,* 248 Mill Street, Grass Valley, CA 95945, 273-4667 or in California (800) 655-4667 • *Nevada City Chamber of Commerce,* 132 Main Street, Nevada City, CA 95959, 265-2692 or (800) 655-NJOY.

Catching the View in Sausalito

They compare it to the Riviera—the houses terraced up the hillside, the glittery water views. With a breathtaking overview of the Bay, the Golden Gate Bridge, and the San Francisco skyline, Sausalito is a town that is definitely worth seeing, as the thousands of day-trippers who arrive every weekend will attest.

Stay overnight, however, and Sausalito can also be a wonderful romantic weekend getaway, and the gateway to some of the Bay Area's most beautiful open spaces. The adjacent Marin Headlands boast clifftop views that are wilder and, if anything, even more spectacular. To make the most of these vistas, you'll want to pick a time when there's the least chance of fog—which makes this an ideal autumn excursion.

Nowadays Sausalito is shared by tourists, artists, and wealthy residents, but it has passed through many incarnations over its colorful history. The permanent development began in 1868, when a group of 20 astute businessmen purchased 1,200 acres of waterfront property, mapped out a town, and started a regular ferry service to San Francisco, luring urbanites to build summer homes here. In 1875 the town boomed when tracks were laid along the waterfront of Richardson Bay and Sausalito became the southernmost railway terminus for the North Pacific Coast Railroad Company. Those were bawdy days, when the town was filled with bordellos, saloons, and gambling halls. During Prohibition Sausalito was the direct route used to ferry illegal booze to San Francisco.

With the opening of the Golden Gate Bridge in 1937, the railroad and the ferry service were no longer needed. Sausalito's new identity came as a shipbuilding center in World War II, bringing 20,000 workers into town. When they moved out after the war, the town was all but deserted. Artists began moving in, attracted by low rents and the area's natural beauty. About that time a famous former bordello madam, Sally Stanford, came into town, purchased the old Vallhalla restaurant, and renovated it in grand 1890s style.

As the town's older buildings were restored and refurbished, the artists and writers were priced out. They moved north, constructing houseboats on dilapidated ferryboats and ship's hulls at the old shipyard sites. Pretty soon tourists began coming to see the houseboats as well as the view, and a new ferry service was launched in 1971.

To get a feel for why people love Sausalito, you need only do what the day-trippers do: start at the harbor, drinking in the view, then walk the town. Staying in town overnight, you have a definite advantage, because you can stroll early, before the mass of tourists arrives.

Begin your walk where the ferries land at the foot of El Portal, a block made welcoming by the Vina del Mar Plaza, a pretty little park with a fountain and two 14-foot-high elephant statues saved from San Francisco's Panama-Pacific Exposition of 1915. Today they serve as unique light posts.

The shops on Bridgeway, the main thoroughfare, are a mixed bag. Some are full of tacky souvenirs; some are far more interesting. Petri's, for example, has American art glass, paperweights, kaleidoscopes, and other nice things, and the Collector's Gallery stocks fine crystal. The Sausalito Country Store will please fans of country crafts and folk art. It is located in the Village Fair, a four-level complex with 50 shops and galleries selling everything from art posters to shells to leather.

Walking up the steep stairs on the west side of the street to Bulkley Avenue takes you away from the crowds to another world—the quiet, shady residential blocks. The houses may look rustic, but their price tags are astronomical, rising as you ascend the hill. Here's where you'll also find the most scenic spot in town for lunch, the Alta Mira Hotel. Be warned that many of the restaurants in town serve up views that far surpass their food, but for lunch it won't matter so much if you are content to feast on scenery.

At the Alta Mira, sadly, the rooms don't quite live up to the location, either. The Sausalito Hotel, the old-timer on El Portal, has few frills but lots of authentic Victoriana. But Sausalito does have one exceptional inn, the Casa Madrona, comprising a series of princely accommodations climbing up the hill from Bridgeway. Every room is different, and each has a name to match its decor—the Gingham Room for blue-and-white Victorian, the La Salle for the feel of a French country manor, the Mariner Room for nautical redwood and brass. Even less expensive rooms have Bay views, but those labeled deluxe are the choice for a special romantic getaway. Many have fireplaces and decks with wonderful vistas. Casa Madrona also has one of Sausalito's best restaurants.

Come back to Vina del Mar Plaza and take a stroll on the boardwalk at the edge of the Sausalito Yacht Harbor to admire the sleek sailing beauties that crowd the shoreline. This is nirvana for sailors, and on a sunny day the Bay is a patchwork pattern of blue water and white sails. Experienced sailors can rent a boat, or you can charter one with a skipper.

Take the bike path beyond the harbor or drive about two miles from the center of town to the northern area along the water to see the colorful houseboat area known as Marinship. It was a major shipbuilding site during World War II, but when the Kaiser shipyards moved out, bohemians and artists came in and built floating homes out of salvaged materials. Near Gate 5 you can walk the docks to see a setting that will start your camera clicking. Each houseboat has its own funky architecture, but all seem to share a love of flowers, and colorful plantings liven the scene.

The time to see the work of some of these artisans is over Labor Day weekend, when the Sausalito Art Festival is in full swing; the only drawback is the added crowds in a town that already has too many visitors.

Another unusual attraction in the Marinship area is the Bay Model Visitors' Center. Supervised by the U.S. Army Corps of Engineers, the Bay Model is a useful scientific tool for engineers and scientists, a working model of the San Francisco Bay and Delta region that covers more than an acre, with tides that rise and fall to simulate the tides of the Bay. It is most interesting for visitors when it is being operated, but since there is no regular schedule, you'll have to phone ahead for dates. Tours of the *Wapama,* the rugged steam schooner at the dock, are offered every Saturday at 11 A.M.

On Sunday it's time to get out of town. If Sausalito's views appear unbeatable, as the saying goes, "You ain't seen nothing yet." The Marin Headlands area of the Golden Gate National Recreation Area offers 12,500 acres of wild coastal bluffs and protected valleys extending from the north end of the Golden Gate Bridge northward to Muir Beach. Long used for lighthouses and military installations, the area offers views that are guaranteed to thrill even the most jaded.

To get there from Sausalito, follow Bridgeway all the way through town toward the Golden Gate Bridge, go under the bridge, take Alexander Avenue heading up, and watch for Marin Headlands signs. Finding the road can be tricky; it's easy to get lost among the military buildings at Ft. Baker. If all else fails, return to Highway 101, get off at Alexander Avenue, and take the first turn leading under the bridge.

Once you're on your way up, stay on Conzelman Road until you reach Point Bonita, a five-mile climb above the bridge towers that affords an astounding view of San Francisco. There are lots of beauty spots along the way where you can stop to ooh and ah, including Battery Spencer and Hill 129, better known as Hawk Hill. The military bunkers you'll pass were in use from the Spanish-American War to World War II.

You can park and walk up the concrete fire road to the top of Hawk Hill to see the thousands of raptors—hawks, kestrels, harriers, eagles, and other birds of prey—that soar overhead in September and October, the peak season for their annual migration. During these months, volunteers from the Golden Gate Raptor Observatory have logged as many as 2,800 birds on a peak day, and recorded 19 varieties of birds. More than 10,000 are spotted in a typical season. Often in October hawks are caught and banded for study, providing visitors a chance to see these majestic birds close up.

Feeling adventurous? Continue to the end of the road, park, and take the half-mile walk to Point Bonita Lighthouse. The path leads along a narrow ridge, through a hand-dug tunnel, and across a narrow footbridge to another amazing perspective: the coastline stretching north and south, the Pacific, and San Francisco's towers gleaming in the distance like El Dorado. The first lighthouse went up here in 1855 to warn ships caught in the fog. A cannon was fired every half hour in foggy weather, day and night. Now there's an automatic sentinel that sends out light and issues periodic booms of warning—not quite as romantic as a cannon, but probably more efficient. The lighthouse is open to visitors on weekends from 12:30 P.M. to 4 P.M.

Battery Wallace, near the Point Bonita trailhead, is a great scenic spot for a picnic, with tables overlooking the Golden Gate Bridge. For more hiking information, including schedules of guided hikes, follow the signs to the visitors' center. Rangers lead many walks focusing on special themes ranging from bird watching, wildflowers, and waterfalls to coastal military activities. Ask also for information about the Miwok Stables, which offer guided horseback rides in the area.

Many walks lead from the cliffs to the beach. An easily accessible spot is Rodeo Beach, a good place for picnics or kite flying. There are more wide, easy coastal trails in the Tennessee Valley, named for the S.S. *Tennessee*, shipwrecked offshore.

If you're not up for a hike, there are other attractions. The California Marine Mammal Center is where sea lions, seals, and other sea creatures that need medical care are nursed back to health. You're likely to find 20 or more animals in residence, with volunteers coaxing them to eat or play or sit still for an injection. Some of the patients are cute; others will break your heart. Come at feeding time, however, and even the feeblest seem to perk up for the fishy pablum that is poured down their gullets.

The newest attraction in the Marin Headlands is the Bay Area Discovery Museum, which moved into several of the old military buildings at East Ft. Baker in April 1991. They are now filled with lively hands-on exhibits for children ages 1 to 10. "Architecture and Design" and "San Francisco Bay" are themes for imaginative displays where kids can use drafting tools, work the crane at a mock building site, and wiggle through an "undersea" tunnel full of starfish, rockfish, and seaweed in a replica of San Francisco Bay. There's a science lab for making plaster casts of a critter paw print, a media center where kids can create their own videos and computer graphics. There are lots of special changing exhibits and weekend workshops for children and their families. The Discovery Store is stocked with imaginative toys, books, and interactive science projects to take home.

It's easy to spend a day enjoying this superb setting. Then maybe wander back into Sausalito for a last dinner and a look at the San Francisco skyline as dusk sets in and the lights go on. It's hard to imagine a more magical ending to a weekend.

Area Code: 415

DRIVING DIRECTIONS   Sausalito is off Highway 101, the first exit north of the Golden Gate Bridge. It is 8 miles from San Francisco, 100 miles from Sacramento.

ACCOMMODATIONS   *Casa Madrona,* 801 Bridgeway, Sausalito, 94965, 332-0502 or (800) 567-9524, E–EE, CP • *Alta Mira Hotel,* 125 Bulkley Avenue, Sausalito, 94966, 332-1350, M–EE • *Sausalito Hotel,* 16 El Portal, Sausalito, 95965, 332-4155, M–EE, CP • *Golden Gate Hostel,* Ft. Barry, Marin Headlands, 94965, 331-2777, scenic spot for hikers and budget-minded weekenders, I.

DINING   *Casa Madrona* (see above), the California cuisine is very good, the view superb, M–E • *Christophe,* 1919 Bridgeway, 332-9244, intimate French bistro, good value, M • *Guernica,* 2009 Bridgeway, 332-1512, Spanish menu, attractive, informal, I–M • *North Sea Village,* 300 Turney Street (at Bridgeway), 331-3300, good and reasonable Chinese, I • *The Spinnaker,* 100 Spinnaker Drive, Sausalito, 332-1500, average seafood with spectacular views, I–M • *Alta Mira Hotel* (see above), go for lunch and the view, I; dinner, M • For breakfast, the unanimous choice is *Fred's Place,* 1917 Bridgeway, 332-4575, a no-frills local tradition for breakfast, with big portions and legendary French toast, I.

SIGHTSEEING   *Bay Model Visitors' Center,* 2100 Bridgeway, 332-3870. Hours: Memorial Day to Labor Day, Tuesday to Friday 9 A.M. to 4 P.M., Saturday and Sunday 10 A.M. to 6 P.M.; rest of year, Tuesday to Saturday 9 A.M. to 4 P.M. Free • *Marin Headlands,* attractions include: *Visitor Center,* Ft. Cronkhite, Rodeo Valley, 331-1540. Hours: Daily 9:30 A.M. to 4:30 P.M.; *California Marine Mammal Center,* Ft. Cronkhite, 289-7334. Hours: Daily 10 A.M. to 4 P.M. Free; *Bay Area Discovery Museum,* 557 East Ft. Baker, Sausalito, 289-7268. Hours: Wednesday to Sunday 10 A.M. to 5 P.M., open Tuesdays also June 15 to September 15. Admission, $5; free on the first Thursday of each month; *Golden Gate Raptor Observatory,* schedules and information from Visitor Center • *Miwok Stable,* 701 Tennessee Valley Road, 383-8048. Hours: Tuesday to Sunday 9 A.M. to 4:30 P.M.

INFORMATION *Sausalito Chamber of Commerce,* 333 Caledonia Street, Sausalito, CA 94965, 332-0505.

Carving Out Fun at Half Moon Bay

Get ready to carve a healthy slice of fall fun in Half Moon Bay. For more than 20 years this little seaside town in the heart of pumpkin-growing country has been headquarters in mid-October for a rousing Art and Pumpkin Festival celebrating the annual harvest. Pumpkin-carving and pie-eating contests and all kinds of pumpkin pageantry— musical entertainment from jazz to rock, parades, a costume ball, mimes, magicians, and clowns—are all designed to pay homage to fall's favorite plump orange symbol. The *Art* in the festival name is for the excellent outdoor arts and crafts displays that accompany the pumpkin proceedings.

Come and enjoy the hoopla, then escape the crowds for some of the many other pleasures of this area—miles of nearby beaches, groves of tall redwoods, dining in a quaint fishing harbor, and staying in some very special inns. Far from least, there's the chance to pick your own perfect pumpkin and bring it home for Halloween. Just be sure to reserve your room well ahead for the big weekend.

The purpose of the original Pumpkin Festival was to raise money to help spruce up a fading Main Street. Proceeds over the years have paid for trees, flowers, park benches, old-fashioned streetlights, and a new park with a gazebo. The event is still sponsored by the Main Street Beautification Committee, but festival crowds have grown so large that local nonprofit groups now share the bounty. Many of them also set up food booths as their big fund-raising effort for the year.

The pumpkin doings actually start on the Monday before the festi-val, when growers from all over Northern California compete in the Great Pumpkin Weigh-Off at Kitty Fernandez Park on Main Street. Some of the champions have topped 500 pounds. The mighty winner each year gets a hefty cash prize and is the star of the Great Pumpkin parade on Saturday at noon, which also includes marching bands and classic cars.

Half Moon Bay is an appealing town even without special doings. It is one of the oldest settlements on this coastline, with some of the buildings on Main Street dating back more than 130 years. The first Mexican settlers called it San Benito, then Spanishtown, but the name that stuck was inspired by the crescent-shaped harbor. In the late 1800s many European settlers moved in to take advantage of the region's fortunate combination of fishing and fertile farmland.

You can best appreciate the breezy, old-fashioned charm of this community of some 9,000 residents on a walk down the short Main Street. A must stop is the Half Moon Bay Bakery. Many of the town's early settlers were Portuguese, and you can still buy delicious Portuguese sweet bread here, baked in a traditional brick oven. Stop at the old-fashioned Cunha Country Store for sandwich makings to go with that bread and you're ready for a dandy beach picnic later on.

Though the town is firmly resisting touristy development (they call it "Carmelization"), there are several interesting small shops and galleries along Main. The Coastal Arts League Museum, with changing exhibits that often include works by local artists, is on Highway 1, known here as the Cabrillo Highway.

The Tin Palace on Main Street, a renovated auto showroom, offers a variety of wares, including toys and handmade quilts. One of the most handsome shops on Main is the Cavanagh Gallery, with folk art, handcrafts, gifts, and fine reproductions of country furniture. Some of the furniture is used in the attractive rooms in the Half Moon Bay Inn.

This is only one of several pleasing lodgings in town. The Zaballa House is choice, an elegantly furnished recent restoration of the town's oldest building, circa 1859. The Old Thyme Inn, an antique-filled 1899 home at the other end of Main Street, is another charmer. Both inns have some rooms with claw-foot tubs, fireplaces, and whirlpools. For a special occasion, splurge for the Old Thyme Inn's Garden Suite, with a double whirlpool beneath a skylight.

Another romantic getaway is the Mill Rose Inn, a luxurious Victorian hideaway with brass beds, fancy wallpaper, and a Jacuzzi tub in a flower-filled gazebo. Lovely English gardens surround this intimate inn, making it a popular choice for weddings. But you don't have to be a honeymooner to enjoy one nice touch here—a champagne breakfast in bed.

Some of the choicest lodgings are north of town. The loveliest inn in the area is the Seal Cove Inn at Moss Beach. Owner Karen Brown Herbert has spent many years writing about inns and she has put her experience and taste to work beautifully in this lavish hideaway, a cross between English country and California chic, with a romantic view of the distant sea framed by a beautiful garden and towering cypress trees.

Ocean lovers may also find romance at the contemporary Cypress Inn, just above Half Moon Bay, where every room has a deck with an ocean view and you step out the door onto a five-mile strand of sandy beach. There's also a fireplace in each room to warm a cool night. The breezy inn is furnished with wicker and filled with colorful folk art.

And there's an in-house masseuse offering massages accompanied by the sounds of the sea just outside.

If you prefer the amenities of a modern small hotel, the Pillar Point Inn is just a few miles away in Princeton. It is directly across from Pillar Point Harbor, a haven for boaters and for diners out for a tasty seafood dinner. For families who are more comfortable in a motel, the pleasant Half Moon Bay Lodge offers views of the Half Moon Bay golf course, and the Harbor View Inn, a motel four miles north in Granada, has moderate rates and is convenient to Pillar Point Harbor. If you don't need frills, kids as well as grown-ups will enjoy a stay at either of two of America's most unusual hostels, the Pigeon Point Lighthouse in Pescadero and the Point Montara Lighthouse in Montara, both a short drive away. Each has family rooms and rooms for couples as well as group accommodations.

On Saturday, you will probably be happily occupied with pumpkin pursuits. But when you've had enough festival, you'll find it's great fun driving out of town to see the pumpkin farms along Highway 92, packed end-to-end with big orange beauties. There are big guys for jack-o'-lanterns, smaller ones for pies—you're sure to find the perfect take-home souvenirs. And there is plenty of farm-fresh produce to be found in this rich agricultural center.

Write ahead for the "Coastside Harvest Trails" brochure, a guide to the many fruit and vegetable farms in the area where you can pick up other fresh bounty besides pumpkins. G. Berta's on Highway 92, for example, lists French carrots, broccoli, cauliflower, and leeks as fall specialties.

Sunday's possibilities are varied. There are miles of state beaches for combing, and many places for viewing sea life and birds. To the south, Pescadero Marsh Natural Preserve offers trails into the marshes, a sanctuary for hundreds of birds, mammals, and amphibians. On weekends a park ranger and docent lead informative hikes. The Pigeon Point Lighthouse is also open for tours on Sundays. A national historic landmark dating to 1872, it still has its original Fresnel lens.

Bikers can take the horse trail on the bluffs, which runs for six miles along the ocean from Half Moon Bay north to Moss Beach. There are scenic spots for picnicking all along the way. Bikes are for rent at the Bicyclery on Main Street in Half Moon Bay.

The Fitzgerald Marine Reserve in Moss Beach is one of Northern California's largest natural tide pool reserves, and holds a cache of treasures at low tide. A few miles farther north, the Point Montara Lighthouse complex is one of the most-photographed in the state. The red-roofed yellow buildings lining the cliff above the ocean make for a pretty picture. At McNee Ranch State Park nearby, walking trails on Montara Mountain take you 2,000 feet above sea level for wonderful views.

Another kind of outing is a walk into the Purissima Creek Redwoods. Situated inland from Half Moon Bay, this serene and stately preserve of lush giants lies on the western slopes of the Santa Cruz mountains. There are some challenging mountain bike trails here.

For a real change of pace, how about splurging on a whale-watching expedition by seaplane? Blue whales are usually around in the fall, humpbacks from June to November.

Whatever you do, don't leave without a look at picturesque Pillar Point Harbor. A seafood dinner with a harbor view ends the weekend in a nicely nautical mood.

Area Code: 415

DRIVING DIRECTIONS Half Moon Bay is on Highway 1. From Highway 101 or I-280, take Highway 92 west. Continue past Highway 1, the Cabrillo Highway, and turn onto Main Street, the heart of town. Half Moon Bay is 28 miles from San Francisco, 43 miles from San Jose, 155 miles from Sacramento.

ACCOMMODATIONS *Zaballa House,* 324 Main Street, Half Moon Bay, 94019, 726-9123, M–E, CP • *Old Thyme Inn,* 779 Main Street, Half Moon Bay, 94019, 726-1616, M–EE, CP • *Mill Rose Inn,* 615 Mill Street, Half Moon Bay, 94019, 726-9794, EE, CP • *Half Moon Bay Bed & Breakfast Inn,* 413 Main Street, Half Moon Bay, 94019, 726-9363, M, CP • *Seal Cove Inn,* 221 Cypress Avenue, Moss Beach, 94038, 728-7325, EE, CP • *Cypress Inn,* 407 Mirada Road, Miramar Beach, Half Moon Bay, 94019, 726-6002, EE, CP • *Pillar Point Inn,* 380 Capistrano Road, Princeton-by-the-Sea, 94018, 728-7377, E–EE, CP • *Half Moon Bay Lodge* (motel), 2400 South Cabrillo Highway (Highway 1), 94019, 726-9000, M–E • *Harbor View Inn* (motel), 11 Avenue Alhambra, El Granada, 94018, 726-2329, I • *Point Montara Lighthouse and AYH Hostel,* 16th Street at Cabrillo Highway (Highway 1), Montara, 94037, 728-7177, I • *Pigeon Point Lighthouse AYH Hostel,* Pescadero, 94060, 879-0633, I.

DINING *Pasta Moon,* 325 Main Street, Half Moon Bay, 726-5125, local favorite for excellent Italian food, homemade pastas, I–M • *San Benito House,* Main and Mill streets, Half Moon Bay, 726-3425, many say best in town, M • *The Foglifter,* Highway 1 and Eighth Street, Montara, 728-7905, unpretentious ambience, creative chef, I–M • *Moss Beach Distillery,* Beach and Ocean streets, Moss Beach, 728-5595, seafood, lively ambience, ocean views, M • *The Shore Bird,* 390 Capistrano Road, Princeton-by-the-Sea, 728-5541, seafood in a great spot overlooking the harbor, I–M • *Chart House,* 8150 Cabrillo Highway, Montara, 728-7366, steak and seafood overlooking Montara Beach, M.

SIGHTSEEING *Half Moon Bay Art & Pumpkin Festival,* Main Street, Half Moon Bay, 726-7133, held annually in mid-October. Phone for current dates and schedule • *Coastal Arts League Museum,* 225 South Cabrillo Highway, Half Moon Bay, 728-7770. Hours: Thursday to Sunday noon to 5 P.M. Free • *Pigeon Point Lighthouse,* Highway 1, Pescadero, 879-0633. Hours: Sunday only, 45-minute tours on the hour, 11 A.M. to 3 P.M., weather permitting. Adults, $2; children, $1 • *Pescadero Marsh Natural Preserve,* Highway 1 and Route 84, Pescadero, 879-2170. Hours: Daily sunrise to sunset • *Fitzgerald Marine Reserve,* California Street, Moss Beach, 728-3584. Hours: Daily sunrise to sunset, walking trails, guided tours on Sunday. Phone for schedules. Free • *Purissima Creek Redwoods,* Higgins Purissima Road, Half Moon Bay. Hours: Daily sunrise to sunset. Free.

INFORMATION *Half Moon Bay Coastside Chamber of Commerce,* 520 Kelly Street, Half Moon Bay, CA, 726-8380, 726-5202 to request written information • *"Coastside Harvest Trails,"* 765 Main Street, Half Moon Bay, CA 94019, 726-4485, free map and listing of area farms, shopping, and sightseeing.

Finding the Heart of San Francisco

Be prepared. If you are like most of the wildly partisan 750,000 residents and the 3 million visitors who flock here each year, you, too, will lose your heart to San Francisco. Who can resist a city on a heavenly bay where every one of the 40 hilltops seems to offer a more spectacular view? Gloriously gaudy Victorian homes, sleek skyscrapers, grand beaux arts architecture, majestic bridges, a diversity of ethnic neighborhoods and lifestyles, an incomparable waterfront, and world-class dining—all of these add to the allure of California's beautiful city by the Bay. Wrapped in romantic fog or glowing golden in the sunlight, it is a city that never fails to enchant.

Many books have been written entirely on San Francisco for those with time for in-depth visits. This chapter is intended for first-timers who want to make the most of a weekend in the city, hoping to glimpse the heart that makes it tick. Autumn is the hands-down winner for best time to visit. It is the city's most agreeable season, with warm days and little fog.

San Francisco is basically a hilly peninsula of 47 square miles with water, water everywhere—the Pacific Ocean to the west, the Bay to the east, the two joined by a narrow strait spanned by the Golden Gate Bridge. It was the discovery of gold that changed a sleepy port town forever, spiraling the population from 900 to 56,000 in one fateful year, 1849–50. The mansions on Nob Hill bear witness to ensuing years, when fortunes were made by people like Levi Strauss, who sold clothing to the prospectors, and the famous quartet of Huntington, Hopkins, Stanford, and Crocker, who became tycoons after completion of their transcontinental railroad.

Everyone knows about the 1906 earthquake and the fire that followed, destroying four fifths of the town. Fortunately, many of the residential areas west of Van Ness were not destroyed, and protecting these early homes spawned a passion for preservation that has never waned. Even the cable cars that began service in 1872 are precious and protected in San Francisco.

Within a decade the city rebuilt, during a "City Beautiful" movement that gave rise to many fine beaux arts buildings such as the domed City Hall. The resurrection was celebrated with the 1915 Panama-Pacific International Exposition. The Palace of Fine Arts in the Marina District was the centerpiece for that exposition.

Striking modern architecture came later, including the Transamerica Pyramid, the focal point of the city's rising skyline, and the Embarcadero District, a well-planned blend of businesses, residences, and parks studded with sculptures. New structures were built to withstand earthquakes, and while bridges and older Marina structures crumbled in 1989, the city's skyscrapers stood firm.

To see these facets of the city, the best starting point is Union Square, a palm-studded green oasis bound by Stockton, Geary, Post, and Powell streets in the heart of the shopping and theater districts. Staying within a few blocks of Union Square allows walking to shopping, Chinatown, the financial district, the Embarcadero, the growing art scene in SOMA ("south of Market Street"), and many other attractions, plus easy access to public transportation to get to other areas.

Nearby hotels include many moderately priced choices as well as the towers atop Nob Hill and the most deluxe city properties. "Moderate" in the city spills into the expensive category, but many pleasant hotels such as the European-style Savoy and Regis, the light and airy Juliana and the Villa Florence, the sleek modernistic Diva, and some charming small inns like the Nob Hill Inn, the Inn at Union Square, and the Petite Auberge can be booked for between $100 and $125 a night, sometimes less on weekend packages. Among even less expensive choices, the Beresford Arms stands out.

Personal picks among the city's ultradeluxe hotels are the Ritz Carlton, for those who want grand, new, and sumptuous luxury, and the Clift, whose gracious, understated elegance and caring personal service keep it at the top even in the face of stiff new competition. The Redwood Room at the Clift, with its burnished walls, is the city's most gracious watering hole.

Much of San Francisco is wonderfully walkable, and some of the excellent walking tours are a highly recommended way to learn about the city. On your own, steep hills can make the going tough. With a transit map and a MUNI Passport, a one- or three-day transit ticket, you can walk when you feel like it, and hop on buses, cable cars, or underground MUNI Metro trains at will to get you to your next destination.

To get a MUNI Passport, from Union Square, walk away from the hills on Powell Street to Market Street and stop in at the Visitors' Information Center on the lower level at Hallidie Plaza, or at the cable car ticket booth at the corner. Passes give big fare discounts and also eliminate worry about having exact change to board. (Note that the three-day pass costs less than two one-day passes.)

The things that most first-timers want to see most of all are cable cars, hills, Victorian houses, and Fisherman's Wharf, and this can be accomplished neatly just by boarding the Powell Street cable car, which climbs to the mansions of Nob Hill and descends to the waterfront. The Hyde-Powell trolley line has the most curves and best views, including a dizzying look down at Lombard Street, one of the steepest and most zigzag of the city's many hills, widely known as "the crookedest street in the world."

To take the trolley without long waits, come early, before the lines form, or take a tip from the natives and don't board at the start of the line on Market. Look at the route on the map, find an intersection with a yellow rectangle painted on the pavement between the cable rails, and just step into the street and wait as the car approaches. It will stop for you. If you should be lucky enough to get a seat, the outside left side offers the best view.

Get off at Nob Hill to admire the architecture, the fine Grace Cathedral, and one of the classic San Francisco views. Stop at the Trolley Car Museum at Washington and Mason streets later if you want to find out how these landmarks-in-motion are kept in service.

San Franciscans sneer at Fisherman's Wharf, with its crowds, tourist-trap shops, and seafood stands, but don't let a local friend talk you out of the trip. Those of us not lucky enough to live here tend to overlook the touristy and see the wonder—the panorama of the Bay and the Golden Gate Bridge, the working fishing fleet, and the fun of buying a fresh Dungeness crab cocktail or clam chowder in a sourdough bread bowl and settling down on a bench to munch while sea lions put on a show, frisking around in the harbor and adding a cacophony of barks to the salty air.

If you have the time, various boat trips let you cruise the harbor, ride to picturesque Marin County, or see the infamous prison on Alcatraz Island. All give you a closer look at that most famous of all San Francisco symbols, the lofty Golden Gate Bridge. The San Francisco Maritime National Historic Park is nearby at Aquatic Park (see more about the waterfront in "Kidding Around in San Francisco," page 224).

The Anchorage complex near Fisherman's Wharf, Pier 39, Ghirardelli Square, a onetime chocolate factory, and the Cannery, a former fruit packing plant, are the main shopping centers on the waterfront. They are less interesting than they used to be, as many of the tenants now are chain stores with branches almost everywhere. But you can still watch chocolate being made at the Ghirardelli Chocolate Manufactory, and there's always fun from the street entertainers hanging around—balloon sculptors, jugglers, mimes, and a "human jukebox."

One of the best things to do along the waterfront is simply to walk away from the crowds toward the bridge on the Golden Gate Promenade. No city in the world has a more remarkable walkway than this four-mile path beside the Bay leading past Aquatic Park along the water all the way to the bridge. Stop at Ft. Mason, an old military base that has been converted into a unique, community-based arts center, with old warehouses now housing small avant-garde troupes for theater, music, and dance, plus galleries and small museums that otherwise might not be able to afford space. You may have to save the museums for a second visit, but do have lunch at Greens in Building A for delicious vegetarian food, homemade bread, and one of the city's most breathtaking views.

Ft. Mason is also headquarters for the Golden Gate National Recreation Area; if you want to include city hiking on your agenda, stop here for information.

When you are rested and ready to continue walking, go beyond Ft. Mason to Marina Green, where joggers and kite flyers hold sway. Beyond is the Palace of Fine Arts, impressive with its Corinthian colonnade and Greco-Roman rotunda, and a pleasant walk, but not really a must on limited time—unless you have kids along for a visit to the Exploratorium here. Next comes the Saint Francis Yacht Club, with a forest of masts in its harbor, followed by playing fields and the Presidio, a military base on prime waterfront that is being incorporated into the National Park Service land. As both army post and national park, it offers forests, creeks, trails, views, and military history.

Turn inland at Marina Green to walk through some of the streets of the charming Marina neighborhood, where pastel low-rise stucco homes are reminiscent of the Mediterranean. A few blocks up is Chestnut Street, a favorite hangout for young San Franciscans. When you want to head farther uphill, the bus on Fillmore Street will drop you on Union Street, one of the city's most appealing enclaves and another prime gathering place for young singles action.

This section was once a valley known as Cow Hollow, a green dale of dairy farms, and later a modest residential area. Nowadays, on the streets between Fillmore and Van Ness, former clapboard homes, carriage houses, stables, and barns have become home to flower-filled mews and coffeehouses, lively cafés, chic boutiques, and pricey antiques stores. Of special interest to architecture buffs is the Octagon House, 2645 Gough Street at Union Street, an 1861 heirloom maintained by the National Society of Colonial Dames. It can be admired anytime but toured only on Wednesdays and Sundays.

Continuing still farther uphill, stop at Broadway and turn right for Pacific Heights, where many of the city's grandest mansions sit high above terraced gardens. Pause where Broderick crosses Broadway for one of the city's incomparable views—the Marina, the Palace of Fine Arts, the Bay, and the Golden Gate Bridge spread before you.

Some nearby mansions of special note within the next several blocks include the Spreckels Mansion, 2080 Washington Street; the Whittier Mansion, 2090 Jackson Street; and the Bourn Mansion at 2550 Webster Street. The Haas Lilienthal House, 2007 Franklin Street, is a fully furnished Eastlake Victorian and headquarters for the Foundation for San Francisco's Architectural Heritage.

Check the MUNI map for the closest eastbound bus to bring you back to Stockton Street, where it is only a few blocks farther to Union Square.

Shopping may or may not be on your city agenda, but a stroll around Union Square will show you some of the city's top stores—Macy's, Nieman-Marcus, and Saks Fifth Avenue among them. Post Street seems to have the poshest of the boutiques. Don't fail to walk into Gumps, a local institution and a mini-museum of jade and other Oriental imports.

More major shopping is just a short stroll away at the San Francisco Shopping Centre, Market and Fifth streets, a vertical mall beneath a dramatic atrium shared by Nordstrom, the Emporium, and many fashionable smaller shops.

This puts you at the edge of SOMA, which is rapidly emerging as the city's newest arts center. Within the past few years, the neighborhood has gained two major attractions, the Center for the Arts at Yerba Buena Gardens and, right across the street, the San Francisco Museum of Modern Art.

The Center is a striking modern $44 million dollar complex with galleries for changing exhibitions and theaters with a wide variety of offerings, often focusing on the talents and interests of the city's many ethnic groups. It overlooks a five-acre downtown park with terrace cafés, an outdoor performance area, and a walk-through waterfall leading to a memorial for Dr. Martin Luther King.

Equally impressive is the light, soaring showplace designed for the

Museum of Modern Art by Mario Botta, which opened its doors in 1995. It is the nation's second largest showcase for modern art. You can't miss the building, with its steel-and-glass skylight mounted at 45 degrees on a granite-banded turret to allow sunlight into the museum atrium. The circular design emblazoned on top is the easily recognizable symbol of the museum.

More museums are on the way in this exciting new neighborhood, including a Mexican Museum, a Jewish Museum, and the California Historical Society. Already in place are the Ansel Adams Center, dedicated to fine photography, with changing shows and a permanent exhibit of Adams's work, and San Francisco's Old Mint Museum, in a classic building dating from 1874.

With all of this, plus the Moscone Convention Center on the next block, it is not surprising that restaurants and clubs are blooming in SOMA, along with an arty new hotel, the Milano.

Earlier development can be seen on the eastern edge of SOMA at 101 Spear, where the art deco Rincon Annex Post Office complex has become a mix of offices, condos, shops, and popular new restaurants. Walk a block beyond, heading toward the water, to Steuart and the Embarcadero area. The water views here are better than ever since the Embarcadero Freeway was removed after the 1989 earthquake. The ferry terminal is home port for commuter boats to Sausalito.

Turn north to Market Street to see the attractive mix of buildings and greenery at Maritime Plaza. A quick Metro underground ride will whisk you back to Union Square, or you can take the flat, easy walk along Market Street (roughly ten blocks), passing the Financial District, the center of which is Montgomery Street, San Francisco's Wall Street and home to the Pacific Coast Stock Exchange. The walk gives you the chance to stop and see the dazzling renovation of the Victorian Garden Court at the Sheraton Palace Hotel at Market and New Montgomery streets. It's a grand place for afternoon tea.

San Francisco's Chinatown is another essential sight. By day you can see markets selling exotic greens and trussed ducks, most clustered in the 1000 to 1200 blocks on Stockton Street. By night the neon glitters brightest over hosts of restaurants on Grant Street, spilling over to Kearny. Don't go by the facades—some of the most unlikely hole-in-the-wall places have the best food. When you see the line outside the unpromising premises of House of Nanking on Kearny, for example, join it—those people are waiting with good reason.

If you can find time and energy for a 1.9-mile walk, Grant Street from Market Street to Pier 39 will show you many facets of San Francisco. It begins in high style near Union Square with shops like Brooks Brothers and Tiffany, opening onto Campton Place and Tillman Place for more shops and a chic hotel. At Bush Street, an ornamental gate marks the official beginning of Chinatown. Walk on past grimacing temple dogs and golden lions and many small shops crammed with Chinese goods, from art objects to souvenir trinkets. If you want to learn something about the biggest Chinese stronghold outside Asia, detour for the Chinese Historical Society of America on Commercial Street between Kearny and Montgomery streets. The Chinese Culture Center on the third floor of the Holiday Inn on Kearny has changing exhibits of Chinese arts and crafts.

At Broadway, Chinatown gives way to the neon lights of clubs on Broadway, then continues into Italian North Beach, and moves on to the Embarcadero and the Bay.

If you settle for visiting Chinatown at night, you'll still see a lot; the shops stay open late. The city's fine Civic Center can also be seen at night by taking in an evening performance of the opera, ballet, or symphony, all of which are housed in this handsome mix of beaux arts, Renaissance, and modernist architecture. Check the STBS booth on the Stockton Street side of Union Square for day-of-performance tickets at half price for events that are not sold out, including theater, concerts, and dance.

An evening at the Civic Center gives you the opportunity to sample the fare at the lineup of good dining along Van Ness Street's "Restaurant Row" or nearby at some favorites such as Stars and the Zuñi Café. But then, dining in this city is literally a movable feast, for wherever you go there are wonderful choices, more than 4,000 restaurants in all, from haute to hip.

There are two more quintessential San Francisco sights. Take in one of the city's best panoramas from the Coit Tower at the summit of Telegraph Hill. Take the No. 30 bus from Stockton and Sutter streets north to Union Street (Washington Square) and transfer to the No. 39 Coit bus to the top of the hill. The tower, a 210-foot cylindrical column, was built in 1934 as a WPA project. One way down is to take the Fillmore steps leading to the Embarcadero area, a steep descent on a wooden stairway past quaint wooden houses and terraced gardens.

Another possibility is to return to Washington Square and take a stroll around North Beach. Cradled by Telegraph Hill on the east and Russian Hill on the west, this lively Italian area offers espresso houses, gelato parlors, delicatessens brimming with prosciutto and mozzarella, tempting bakeries, and a host of good restaurants. Upper Grant Street has some colorful spots, including landmarks such as the Italian & French Baking Company and the Panama Canal Ravioli Factory. At night the North Beach mood changes a bit when the lights go on at strip joints on Broadway.

The final essential city sight is Golden Gate Park, offering 1,017 acres of escape, with a Conservatory of Flowers, a Japanese Tea Garden, lakes for paddling, a science museum, and an aquarium. Two of city's top three art museums are here: the M. H. de Young Memorial

Museum, housing a collection of American art and major traveling exhibits; and the Asian Art Museum, holding the priceless Avery Brundage collection of nearly 10,000 Oriental treasures.

One admission gets you into both these museums plus the stately California Palace of the Legion of Honor in Lincoln Park, a museum modeled after its namesake in France and with an oceanfront setting as marvelous as its displays of European masterpiece paintings and Rodin sculptures. This is out of the way, but the half-hour ride on the No. 2 Clement bus going from Sutter Street in midtown to the Palace provides a mini-tour of neighborhoods and the mix of modestly priced ethnic restaurants on Clement between Second and Tenth avenues that are favorites for San Franciscans on a budget. Russian, Vietnamese, Greek—just name your cuisine. This area also now holds about a third of the city's Chinese population.

Get off at Clement and 33rd and walk through the golf course to the Palace or transfer here to the No. 18, the 46th Avenue bus running directly to the museum. The No. 18 bus loops back to another favorite ocean viewpoint, the Cliff House, overlooking Ocean Beach and Seal Rocks.

If you can manage more, the choices are great. There's colorful browsing in the Castro District, the stronghold of the city's vital gay population, where shopkeepers have transformed 1880s Victorians into imaginative boutiques, bookstores, and watering places. Haight-Ashbury, the hippie heaven of the 1960s, is now a gentrified scene with antiques stores, funky shops, and used-clothing stores. And yes, you may sight a few remaining punks and hippies. The Japan Center, a focal point for the city's 12,000 Japanese residents, offers just a few shops, so it is mainly of interest for plush sushi bars and restaurants, all crowned by five-tiered pagodas. If you want to see a classic cluster of Victorian houses in rainbow hues, head for Alamo Square, on the way to Golden Gate Park.

In addition to the old adobe mission, San Francisco's oldest structure, the not-so-fancy Mission District offers Spanish flavor, especially along 24th Street, and the chance to see some 200 community murals, some as small as a door, others the size of a building. More than 30 of these are right on 24th Street, along with the Mission's art center, the Galeria de la Raza, at 24th and Bryant.

If the day is fine and you've had enough city, you are in the town with the largest urban park in the world, the Golden Gate National Recreation Area, with 114 square miles of green and miles of walking trails, many of them along the ocean and Bay. Then, of course, all those boat rides are waiting back in the harbor, not to mention the zoo and all the additional family attractions mentioned in "Kidding Around in San Francisco," pages 224 to 228—places you certainly need not be a kid to enjoy. Or you could rest your feet by getting into your car for a final city overview on the 49-mile scenic tour to catch the sights you've missed. Follow the sea gull signs or pick up a printed guide from the visitors' information center.

Let's face it, there's never enough time for everything in this effervescent city. You'll no doubt leave agreeing with Rudyard Kipling, who said: "San Francisco has only one drawback—'tis hard to leave."

Area Code: 415

DRIVING DIRECTIONS San Francisco is located directly on Highways 1 and 101 coming north or south and can be reached via I-80 across the Bay Bridge from the east. The western border is the Pacific Ocean.

PUBLIC TRANSPORTATION Almost all major airlines and bus lines serve the city. In town, public transportation is via buses, railway, and cable cars operated by the Municipal Railway; information from 673-MUNI.

ACCOMMODATIONS **Top-of-the-line:** *Clift Hotel*, Geary and Taylor streets, 94102, 775-4700 or (800) 332-3442, EE • *The Ritz Carlton,* 600 Stockton Street, 94108, 296-7465 or (800) 241-3333, EE • *Mandarin Oriental,* 222 Sansome Street, 94104, 885-0999, luxury 37 stories up, great views, EE • *Fairmont Hotel,* 950 Mason Street, Nob Hill, 94106, 772-5000 or (800) 527-4727, best of the Nob Hill old-timers, EE • *Stanford Court,* 905 California Street, Nob Hill, 94108, 989-3500 or (800) HOTELS-1, another hilltop celebrities' favorite, EE • *Campton Place,* 340 Stockton Street, 94108, 781-5555, gracious, small, serene, EE • *Hotel Nikko,* 222 Mason Street, 94102, 394-1111, big but with stunning contemporary Japanese decor, EE • **Vintage Victorian charm:** *Sherman House,* 2160 Green Street (one block off Union Street), 94123, 563-3600, ultimate elegance, EE, CP • *The Mansions,* 2220 Sacramento Street, 94115, 929-9444, quirky Old World charm, E–EE, CP • **Small and posh:** *Donatello,* 501 Post Street, 94102, 441-7100 or (800) 227-3184, in California (800) 792-9837 • *Inn at the Opera,* 333 Fulton Street (near the Civic Center), 94102, 863-8400, EE, CP • *The Inn at Union Square,* 440 Post Street, 94102, 397-3510 or (800) 288-4346, E–EE • *White Swan Inn,* 845 Bush Street, 94108, 775-1755, EE, CP • *Petite Auberge,* 863 Bush Street, 94108, 928-6000, E–EE, CP • *Hotel Milano,* 55 Fifth Street, 94103, 543-8555 or (800) 447-7462, E–EE • **Inn charm at more reasonable rates:** *The Savoy,* 580 Geary Street, 94102, (800) 227-4223, E • *The Bed & Breakfast Inn,* 4 Charlton Court (off Union Street), 94117, 921-9784, shared bath, M; private bath, E–EE • *Nob Hill Inn,*

1000 Pine Street, 94109, 673-6080, M–EE, CP • **Pleasant small hotels:** *Hotel Juliana*, 590 Bush Street, 94108, 392-2540 or in California (800) 372-8800, E, CP • *Villa Florence*, 225 Powell Street, 94102, 397-7700 or in California (800) 243-5700, E, CP • *Hotel Vintage Court*, 650 Bush Street, 94108, 392-4666, E, CP • *Hotel Triton*, 342 Grant Avenue, 94108, 394-0500 or (800) 433-6611, E–EE, CP • *Hotel Diva*, 440 Geary Street, 94102, 885-0200 or (800) 553-1900, E, CP • *Regis Hotel*, 490 Geary Street, 94102, 928-7900 or (800) 82-REGIS, M–E • *Monticello Inn*, 127 Ellis Street, 94102, 392-8800 or (800) 669-7777, E, CP • *Kensington Park*, 450 Post Street, 94102, 241-2929 or (800) 553-1900, M–E • *Cartwright Hotel*, 524 Sutter Street, 94102, 421-2865 or (800) 227-3844, E–EE • **Good values:** *Hotel Beresford*, 635 Sutter Street, 94102, 673-9900, M, CP • *Hotel Beresford Arms*, 701 Post Street, 94109, M, CP • *Golden Gate Hotel*, 775 Bush Street, 94108, 392-3702 or (800) 835-1118, M, CP • *Hotel Union Square*, 114 Powell Street, 94102, 397-3000 or (800) 553-1900, M–E, CP • *San Remo*, 2237 Mason Street, 94133, 776-8688 or (800) 352-REMO, bargain rates for those willing to forgo private baths, I • **Motels:** For families or anyone preferring a motel, these are convenient and pleasant, all M: *Cow Hollow Motor Inn*, 2190 Lombard Street, 94123, 924-5800 • *Chelsea Motor Inn*, 2095 Lombard Street, 94123, 563-5600 • *Coventry Motor Inn*, 1901 Lombard Street, 94123, 567-1200.

DINING   Critic's top choices: *Masa's*, 648 Bush Street, 989-7154, exquisite nouvelle French, EE • *Fleur de Lys*, 777 Sutter Street, 673-7779, French haute cuisine, E–EE • *La Folie*, 2316 Polk Street (between Union and Green), 776-5577, charming and excellent French food, E–EE • *Aqua*, 252 California, 956-9662, superb seafood, E–EE • *Chez Michel*, 804 Northpoint, 775-7036, the city's newest French star, the only fine dining near Ghiradelli Square and great value for the price, M • *Acquerello*, 1722 Sacramento Street at Van Ness, 567-5432, highly regarded Italian, E • *Postrio*, 545 Post Street, 776-7825, Wolfgang Puck's smash success, ultimate California cuisine, E–EE • *Stars*, 150 Redwood Alley (near the Civic Center), 861-7817, Jeremiah Tower's famous brasserie, M–EE • *Campton Place*, 340 Stockton Street, 781-5555, elegant setting for top California cuisine, E–EE • *The French Room*, Clift Hotel, 495 Geary Street (at Taylor Street), 775-4700, grand dining, exquisite traditional setting, prix fixe, EE • *Ritz Carlton Dining Room*, 600 Stockton Street, 296-7465, rave reviews for New American classics, E–EE • **Union Square area:** *Kuleto's*, 221 Powell Street, 397-7720, California-Italian cuisine, M–E • *Brasserie Savoy*, 580 Geary Street, 441-2700, casual, chic, M • **Van Ness area:** *Stars Café*, 555 Van Ness Avenue, 861-4344, lower-priced sibling next door to the original Stars, highly recommended, M • *Swan Oyster Depot*, 1517 Polk Street, 673-1101, excellent and reasonable seafood, M • *Golden Turtle*, 2211 Van Ness Avenue, 441-4419, top Vietnamese, I–M • **Embarcadero area:** *Square One,* 190 Pacific Avenue, 788-1110, raves for the owner-chef's home-style Mediterranean cuisine, M–E • *Fog City Diner,* 1300 Battery Street, 982-2000, a city institution, creative menus in a diner setting, M–E • *Etrusca,* 121 Spear Street, Rincon Center 2, 777-0330, tasty Italian, M–E • *Wu Kong,* 101 Spear Street, Rincon Center 1, 957-9300, great for dim sum, I–M • *Splendido's,* 4 Embarcadero, 986-3222, trendy, chic pizza, light fare, M • **North Beach area:** *Moose's,* 1652 Stockton Street, 989-7800, a real winner, attractive airy Mediterranean-Italian menu, M • *Washington Street Bar and Grill,* 1707 Powell Street (at Union), 982-8123, long-time neighborhood gathering place, jazz, M • *Caffe Roma,* 414 Columbus Avenue, 391-8584, favorite coffeehouse and café, I • **SOMA area:** *Restaurant Lulu & Lulu Bis,* 816 Folsom Street, 495-5775, wood-fired rotisserie, Tuscan influence, M; Lulu Bis serves family-style at long tables, prix fixe, EE • *Bistro M,* 55 Fifth Street, 543-5554, attractive modern brasserie decor, good food, M • **Union Street area:** *Doidge's Kitchen,* 227 Union Street, 921-2149, a tradition for breakfast, I • *Perry's,* 1944 Union Street, 922-9022, where the chic young meet and greet, good for light fare, Sunday brunch, I–M • **Chinatown:** *House of Nanking,* 919 Kearny Street, 421-1429, hole in the wall, long lines, but worth it for extraordinary food, I • *Hong Kong Tea House,* 835 Pacific Avenue, 391-6365, forget the decor, delicious dim sum, I • **All around town:** *One Market,* One Market Street (at Steuart), 777-5577, American brasserie, noted chef, M–E • *Boulevard,* One Mission Street, 543-6084, American home cooking, very well reviewed, M–E • *Zuñi Café,* 1658 Market Street, 552-2522, arty, casual, fun, always packed, M–E • *Tommy Toy's Chinoise,* 655 Montgomery Street, 397-4888, upscale Chinese, business district favorite, M • *Thep Phanom,* 400 Waller Street (at Fillmore), 431-2516, top Thai, in lower Haight, I • *Hayes Street Grill,* 320 Hayes Street, 863-5545, widely praised California bistro near the Civic Center, M–E • *Tadich Grill,* 240 California Street, 391-2373, long-time business district favorite for seafood, M–E • *Pacific Heights Bar and Grill,* 2001 Fillmore Street, 567-3337, popular for oyster bar, seafood, social scene, M • *Bix,* 56 Gold Street, 433-6300, chic downtown supper club, M–E • *Greens,* Building A, Ft. Mason, 771-6222, wonderful vegetarian dishes and fresh-baked breads, even better harbor views, I–M.

SIGHTSEEING *M. H. de Young Memorial Museum,* Golden Gate Park, 750-3600 or 863-3330, information tape. Hours: Wednesday to Sunday 10 A.M. to 5 P.M. Adults, $5; ages 12 to 17, $2; under 12, free. Free on the first Wednesday and Saturday (10 A.M. to noon) of the month. One admission ticket on the same day includes the adjoining *Asian Art Museum,* 668-8921, as well as *California Palace of the Legion of Honor,* Lincoln Park, 750-3600 • **SOMA attractions:** *San*

Francisco Museum of Modern Art, 151 Third Street, 357-4000. Hours: Tuesday to Sunday 11 A.M. to 6 P.M., Thursday to 9 P.M. Adults, $7; under 13, free. *Center for the Arts at Yerba Buena,* 701 Mission Street (at Third). Gallery hours: Tuesday to Sunday 11 A.M. to 6 P.M. Adults, $4; under 16, $2; for information on performing arts events, phone 978-ARTS • *Ansel Adams Center for Photography,* 250 Fourth Street, 495-7000. Hours: Tuesday to Sunday 11 A.M. to 5 P.M. Adults, $4; students, $3; under 12, free • *Old U.S. Mint,* Fifth and Mission streets, 744-6830. Monday to Friday 10 A.M. to 4 P.M. Free • *Ft. Mason Museums,* Buchanan and Marina Boulevard, include *San Francisco Craft and Folk Museum,* Building A, 775-0990. Hours: Tuesday to Friday and Sunday 11 A.M. to 5 P.M., Saturday 10 A.M. to 5 P.M. Admission, $1 • *Mexican Museum,* Building D, 441-0404. Hours: Wednesday to Sunday noon to 5 P.M. Adults, $3; students, $2; under 10, free • *Museo Italo Americano,* Building C, 673-2200. Hours: Wednesday to Sunday noon to 5 P.M. Free • *San Francisco African-American Historical and Cultural Society,* Building C, 441-0640, art exhibits, field trips to black historical sites. Hours: Wednesday to Sunday noon to 5 P.M. Donation • **Other attractions:** *Haas-Lilienthal House,* 2007 Franklin Street (at Jackson), 441-3004. Hours: Tours Wednesday noon to 3:15 P.M., Sunday 11 A.M. to 4:15 P.M. Adults, $4; children, $2. • *Mission Dolores,* 16th and Dolores streets, 621-8203. Hours: Daily 9 A.M. to 4 P.M. Donation, $1 • *Galleria de la Raza/Studio 24,* 2851 24th Street, 826-8009, Chicano and Latin art. Hours: Tuesday to Saturday noon to 6 P.M. Free • *Chinese Historical Society of America,* 650 Commercial Street, 391-1188. Hours: Tuesday to Saturday noon to 4 P.M. Donation • *Chinese Culture Center,* 750 Kearny Street, 3rd floor, Holiday Inn, Chinatown, 986-1822. Hours: Tuesday to Saturday 10 A.M. to 4 P.M. Free. See also the *National Maritime Museum, Cable Car Museum, California Academy of Sciences, Aquarium, Planetarium, Exploratorium,* and other attractions, pages 227 to 228.

BOAT RIDES *Red and White Fleet,* Piers 41 and 43½, Fisherman's Wharf, 546-2700 or (800) 229-8724, ferries daily for Sausalito and Tiburon; to Angel Island daily in summer, weekends in winter. Phone for current schedules and rates. Alcatraz trips, see page 227 • *Blue and Gold Fleet,* Pier 39, Fisherman's Wharf, 704-5555, sightseeing bay cruises, phone for current information.

WALKING TOURS Phone for current schedules, rates • *City Guides,* Friends of the San Francisco Public Library, 557-4266, history, architecture, culture, neighborhoods • *Heritage Walks,* Foundation for San Francisco's Architectural Heritage, 441-3004, architectural walks • *All About Chinatown,* 982-8839 • *Wok Wiz,* 355-9657, more Chinatown • *Friends of Recreation and Parks,* 221-1311, Golden Gate Park tours, weekends May to October • *Cruisin' the Castro,* 550-8110 •

Precita Eyes Mural Center, 285-2287, Mission District murals • **Hiking:** *Golden Gate National Recreation Area,* Ft. Mason Information Center, 441-5706; general information, 556-0560.

INFORMATION *San Francisco Convention & Visitor Bureau,* P.O. Box 6977, San Francisco, CA 94101, 391-2000 • *Visitor Information Center,* Hallidie Plaza, Powell and Market streets, lower level. Hours: Monday to Friday 9 A.M. to 5:30 P.M., Saturday 9 A.M. to 3 P.M., Sunday 10 A.M. to 2 P.M. Daily events information, 391-2001.

WINTER

Overleaf: *Winter wonder in Yosemite. Photo courtesy of Eleanor Berman.*

An Old-Fashioned Christmas in Petaluma

Here comes Santa Claus, steaming into town on a gala riverboat. And there go the townspeople, decked out in their best Victorian finery for the "Saturday Stroll," a Christmas card come to life.

In the little town of Petaluma they really know how to make the most of the holidays. There is merriment on the menu here from Thanksgiving weekend right through December, in a town whose old-fashioned look makes a perfect traditional setting. To add to the fun, this is Christmas tree country, with lots of opportunity to cut your own tree on the farm.

Before you go into town, stop at the headquarters of the Petaluma Visitors' Program, off Highway 101 at the Highway 116 exit, to pick up walking tours and information about the area.

If downtown Petaluma looks familiar, it may be because the wealth of period architecture has made it the backdrop chosen for countless commercials and classic movies such as *Peggy Sue Got Married* and *American Graffiti*.

The town's earliest history can be seen at the Old Adobe, a ranch built by Mexican General Vallejo in the 1830s. Now part of a state park, the building is California's largest adobe, nicely restored and with displays of clothing, tools, and other artifacts of its period.

Petaluma became a thriving river port in the 1850s, accounting for the wealth that built the earliest downtown structures. Disillusioned gold miners later settled here and became farmers. Then, in the late 1800s, an incubator was perfected in Petaluma, and the town gained new prosperity and renown as the "Egg Capital of the World." Most of the poultry farms are gone today, but this is still a prime dairy center.

Miraculously untouched by the 1906 earthquake, Petaluma has kept its fine stock of nineteenth-century buildings. There are walking tours of the A Street Historic District, where many of the older homes are located, or you can get an idea of some of the residences with just a short stroll on Sixth Street.

Another printed walking tour points out the even more interesting period architecture downtown, including some rare ornate cast-iron buildings. The Great Petaluma Mill, a riverfront landmark, includes an 1854 warehouse that is the town's oldest building. It has been converted to an attractive shopping complex, but memorabilia and antique machinery still tell of the time when this was one of Northern California's largest feed mills.

Here and in many of the vintage buildings, today's occupants include antiques and gift shops, making this a prime spot to hunt for unique gifts. Old Mill Antiques, in the Mill complex, is Sonoma County's largest collective, There are many more shops on Petaluma Boulevard, especially clustered on the 100 block, and on Kentucky Street between numbers 141 and 152. Any shop can give you a directory with a listing of more than a dozen local stops. All the dealers usually join in hosting an open house the first Sunday in December, with refreshments.

If you are looking for bargains, visit Petaluma Village Factory Outlets, located between Highway 101 and Petaluma Boulevard North, just south of Corona Road. The 50 shops include some of the best-known fashion labels, all selling at substantial discounts.

Petaluma gets into the Christmas spirit in a big way, with decorations, parades, and open houses. The fun starts early when Santa arrives on the Saturday after Thanksgiving, gliding down to the landing at the Petaluma River Turning Basin aboard a paddlewheel steamboat that is suitably decked out for the season. When Santa disembarks, he continues his ride in style in the Antique Wagon and Horse Procession, featuring antique stagecoaches, mule and horse teams, and riders in both Victorian dress and costumes from Raggedy Ann to Davy Crockett.

Early in December, some of the town's finest homes are open for the annual evening Heritage Homes Christmas Parlour Tour. They are filled with Victorian decorations for the holidays, including exquisite trees with old-fashioned trimmings. Hosts are on hand in period costumes to tell about the special history of their homes and to offer refreshments.

Festivities that day start in the afternoon, when the Petaluma Historical Library and Museum holds an annual Victorian Holiday Tea in its majestic columned 1904 building, known for its stained-glass dome. Tables are set with fine china teapots and laden with Christmas confections.

The town has gained the nickname of "City of Lights" for its many holiday decorations. A self-guided driving tour map is available to take you to the best of the showplaces.

Pick the right date and you can combine the tour with a visit to the Adobe Luminaria Fiesta, celebrating Christmas in early California–style at the Petaluma Adobe State Historic Park. A thousand sandbag candles (luminarias) are lit at dusk, accompanied by entertainment from Spanish carolers and dancers. Later that evening, four local yacht clubs navigate a flotilla of colorfully lit and decorated boats into the Petaluma River's downtown harbor in the annual Lighted Boat Parade.

Be sure to save time for a country outing to a farm where you can cut your own Christmas tree. Wreaths are another local specialty. The free Sonoma "Farm Trails" brochure lists almost a dozen places in Petaluma to find handsome firs and pines, usually priced by the foot. There are more choices in neighboring Sebastopol, including Country

Christmas Tree Farm, the largest in Sonoma County. Write for the map before you go, or pick one up at the Visitors' Program office. Some farms will tie your tree on your car, but others won't, so come prepared with cord and an old blanket to protect the car from sap.

Little Hills Christmas Tree Farm has extra attractions for the kids in the form of an animal corral, hot cider, and Santa himself on hand to say hello, usually accompanied by his friendly camel. Lucky Duck Christmas Tree Farm offers visits with ducks and geese.

While you are in the country, you may want to stop for fresh eggs, homemade sausage, smoked turkeys, dressed pheasant or wild turkey, fresh mushrooms, homemade jellies, dried flowers and herbs, and other goodies, all at Petaluma farms listed on the "Farm Trails" map. Two Petaluma cheese factories also welcome visitors for tours.

Families should plan to take in the annual Christmas production of the Children's Theater Workshop at the Cinnabar Theater, an innovative Petaluma performing arts ensemble. Shows are given Friday through Sunday through mid-December.

And the annual holiday extravaganza at the Redwood Empire Ice Arena in Santa Rosa is just a 17-mile drive north. Among the stars on ice each year is everybody's favorite beagle, Snoopy, whose creator, cartoonist Charles Schulz, owns the Ice Arena. Snoopy's Gallery, adjoining the arena, has a Charles Schulz mini-museum upstairs, including his own favorite drawings. The shop itself is chockablock with gift ideas, as are the shops around Railroad Square in Santa Rosa.

Two other worthwhile Santa Rosa stops are the Museum, which has a special Christmas exhibit each year featuring a different country's holiday costumes, and, if your timing is right, the annual free holiday open house and gift sale at the Luther Burbank House, which is beautifully decorated for the season. The event usually takes place the first weekend in December. And the first two weekends of December usually bring an annual Christmas Crafts Fair and Celebration at the Sonoma County Fairgrounds in Santa Rosa, offering entertainment as well as the chance to pick up interesting gifts.

If you need still more diversion, check the holiday schedule in Sonoma, a short drive to the east. One of the loveliest events here is the annual Christmas at Sonoma Mission. Actors portraying General and Mrs. Vallejo are on hand to welcome visitors and begin the lighting of the candles. The plaza tree is lit, and there is outdoor caroling in the plaza before everyone joins the candlelight procession into the Mission for Christmas readings and singing. The evening ends with refreshments in the Barracks Courtyard.

Advance schedules of these events are necessary in order to coordinate them with your Petaluma plans. You might even prefer to stay in Santa Rosa or Sonoma, where the lodging and dining choices are wider. But whether you come for the day or stay for the weekend, Petaluma's old-fashioned Christmas spirit is guaranteed to be contagious.

Area Code: 707

DRIVING DIRECTIONS   Petaluma is located off Highway 101, 39 miles north of San Francisco, 90 miles from Sacramento.

ACCOMMODATIONS   Local choices are limited to one bed-and-breakfast inn, motels, and a farm • *Cavanagh Inn,* 10 Keller Street, Petaluma, 94952, 765-4657, Victorian within walking distance of downtown, M–E, CP • *Best Western Petaluma Inn,* 200 South McDowell Boulevard, Petaluma, 94954, 763-0994, motel, I–M • *Quality Inn,* 5100 Montero Way, Petaluma, 94954, 664-1155, motel, I–E • *Silver Penny Farm,* 5215 Old Lakeville Road No. 1, Petaluma, 94954, 762-1498, a farmhouse and cottages on 17 scenic acres, used as a retreat by the Archdiocese of San Francisco. Cottages and rooms are available to individuals for overnight stays, I–M. See also Sebastopol, pages 101 to 105; Santa Rosa, pages 142 to 146; and Sonoma, pages 110 to 115.

DINING   *Steamer Gold Landing,* 1 Water Street, 763-6876, in historic building on the river, American menu, dancing, M • *Buona Sera,* 148 Kentucky Street, 763-3333, highly rated Italian, M • *Fino Cucina,* 208 Petaluma Boulevard North, 762-5966, deco decor, more tasty Italian, I–M • *De Schmire,* 304 Bodega Avenue, 762-1901, open kitchen, hanging ferns, country French food, M • *Sonoma Joe's,* 5151 Montero Way, 775-5400, California cuisine, I–M • *The Old River Inn,* 222 Weller Street, 765-0111, Victorian on the river, Italian and French, M • *Johnson Oyster & Seafood,* 253 North McDowell Boulevard, 763-4161, try the fried oysters, I–M • *Dempsey's,* 50 East Washington Street, 765-9694, brew pub on the river, I • *Aram's,* 131 Kentucky Street, 765-9775, coffee shop with Armenian specialties, good for lunch or tasty desserts (closes at 6 P.M.), I.

SIGHTSEEING   **Christmas activities:** For current Petaluma schedule, contact the *Petaluma Visitors' Program* at the address below. For schedule of Santa Rosa, Sonoma, and other Sonoma County events, contact *Sonoma County Convention & Visitors' Bureau,* 5000 Roberts Lake Road, Suite A, Rohnert Park, 94928, 586-8100 or (800) 326-7666 • *Cinnabar Performing Arts Theater,* 3333 Petaluma Boulevard North, Petaluma, 763-8920, phone for current offerings • *Petaluma Adobe State Historic Park,* 3325 Adobe Road (at Casa Grande), Petaluma, 762-4871. Hours: Daily 10 P.M. to 5 P.M. Adults, $2; ages 6 to 12, $1 • *Petaluma Historical Library and Museum,* 20 Fourth Street, Petaluma, 778-4398. Hours: Thursday to Saturday and Monday 10 A.M. to 4 P.M., Sunday 1 P.M. to 4 P.M. Free • *The Cheese Factory,* Petaluma–Point Reyes Road, Petaluma, 762-6001. Hours: Daily tours 10 A.M. to 4 P.M. Free • *The Creamery Store,* 711 Western Avenue (at

Baker Street), Petaluma, 778-1234. Hours: Tours on the hour, Monday to Saturday 11 A.M. to 3 P.M. Free • *Redwood Empire Ice Arena,* 1667 West Steele Lane, Santa Rosa, 546-7147, phone for current holiday schedules and rates.

CHRISTMAS TREE FARMS   Phone for directions • *Little Hills Farm,* 763-4678 • *Lucky Duck Farm,* 763-9710 • *Country Christmas Tree Farm,* 823-3309. For farm map listing additional tree farms, send a self-addressed envelope with two stamps to *Sonoma County Farm Trails,* P.O. Box 6032, Santa Rosa, CA 95406, 544-4728, or pick one up at the Petaluma Visitors' Program.

INFORMATION   *Petaluma Visitors' Program,* 799 Baywood Drive, Suite 1 (off Highway 101 at Highway 116 exit), Petaluma, CA 94954, 769-0429.

Christmas Trees in Redwood Country

The spirit of Christmas past is alive and present at the Benbow Inn, a bit of old England transplanted to Northern California. The entire month of December at this national historical landmark in Garberville is devoted to old-fashioned festivities that are guaranteed to cheer.

Come for the holidays or just for a weekend and add a different kind of Christmas tree to your agenda—the magnificent redwoods nearby along the famous Avenue of the Giants. Even in a state filled with scenic drives, this one is a standout.

The festive mood is set as soon as you enter the door of the Benbow, for the inn is adorned top to bottom with greenery, crowned by a 15-foot animated teddy bear Christmas tree. There's a multicourse dinner on Christmas Day, a champagne dinner dance on New Year's Eve, and entertainment almost every night. And, of course, there's a visit from Santa Claus, who doesn't want to miss out on the fun.

There's a definite feeling of old England to the setting, from the half-timbered facade to the dark columns, arches, huge Oriental rug, and big fireplace in the lobby. Another very British touch is tea and scones served along with hot cider each afternoon.

The building was commissioned by the Benbow family more than 60 years ago, and designed by noted architect Albert Farr. It opened in 1926, and played host to many notable guests in its early days. The hotel had faded a bit until recently, when new owners restored the original elegance of the main building, filling the public rooms with fine furnishings, paintings, needlepoint, and objets d'art. Even the smaller, modestly priced guest rooms upstairs have fine reproduction furnishings and come stocked with nice things like sherry, coffee and tea, and a basket of paperback mysteries. Four luxurious terrace and garden rooms were added during the restoration, three with wood-burning fireplaces that are just the thing to warm a winter night. A Garden Cottage, with a four-poster bed and a whirlpool bath, is the perfect romantic hideaway.

The dining room is formal, with a beamed ceiling and dark Windsor chairs. The continental menu is always fine, but the chef outdoes himself with his holiday extravaganzas.

If the weather cooperates, you can walk this feast off among the redwoods; if not, you will at least have an unforgettable drive in store. Allow a minimum of an hour and a half to enjoy these majestic trees even if you never leave the car.

The Avenue of the Giants begins about three miles north of Garberville. It is actually the old Highway 101 winding along the Eel River, now a bypass parallel to the new 101. The 33-mile byway runs right into the dim, fragrant, mysterious forest groves of Humboldt Redwoods State Park, almost close enough to touch the stately trees.

Within this one park is the largest concentration of old-growth redwoods in the world, 17,000 acres of virgin trees, including some of the largest and oldest still standing. The oldest recorded coastal redwood found here was 2,200 years old.

Driving-guide pamphlets are usually available at either entrance to the park. The visitors' center located roughly 15 miles into the park has informative displays, a slide show, literature about redwoods, and more maps to guide the rest of your route. The maps point out many stops along the way where you can get out and walk, feeling even more intimately the immense size of the trees.

Winter weather is often mild and snow is rare, but it may rain, so come prepared with a poncho and proper footwear. Don't let the rain discourage you from at least a short walk. The trees form an effective umbrella, so only a real downpour can spoil the trip. The forest is often at its most awesome on a misty winter day. The very best part of a winter visit is having this 20-million-year-old forest almost to yourself.

Two short walks should not be missed. The first is the Founders Grove, an easy 20-minute self-guided loop that explains how a redwood forest grows, and takes you past two memorable trees. The grove was dedicated in 1931 to honor the founders of the Save the Redwoods League. The Founders Tree, which stands over 346 feet high, is estimated to be between 1,300 and 1,500 years old. The Dyerville Giant, one of the tallest trees in the world, was last measured in 1972 at 362 feet tall and 17 feet in diameter. It is even taller today and may well grow into the tallest tree on earth.

Nearby on the other side of the road is the Rockefeller Loop Trail, another short half-mile walk through unbelievably tall redwoods. There is also an outstanding drive along Albee Creek and Honeydew roads, winding for six miles through the 9,000-acre Rockefeller Forest, the largest remaining old-growth forest. It gives a sense of what much of the northern coast must have looked like hundreds of years ago. There are two parking areas leading to trails into the forest.

If the sun shines, consider slightly longer hikes such as the 1.7-mile Grove Trail through many of the memorial groves, or the 2.1-mile Big Tree Loop.

It's worth noting that fishing in the Eel River is at its best in late fall and winter, when the salmon and steelhead make their way from the ocean upriver to spawn. When the fish are running, fishing is the most popular winter activity in the park. Rock hounding for jade and jasper along the South Fork of the Eel is another recommended pastime on a nice day.

At the end of the Avenue of the Giants you can extend your outing north into Scotia, one of the last of the company-owned mill towns. One brochure aptly describes its neat look-alike homes as reminding one of a miniature model railroad town come to life. The Scotia Inn is worth a stop; it's quite grand for this tiny town. The Pacific Lumber Company, the town patron, offers free tours through its sprawling mill on workdays.

A bit farther north is Ferndale, a delightful Victorian town filled with fine architecture and unusual shops. Ferndale is really worth an unhurried trip on its own; it is about 45 minutes from Garberville via the main highway. See pages 32 to 37 for more about the town.

For a souvenir of your redwood visit, take the Myers Flat exit and follow the signs to the Drive-Thru Tree, which provides an irresistible photo opportunity. Needless to say, there is a gift shop as well, one of many in towns along the Avenue of the Giants selling redwood burl slabs, bowls, and carvings. You can see demonstrations of the burls being turned into bowls. They cost much less here than in city shops and make fine last-minute Christmas gifts. The Benbow Gallery, near the inn, has other ideas—fine art and crafts, sculpture, and photography.

With driving and shopping done, it's back to the inn for a fine dinner and maybe some caroling or a concert. Have yourself a merry little Christmas indeed.

Area Code: 707

DRIVING DIRECTIONS Follow Highway 101 north to Garberville, about 200 miles north of San Francisco, 227 miles from Sacramento.

ACCOMMODATIONS   *Benbow Inn,* 445 Lake Benbow Drive, Garberville, 95442, 923-2124 or (800) 355-3301, wide variation in room sizes and prices, M–EE. Ask for current Christmas package rates; hotel closes for the winter after the holidays • *Best Western Humboldt House* (motel), 701 Redwood Drive, Garberville, 95440, I, CP • *Scotia Inn,* Main and Mill streets, Scotia, 764-5683, nicely maintained by the local mill, I–M, CP.

DINING   *Benbow Inn,* Garberville (see above), M–E • *Scotia Inn,* Scotia (see above), M • *Waterwheel Restaurant,* 948 Redwood Drive, Garberville, 923-2031, casual, breakfast, lunch, and dinner, I–M.

SIGHTSEEING   *Avenue of the Giants,* old Highway 101 north of Garberville between Phillipsville and Jordan Creek; follow Auto Tour signs. Printed tour guide brochures available at entrances on either end. Free • *Humboldt Redwoods State Park Visitors' Center,* Avenue of the Giants, 946-2263. Hours: In summer, daily 9 A.M. to 5 P.M.; some off-season dates; phone for current information • *Drive-Thru Tree,* 13078 Avenue of the Giants, Myers Flat exit, 943-3154. Hours: In summer, daily 8 A.M. to 8 P.M.; rest of year, 9:30 A.M. to 5 P.M. Adults, $1; children, free • *Pacific Lumber Company,* Scotia, 764-2222. Hours: Self-guided tours 7:30 A.M. to 10 A.M. and 12:30 P.M. to 2:30 P.M. workdays. Free.

INFORMATION   *Avenue of the Giants Association,* P.O. Box 1000, Miranda, CA 95553, 923-2265 • *Garberville–Redway Chamber of Commerce,* 773 Redwood Drive, Garberville, CA 95542, 923-2613.

Winter Wonders at Yosemite

In the still majesty of winter, Yosemite National Park is a magical place. Whipped cream toppings crown the tall trees and powdered sugar icing dusts the mountaintops ringing the valley. Streams and lakes sparkle in the sunlight like jewels in a pristine field of white.

This quiet season offers an amazing variety of activity, yet reser- vations are easy to come by and rates are about 25 percent less than the rest of the year. No wonder winter is many people's favorite season at Yosemite.

These days you don't even have to worry about road conditions, unless you prefer to drive. Take Amtrak or fly to Fresno or Merced and there are bus connections directly to Yosemite. Once arrived, there's no need for a car, as free shuttles cover the entire valley, the heart of the park.

Temperatures are milder down in the valley, so the waterfalls and rivers are flowing most of the winter, and snow is moderate, allowing visitors to get around easily. It's at higher elevations like Badger Pass, 3,000 feet above, that the snowfall hits 180 inches, ideal for skiing downhill or cross-country in a fairyland setting. The cross-country trails along Glacier Point Road offer fantastic views of the valley below.

No need to worry about getting to Badger Pass, either. There is regular free service on buses well equipped for any weather. The ride up is a sightseeing thrill even if all you do is stay for lunch. The valley vista just before Wawona Tunnel on the way up is one of the park's best.

Nonskiers can try the fun of a ranger-guided tour on snowshoes, hop aboard a snowcat tour, or come back to the valley to glide around the big outdoor ice skating rink at Curry Village. Night skating under the stars is a rare experience, and there's a warming hut to welcome you afterward with a hot drink.

For most people, the favorite Yosemite activity is simply exploring the seven-mile valley, admiring the towering surrounding peaks and the waterfalls cascading down their sides. Enough paths are plowed to ensure that there is always room to walk in a wonderland of white, savoring the sight of famous sentinels of the park with snowcaps glinting in the sun.

The unusual shapes of the mountain formations are what makes them so unique. They were carved by glaciers millions of years ago. Ice filled the valley, widening and deepening it into a U shape with hanging valleys from which the waterfalls flow. The fracturing and polishing of the granite by the massive ice movement produced features such as the sheer faces of El Capitan and Half Dome, the Royal Arches, the rounded top of Sentinel Dome, the points of Cathedral Spires, and the sloping Three Brothers. The park lakes were formed when the glacier began to melt.

Half Dome is the tallest formation, rising an awesome 4,733 feet above the valley floor. Mighty El Capitan stands at 3,593 feet above the valley. Among the waterfalls, Yosemite Falls is king, with upper and lower sections that total 2,425 feet. Bridalveil Fall is a favorite sight for the wind currents that often swirl the waters into a sideways mist. At 620 feet, it seems small—until you realize that it is the height of a 62-story building.

The morning Photo Walk is a good introduction, taking you to some prime lookouts. More favorite winter walks are easy half-mile strolls to Yosemite Falls or Bridalveil Fall and the walk around Mirror Lake, which is just more than a mile. When the paths are clear, bikes are another great way to see the sights. They are for rent at Yosemite Lodge.

You can also take your car or use the shuttle bus to cover the auto loop, which passes all the important sites. Or sign up for a two-hour bus tour of the valley, with photo stops for the most scenic views. You'll want to do some photography on your own, since the colors are best early and late in the day. Sunset is downright miraculous, particularly at El Capitan. The eastern end of the park near Yosemite Falls is best in the morning. No matter how much film you bring, it won't be enough.

For photo inspiration, visit the Ansel Adams Gallery in Yosemite Village, a gift shop with a wonderful selection of photographs by the man whose work captured the soul of Yosemite.

If the beauty around you inspires the artist in you, check the schedule of art classes at the Art Activity Center, between the Gallery and the Valley Post Office.

The visitors' center nearby is always worth a stop, both for information and for changing exhibits. For first-time visitors, there is an orientation slide show called "One Day in Yosemite" to help make the most of a short stay.

Next to the center is the Indian Cultural Exhibit, telling the story of the valley's native Miwok and Paiute people and sometimes offering demonstrations of skills such as basket weaving and beadwork. The Museum Gallery next door has changing exhibits on the park.

A short trail behind the center leads through the Indian Village of the Ahwahnee, a reconstructed early settlement. Another nearby one-mile nature trail, "A Changing Yosemite," shows how the park has altered over the years and will continue to change in the future.

Yosemite is a great winter getaway for families. The Badger Pass area, the oldest ski area in California, is a perfect place to learn to ski. A special Badger Pups program for ages four to six combines beginning lessons and baby-sitting. The area is small enough so that kids can roam and always be sure of finding their parents when they return to the small lodge. Children who participate in snowshoeing, nature walks, and other outdoor programs earn Junior Snow Ranger certificates and badges. Free ranger talks are held in the early evening and are interesting for all ages. And children are as awed as their elders by the peaks that make this park unique.

Members of an army battalion scouting Indians were the first Americans to enter the valley in 1851. They bestowed the Indian name that sounded to them like *yo-sem-i-ty*, but chose new titles for the famous cliffs according to the way they looked—North Dome instead of *to-ko-ya*, El Capitan instead of *to-tock-an-noo*.

Word of the wonders spread, and people came trekking in to see them. Landscape architect Frederick Law Olmsted was among those who petitioned Congress to protect the area, and in 1864 Abraham Lincoln signed the Yosemite Grant, entrusting the state of California with both the valley and the Mariposa Big Trees Grove of giant sequoia trees to the south. It was a landmark act, the forerunner of our national park system.

Until 1874, when stage roads replaced trails, the only way in was on foot or horseback, and there were few comforts. Still, the surroundings continued to lure. John Muir, who walked his way from Oakland to Yosemite in 1868, was one of those who formed a lifelong love affair with the area. Alarmed by the loss of vegetation he saw from farm animals overgrazing the land, Muir was prominent among those who lobbied Congress for protection, and in 1890 the high country surrounding the valley became Yosemite National Park. After much maneuvering, California returned its original grant to the government in 1906, and the valley and the Mariposa Grove were incorporated into the national park.

The very next year the Yosemite Valley Railroad was completed from Merced to El Portal, 12 miles west of Yosemite, providing the first easy access. In 1913 cars were permitted in the park for the first time—and they haven't stopped coming since.

The name Curry has been associated with Yosemite since 1899, when a new camp for tourists called Curry's opened, offering beds in tents for $2 a day. In 1925 the Curry family was granted the concession to manage the growing number of lodgings and eating places in the park, and family members remained at Yosemite until the late 1970s. They supervised work on a hotel called the Ahwahnee, a grant structure that opened in 1927 and remains the prime place to stay at Yosemite. The rock and beamed front fits beautifully into the setting. An interesting note: The beams are actually concrete cleverly stained to look like redwood. The soaring dining room and the collection of priceless Indian baskets, paintings, and photos make a visit a must. If you can't afford dinner, come for breakfast or lunch.

While most of winter may be a quiet season at Yosemite, holiday traditions here are legendary. The Bracebridge Dinner at Christmas, a seven-course meal and pageant, and the New Year's Eve Dinner-Dance at the Ahwahnee are so popular that reservations are done by lottery, with applications required a year in advance.

A less extravagant but very pleasant option is the "Old-Fashioned Christmas" program held annually at the Pioneer Yosemite History Center at the southern end of the park. Activities include caroling, candlelight tours, storytelling, tree-trimming, and stagecoach rides. Lodging is at the National Landmark Wawona Hotel, the 1870s Victorian that traditionally is draped with natural garlands and filled with Christmas cheer. Reserve early, but you won't need a lottery for this one.

For people who can get away midweek, two newer Yosemite traditions are worth knowing about. The Vintners' Holiday in November and early December is hosted by well-known wine critics. Each session features specific vineyards, whose products are used for tastings, and festive dinners complementing the wines.

January brings the annual Chefs' Holiday at the Ahwahnee, when a series of great chefs and cooking experts offer talks, demonstrations, and a Chef's Dinner, a five-course feast prepared by the featured chef. When there is room, the dinners are open to all, though advance reservations are essential.

Activities may make the days fly by, but they aren't the prime reason to visit Yosemite in winter. The greatest pleasure of all remains a quiet and private one—simply contemplating the beauty of this extraordinary valley, a vision that is all the lovelier with a crown of winter white.

Area Code: 209

DRIVING DIRECTIONS   In winter, the recommended route to the park is Highway 140 via Mariposa. It is the least mountainous and snow chains are rarely needed, though it is necessary to carry them when driving anywhere in the Sierra Nevada in winter. They could be required at any time. The Tioga Road from Lee Vining to Crane Flat and Glacier Point Road beyond Badger Pass are closed in winter. Highway 41 from Fresno frequently requires chains, as does curvy Route 120 west to the Big Oak Flat entrance. Yosemite is 210 miles from San Francisco, 89 miles from Fresno, 81 miles from Merced, about 175 miles from Sacramento. For recorded weather and road conditions, phone 372-0200.

PUBLIC TRANSPORTATION   Daily Amtrak train service from Oakland and Sacramento to Merced, met by a Yosemite VIA bus that continues into the valley. Free bus to the Oakland station from San Francisco or from the Stockton station to Sacramento is included in the train fare. Amtrak also has daily service from San Diego and Los Angeles to Fresno, with connecting buses. For information, phone Amtrak, (800) USA-Rail, or Yosemite VIA Bus Line, 742-5266 or (800) 842-5463 in California. Bus service is also available from the Fresno airport or downtown Fresno; phone 442-5240 or (800) 996-7364 in California. Free shuttle bus service in the park makes cars unnecessary.

ACCOMMODATIONS   For all Yosemite reservations, write or phone Central Reservations, Yosemite Concession Services Corporation, 5410 East Home, Fresno, 93727, 252-4848. Special hot line for winter reservations, 454-2000. Rates range from a tent-cabin for under $40 to over $200 for a room at the Ahwahnee. Less-expensive rooms with shared baths are available in the Lodge and Curry Village. *Ahwahnee Hotel,* EE; *Yosemite Lodge.* I–M; *Curry Village,* I–M; *Wawona Hotel,* open Easter to October, Christmas holidays, Thanksgiving, and winter weekends, I–M. Also open in season: *Tuolumne Meadows*

Lodge, tent-cabins, I; *White Wolf Lodge,* cabins and tent-cabins, I. For park campground reservations, phone MISTIX, (800) 365-2267.

DINING *Ahwahnee Hotel,* 372-1489, the beautiful beamed dining room is a must, open for all meals; breakfast, I; lunch, I–M; reservations required for dinner, E–EE • *Mountain Room Broiler,* Yosemite Lodge (see above), grill specialties, M–E • *Four Seasons Restaurant,* Yosemite Lodge (see above), California-American menu, M; breakfast, I • *Yosemite Lodge Cafeteria,* open for three meals daily, I • *Degnan's Delicatessen,* Yosemite Village, sandwiches, salads, I • *Degnan's Fast Food,* Yosemite Village, pizza, sandwiches, snacks, I • *Wawona Hotel Dining Room,* 375-6556, dinner reservations required, M–E.

Also available in summer: *The Loft,* above Degnan's Deli, Yosemite Village, sandwiches, soups, salads, pasta, I–M • *Tuolumne Meadows Lodge,* 372-8413, rustic tent village beside the river, breakfast, I; dinners, I–M (advance reservations essential) • *Curry Pavilion Cafeteria,* breakfast and dinner, I • *Curry Village Hamburger Deck,* all meals, snacks, I • *Village Grill,* Yosemite Village, all meals, I–M. Picnic lunches are available at all Yosemite lodgings with advance notice.

SPECIAL EVENTS *Christmas Bracebridge Dinner or New Year's Eve Dinner-Dance.* Send separate applications addressed to Bracebridge Dinner or New Year's Eve Dinner-Dance, Yosemite Reservations, Yosemite National Park, CA 95389. Applications are available from December 15 to January 15 only and are accepted until February 15, the year preceding the event. Winners are notified in early spring • *Yosemite Vintners' Holidays,* mid-November to mid-December, and *Yosemite Chefs' Holidays,* three weeks in January; for schedules and reservations, contact Yosemite Holidays, 5410 East Home Avenue, Fresno, CA 93727, 454-2000.

SIGHTSEEING *Yosemite National Park,* 372-0264; recorded information, 372-0200. Admission, $5 per car • *Yosemite Valley Visitors' Center,* Yosemite Village, 372-0299. Hours: Daily 9 A.M. to 5 P.M. For current update on ranger-led walks, ski instruction, snowshoe treks, evening programs, and all other activities at Yosemite, check the free publication *Yosemite Guide,* available at entry gates, the visitors' center, or any park lodging. For Badger Pass ski conditions, phone 372-1000 • *Indian Village of the Ahwahnee,* behind visitors' center, Yosemite Village. Hours: Self-guided trail open daily in daylight hours • *Yosemite Museum,* next to visitors' center. Winter hours: Friday to Tuesday 10 A.M. to noon, 1 P.M. to 4 P.M. • *Badger Pass Ski Conditions,* 372-1000.

INFORMATION *Yosemite National Park,* c/o National Park Service Public Information Office, P.O. Box 577, Yosemite National Park, CA 95389, 372-0265.

Back to Nature near Santa Cruz

It isn't easy being an elephant seal. You'd think that mating season would be a happy time, but not for these males. It means they must come ashore and fight for the right to mate. The huge bulls, 14 to 16 feet long and weighing up to nearly 2½ tons, wage ferocious, roaring, and sometimes bloody battles that are amazing to behold. During breeding season, from December to March, the seals and their mating rituals have become a major tourist attraction at Año Nuevo State Reserve, about 20 miles north of Santa Cruz, where weekend nature tours are sold out far in advance.

Plan ahead and you can have a fascinating double nature encounter, for this is also the time of year when monarch butterflies are in residence by the thousands at Natural Bridges State Beach, just outside Santa Cruz, the only official monarch preserve in California. And it is also a chance to explore Santa Cruz County's blend of mountains and sea and to enjoy the town itself without crowds. On a mild, sunny winter day, walkways that teem with people in summer become serene strolls with fabulous views of surf and surfers in action.

Try to get an early reservation for the elephant seal walks. Tours last two and a half hours and cover three miles, much of them through loose sand, so choose appropriate footwear and a warm jacket. Bring binoculars for close-up views; elephant seals can be dangerous, and visitors are warned to stay at least 40 feet away.

The first view of so many mammoth seals resting like logs on the sand amazes, and the name "elephant" becomes easy to understand when you see their long dangling noses. The reason they all lie dead still is to conserve energy between those bloody bouts.

On the tour you'll learn that these enormous creatures spend most of their lives at sea, coming ashore only to molt, mate, and give birth. They were slaughtered by the thousands in the last century for their oil-rich blubber. By 1892 only 50 to 100 were left in one remaining colony off the coast of Baja California. In the 1920s both the Mexican and U.S. governments gave them protected status, and slowly they began to reappear in Southern California waters.

They were first sighted on Año Nuevo Island in 1955. The state purchased the rocky 13-acre island and a strip of adjacent mainland in 1958 to create the present reserve, a sanctuary for all kinds of marine mammals and birds that now includes some 4,000 acres of coastal mountains, bluffs, dunes, and beaches. Elephant seals have been breeding here since 1961, with numbers increasing each year. Some 2,000 seals now come ashore at Año Nuevo.

The first males arrive in December. The victors of the violent battles that ensue do most of the breeding that repopulates the colony, with much of the duty falling on the "alpha" bull, the top fighter.

Later in December the females appear, forming harems on the beaches. They are smaller than the males, but still average 12 feet in length and 1,200 to 2,000 pounds. Six days after coming ashore, the females give birth to pups that were conceived the previous year. Then, after about 24 days of nursing, they are ready to mate again. The fertilized egg does not implant in the uterus wall for three months, and as the gestation period is eight months, the young will be born here the following winter.

By March most of the adult seals are gone, leaving the awkward pups behind. The babies molt, their original black fur replaced by shiny new silver, learn to swim, then, during the last three weeks of April, leave one by one, swimming northward.

Elephant seals find their way back to Año Nuevo when it is time for the annual molts, with females and juveniles arriving from April to May, young adults from May to June, and full-grown adult males from July to August. Molting seals basking on the beaches are visible from viewpoints on a designated trail. From April through November you can visit the island anytime by getting a hiking permit at the Wildlife Protection Area at Año Nuevo Point.

From Año Nuevo it is a short drive down the coast to Natural Bridges State Beach. The park offers picnic areas and rocky tide pools for exploring, but the real attraction is the Monarch Natural Preserve. These regal orange-and-black butterflies are also long-distance travelers, flying from as far away as western Canada on their annual migration to the California coast. When the days grow shorter in October, it is nature's signal to the butterflies to seek shelter in a warmer climate, and this preserve gives its winter guests just what they need for survival—eucalyptus trees for food and a canyon location providing shelter from the wind. Visitors can view the butterflies along a scenic walkway and also learn about them at an educational demonstration milkweed patch that shows the miracle of metamorphosis from egg to caterpillar to butterfly beauty.

Once again, you'll need binoculars for the best view of the thousands of butterflies in the trees, for though they are near at hand, they group together into clusters as protection from wind, rain, and cold. Until you look closely, they look for all the world like clumps of dead leaves. Sunshine and temperatures above 55 degrees lure them out to play, and it is when they spread their velvety wings that their glorious color can be seen.

When daylight hours begin to increase in late January and early February, the mating instinct takes over. On warm afternoons courting pairs can be seen drifting down to the ground like falling leaves. Most of the butterflies are gone by early March, on their way north again.

Because butterflies live only six to nine months, there are no leaders to direct a new generation back to Santa Cruz each fall. How they return unerringly to these wintering grounds is one of nature's mysteries.

You can learn still more about nature and the sea around you with a visit to the Long Marine Lab, next door to Natural Bridges. This research and instructional facility of the University of California at Santa Cruz invites the public in to view dolphin and sea lion tanks, an aquarium, a touch tank, and marine exhibits that include the 85-foot skeleton of a blue whale.

After seeing the seals and the butterflies, the next choice is yours: mountains or sea. Inland in the Santa Cruz mountains is Big Basin Redwoods State Park, California's first state park, with more than 100 miles of hiking trails, dramatic waterfalls, and some prize redwood groves. The half-mile Redwood Trail loops past some of the most impressive trees.

More majestic trees, with apt names such as "Giant" and "Neck-breaker," are in the Redwood Grove of Henry Cowell Redwoods State Park, south of Big Basin. One of the favorite ways to see these trees is aboard the Roaring Camp & Big Trees Narrow-Gauge Railroad in Felton, a nostalgic trip on an authentic 1880s steam train. This is the steepest narrow-gauge grade in North America, and it may have the tightest turns. It's truly a thrilling ride, right up to the stop atop Bear Mountain in a sun-dappled grove of big trees. You can picnic on the mountain and take a later train back or return to the depot for a chuck-wagon barbecue in Roaring Camp, a replica of an 1880s logging town with a picturesque covered bridge. A short nature trail from the town takes you back into Henry Cowell Redwoods State Park next door. In summer there's an additional train ride directly to the Santa Cruz Beach boardwalk.

If mountains are your weekend preference, the best for lodging are two small homey inns in Ben Lomond. Rustic, redwood Fairview Manor even has its own walking paths; it is set on two and a half private acres on the San Lorenzo River. Breakfast is delightful here, served family style on a redwood picnic table in front of a big picture window facing the woods and the river. Chateau Des Fleurs in town offers Victorian charm. The pale blue house, circa 1879, has stained-glass accents and upstairs rooms with antique brass and iron beds, pretty florals, and fluffy comforters on the beds.

If romance is on your mind, you may choose to stay in Santa Cruz at the Babbling Brook Inn, one of the most romantic hideaways on the coast. Rooms with tasteful French country decor are privately tucked away on a hillside with waterfalls cascading into a meandering brook with its own mill wheel. Most of the rooms have fireplaces and private decks; two have whirlpool tubs.

The other best choices in town are Victorian mansions. Cliff Crest, an 1887 Queen Anne, offers spacious rooms, big breakfasts, and a solarium for sunning, and Chateau Victorian, a more formal inn, has fireplaces in every room and nice outdoor patios and decks. All lodgings are within a reasonable downhill walk of the beach. More attractive options can be found south of Santa Cruz in Capitola, a busy seaside town noted for its begonia nurseries, or in the neighboring hills of Aptos and Soquel, an antiquing center.

Santa Cruz, the northern tip of Monterey Bay, is best known for surfers and for its Boardwalk beachfront amusement park, but this is also a town with a delightfully revived downtown and a host of good restaurants in town and in neighboring communities.

A fixture since the mid-1800s, the Boardwalk is a little tacky, a little nostalgic—and the nostalgia shines best on off-season weekends, without the summer crush. Rides vary from the thriller Giant Dipper roller coaster to a gentle 1911-vintage merry-go-round, complete with hand-carved horses and a 342-pipe organ. Both these rides have been named historic landmarks. There are vintage arcade games as well, and a miniature golf course, plus big-band dancing and concerts almost year-round.

Winter stays lively throughout the town, what with the January Fungus Fair, a celebration of mushrooms at the local museum; the Clam Chowder Cook-Off in February; and a Jazz Festival on the wharf in March.

The municipal wharf is just a stroll away from the Boardwalk. Built nearly 100 years ago, it is a favorite spot for fishing or dining on the day's catch, as well as for pelican and sea lion watching. Deep-sea fishing trips and bay cruises depart from the wharf, including whale-watching tours in winter.

Whether you'll want to go to sea or take advantage of Santa Cruz County's 29 miles of beaches depends on whether the sun shines on your weekend, but the drive past the stately homes on the bluffs along West Cliff Drive is always a winner. Along the drive is scenic Lighthouse Point, one of the most photographed sites on the coast. The lighthouse is now a surfing museum, with some colorful displays of surfing history and examples of some of the earliest boards, including a 100-pound slab of redwood measuring 15 feet in length. Steamers Lane below is a good place to look for latter-day surfers in action. This is also a good vantage point for Seal Rock, home to a noisy colony of sea lions. Remember to keep those binoculars with you.

The central portion of Santa Cruz has been completely rebuilt since it suffered serious damage in the 1989 earthquake. Pacific Street has blossomed with a lineup of interesting boutiques, galleries, coffeehouses, and cafés. You need only stroll three or four blocks to find a host of temptations, everything from Southwestern jewelry and clothing at Western Vision to a variety of crafts at the Many Hands Gallery to antique jewelry at Judy Wymant. The Bookshop Santa Cruz is one of the best independent bookstores on the coast.

The McPherson Art and History Center is another focal point in the new downtown. As the name suggests, this modernist cultural center for the community offers both a gallery of town history and changing exhibitions in two handsome art galleries.

One long-time landmark site that remains is the Spanish-style City Hall, on Center Street. At the Visitors' Council office, you can also pick up a tour map of some of the town's fine Victorian homes.

There are many other sights to keep you occupied. The Santa Cruz City Museum has natural history exhibits on Monterey Bay, including a tide pool touch tank, and displays of rocks, fossils, and Indian culture. It sponsors an annual winter Fungus Fair and spring Wild Flower Show. In Santa Cruz Mission State Historic Park you can see the 1822 adobe built to house the Native Americans who worked at the Mission, the only authentically restored Indian living quarters in the California Mission chain.

If you need further diversions, visit the Mary Porter Sesnon and Eloise Pickard Smith art galleries at the University of California at Santa Cruz. There are many antiques stores along Soquel Drive on the way to Aptos, and some excellent stops for lunch or dinner. The Visitors' Council has a booklet listing dozens of art galleries, or you can pick up a guide to Santa Cruz County wineries, most in scenic locations in the hills. Santa Cruz Memorial Park has some unusual attractions, a life-size wax sculpture of *The Last Supper* and a Shroud of Turin collection with a life-size replica of the Shroud copied from the original.

Whatever you do, take time for a drive uphill on Bay Street to the UC–Santa Cruz campus. Pick up a self-guided tour map at the main entrance information booth. The campus is a unique complex, built in a cluster pattern with half a dozen separate colleges separated by woodland, each with its own strikingly individual architecture. The site is a former hilltop ranch, and the views of Santa Cruz and the sea are matchless. There's also a fine Arboretum, offering guided tours on weekends.

The campus adds to the diverse evening offerings in Santa Cruz with a full slate of theater, concerts, and dance. There are also concerts by the Santa Cruz Chamber Players, and performances by the year-round Actors Theatre. The summer schedule is even busier, including Shakespeare Santa Cruz at the university and the major Cabrillo Music Festival. Check the Visitors' Council for current offerings.

Winter is also the season for whale watching, as the California Gray Whale makes its annual migration to Mexico. A favorite point from which to see the whales is Greyhound Rock in Davenport, or you can sign up for a whale-watching tour.

The final attraction in Santa Cruz claims to be another natural wonder, but you'll have to judge for yourself. The Mystery Spot east of town is a freaky area where a compass will indicate the opposite of the right direction, kids can climb the walls without falling off, and balls roll uphill as well as down. Even if you're skeptical about what kind of gravitational force is at work, you'll have to admit it's unique.

Area Code: 408

DRIVING DIRECTIONS Santa Cruz is on Highway 1, 70 miles south of San Francisco, 45 miles north of Monterey, 145 miles from Sacramento.

PUBLIC TRANSPORTATION San Jose and Monterey Peninsula airports, each 35 miles.

ACCOMMODATIONS Note that most inns have lower rates in winter • *Babbling Brook Inn,* 1025 Laurel Street, Santa Cruz, 95060, 427-2437, M–EE, CP • *Cliff Crest,* 407 Cliff Street, Santa Cruz, 95060, 427-2609, M–E, CP • *Chateau Victorian,* 118 First Street, Santa Cruz, 95060, 458-9458 • *Mangels House,* P.O. Box 302, Aptos, 95001, 688-7982, spacious home in parkland, M–E, CP • *Apple Lane Inn,* 6265 Soquel Drive, Aptos, 95003, 475-6868, homey, animals, M–EE, CP • *El Salto,* 620 El Salto Drive, Capitola, 95010, 462-6365, a cluster of guest rooms and cottages in a garden setting by the sea, E–CC, SP • *The Inn at Depot Hill,* 250 Monterey Avenue, Capitola, 95010, 462-3376, exquisite and luxurious, though smack in the middle of town, EE, CP • *Fairview Manor,* 245 Fairview Avenue, Ben Lomond, 95005, 336-3355, E, CP • *Chateau Des Fleurs,* 7995 Highway 9, Ben Lomond, 95005, 336-8943, M–E, CP.

DINING *The Library at Chaminade,* 1 Chaminade Lane, Santa Cruz, 475-5600, California cuisine, elegant, part of a conference center, prix fixe, EE • *India Joze,* 1001 Center Street, Santa Cruz, 427-3554, creative East Asian and Middle Eastern cuisine, artsy decor, in the Santa Cruz Art Center, M • *Café Bittersweet,* 2332 Mission Street, Santa Cruz, 423-9999, cozy European-style café, many say best in town, E • *O'mei,* 2316 Mission Street, Santa Cruz, 425-8458, exceptional gourmet Chinese fare, I • *Gabriella Café,* 910 Cedar Street, Santa Cruz, 457-1677, California cuisine, highly praised, M • *Crow's Nest,* 2218 East Cliff Drive, Santa Cruz Yacht Harbor, Santa Cruz, 476-4560, seafood, bay views, popular, lively, M • *Casablanca,* 101 Main Street, Santa Cruz, 426-9063, continental, bay views, M–E • *Ristorante Avanti,* 1711 Mission Street, Santa Cruz, 427-0135, local favorite for Italian, M • *Tyrolean Inn,* 9600 Highway 9, Ben Lomond, 336-5188, German, I–M • *Ciao! Bella!!,* 9217 High 9, Ben Lomond, 336-9221, Italian, M • *Shadowbrook,* Wharf and Capitola roads, Capitola, 475-1511, spectacular setting on the sea, cable car down to restaurant, dancing, romantic, worth a visit, E • *Café Sparrow*, 8042 Soquel Drive, Aptos, 688-6238, charming setting for country French fare, M • *Chez Renee*, 9051 Soquel Drive, Aptos, 688-5566, Mediterranean and California fare, M–E • *Theo's*, 3101 North Main Street, Soquel, 462-3657, French country decor, own organic garden, I–M • Two lively local brew pubs for homemade brew, informal food, and camaraderie are *Santa Cruz Brewing Co. & Front Street Pub*, 516 Front Street, 429-8838; and *Seabright Brewery*, 519 Seabright Avenue, Santa Cruz, 426-2739, both I–M. For light meals try *The Crepe Place*, 1134 Soquel Avenue, Santa Cruz, 429-6103, I. For breakfast, the stars are *Zachary's*, 819 Pacific Avenue, 427-0646, I; and *The Broken Egg*, 7887 Soquel Drive, Aptos, 688-4322.

SIGHTSEEING   *Año Nuevo State Reserve*, New Years Creek Road (off Highway 1), Pescadero, 879-0595. Reservations for elephant seal tours, MISTIX, (800) 444-7275 beginning November 1. Tour fee, $2. Parking, $6 • *Natural Bridges State Beach*, West Cliff Drive, 423-4609. Hours: Daily 8 A.M. to dusk. Parking, $6 • *Roaring Camp & Big Trees Narrow-Gauge Railroad*, Graham Hill Road (off Highway 9), Felton, 335-4400. Hours: 75-minute steam train rides October to mid-June on weekends, weekdays also in summer. Check current schedules. Adults, $12; ages 3 to 15, $8.75; also 2½-hour excursions on the Santa Cruz Big Trees and Pacific Railway: adults, $14; children, $8.95 • *Long Marine Lab*, 100 Shaffer Road (past the end of Delaware Street just north of Natural Bridges State Park), Santa Cruz, 459-4308. Hours: Tuesday to Sunday 1 P.M. to 4 P.M. Donation • *McPherson Center for Art & History*, 705 Front Street, Santa Cruz, 454-0697 • Hours: Tuesday through Sunday 11 A.M. to 4 P.M., to 8 P.M. on Thursday. Admission to both art and history museums: adults, $3; students, $2; under 12, free • *Santa Cruz City Museum*, 1305 East Cliff Street, Santa Cruz, 429-3773. Hours: Tuesday to Friday 10 A.M. to 5 P.M., weekends 1 P.M. to 4 P.M. Donation • *University of California at Santa Cruz*, Bay and High streets, 459-4008. Parking fee, $3. Hours: Student-led tours by reservation, Monday to Friday 10:30 A.M. and 1:30 P.M. • *Arboretum*, High Street, 427-2998. Hours: Open daily 9 A.M. to 5 P.M. Guided tours Wednesday, Saturday, and Sunday 2 P.M. to 4 P.M. • *Santa Cruz Surfing Museum*, Lighthouse Point, West Cliff Drive, Santa Cruz, 429-3429. Hours: Thursday to Monday noon to 4 P.M., also Wednesday in summer. Donation $1; children free • *Santa Cruz Mission Adobe*, 134 School Street, Santa Cruz, 425-5849. Hours: Wednesday through Sunday 10 A.M. to 4 P.M. • *Santa Cruz Memorial Park*, 1927 Ocean Street Extension, Santa Cruz, 426-1601. Hours: Monday to Saturday 8 A.M. to 5 P.M. • *The Mystery Spot*, 1953 Branciforte Drive, Santa Cruz, 423-8897. Hours: Daily 9:30 A.M. to 5 P.M. Adults, $3; ages 5 to 11, $1.50 • *Mary Porter Sesnon Gallery*, UC–Santa Cruz, 459-2314. Hours: Tuesday to Sunday noon to 5 P.M. during academic year. Free • *Eloise*

Pickard Smith Gallery, Cowell College, UC—Santa Cruz, 459-2953. Hours: Tuesday to Sunday 11 A.M. to 5 P.M. Free • *Big Basin Redwoods State Park,* 21600 Big Basin Highway, Boulder Creek, 338-6132 or (800) 444-7525. Hours: Daylight hours. Parking, $5 • *Henry Cowell Redwoods State Park,* 101 Big Trees Park Road, Felton, 335-9145. Hours: Daylight hours. Parking fee, $5 • **Whale watching:** *Stagnaro's,* Santa Cruz Municipal Wharf, 427-2334.

INFORMATION *Santa Cruz County Conference and Visitors' Council,* 701 Front Street, Santa Cruz, CA 95060, 425-1234.

Taking the Cure at Calistoga

Feeling stressed? Need a rest? Winter getting to you? Pack your bags and take off for a sure cure in Calistoga.

Calistoga is unique in the Napa Valley, a funky town that found fame not just from grapes but from two other natural assets—mud and hot water.

This is mineral water, of course, which has always fascinated people who believe that natural hot springs possess healing powers. In the 1800s the rich and famous made a beeline to soak in similar waters at Saratoga Springs, New York, making it America's most fashionable resort.

Saratoga was the inspiration for Sam Brannan, a colorful character who had made a mint in the Gold Rush. According to local lore, Brannan was California's first millionaire, first newspaper publisher, first land developer, founder of the first bank and school, and the man who built the first railroad and telegraph line.

Always in the market for a new first, in 1859 he bought a square mile of land at the top of the Napa Valley just below Mt. St. Helena, a place where natural geysers spout water as hot as 212 degrees. His goal was to create the Saratoga of California. The story goes that while toasting the new town at a banquet, Brannan got his words mixed up, calling it "the Calistoga of Sarafornia"—and the name stuck.

Calistoga offered a bonus in the volcanic ash and peat moss that were in generous supply here, the makings for a treatment that would ultimately become better known than the hot springs—the famous Calistoga mud bath.

Today, with the revival of interest in spas and natural healing, Calistoga is more popular than ever. No longer just for people in search of cures for aches or arthritis, Calistoga's spas attract a large percentage of young and fashionable patrons who simply want to relax and de-stress.

This new breed of spagoer is changing things. In addition to mud baths and massage, you can try trendier treatments such as Japanese enzyme baths, herbal wraps, reflexology, or an acupressure facelift. Growing numbers of visitors have also spawned some delightful inns in the area.

Nor is the fun over after you try the treatments. There are some natural wonders to see, such as Calistoga's own "Old Faithful" geyser and a petrified forest, and several top wineries can be found around this northernmost Napa town.

Sandwiched between scenic hills, lined with wooden arcaded shops, and with an old train station at the end, Calistoga's Lincoln Street would look right at home in a movie western. But no western ever had signs like these: "Dr. Wilkinson's Hot Springs and Mud Baths," "International Spa," "Pine Street Inn and Eurospa." The oldest of the spas is Indian Springs, the newest incarnation of the original resort founded by Sam Brannan and going strong since 1865. Dr. Wilkinson has become a kind of guru of the mud bath set; he has been in business since 1946, and his own longevity seems to attest to the benefits of his regimens. The newest entry and one of the most attractive is the Lavender Hill Spa, which specializes in couples; it is out of downtown, on a terraced hillside off the highway.

Whichever spa you choose, the classic treatment is the same. First you step into the warm mud bath—and discover that this isn't the gooey stuff of your young mud pie days but a mix made buoyant by volcanic ash. Instead of sinking, you almost float, and the mixture has to be applied to arms and legs, something like a facial for the body. The face itself is not covered with mud, but with a light scented mask. Ten minutes spent relaxing in the mud is supposed to do good things for you, such as deep-heating muscles and joints, detoxifying the body, warming away tension and aches, and giving the skin a soft, healthy glow.

How does it feel to be immersed in mud? Some people absolutely love it; some find it vaguely distasteful. You really can't judge how you'll feel until you try it for yourself. Some couples like the experience so much they share it in private rooms with his-and-her tubs. The newest innovation, the enzyme bath, is a variation that puts you in a steamy pile of cedar and fir shavings, to the tune of New Age music. Some say this feels cleaner, but overall it generates the same extreme reactions—love and hate.

After the mud bath, the next step is to wash off well in the shower and proceed to a hot mineral water bath in a Jacuzzi tub, letting your body soak in the benefits of the minerals. Next comes a stay in the steam room, where the steam also comes from mineral water. By now your body feels like gelatin, and you are taken to a private booth, wrapped in a soft blanket, and left to relax and cool down. The odds are good that you'll soon be sound asleep.

You can stop there, but most people wind things up with a wonderful massage. They don't come much better than in Calistoga.

These are the basics, taking about two hours, but there are many other treatments to try, such as facials—plain or followed by a mud mask—or the "facelift," a one-hour facial massage concentrating on restoring skin tone. A skin-glow rub consists of a light massage with fine sea salt, followed by a scented loofah scrub, leaving your skin feeling as soft and smooth as a newborn's. It's easy to spend four hours being rejuvenated, and many spas offer a whole day of pampering.

The ideal time for the shorter routine is late afternoon, when you can come back and nap a little before dinner, but that time fills first, so reserve well ahead. Whenever you are scheduled, after you've had your tensions soaked, kneaded, and napped away, you should feel fabulous.

Some spas have their own motel accommodations, putting you just steps from your room, but unless you are attracted by their moderate rates, Calistoga has many better lodgings to offer. Just a short walk from Lincoln Avenue is the Brannan Cottage Inn, the original complex built by Sam Brannan for his Calistoga Hot Springs Resort, which is on the National Register of Historic Places. The cottage rooms have been nicely restored and furnished in pretty country style, with lots of pine and wicker. Two more pleasant choices within walking distance of town are the Elms Inn, a handsome Victorian house, and Scott Courtyard, six suites in bungalows around an attractive court with a pool and hot tub. Those on a budget may be interested in the two cottages that make up Oakwood, another in-town bed-and-breakfast inn.

Even nicer oases can be found north of town on Highway 128, known as Foothill Boulevard, a busy road that calms down when it splits off from Highway 29 just north of Calistoga. Foothill House is a restored farmhouse with a fireplace in each guest room, and the Calistoga Country Lodge is my favorite, with whimsical Southwestern decor, lots of cow-motif statues and upholstery, and a pool with lovely valley views.

Other possibilities include the stylishly furnished Meadowlark Country House, nicely secluded and with a pool. The antique-filled Larkmead Country Inn is located in the vineyards next to the Hanns Kornell Champagne Cellars. The Silver Rose Inn, a larger complex with gardens and a fountain, has nine elaborately furnished rooms and suites, each decorated in a different theme, from teddy bears to western boots and saddle, but all sharing the lovely location with views of the vineyards.

The real find for escapists is Quail Mountain, a stunning contemporary home in a 26-acre forested range high above the valley. Each of the three rooms has a private deck, and there is a pool plus a hot tub on a deck surrounded by tall trees.

Another kind of option is the Mountain Home Ranch, off in the wooded mountains outside of town. Meals are family style, and accommodations are rustic, without telephone or TV. Guests can fish in a lake, swim in the pool, and play tennis.

What to do in town in Calistoga when you aren't at the spa? One highly recommended stop is the Sharpsteen Museum, whose creative display takes you back to the 1860s with well-done dioramas and 3-D shadow boxes, exact even down to details like ladies' fans and kitchen furnishings. The museum was the idea of Ben Sharpsteen, a onetime Disney producer who retired to Calistoga, and it quickly became a community project that is one of the town's prides. One of the early Brannan cottages was moved to adjoin the museum, and a handsome garden was planted in between. The cottage is furnished in Victorian style.

The town itself is only a few blocks long and won't take long to cover. This is not a shopper's mecca, but it does have a few galleries of interest on Lincoln Avenue, especially the Artful Eye for contemporary crafts.

A main attraction in town is the 1868 railroad depot, one of California's oldest. It now houses the local information office, a café, a good wine store, and a variety of shops. There are more stores in half a dozen restored Pullman cars right next door, though the exterior is more interesting than the wares of most of the shops inside. Behind the train cars there's an antiques store that is worth a look.

The Calistoga area is prime for winery visits. Sterling Vineyards is unique for the aerial tram that shuttles visitors from the parking lot to the hilltop winery for superb views of the Napa Valley. There is a self-guided winery tour and a tasting room with a terrace that offers fabulous views.

Hanns Kornell Champagne Cellars, a well-known sparkling wine producer, has historic aging cellars and offers interesting tours of the champagne-making process. Chateau Montelena, a highly regarded maker of premium wines, requires an appointment for a tour, but you are welcome to drive up to see the native stone building, dating from 1882, and the beautiful Oriental garden setting that has been created on the grounds. Arching bridges connect a series of islands in picturesque Jade Lake. Two of the pagodas can be used for picnicking, but only if you call ahead to reserve the space.

Cuvaison, with a mission-style building on nicely landscaped grounds, is an alternate for scenic picnicking. And Clos Pegase merits a look for the dramatic stucco Mediterranean-inspired building designed by noted architect Michael Graves.

Turning from wine back to water, those who have never seen a natural geyser in action can visit California's own "Old Faithful," almost next door to Chateau Montelena. It is one of the few geysers in the world that perform at regular intervals. Thousands of gallons of 350-degree water ascend some 60 feet into the air in dependable repeat performances every 40 minutes. The show lasts about four minutes. The only thing that shifts this regular schedule seems to be an earthquake. From two days to two weeks before a quake occurs within a 500-mile area, the eruptions have been found to be farther apart, making them an early warning system that is under study by scientists.

Incidentally, Calistoga's mineral water is bottled and sold in city stores by Crystal Geyser Natural Beverages and the Calistoga Mineral Water Company.

Another natural phenomenon in the area is the Petrified Forest, where giant redwoods uprooted by volcanic action millions of years ago have gradually turned to stone. It's not a must-see, but it is interesting if you like that sort of natural curiosity.

If you want to go biking in vineyard country, you might want to try "Cruizin' with Jules," two- or four-hour rental-bike tours that take you to the top of Napa's hillsides so you can see the scenery with maximum coasting and minimum work. Balloon tours are another popular way to see the sights, and Calistoga also boasts a glider port right in the middle of town, where you can soar above the valley with an experienced pilot.

If the weather makes you want to enjoy the natural beauty of the upper Napa Valley close up, Bothe–Napa Valley State Park provides 1,800 acres of hiking trails and picnic grounds, or you can head a few miles north to Robert Louis Stevenson State Park, whose beauty inspired Stevenson to write *Silverado Squatters,* a book about his stay here with his bride in 1880. Stevenson called 4,500-foot Mt. St. Helena "the Mont Blanc of the Coast Range." The five-mile trail to the top rewards with wonderful vistas of the Napa and Sonoma valleys. Note that this is a wilderness park without services.

Too much to fit into one weekend? Better plan a return visit—and another round of soaks and massage. In Calistoga, it's true that you can't get too much of a good thing.

Area Code: 707

DRIVING DIRECTIONS   From Highway 101, take Route 37 east, then Highway 29 north to Calistoga. Coming from I-80, take Route 12 west to Highway 29 north. An alternate to Highway 29 to avoid traffic is the parallel Silverado Trail from Napa. Calistoga is 77 miles from San Francisco, about 79 miles from Sacramento.

ACCOMMODATIONS   Most inns offer their lowest rates in winter. • *Brannon Cottage Inn,* 109 Wapoo Avenue, Calistoga, 94515, 942-4200, EE, CP • *The Elms,* 2300 Cedar Street, Calistoga, 94515, 942-9476, E–EE, CP • *Quail Mountain,* 4455 North St. Helena Highway, Calistoga, 94515, 942-0316, E, CP • *Foothill House,* 3037 Foothill

Boulevard, Calistoga, 94515, 942-6933, E–EE, CP • *Calistoga Country Lodge,* 2883 Foothill Boulevard, Calistoga, 94515, 942-5555, E, CP • *Scott Courtyard,* 1443 Second Street, Calistoga, 94515, 942-0948, E, CP • *Silver Rose Inn,* 351 Rosedale Road, Calistoga, 94515, 942-9581 or (800) 995-9381, E–EE, CP • *Oakwood,* 1503 Lake Street, Calistoga, 94515, 942-5381, M, CP • *Meadowlark Country House,* 601 Petrified Forest Road, Calistoga, 94515, 942-5651, E–EE, CP • *Larkmead Country Inn,* 1103 Larkmead Lane, Calistoga, 94515, 942-5360, M–E, CP • *Mountain Home Ranch,* 3400 Mountain Home Ranch Road, Calistoga, 94515, 942-6616, June to Labor Day, M–EE, MAP; February to June and September to December, I–E, CP.

CALISTOGA SPAS This is a partial list; write to the Chamber of Commerce for a complete roster. • *Dr. Wilkinson's Hot Springs Spa,* 1507 Lincoln Avenue, 942-4102, long-established and reliable, mud and mineral baths, massage, facials, cerofango treatments, acupressure facelifts, indoor and outdoor pools. Motel, I; rooms in Victorian guest house, M; guest cottages, I–EE • *Lincoln Avenue Spa,* 1339 Lincoln Avenue, 942-5296; mud, herbal, mint, and sea mud wraps; massage; herbal facials; acupressure facelifts. Lodging packages available with Golden Haven Hot Springs Spa Resort, I–M • *Calistoga Spa Hot Springs,* 1006 Washington Street, 942-6269, mud and mineral baths, four heated mineral pools, including wading pool, I–M • *International Spa,* 1300 Washington Street, 942-6122. Aromatherapy, seaweed mineral baths, massage, herbal blanket wraps, herbal facials, foot reflexology. Motel rooms next door at adjoining *Roman Spa Resort,* indoor and outdoor pools, sauna, I–M • *Indian Springs Hot Springs Spa and Resort,* 1712 Lincoln Avenue, 942-4913. Volcanic ash mud baths, mineral baths, massage, big geyser-fed outdoor warm-water pool, tennis courts, 16 cottage suites, E–EE • *Lavender Hill Spa,* 1015 Foothill Boulevard (Highway 29), Calistoga, 942-4495. Specializes in couples, offering fango mud, seawood, summer mint, and rosemary, and aromatherapy mineral salt baths, facials, massage, foot reflexology, and herbal wraps. No lodging.

DINING *Catahoula,* Mount View Hotel, 1457 Lincoln Avenue, 942-2275, ex-Campton Place chef serving up nouvelle-Southern cuisine, best in town, M • *All Seasons Café,* 1400 Lincoln Avenue, 942-9111, long-time favorite for creative bistro menu, wide wine selection, M • *Wappo Bar & Bistro,* 1226-B Washington Street, Calistoga, 942-4712, eclectic menu, excellent reviews, M • *Calistoga Inn and Napa Valley Brewing Company,* 1250 Lincoln Avenue, 942-4101, informal, snacks to full meals, brewery on premises, I–M.

SIGHTSEEING *Sharpsteen Museum and Sam Brannan Cottage,* 1311 Washington Street, 942-5911. Hours: April to October, daily 10

A.M. to 4 P.M.; rest of year, noon to 4 P.M. Free • *Old Faithful Geyser,* 1299 Tubbs Lane, 942-6463. Hours: Daily 9 A.M. to 5 P.M.; in summer to 6 P.M. Adults, $5; ages 6 to 12, $2 • *Petrified Forest,* 4100 Petrified Forest Road, 942-6667. Hours: Daily 10 A.M. to 5 P.M., in summer to 6 P.M. Adults, $3; ages 4 to 11, $1 • *Bothe–Napa Valley State Park,* Highways 29/128, three miles south of Calistoga, 942-4575. Parking, $5 • *Robert Louis Stevenson State Park,* Highway 29, eight miles north of Calistoga, c/o Bothe–Napa Valley State Park, 942-4575. Free.

WINERIES   *Sterling Vineyards,* 1111 Dunaweal Lane (off Highway 29), 942-3344, self-guided tours. Hours: Daily 10:30 A.M. to 4:30 P.M. Tram ride: $5; under 16, free • *Clos Pegase,* 1060 Dunaweal Lane, 942-4981. Hours: 10:30 A.M. to 5 P.M., free tours 11 A.M. and 2 P.M. • *Chateau Montelena,* 1429 Tubbs Lane, 942-5105. Hours: Daily 10 A.M. to 4 P.M., tours and picnicking by appointment. Charge for wine tasting • *Hanns Kornell Champagne Cellars,* 1091 Larkmead Lane, 942-0859. Hours: 10 A.M. to 5 P.M., regular free tours held until 3:45 P.M. • *Cuvaison Winery,* 4550 Silverado Trail, 942-6266. Tours by appointment, 10 A.M. to 5 P.M.

ACTIVITIES   **Bike rentals:** *Jules Culver Bicycles,* 1227F Lincoln Avenue, 942-0421, also "Cruizin' with Jules" downhill bike tours; *Palisades Mountain Sport,* 1330-B Gerrard Street, 942-9687 • **Balloon tours:** *Once in a Lifetime Balloon Company,* 1458 Lincoln Avenue, #12, 942-6541 • **Glider rides:** *Calistoga Gliderport,* 1545 Lincoln Avenue, 942-5000.

INFORMATION   *Calistoga Chamber of Commerce,* Calistoga Depot, 1458 Lincoln Avenue, Calistoga, CA 94515, 942-6333.

A Peak Experience at North Tahoe

Standing atop a powdery mountain and looking down at America's loveliest Alpine lake is an ultimate scenic ski experience, a vision so celestial that one of Lake Tahoe's ski areas has aptly been dubbed "Heavenly." The extraordinary depth of the lake, averaging 989 feet and as much as 1,645 feet at the deepest point, means that the water does not freeze, remaining a shimmering mirror year-round.

And you needn't be a skier to enjoy this mountain majesty. It can be viewed from on high via cable cars or at water level aboard a cruise boat. The famous 70-mile drive around the lake is even more beautiful when the mountains are covered with a coat of white.

So while it may be heaven for skiers, winter at Tahoe is wonderful even if you don't know a schuss from a slalom. There's activity galore—ice skating, sleigh riding, and snowmobiling, plus a host of shops and galleries to browse. And if all that isn't enough, Lady Luck beckons just across the border at the Nevada gambling casinos.

The peak excitement at North Lake Tahoe comes during the annual Snowfest in early March, a celebration that has grown over the past decade into the biggest winter carnival in the West. Festivities literally start off with a bang with the opening-night fireworks, a downhill torchlight parade, and a laser light show at Squaw Valley. For the next ten days there are races on the slopes, parades in town, costume competitions, kids' events, dances, and crazy contests from ice-cream eating to a snowman-building competition. The ice-carving competition brings out the artistic with intricate entries such as an aquarium complete with fish. And they really get into the dress-your-dog competition; past entrants have been togged out as a bride and groom, a native with dreadlocks, a cowboy with boots and lasso, and the Phantom of the Opera, complete with cape, top hat, and mask.

There's no better time to enjoy the fun and explore the skiing and other diversions of North Tahoe. Those who are used to skiing at Heavenly or other areas near South Lake Tahoe will find this part of the lake less congested, particularly the attractive wooded western lakeshore. And since the biggest casinos are a long drive away, there is much less emphasis on gambling here. Tahoe City is a small, unpretentious place with some interesting shopping complexes and dining places, and Truckee, a town that still looks a lot like it did 100 years ago, has its own share of intriguing small shops and restaurants.

The jewel in North Tahoe's mountain crown is Squaw Valley USA, a world-class resort nestled below six lofty Sierra peaks. These vast slopes offer open bowls and trails, 33 lifts, miles of runs for the beginner and intermediate skiers, and some of the most challenging advanced skiing to be found anywhere. The steep KT-22 trail is a legendary challenge among experts.

Skier or not, you'll find a ride on the Squaw Valley Cable Car to be an unsurpassed thrill, a 2,000-foot glide to the High Camp complex, where you are parallel with the peaks and can see across a vast mountain panorama to the lake. The recently added Bath and Tennis Club at High Camp allows you to dine as well as enjoy an all-year Olympic-size ice skating rink and heated tennis courts, all 8,200 feet up in the sky.

Parents will appreciate the separate Squaw Valley Children's World lodge, with infant care, supervised snow play, and a junior ski school for children ages 6 months to 12 years. Three pony tows and a platter tow top this area exclusively for kids. Reserved parking makes it easy to drive up and drop off the little ones.

The Olympic Winter Games held in 1960 left Squaw Valley a happy legacy of slopeside accommodations, shops, and restaurants, but the best was yet to come with the opening of the Resort at Squaw Creek, a luxurious lodging set apart from the main valley on 620 acres. It boasts its own ice skating rink and health club as well as on-site lifts and trails that connect to the big mountain. Every room has a mountain view. For those who can afford the tab, this is Squaw Valley's prime place to stay. In summer there's the added lure of a Robert Trent Jones golf course.

The rest of the valley lodgings also offer shuttle or walk-to-the-slopes convenience. Many are suites with convenient kitchens, but they come with a high price tag. More budget-conscious rooms can be found in lodges farther from the slopes and in bed-and-breakfast inns in Tahoe City or Truckee.

Free daily bus service provided to most area ski mountains allows you to sample not only Squaw but some of its smaller neighbors such as Alpine Meadows, the locals' favorite, and Northstar, an attractive self-contained contemporary resort with its own ski mountain. Many families enjoy staying at Northstar, where you can walk to everything and the crowds are small.

Cross-country skiers will appreciate the Ski Tahoe North interchangeable ticket that allows sampling seven resorts and more than 500 kilometers of groomed trails.

For those who would rather shop than ski, the North Tahoe area has some of the best offerings around the lake. The Boatworks Mall in Tahoe City, an attractive amalgam of redwood and skylights right on a lakefront marina, has a dozen quality shops offering everything from games to gemstones. The Sierra Galleries have a selection of fine art and sculpture, and the Heritage Gallery features graphics, including a collection of vintage photos of Lake Tahoe. More shops beckon in the nearby Lighthouse Center and Roundhouse complexes, and there are more galleries on Main Street. One of the most interesting stops is High Country Silverworks on North Lake Boulevard, featuring a huge variety of fine handcrafts and jewelry.

While you are browsing, take a look at the famous "Fanny Bridge" over the Truckee River just south of Lucky's supermarket. It was named for all the summer tourists bent over to watch the giant rainbow trout leaping in the river. Nearby is the Gatekeeper's Cabin, restored by the North Lake Tahoe Historical Society and open to the public in summer.

Truckee is a total change of mood—and time. Commercial Row, the main street, with its arcaded shops and old depot, is straight out of the 1890s. Plan to stay awhile; almost every little shop on this short street is worth a visit. Tiffany lamps, handwoven rugs, blown glass, pottery, and outdoor wear are just a few of the items available. Truckee has its own share of good restaurants as well.

Since Amtrak comes right into town, you could avoid winter driving by taking the train to Truckee and then taking advantage of free bus shuttles to skiing.

If you bring your car, pick the sunniest day of your stay for a drive around the lake. Allow about two hours for the 72-mile loop if you are not making stops. For some details on the sights, see pages 75 to 77, but you'll need no guide to know you are taking one of America's most scenic routes. A cruise offers another beautiful perspective that lets you fully appreciate the majesty of the surrounding mountains.

What with the lake, the shops, and a number of outdoor diversions, the days will fly by even if you're not making the snow fly. There are even a couple of small museums that merit a look. The Donner Museum marks the place near Truckee where the Donner Party braved the awful winter of 1846–47; the museum has artifacts, movies, and a slide show that tell of their ordeal. And the Western American Ski Sport Museum at Boreal Ridge will show you how skiing has changed from 1860 to the present. The exhibit includes vintage ski movies.

When the sun goes down, North Tahoe's après-ski spots wake up. Look for live music at Humpty's Pierce Street Annex and Rosie's Café in Tahoe City, at the Olympic Village Inn at Squaw Valley, and at Cottonwood in Truckee.

Or you may hear the siren call of the casinos over in Nevada. Casinos like Cal-Neva Lodge, on the north side of the lake, are small-time compared to the glitzy hotels adjoining South Lake Tahoe, but they have their fair share of gaming tables and slot machine action. The classiest of the casinos is farther east at the Hyatt Regency in the posh resort community of Incline Village, and it is worth the extra few minutes' drive. Watch for Incline Village signs—the hotel itself has no signs on the highway.

Whatever happens at the casinos, you'll likely agree that a North Tahoe weekend is a winner.

Area Code: 916

DRIVING DIRECTIONS   Follow I-80 east to Truckee; turn south on Highway 89 for Squaw Valley and Tahoe City. From the south, take Route 50 east and turn north on Highway 89. Carry chains; winter storms can come up suddenly, and chains are required on some portions of the road in bad weather. For winter road conditions, phone (916) 445-7623. North Lake Tahoe is about 200 miles from San Francisco, 88 miles northeast of Sacramento.

PUBLIC TRANSPORTATION   Amtrak serves Truckee from San Jose, Oakland, Richmond, Martinez, and Sacramento; phone (800) USA-RAIL for information. Reno, Nevada, is the closest airport, about

45 minutes away, with shuttle service to Truckee. It is easy to manage without a car if you stay at a resort or in Tahoe City or Truckee. Ski areas offer free shuttles, and the local TART bus system will take you from town to town for a pittance.

ACCOMMODATIONS *The Resort at Squaw Creek,* Olympic Valley, 96146, 583-6300 or (800) 3CREEK3, posh resort, great views from every room, EE • *Northstar at Tahoe,* P.O. Box 129, Truckee, 96161, 562-1113 or (800) 533-6787, E–EE • *Olympic Village Inn,* 1909 Chamonix Place, Olympic Valley, 96146, 581-6000 or (800) VILLAGE, nicely furnished suites, mini-kitchens, stereo, heated pool, hot tub, shuttle to lifts, E–EE • *Squaw Valley Inn,* 1920 Squaw Valley Road, Olympic Valley, 96146, 583-1576 or (800) 323-7666, comfortable rooms, E–EE • *Squaw Valley Lodge,* 201 Squaw Peak Road, Olympic Valley, 96146, 583-5500 or (800) 922-9970, studio and one-bedroom suites, kitchens, EE • *River Ranch,* Highway 89 and Alpine Meadows Road, Tahoe City, 95730, 583-4264 or in California (800) 535-9900, historic rustic lodge, attractive rooms with balconies overlooking the river, M • *Mayfield House,* 236 Grove Street, Tahoe City, 96145, warm and pleasant B&B, M–E, CP • *Chaney House B&B,* P.O. Box 7852, Tahoe City, 96145, 525-7333, striking stone house in the pines, E, CP • *Rockwood Lodge,* 5295 West Lake Boulevard, Homewood, 96141, 525-5273 or (800) LE-TAHOE, stone-and-timber home on the lake, attractively furnished, E–EE, CP • *Sunnyside,* 1850 West Lake Boulevard, Tahoe City, 96145, 583-7200 or in California (800) 822-2SKI, attractive lodge on the lake, modern furnishings, M–E, CP • *Charney Chalet Resort,* 6549 North Lake Boulevard, Tahoe Vista, 96148, 546-2529, motel in the pines, some lake views, I–M • *The Cottage Inn,* 1690 West Lake Boulevard, Tahoe City, 96145, 581-4073 or (800) 581-4073, cottages, Scandinavian furnishings, sauna, E–EE, CP • *Alpenhaus,* 6941 West Lake Boulevard, Tahoma, 96142, 525-5000, rustic Alpine-style inn, M–E, CP • *Richardson House,* P.O. Box 2011, Truckee, 95734, 587-5388, modest B&B in town, I–M, CP.

DINING *Glissandi,* Resort at Squaw Creek (see above), elegant splurge, EE • *Wolfdale's,* 640 North Lake Boulevard, Tahoe City, 983-5700, creative menus, Japanese accent, M–E • *Christy Hill,* 115 Grove Street, Lakehouse Mall, Tahoe City, 583-8551, highly rated California cuisine, E • *Rosie's Café,* 571 North Lake Boulevard, Tahoe City, 583-8504, the local hangout, great lunches, I; varied dinner menu, M • *River Ranch,* Tahoe City (see above), continental dishes, game, I–M • *Za's,* 395 North Lake Boulevard, 583-1812, local favorite for bargain-priced Italian food, I–M • *Jake's on the Lake,* 780 North Lake Boulevard, Tahoe City, 583-0188, reliable standby for steak and seafood, M • *Backstage Bistro,* Squaw Valley, 581-0454, very popular, M (in summer same owner has *Chambers Landing,* 6300 Chambers Lodge Road,

Homewood, 525-7262, M) • *Sunnyside,* Tahoe City (see above), known for French-fried zucchini and gin fizzes, M; also café menu, I–M • *La Playa,* 7042 North Lake Boulevard, Tahoe Vista, 546-5903, beach bar, lake views, French country and seafood, M–E • *Le Petit Pier,* 7238 North Lake Boulevard, Tahoe Vista, 546-4464, water views, continental menu, E–EE • *Swiss Lakewood,* 5055 West Lake Boulevard, Homewood, 525-5211, game, seafood, beef fondue in winter, M–E • *Creekside Grill,* Olympic Village Inn, Olympic Valley (see above), I–M • *The Alpenhaus,* Tahoma (see above), M–E • *The Basque Club,* Northstar Village, 562-2460, five-course traditional Basque meal, M • *The Left Bank,* 10096 Commercial Row, Truckee, 587-4694, country French with Oriental touch, E • *O.B.'s Pub and Restaurant,* 10048 Commercial Row, Truckee, 587-4164, popular, fajitas to fish and chips, I • *Cottonwood,* 10142 Rue Hilltop, Truckee, 587-5711, great views, eclectic menu, live jazz on weekends, M • *The Passage,* Truckee Hotel, Commercial Row, Truckee, 587-7619, seafood, international menu, I–M.

SIGHTSEEING *Squaw Valley Scenic Cable Car Ride,* Squaw Valley USA, 583-6985. Hours: Daily, weekends 8:30 A.M. to 9 P.M., weekdays 9 A.M. to 9 P.M. Adults, $12; children, $5; after 4 P.M. $5 for all • *Donner State Park Memorial Museum,* off I-80 near Donner Lake, 587-3841. Hours: Daily 10 A.M. to 4 P.M. Adults, $2; ages 6 to 12, $1 • *Western America Ski & Sport Museum,* Boreal Ski Area, off I-80 at Boreal Ridge exit, 587-3841. Hours: Tuesday to Sunday 11 A.M. to 5 P.M. Free • **Lake Tahoe cruises:** *North Tahoe Cruises,* Lighthouse Marina, 700 North Lake Boulevard, Tahoe City, 583-0141; *North Shore Cruises,* Tahoe Yacht Harbor, Tahoe City, 583-5570 •

ACTIVITIES **Sleigh rides** (by prior reservation only)*: Sugar Bowl,* 426-3651; *Northstar,* 562-1230 (Northstar rides can be combined with dinner at the Basque Club) • **Hot-air balloon rides:** *Mountain High Balloons,* 587-6292 • **Snowmobiling:** *Zephyr Cove Snowmobile Center,* 882-0788; *TC Sno Mo's,* 581-3906; *Eagle Ridge Snowmobile Outfitters,* 546-8667 • **Horseback riding:** *Northstar,* 562-1230, trails open all year, weather permitting.

INFORMATION *Tahoe North Visitors' and Convention Bureau,* P.O. Box 5578, Tahoe City, CA 96145, 583-3494 or (800) TAHOE-4-U.

A Whale of a Time at Point Reyes

Not very far from the Bay Area buildup is a wild, salt-sprayed peninsula that lures geologists, nature lovers, escapists, and whale watchers from miles around.

Point Reyes, a strip separated from the rest of Marin County by Tomales Bay, was named a national seashore in 1962, preserving a diverse 69,000 acres of hills and meadows, cliffs and headland, estuaries and ocean beaches—much of it within sight of dense pine forests. Deer and tule elk wander the meadows, sea lions bask on the rocks, and as many as 361 species of birds have been sighted in the area, from huge hawks and eagles to flocks of egrets, herons, pelicans, and other shorebirds. A legendary lighthouse adds to the scene.

This is great country for exploring, on foot, by bike, or on horseback. Mild weather as early as February carpets the land with wildflowers, and in winter Point Reyes offers one of the best viewpoints on the West Coast for watching gray whales migrating south to Baja California.

Small, sleepy towns like Olema, Point Reyes Station, and Inverness supply a variety of inns, a few galleries, and just enough good dining to keep visitors happy. The number-one lodging pick has to be the Blackthorne Inn, nestled in a wooded canyon like a four-story redwood-and-pine treehouse, with private decks and hot tubs hidden off spiral staircases. The eight-sided "Eagle's Nest" on top will delight romantics.

Ten Inverness Way is a cozy choice in a pretty garden in town, with patchwork quilts on the beds and a welcoming fireplace in the living room. Holly Tree Inn is in a country setting and offers airy spaces decorated with Laura Ashley prints. The owners also offer some of the many private cottages that are available in the area.

Other choices include rustic but cozy digs up the hill at Manka's Inverness Lodge, above one of the best restaurants in the area; two of the rooms have balconies with bay views. Sandy Cove Inn is a charming tiny cottage colony right on the water, and the ranch-style Point Reyes Country Inn and Stables is out in the country, with balconies or garden patios to enjoy the scene.

The national seashore can fill a weekend by itself. Start at the attractive rustic Bear Valley visitors' center just past Olema for guidance in seeing its many aspects. There's a 20-minute introductory film called *Something Special,* and you can inquire here about the many ranger-guided activities, which include bird walks, tide pooling, hikes, tours of the historic boathouse, an evening lighthouse tour, and an informative walk along the Earthquake Trail. Native American volunteers also offer demonstrations of traditional Indian skills and talks on their culture at Kule Loklo, a reconstructed Coast Miwok Indian village.

Another special place open to visitors is the Morgan Horse Ranch, a working farm where horses are trained for use by National Park Rangers. The story of the restored Pierce Ranch, a dairy ranch dating back to 1858, can be learned on a self-guided tour.

Pierce Point, not far from the ranch, is the best place to spot the majestic antlered tule elk that have been carefully nurtured in the park. The herd, originally 13 elk brought into the park in 1976, now numbers more than 100.

Before you make the trip to Point Reyes Lighthouse, ask at the visitors' center about the weather, since the headlands where the historic 1870 lighthouse stands 294 feet above the sea are often shrouded in fog. It is said to be the windiest and foggiest spot on the West Coast, a notorious hazard for boats. On a clear day, however, the views are stunning. One of the advantages in coming off-season is that you avoid the worst of the fog season, in summer.

You can reach a good vantage point on an easy half-mile walk from the parking lot to an observation deck, but a descent of 300 steps from the parking area leads to the prime spot for whale watching. The peak times are usually mid-January for the southward migration, mid-March to watch the returning whales with their young calves. Since parking at the lighthouse is limited, a shuttle bus from the South Beach entrance runs on crowded weekends or holidays. Check for current information and for weather conditions before you plan a trip. The lighthouse has its own visitors' center building, with exhibits on whales, wildflowers, geology, and lighthouses. Naturalists are also available to provide some fascinating whale lore.

Another way to see the whales is on expeditions run by the Point Reyes–Farallon Islands National Marine Sanctuary. The islands are a strip paralleling the coast from the tip of Point Reyes to south of the Golden Gate.

Point Reyes has special fascination for geologists because it is land in motion. The area sits astride the meeting place of two of the great land plates forming Earth's crust, the Pacific and American plates. The point where the two don't quite meet, the infamous 700-mile San Andreas Fault, is constantly in flux. It was a point of tremendous pressure buildup back in 1906, as the plates slipped and strained against each other. The town of Olema became the epicenter of the devastating 1906 San Francisco earthquake, which thrust the Point Reyes Peninsula 20 feet to the northwest. The area was much less affected by the more recent California quakes in 1989 and 1992, which peaked farther south and north.

Not far from the visitors' center is the Earthquake Trail, a walk of just over half a mile along the fracture zone of the 1906 quake. There are pictures of the damage done and information about present theory on earthquakes. You can actually stand with one foot on either side of the San Andreas fault.

The Woodpecker Trails and a Nature Walk are other easy walks near the center.

One of the most popular hikes in the area is the Bear Valley Trail, running along Bear Valley Creek through forests of fir and redwood trees to Arch Rock and a wonderful coastline vista. A longer trek, seven miles round-trip, leads to Tomales Point, where the peninsula narrows and you can see ocean waves on one side, calm Tomales Bay on the other. The Point is another good bet for spotting tule elk.

Chimney Rock lies at the other end of the peninsula between the ocean and Drakes Bay, reached via a turnoff on the lighthouse road. In spring the cliffs are covered with wildflowers. If you want to picnic on the small protected beach, the Inverness Store Deli can supply all the fixings.

Some beach destinations are reachable by car. Point Reyes Beach runs on and off for nearly 30 miles, divided into north and south portions. These are great areas for beachcombing, but don't go near the water. Riptide currents and undertow make it treacherous.

Limantour Road leads to a lovely beach with calm water where you can wade with the birds, weather permitting. If there is sun, this is also a place for basking. The Estero de Limantour, close by, is a favorite spot for bird-watchers.

Even when the weather is hazy at Point Reyes, you may find sunshine at Hearts Desire Beach in Tomales Bay State Park, at the sheltered opposite side of the peninsula. It can be reached by car off Sir Francis Drake Boulevard.

For a change of pace, visit Johnson's Oyster Company, on Sir Francis Drake Boulevard within the national seashore boundaries. The owners have been oyster farmers for many generations, using the traditional method of seeding the shells, then hanging them on racks in the shallow water of the bay. It takes 18 months before the oysters are ready for sale. There's lots to see here—an incubation room where oysters are cared for in huge tubs of water until they big enough to go outside, boats being loaded and unloaded, and oyster-filled nets being hauled out of the water. Sample the tasty critters in a cocktail sauce, or buy them in the shell to take home.

It does sometimes rain in winter, but there are diversions if the weather is uncooperative. Point Reyes Station, population 675, is the liveliest town nearby, a onetime rail junction that still has some quaint Old West flavor. One of the most interesting shops in town is Black Mountain Weavers, a cooperative with a wide selection of crafts. The William Lester Gallery and the Borge Gallery have many paintings of Marin land and seascapes. The Station House Café, which looks like an ordinary diner, is known for its excellent California cuisine and has live music on weekends; the Point Reyes Roadhouse serves micro-brewery beers on tap and has a super oyster bar and entrées from cheese steaks to Cajun snapper.

Special stops in Inverness are Shaker Shops West, with a selection of authentic Shaker furniture reproductions and hand-crafted gifts, and the Bellwether shop, offering baskets, jewelry, and crafts.

Follow Sir Francis Drake Boulevard inland for half an hour and you'll be in San Anselmo, a pleasant town that is the antiquing center of Marin County, with wall-to-wall shops. Or you could take a drive to secluded little Bolinas, a community south of the national seashore prettily set on bluffs overlooking the Pacific. Bolinas has gained notoriety because residents keep taking down the signs that would direct visitors into town. Driving south, look for the turnoff on the right on Highway 1 just after Rancho Boliulines, a private residence, and you'll be on the Bolinas–Olema Road, leading into town.

The spirit of the 1960s is still alive and well in Bolinas, a town with a mix of overage hippies, artists, craftspeople, retirees, and some wealthy folks who've built beautiful homes to appreciate the natural surroundings. Take a drive around, and stay for a while. Learn a little bit of local lore at the town museum, and look into the little crafts shops. Stop at the local gathering place, the Bolinas Bay Bakery and Café, for breakfast or lunch, and try the renowned cinnamon buns. Smiley's Schooner Saloon, with its old oak bar and gleaming brass, is the perfect place to while away part of the afternoon on a dreary day.

Bolinas Lagoon, on Highway 1, should be noted by anyone who is interested in bird life. It is a sanctuary for thousands of shorebirds, and the sandpits and dunes are often occupied by seals. Another interesting spot is the Point Reyes Bird Observatory Banding Station at the Palomarin Trailhead of the national seashore. The public is welcome to observe bird research in action. To get there, watch for Mesa Road, a turnoff from the Bolinas–Olema Road. Many hiking trails can also be reached from this trailhead.

Or, if none of the above appeals, you can always head back to your inn, sit back, and just enjoy the peace and quiet. It's one of the many rare finds at Point Reyes.

Area Code: 415

DRIVING DIRECTIONS Point Reyes National Seashore can be reached via roller-coaster scenic Highway 1, or take Highway 101 north, then head west on Francis Drake Boulevard to Olema. The Point Reyes National Seashore Bear Valley Visitors' Center is a half-mile west of Olema, about 60 miles from San Francisco, 135 miles from Sacramento.

ACCOMMODATIONS *Blackthorne Inn,* 266 Vallejo Avenue, P.O. Box 712, Inverness Park, 94937, 663-8621, M–EE, CP • *Ten Inverness Way,* Box 73, Inverness, 94937, 669-1648, M–E, CP • *Sandy Cove Inn,* 12990 Sir Francis Drake Boulevard, P.O. Box 869, Inverness, 94937, 669-COVE, E • *Manka's Inverness Lodge & Restaurant,* off Sir Francis Drake Boulevard, P.O. Box 1110, Inverness, 94937, 669-1034, M–EE • *Holly Tree Inn and Cottages,* 3 Silverhills Road, Box 642, Point Reyes Station, 94956, 663-1554, E–EE, CP • *Point Reyes Seashore Lodge,* 10021 Highway 1, P.O. Box 39, Olema, 94950, 663-9000, modern, well furnished, in-room refrigerators, nice lawn out back, M–EE, CP • *Roundstone Farm,* 9940 Sir Francis Drake Boulevard, Box 217, Olema, 94950, 663-1020, renovated ranch, nice country views, E, CP • *Point Reyes Country Inn & Stables,* 12050 Highway 1, Point Reyes Station, 94956, 663-9696, E • *Thomas' White House Inn,* P.O. Box 132, Bolinas, 94924, 868-0279, small inn, nice views, M, CP • **Individual cottage accommodations:** *Neon Rose,* P.O. Box 632, Point Reyes Station, 94956, 663-9143, E • *Knob Hill,* P.O. Box 1108, Point Reyes, 94956, 663-1784, M • *Fairwinds Farm,* P.O. Box 581, Inverness, 94937, 663-9454, E. For further listings, contact *Coastal Lodging,* P.O. Box 1162, Point Reyes Station, 94956, 485-2678; *Inns of Point Reyes,* P.O. Box 145, Inverness, 94937, 663-1420, or (707) 664-6606; or *Inns of Marin,* 663-2000.

DINING *Manka's Inverness Lodge* (see above), game, oysters, wild berry pie, cozy, one of the area's best, M–E • *Vladimir's,* Sir Francis Drake Boulevard, Inverness, 669-1021, a Czech charmer, M • *Olema Inn,* Sir Francis Drake Boulevard at Highway 1, Olema, 663-9449, gracious dining, M • *Point Reyes Roadhouse and Oyster Bar,* Highway 1, Point Reyes Station, 663-1277, known for local barbecued oysters, I–M • *Station House Café,* Main Street, Point Reyes Station, 663-1515, open breakfast through dinner, highly regarded, I–M.

SIGHTSEEING *Point Reyes National Seashore,* Point Reyes, 94956; *Bear Valley Information Center,* 663-1092, open year-round, phone for seasonal hours and programs; *weather and whale information, 663-9029; Ken Patrick Drakes Beach Visitor Center,* 669-1250; *Lighthouse Visitor Center,* 669-1534; *Morgan Horse Ranch,* 663-1763 • *Johnson's Oyster Farm,* 11171 Sir Francis Drake Boulevard, Point Reyes National Seashore, 669-1149. Hours: Tuesday to Sunday 8 A.M. to 4:30 P.M. Free • *Point Reyes Bird Observatory,* Palomarin Field Station, south end of Point Reyes National Seashore, 868-0655. Hours: Bird banding and netting demonstrations 6 A.M. to noon weekends; visitors' center and nature trail open daily • *Bolinas Memorial Museum,* 48 Wharf Road, Bolinas, 868-0330. Hours: Friday to Sunday 1 P.M. to 5 P.M. Free.

ACTIVITIES   **Horseback riding:** *Five Brooks Stables,* 663-1570 •
Bike rentals: *Trailhead Rentals,* 663-1958.

INFORMATION   *West Marin Chamber of Commerce,* P.O. Box
1045, Point Reyes Station, CA 94956, 663-9232.

Kidding Around in San Francisco

Kids love San Francisco—and vice versa. It almost seems that this was
a city designed with children in mind. Few amusement park rides can
equal the fun of those real-life trolley cars clambering up and down the
hills, and the harbor seals that voluntarily choose to do their frisking
around Fisherman's Wharf couldn't cause more delight if they had
been planted by the city public relations staff. And how do you match
the thrill of actually walking or biking across the Golden Gate Bridge?

Creative museums for children and an aquarium, planetarium, and
zoo are all perennial favorites, and no city offers so many great places
for walks and bike rides with fabulous views. Many of these attractions are free or give families a price break. Even five-star hotels like
the Clift make a point of welcoming kids with Nintendo and Monop-
oly games, Dr. Seuss books, and Disney movies on video.

San Francisco gives every opportunity to introduce youngsters to
fine art, theater, or music, with plenty of lighter diversions to keep
young interest high. Best of all, the places that kids love best in the
city have almost equal appeal for moms and dads. When school vaca-
tions have the kids asking "What can we do now?" a San Francisco
family weekend will give you at least 101 good ideas.

Just like the grown-ups, children first of all want to climb aboard
those entrancing trolley cars, so read up on how to manage the MUNI
transit system (pages 174, 180), get a MUNI Passport and map, and
board a trolley headed up- and downhill to Fisherman's Wharf.

At the wharf, have a look at the figureheads, ship models, and photos in the ship-shaped National Maritime Museum in Aquatic Park,
and the lineup of historic ships at Hyde Street Pier. Prowling the pas-
sageways of the three-masted 1886 square-rigger *Balclutha,* the last of
the historic Cape Horn fleet, is special fun. Living-history programs onboard let you experience some of the excitement of sailing 100 years
ago. Rangers also lead tours of the engine room of the impressive 1890
ferryboat *Eureka.*

Take time out for a chowder and sourdough snack while you watch some of the city's free entertainment—the fishing fleet and the seals. Then take a stroll to see some of the street performers in action around the wharf and its shopping centers, especially at the Cannery. Balloon sculptors seem to win the biggest audience of fascinated kids. If you're feeling flush, the children may lure you into the amusement park at Pier 39, or to see the San Francisco Experience, a multimedia show that simulates the feeling of being in the middle of an earthquake. In 1996, Pier 39 will have yet another lure, Underwater World, an aquarium that "floats" visitors on a moving walkway through an ocean environment. You can also tour the 312-foot submarine U.S.S. *Pampanito* at Pier 45, or board a boat at Piers 39 or 41 for a harbor cruise or a picnic on Angel Island.

You'll have to reserve well ahead if you hope to take the boat trip that older children like best, the tour of infamous Alcatraz Island. There's always standing room only to see the notorious prison where Al Capone and lots of other famous bad guys were put away. A slide show explains the story of Alcatraz, and there are several instructive tours with rangers, but nothing is more vivid than the self-guided audio tour using the voices of actual prisoners and wardens who lived and worked on Alcatraz. It paints a realistic picture of life on "the rock," including punishment in D block, the isolation unit where inmates were allowed out only once a week, and "the Hole," the ultimate punishment, six dark steel-lined boxes.

Alcatraz Island is more than a prison. It is also the site of the first lighthouse on the West Coast and a natural preserve of gardens, tide pools, rocky cliffs, gull nesting areas, and incomparable Bay views, especially from the lighthouse plaza and the west walkway. Allow plenty of time, and bring a jacket when you visit; the prison site was not chosen for its balmy weather.

Back on land, a walk or ride farther on the Golden Gate Promenade around the waterfront past Ft. Mason leads to the impressive Palace of Fine Arts and another treat for children and inquisitive parents. *Museum* isn't really the right word for San Francisco's Exploratorium, a place that has spawned imitators around the country. *Newsweek* magazine compared it to Disneyland for entertainment value, but this time the do-it-yourself experiences are teaching important things about science and perception while they entrance the kids.

The interior of the Exploratorium looks a lot like a huge airplane hangar divided into sections that concentrate on specific topics such as sound and hearing, touch, patterns, electricity, motion, vision, weather, color, and light. What can you do? How about finger painting on a computer screen without benefit of paints? Or watching a video camera record your movements in a kaleidoscope of flowing figures? You can walk into a distorted room where people seem to shrink or grow, or maybe watch a glassblower demonstrating the art of making marbles or a kite maker explaining why his creations will fly. Every area has its own mesmerizing exhibits to push, pull, talk, or listen to, some 700 in all, plus demonstrations that are different every week. Reserve ahead if you want to experience the Tactile Dome, a pitch-black crawl through a variety of touch experiences. The biggest problem at the Exploratorium may be convincing the kids to leave.

If you've brought your bikes, you can probably lure children away by promising a ride along the rest of the Golden Gate Promenade, leading to the bike lane across the famous bridge. The views looking back at the city from 210 feet above the water are guaranteed to thrill, no matter how old or young you are. Another way to get there is via the city bus, which stops at the toll plaza on the city side of the bridge; from there you can judge how much of the 3.4-mile hike to the northern end small legs can handle. Check your MUNI map for the current route.

Families could easily spend a whole day in Golden Gate Park. Attractions include a playground where kids can actually ride an antique carousel, circa 1912, enjoy lakes for boating or watching enthusiasts of miniature sailboats in action, and visit the California Academy of Sciences. The Academy offers an impressive gem and mineral hall, a chance to walk through all the habitats of the state in the "Wild California" hall, a 3-billion-year stroll through evolution in the "Life Through Time" exhibit, or the opportunity to visit the Far Side of Science Gallery, featuring some 160 cartoons by Gary Larson. It also houses the Morrison Planetarium, where there are daily celestial shows and a dazzling Laserium show on certain evenings. Perhaps the favorite attraction is the Steinhart Aquarium, home to more than 14,000 denizens of the deep, including speedy ocean swimmers circling in a giant swirl of seawater known as the Fish Roundabout and a living-coral-reef tank.

Point Lobos is another kids' favorite spot. The Cliff House and its promenade, easily reached on city buses, are perfect vantage points for watching the residents of Seal Rocks out in the Pacific and the surfers below at Kelly's Cove off Ocean Beach. Remember to bring the binoculars along.

Another bus ride or MUNI Metro train ride brings you to the zoo, with more than 1,000 fascinating creatures in residence, from antelopes to zebras. Take a 20-minute Zebra Zephyr tour to get the lie of the land on the 70-acre grounds, then head for your own favorites— the Primate Discovery Center; Koala Crossing, a re-creation of the Australian outback; or Gorilla World, the world's largest gorilla habitat. Some of the rarer species in residence at the zoo are snow leopards, pygmy hippos, white rhinoceroses, and a white tiger.

Tots will find their own Children's Zoo with a nature trail for communing with raccoons and rabbits in their natural habitats and the chance to pet, feed, and play with baby animals. The playground next door has its own handsome antique carousel.

Back in town, you'll find that small fry are intrigued by colorful

Chinatown, by both the bright neon Chinese signs at night and the odd assortment of goods for sale at markets during the day, things like dried snails, lichee nuts, eels, and octopus, which will bring choruses of horrified but fascinated ooohs.

If you happen to have a long weekend, stop in the Wells Fargo Bank's History Museum, open Monday to Friday, to see a re-creation of an Old West Wells Fargo office, gold specimens, and other relics from Gold Rush days. The Old U.S. Mint, restored to its 1800s appearance, also offers some awesome examples of gold bars and a solid gold bear. It is also open weekdays only.

No matter how many times you do it, youngsters never tire of repeating a trolley ride, and older children will enjoy visiting the Trolley Museum to find out what it takes to keep these rolling historic landmarks in service.

For that matter, if your legs can take it, there's nothing children like better than simply clambering up to Nob Hill or down the zigzags of Lombard Street on their own. Guaranteed they'll never complain that there's nothing to do in San Francisco—and much of it won't cost you a cent.

Area Code: 415

DRIVING DIRECTIONS AND PUBLIC TRANSPORTATION
See page 180.

ACCOMMODATIONS AND DINING   See pages 180 to 182.

SIGHTSEEING   *San Francisco Maritime National Historical Park,* 556-3002, includes National Maritime Museum, Aquatic Park at the foot of Polk Street. Hours: Daily 10 A.M. to 5 P.M. Free • *Hyde Street Pier,* foot of Hyde Street, historic ships. Hours: Daily 10 A.M. to 6 P.M. Adults, $3; ages 12 to 17, $1; under age 16, free • *U.S.S. Pampanito,* Pier 45, Fisherman's Wharf, 929-0202, World War II submarine. Hours: June to October, daily 9 A.M. to 9 P.M.; November to June, 9 A.M. to 6 P.M. Adults, $4; ages 12 to 17, $1; under 12, free • *Alcatraz Island,* Red and White Fleet, Pier 41, Fisherman's Wharf, 546-2700 or (800) 229-2784. Hours: Boats depart daily, winter 9:45 A.M. to 2:45 P.M., summer until 4:15 P.M. Adults, $8.75; ages 12 to 18, $7.75; under 12, $4.25. Tickets go on sale at 8 A.M., advance reservations strongly advised; phone at least a day in advance for charge-card reservations ($2 service charge) • *Exploratorium,* Palace of Fine Arts, 3601 Lyon Street (at Marina Boulevard), 563-7337, Tactile Dome reservations 561-0362. Hours: Tuesday to Sunday 10 A.M. to 5 P.M., Wednesday to 9:30 P.M. Adults, $8.50; students, $6.50; ages 6 to 17, $4.50; ages 3 to 5, $2 • *California Academy of Sciences and Steinhart Aquarium,*

Golden Gate Park, 221-5100. Hours: Daily 10 A.M. to 5 P.M. Adults, $7; students, $4; ages 6 to 11, $1.50. *Morrison Planetarium Show,* 750-7141. Hours: Daily Monday to Friday 2 P.M., weekends hourly 1 P.M. to 4 P.M. Adults, $2.50; under age 17, $1.25. Startalks, weekends at noon, daily in summer, $1.25. *Laserium,* 750-7138; check show schedules and fees • *San Francisco Cable Car Museum,* Washington and Mason streets, Nob Hill, 474-1887. Hours: Daily April to October 10 A.M. to 6 P.M., rest of year until 5 P.M. Free • *San Francisco Zoo,* 45th Avenue at Sloat Boulevard, 753-7080. Hours: Daily 10 A.M. to 5 P.M. Adults, $6.50; ages 12 to 15, $3; ages 5 to 12, $1 • *Wells Fargo History Museum,* 420 Montgomery Street, 396-2619. Hours: Monday to Friday 9 A.M. to 5 P.M. Free • *Old Mint Museum,* Fifth and Mission streets, 744-6830. Hours: Monday to Friday 10 A.M. to 4 P.M., docent tours with movie on the hour, last show starts at 3 P.M. Free • *The San Francisco Experience,* Pier 39, second level, 982-7550. Hours: Shows daily every half hour 9:30 A.M. to 9:30 P.M. Adults, $7; ages 5 to 16, $4 • *Ferry rides:* Red and White Fleet, Pier 43½, 546-2700 or (800) 229-2784. Ferries to Angel Island, Sausalito, and Tiburon. Round-trip fares: adults, $8; ages 5 to 11, $4.

INFORMATION *Visitor Information Center,* Hallidie Plaza, Powell and Market streets, lower level, 391-2000. Hours: Monday to Friday 9 A.M. to 5:30 P.M., Saturday 9 A.M. to 3 P.M., Sunday 10 A.M. to 2 P.M. Daily events information 391-2001.

Under the Spell in Carmel

This is fairy-tale country. With its flower-bedecked cottages, labyrinth lanes, courtyards, and twisted pine forests sloping to a talcum beach, the town dubbed Carmel-by-the-Sea casts a spell of enchantment. The setting impressed even Father Junipero Serra. The mission he established here in 1771 was his favorite, and he asked to be buried at the foot of the altar in the cathedral.

In this century, it was artists and writers who succumbed to Carmel's lures. When much of San Francisco's cultural community was left homeless by the earthquake in 1906, many made their way to Carmel. Over the years Jack London, Upton Sinclair, Sinclair Lewis, and Robinson Jeffers were among those who helped establish the town as a bohemian outpost. Later they were joined by noted photographers Edward Weston and Ansel Adams. Though rising rents eventually forced out many of the artists, their legacy remains in the 50-plus galleries in town.

There were two reasons why rents increased: the discovery of Carmel by the wealthy and the arrival of tourists. There are far too many of the latter to suit many residents, who deplore the dozens of shops, the busloads of sightseers, and the long lines of cars that descend in season. Still, a Carmel visit is a visual delight, so the solution for weekenders is to come in the cooler months, when you can appreciate the charm without the congestion.

The town has done its best to keep its quaintness intact, with strict ordinances that outlaw tall buildings and neon signs. Residential streets have no traffic lights, no sidewalks, and no numbers on the Hansel-and-Gretel houses.

Perhaps the best way to appreciate Carmel's special ambience is to begin with some of those residential sections. Follow Ocean Avenue to the water and turn left on the aptly named Scenic Street. Continue south to Santa Lucia Avenue, turn left again, and take almost any turn to the left or right onto San Antonio, Carmelo, Camino Real, or Casanova. Get out and walk for a close-up view of the shingled cottages nestled in the pines and you'll understand Carmel's magic spell.

Go back to Scenic and continue south along the bluff above the beach to admire the area's natural beauty. Just beyond Carmel Point is Tor House, the stone cottage and tower that Robinson Jeffers built in 1918 with local stone. The warm interior and lovely gardens are worth a tour, but since one of the family members still lives in the house, visitors are welcomed only on Friday and Saturday, by advance reservation.

Continuing around the point, you'll pass Carmel River State Beach, a lagoon, and a bird sanctuary. Even in summer these are tranquil escapes, an alternative to the beautiful but busy town beach.

The Carmel Mission is lovely as well as historic. It was the second-oldest mission in California, the home base from which Father Serra established further ministries in the state. A flower-filled courtyard leads to the graceful cathedral, a 1797 mellowed stone church with a Moorish tower and four bells. Within the mission complex are three museums, including a book museum that contains Serra's own 600 volumes. It was California's first library. The cell where Father Serra died reveals his monastic life; its contents are only a slab of wood with a single blanket and no mattress.

Prepare to be tempted when you head for Ocean Avenue, for many Carmel stores are high caliber, and window-shopping is pleasant even if you can't afford to buy.

Art lovers will find wonderful browsing. The heart of the gallery area is between 5th and 6th between San Carlos and Lincoln, but the gallery guide available at most locations will lead to other worthwhile stops as well. The art featured at the handsome Carmel Art Association, a local cooperative on Dolores Street, is not to be missed, and photography fans will want to see the fine work of Adams, Weston, and other masters at Photography West Gallery on Ocean at Dolores and the Weston Gallery on 6th between Dolores and Lincoln.

More shops can be found on Highway 1 at the Barnyard, a beautifully landscaped complex with a notable bookstore-restaurant, the Thunderbird.

Don't get so caught up in shopping that you fail to reserve one full morning or afternoon for Point Lobos State Reserve. Located just four miles south of Carmel, these 1,250 acres along Carmel Bay, with some of the most dramatic views of rocks and surf on this or any other coast, have been called "the greatest meeting of land and water in the world." If it is a busy weekend, come early, as sightseers are limited to 450 at a time to make sure everyone gets the most from a visit.

One of the most fascinating parts of the reserve is its Monterey Cypress Grove, the trees clinging to the cliffs above the surf carved by wind and weather into otherworldly shapes no sculptor could match. Bring along binoculars to make the most of such offshore formations as Bird Island, a refuge for thousands of waterfowl, including cormorants, pelicans, and gulls, and Sea Lion Rocks, where scores of noisy sea lions are at home. From December to May this is also a great spot to watch for the spouting and diving gray whales that migrate to these waters each year. There are easy trails through the Cypress Grove and to all the best vantage points.

Carmel is loaded with lodgings that are a convenient walk to town or beach. The grand La Playa Hotel, a long-time landmark, is fresh from a recent renovation, as is the more moderately priced Moorish-style Cypress Inn, owned by onetime movie queen Doris Day. One of the most appealing lodgings in town is the Mission Ranch, owned by present-day star and onetime Carmel mayor Clint Eastwood. He bought the historic ranch when it was threatened with development and spent millions restoring the original farmhouse and bunkhouse and adding compatible new cottages, providing every creature comfort without losing the original feel of the place. Choicest rooms are in the new Meadow View cottages, with fireplaces and porches looking across the meadows and wetlands to the ocean.

On a more modest scale in town, the Sandpiper, San Antonio House, and the Sea View will please fans of homey bed-and-breakfast inns, while Sundial Inn, Happy Landing, and Vagabond's House offer cottage accommodations with fireplaces set in garden settings.

For dramatic ocean views, nothing touches the luxurious Highlands Inn, perched on a cliff south of town. At least come for a meal; their Pacific's Edge restaurant is often called the best in the area.

Other posh lodgings can be found inland in the Carmel Valley, where the sun shines even when the coast is enveloped in fog. Both Quail Lodge and the Carmel Valley Ranch Resort have notable golf courses, but the privacy, tasteful rooms, and scenic valley views they provide will appeal even if you don't know a putter from a parasol. The most unusual and exclusive valley retreat is Stonepine, a lavish Mediterranean-style chateau guarded by electronic gates and 60-foot Italian stone pines. It was built in the 1930s by Helen Crocker Russell of the San Francisco banking family and is now an ultimate hideaway, with a staff of 30 for 26 guests. The grounds include a fine Equestrian Center.

The only dining problem in Carmel is choosing among the dozens of possibilities. Whichever restaurant you choose, you'll most likely find that the atmosphere is charming—just like the rest of Carmel.

Area Code: 408

DRIVING DIRECTIONS   Carmel is off Highway 1, about 125 miles south of San Francisco, 215 miles from Sacramento.

PUBLIC TRANSPORTATION   Closest entry is Monterey Peninsula Airport, about ten miles. Greyhound bus service also goes into Monterey.

ACCOMMODATIONS   *Highlands Inn,* Highway 1, P.O. Box 1700, Carmel, 93921, 624-3801 or (800) 682-4811, EE • *La Playa Hotel,* Camino Real at 8th, Carmel, 93921, 624-6476 or in California (800) 582-8900, E–EE • *The Sandpiper Country Inn,* Bay View Avenue at Martin Way, Carmel, 93923, 624-6433, M–EE, CP • *Cypress Inn,* Lincoln and 7th, Carmel, 93921, 624-3871 or in California (800) 443-7443, M–EE • *Sea View Inn,* Camino Real between 11th and 16th, Carmel, 93921, 624-8778, M–E, CP • *Mission Ranch,* 26270 Dolores Street, Carmel, 93921, 624-6436, M–EE, CP • *Vagabond's House Inn,* 4th and Dolores, Carmel, 93921, 624-7738 or (800) 262-1262, M–EE, CP • *Cobblestone Inn,* Junipero between 7th and 8th, Carmel, 93921, 625-5222, pick of the in-town motels, M–EE, CP • *Sundial Lodge,* Monte Verde at 7th Street, Carmel, 93921, 624-8578, E–EE, CP • *San Antonio House,* San Antonio at Ocean Avenue, Carmel, 93921, 624-4334, E–EE, CP • *The Happy Landing,* Monte Verde between 5th and 6th, Carmel, 92921, 624-7917, M–EE, CP • *Tickle Pink Inn,* 155 Highland Drive, Carmel, 93923, 624-1244 or (800) 635-4774, upscale motel sharing Highland Inn view, EE, CP • *Stonepine,* 150 East Carmel Valley Road, Carmel Valley, 93924, 659-2245, EE, CP • *Quail Lodge Resort and Golf Club,* 8205 Valley Greens Drive, Carmel Valley, 93923, 624-1581, EE • *Carmel Valley Ranch Resort,* 1 Old Ranch Road, Carmel Valley, 93923, 625-9500 or (800) 4-CARMEL, EE.

DINING   *The Covey,* Quail Lodge (see above), elegant and excellent California-French, E • *Pacific's Edge,* Highlands Inn (see above) spectacular view, fine dining, prix fixe, EE • *Anton & Michel,* Mission between Ocean and 7th streets, Carmel, 624-2406, continental, charm,

E • *Sans Souci,* Lincoln between 5th and 6th streets, Carmel, 624-6220, French menu, gracious setting, E • *Crème Carmel,* San Carlos between Ocean and 7th streets, 624-0444, California-French, E • *Casanova,* 5th Avenue between San Carlos and Mission, Carmel, 625-0501, northern Italian, romantic cottage setting, E • *California Thai,* San Carlos at 4th Avenue, 622-1160, change of pace, well-prepared Thai-California cuisine, M • *La Bohème,* a find, changing set menu, full dinner, M • *Prima 6th Avenue Grill,* 6th Avenue at Mission Street, 624-6562, creative American menu with Italian influence, M • *Piatti,* Junipero and 6th, 625-1766, popular Italian, I–M • *Rio Grill,* Highway 1 and Rio Road, Carmel Valley, 625-5436, creative American, recommended by all despite shopping center setting, I–M • *Mission Ranch Restaurant* (see above), rustic dining room with wonderful views from the deck, M • *Red Lion Tavern,* Dolores between 5th and 6th, 625-6765, English ambience, good pub menu, good fun, I–M.

SIGHTSEEING   *Carmel Mission,* 3080 Rio Road, Carmel, 624-3600. Hours: Monday to Saturday 9:30 A.M. to 4:30 P.M., Sunday from 10:30 A.M. Donation • *Point Lobos State Reserve,* Highway 1, four miles south of Carmel, 624-4909. Hours: 9 A.M. to 6:30 P.M., in winter to 5 P.M. Per car, $6.

INFORMATION   *Carmel Business Association,* San Carlos and 7th, P.O. Box 4444, Carmel-by-the-Sea, CA 93921, 624-2522 • *Monterey Peninsula Chamber of Commerce,* 380 Alvarado Avenue, P.O. Box 1770, Monterey, CA 93942, 649-1770.

Romance on the Rocky North Coast

Sometimes sightseeing isn't the point of a weekend away. Sometimes all you want to discover is each other. When romance is on your mind, there's no better destination than the dramatic stretch of coastline between the towns of Gualala and Elk, south of Mendocino. Follow the road along heart-stopping twists and turns overlooking the sea to find lodgings from cozy inns to luxury digs offering privacy, a bit of pampering, and a backdrop of crashing sea just beyond the window. There are no crowds here, but there's plenty of natural beauty around in parks where you can beachcomb, picnic, or just contemplate the rhythms of the sea.

Romance knows no season, but if you come in winter, the waves are wildest, the fireplaces coziest, and you'll get a bonus—the chance to spot migrating whales offshore. Innkeepers swear that there are plenty of sunny spells between the raindrops.

During Gold Rush days, schooners loaded with redwood for San Francisco set sail from tiny "doghole ports" all along the southern Mendocino County coastline. The logging towns that grew up still have the look of bygone days, with rustic wooden facades and many fine restored Victorians.

The gateway to the county is Gualala (pronounced "Wa-*lah*-la," located where the Gualala River meets the Pacific. The river, a favorite of steelhead salmon fishermen, also offers sandy beaches for picnickers. Gualala Point Regional Park, just south of town, is a prime place for whale watching, horseback riding, and beachcombing.

A logging center until the 1960s, Gualala is now developing into an arts enclave, with many painters, sculptors, photographers, and musicians in residence. Check with Gualala Arts (884-1138) for any current exhibits, plays, and concerts. The little town also offers a couple of galleries, shops, a 1903 hotel with a no-frills menu and a lively bar, some small cafés, and three prize inn finds for romantics.

The Whale Watch Inn is a posh, contemporary cluster of five small buildings, just 18 rooms total, all with commanding Pacific views. The sitting room–lobby has comfortable contemporary leather sofas around a circular fireplace, and a wall of windows looking out to sea. There's a private stairway to the beach. Each room or suite offers cozy down comforters; many have fireplaces, whirlpools, and skylights; and all have decks with ocean views. The furnishings vary from art deco to French country, tasteful and something for every taste.

You can't miss Gualala's St. Orres—the onion domes, stained glass, stencil decoration, and other architectural details inspired by the area's early Russian settlers are totally unique. (You can see the remains of that Russian colony at Ft. Ross, on the coast to the south.) The domes provide a dramatic three-story ceiling for the highly regarded dining room. The handcrafted rooms in this main building are small, albeit modestly priced, and they share bathrooms—his, hers, and ours, with a shower for two. The choicest are rooms 1 and 2 in front, each with stained-glass French doors that open to the balcony overlooking the ocean.

The real lovers' lairs are the cottages. The Meadows lodgings are reached through the gardens and across a little footbridge. Wildflower, a cabin with a wood-burning Franklin stove, a skylight, and a very private outdoor hot-water shower, is for rustics and budget watchers. The Tree House and the Rose Cottage are more luxurious; both have sundecks with sea views. Across St. Orres Creek from the hotel, seven Creekside cottages share the use of a spa facility that includes a hot tub, sauna, and sundeck. There are several moderately priced choices here, with ocean or forest views.

Nostalgia buffs will fall in love with Gualala's Old Milano Hotel, a charm-filled pristine white 1905 building with a railed front porch. The hotel is on the National Register of Historic Places. The candlelit dining room is an area favorite. Room decor is Victorian, with pretty prints and quilts; the grounds include three acres of gardens. A big lawn rolls right down to the cliffs above a dramatic cove, and there's a hot tub on a cliffside overlooking the Pacific.

Six rooms upstairs share two baths, but the master suite comes with a private bath as well as a sitting room with wonderful ocean vistas. Even more romantic are the garden accommodations, the Vine Cottage or the Caboose, an actual railroad car turned into a cozy lodging with a wood stove and two upstairs brakeman's seats for sunset watching.

Up the coast, Point Arena is a favorite spot for surfers when the waves are high, for sea kayakers and rowers on calmer days, when you can paddle among the offshore rocks and say hello to the sea lions. The town of Point Arena is coming back to life, with both new construction and restoration of old buildings, including a classic 1927 vaudeville theater. The fishing pier at Arena Cove, lost to a 1983 storm, has been rebuilt in sturdy concrete. Try your luck or buy some of the catch of the day from local fishermen. The cove is also a good place for beachcombing or for watching the surfers when they are out.

Point Arena Lighthouse is definitely worth a visit. Rebuilt after the 1906 earthquake, the 115-foot lighthouse is now automated, and the old facilities have been turned into a maritime museum telling of the perils that confronted the many ships now lying in a watery graveyard in the deep off the point. You can climb the light tower and admire the big lens in the light room. A nonprofit group has turned the old Coast Guard quarters into guest houses that allow you to share the extraordinary view. This is one of the best outposts for whale watchers.

When you continue north to Manchester, you are in the "banana belt," an area where sheltering mountains and prevailing winds keep away cold and fog. Dairy herds roam the hillsides on picturesque pastureland bordered by ocean cliffs to the west, redwood and Douglas fir forests to the east.

The fertile bottomland of the nearby Garcia River attracts birdwatchers in winter to see the rare tundra swan, known as the whistling swan. The birds fly in all the way from Siberia, drawn to the rich feeding area. One good place to see them is along Miner Hole Road; turn west at mile marker 17.54, north of Point Arena.

Manchester State Beach offers a five-mile sweep of sand, plus meadows and dunes, another fine place for communing with nature.

Elk is another logging town that has kept much of its frontier feel. Off the coast here are tall rock formations known as sea stacks, best explored in kayaks or boats. Greenwood State Park gives more access to the coast, a one-mile beach ideal for beachcombing and tide pooling. The park includes the site of the mill lumberyard and wharf from the old logging days.

Tiny Elk also boasts three superb hideaways. The Harbor House, set on a bluff overlooking Greenwood Landing, is a California classic. Built of redwood from the nearby forest, the handsome house is an enlarged version of the "home of redwood" exhibit building at the 1915 Panama-Pacific International Exposition in San Francisco, and it is beautiful, especially the inviting redwood-paneled living room with its oversize fireplace. A stroll down the steps leads to a glade by the beach, complete with a tiny waterfall. Carved wooden benches are strategically placed for contemplating the sea.

The six bedrooms in the house are big and well furnished, with printed wallpaper and lots of antique pieces. Four rustic cottages are less elegant but more private. Every room comes with a fireplace or parlor stove. At dinnertime everyone sits down together for a set menu, just like family.

The Sandpiper House Inn, built by the same lumber company in the same year, is a smaller bed-and-breakfast treasure perched on a rugged cliff above the cove. The gray shingled exterior is unpretentious, but the interior is distinctive, with coffered ceilings and fine raised redwood paneling in the living and dining rooms. Beyond the house, a rose arbor leads to lavish perennial gardens extending to the edge of the bluff, where a path descends onto a private beach. Most of the tasteful, antique-accented bedrooms have full views across the garden to the water.

The Greenwood Pier Inn, atop the bluff just down the road, is delightfully quirky, a group of fairy-tale cottages with peaked roofs and skylights, connected by flower-bordered paths amid a profusion of flowers.

Artist-owners Kendrick and Isabel Perry came up with the fanciful architecture and the extraordinary tilework and artistic collages inside. Kendrick doubles as head gardener and chef of the small restaurant; Isabel runs the treasure-filled country store and garden shop at the complex entrance. Breakfast is delivered to your door, so you can wake to the heavenly views. The choicest aeries are in the flower-bedecked trilevel Sea Castle, on the edge of the cliff, where winding stairs lead up to windowed turrets overlooking the sea-carved stone arches below.

Along this magnificent coastline, any of these special places can provide a perfect setting for love to bloom. The rest is up to you.

Area Code: 707

DRIVING DIRECTIONS   The stretch from Gualala to Elk is about 33 miles along Highway 1, paralleling the Pacific. Take curvy Highway 1 or cut coastal driving time by taking Highway 101 north. From 101, turn west at Geyserville to Canyon Road and Skaggs Springs

Road, arriving on Highway 1 about 12 miles south of Gualala, or continue on Highway 101 to Cloverdale and take Highway 128 west through the Anderson Valley wine country to Boonville, then Mountain View Road, meeting Highway 1 just north of Point Arena. Note that the connecting roads are scenic but slow. Elk, the farthest point, is about 150 miles from San Francisco, 190 miles from Sacramento.

ACCOMMODATIONS *Whale Watch Inn,* 35100 Highway 1, Gualala, 95445, 884-3667, EE, CP • *St. Orres,* P.O. Box 523, Gualala, 95445, 884-3303, hotel, I; cottages, M–EE • *Old Milano Hotel,* 38300 Highway 1, Gualala, 95445, 884-3256, M–EE • *Harbor House,* 5600 Highway 1, Elk, 95432, 877-3203, EE, MAP, special winter rates January to March • *Sandpiper House,* 5520 Highway 1, Elk 95432, 877-3587, E–EE, CP • *Greenwood Pier Inn,* 5928 Highway 1, Elk, 95432, 877-9997, E-EE, CP • *Point Arena Lighthouse Keepers,* P.O. Box 11, Point Arena, 95468, 882-2777, two- and three-bedroom lodgings, M–E; phone for information.

DINING *St. Orres,* Gualala (see above), 884-3335, prix fixe, EE • *Old Milano Hotel,* Gualala (see above), E • *Harbor House,* Elk (see above), dinner for nonguests by prior reservation only, prix fixe, E • *The Food Company,* 38411 Highway 1, Gualala, 884-1800, likely spot for lunch, I–M • *Gualala Hotel,* P.O. Box 675, Highway 1, Gualala, 884-3441, I–M • *Top of the Cliff,* Seacliff Center, Highway 1, Gualala, 884-1539, panoramic views, E–EE • *Roadhouse Café,* 6061 Highway 1, Elk, 877-3285, breakfast and lunch, don't miss the scones, I • *Greenwood Pier Café* (see above), California cuisine, open weekends only, M • *Bridget Dolan's Pub,* 5910 Highway 1, Elk, 877-3422, Irish fare and brew on tap, I–M.

SIGHTSEEING *Point Arena Lighthouse,* P.O. Box 11, Lighthouse Road, 882-2777. Hours: Daily 11 A.M. to 2:30 P.M. Adults, $2; children, $.50 • *Mendocino Coast State Parks,* 937-5804, phone for information and hours for all area parks • **Horseback riding:** *Roth Ranch,* Gualala, 884-3124 • *Kayaking: Force 10,* Elk, 877-3505 • **Bike and boat rentals:** *Adventure Rents,* Gualala, 884-4FUN.

INFORMATION *Mendocino County Tourism Bureau,* 239 South Main Street, Willits, CA 95490, (800) MENDO • Ft. Bragg–Mendocino Coast Chamber of Commerce, P.O. Box 1141, Ft. Bragg, CA 95437, 964-3153.

Castle Country near Cambria

The sand castles are on the beach; the real castle is just up the road. With so much going for it, the wonder is that Cambria has retained its low-key charm. Even the growing lineup of art galleries on Main Street hasn't changed the feel or appeal of this small town where the pines meet the sea. The art only adds a new attraction to the full agenda in store for weekenders.

William Randolph Hearst's dream castle, located in the hills eight miles north, came along just in time to save Cambria and change its fate forever. Settled by ranchers and homesteaders in the 1860s, Cambria in its early days was an active farming and lumbering center and a busy port. Then came a double blow—a devastating fire in 1889 and the coming of the railroad, which supplanted the ships. The town was left by the wayside, a peaceful, isolated dairy farming area without even a decent access road.

Once construction of the castle got under way in 1919, it provided enough jobs to begin Cambria's revival. Residents built and maintained the estate and formed the household staff when Hearst and his guests were in residence. A road into town finally was built in 1924, and real estate entrepreneurs began to see possibilities. In 1927 the Cambria Development Company divided a large tract of land called Cambria Pines into small lots and advertised them nationwide at modest prices, putting the town on the map. The prices, in fact, were so reasonable that many people bought sight unseen.

Those who did so were wise, for when Hearst Castle opened to the public in 1958, Cambria bloomed as seaside headquarters for those who came to tour. Though still a small town of just over 3,000, it has become a popular haven for both artists and retirees. Moonstone Beach Drive is lined with choice sea-view accommodations, and Main Street and Burton Drive boast more than a dozen art galleries, plus gift shops and antiques merchants.

While Cambria could provide a pleasant seaside getaway on its own, the Hearst San Simeon State Historic Monument remains the prime reason for a visit. Advance reservations are always recommended, but you must call ahead if you want to come in December for a special treat—the castle decked out in Yuletide splendor. Docents in period dress show off the towering tinsel-covered trees and a replica of the Hearst family's original nativity scene.

With any luck, you'll also be able to enjoy strolls on Cambria's beach when you come, since the weather is mild along this section of the central coast most of the year. The local chamber of commerce lists 50 to 70 degrees as the year-round average temperature and promises surfing, hiking, bicycling, tide pooling, beachcombing, rock hunting, and fishing year-round. Off-season prices at the lodgings along Moonstone Beach make things even nicer. Many have fireplaces so you can sit back and enjoy the view in warm comfort, even if the weather is chilly.

The Beach House is the choice of the inns for its views from the front bedrooms and the sitting room, though there are some charming choices in town as well. This is also a town where many of the motels on the stretch across from the beach have inn ambience, are unusually well furnished, and come with nice features like fireplaces and in-room refrigerators.

Visitors to Hearst Castle arrive first at a visitors' center not far off Highway 1, where there are exhibits telling of the exploits of William Randolph Hearst. From here everyone is taken up the hill by bus to visit Hearst's ultimate fantasy, a 115-room mansion with 38 bedrooms and 41 baths, 14 sitting rooms, a movie theater, two libraries, a baronial dining hall, and an 82-foot living room.

The inventory lists 20,000 art objects and antiques, gathered by the great publisher from all over the world. Gothic and Renaissance tapestries, fine wood carvings, huge French and Italian mantels, and collections of silver, Oriental rugs, Roman mosaics, and a variety of statuary are only some of the treasures Hearst lived among when he was in residence in his castle.

It is difficult to visit without thinking of Orson Welles and the movie classic *Citizen Kane,* which offers a thinly disguised portrayal of Hearst's life. As the movie suggests, the tycoon presided here with his mistress, movie star Marion Davies; it is said that his wife never set foot in the house. The never-ending stream of guests included a Hollywood Who's Who of the day, stars like Laurence Olivier, Rudolph Valentino, Charlie Chaplin, and Greta Garbo. Winston Churchill and President Calvin Coolidge were also visitors, for Hearst's vast publishing and film empire gave him enormous political power.

Hearst placed his mansion on an isolated knoll overlooking the sea and surrounded it with 127 acres of gardens, terraces, and palatial guest houses. He called the estate "La Cuesta Encantada" ("The Enchanted Hill"), and his twin-towered Spanish-Moorish mansion "La Casa Grande." Guest cottages were grouped around the main house, much as in a tile-roofed Mediterranean village. Julia Morgan, a Berkeley architect and graduate of the Paris School of Beaux Arts, was chosen to bring his plans to reality.

The expansive landscaping required water to be piped from natural springs five miles away and mountains of topsoil to be carted in to transform a rocky hilltop into a garden of exotic beauty. The different levels of the grounds required hundreds of feet of retaining walls and balustrades. Hearst assembled a zoo that included 70 species roaming freely in 2,000 fenced acres. Exotic residents included a leopard, a panther, and a polar bear. Wildlife such as zebra, tahr goats, elk, and

Barbary sheep still have free range on the grounds and can be spotted on the bus ride up the hill.

Among the most lavish areas of the estate are the swimming pools. The 345,000-gallon outdoor Neptune Pool is in a setting inspired by Greco-Roman temples, complete with colonnades and statues. The indoor Roman pool is so large that two tennis courts are situated on the roof above. The pool room is dazzling, lined with multicolored Venetian glass tiles and gold leaf layered between clear glass tiles.

Hearst continued adding to the estate for more than two decades, spending millions on the project. It was still unfinished when he died in 1951. The Hearst Corporation, unable to sell the property, donated it to the state in 1957. Four tours of various parts of the estate are offered, plus a very special evening tour offered in spring and fall.

Tour One, which takes in the castle's first floor, one guest house, and some of the gardens, is recommended for a first visit. A short film of life at the castle during the 1920s and 1930s is shown in the movie theater. Return guests can take Tour Two, covering the upper floors, the kitchen, a library filled with 5,000 books and superb Greek vases, and Hearst's own Gothic Suite, occupying the entire third floor of the castle.

Tour Three takes in another guest house plus the north wing, three floors of ten luxurious guest bedrooms finished during Hearst's final years at the castle. The marble bathrooms are the most lavish on the estate. Tour Four, offered April to October only, includes the grounds and gardens of San Simeon, plus a tour of the 17-room La Casa del Mar, the largest of the guest houses, the Hidden Terrace, and the Wine Cellar.

The evening tour is a "living history" program, featuring docents in 1930s dress appearing as Hearst's guests and domestic staff, adding life to the proceedings. The tours begin at sunset and take in the highlights of the estate.

If touring inspires you to start your own art collection, you've come to the right town. Though Cambria's offerings might not have satisfied Hearst, there is something here for almost every more modest modern taste.

The browsing area is divided into two areas, East Village and West Village, with galleries and shops galore on West Main Street and on Burton Drive to the east. Main Street in the West Village area has some of the most impressive art, as well as the town's antiques shops. Mike Cluff is a recommended stop for a wide variety of excellent work, including limited editions by the talented folk artist Watanabe. Next door is the Great American Characters Gallery, offering original animation drawings from classic Warner Brothers cartoons, a must-see for Bugs Bunny fans. The Soldier Factory and Art Gallery is unique, with its lineup of toy soldiers, limited-edition Civil War prints, and prints of historic air battles. Also on Main Street is the Schoolhouse Gallery, the home of Allied Arts, showing and selling work by over 350 local artists in the town's historic Victorian-era schoolhouse.

Collectors and admirers of art glass won't want to miss the Seekers Gallery, on Burton Drive, showing museum-quality work by more than 100 leading artisans. Burton is lined with more intriging stops, including the offbeat What Iz Art, which calls itself "an indoor amusement park for the creative mind."

Almost every shop offers the local gallery guide, but you'll need little guiding, since the town is small. Part of the fun of Cambria is strolling the pleasant streets to make your own discoveries, from Indian jewelry to large-scale oils.

When you are ready to relax, head back to Moonstone Beach for a walk along the surf, or drive a few miles north to San Simeon State Beach Park, where Leffingwell Landing rewards beachcombers with agates, jade quartz, and other beach treasures. The park bluffs are good sites for spotting sea otters, seals, and whales in winter.

Perhaps you'll be inspired to build a miniature sand castle of your own—with a tip of the pail to Mr. Hearst, the greatest castle builder of them all.

Area Code: 805

DRIVING DIRECTIONS   Cambria is located on the coast just off Highway 1, 8 miles below San Simeon. It is 94 miles south of Monterey, 245 miles from San Francisco, 322 miles from Sacramento. Highway 101 is longer in miles, but is much quicker than the hill coastal route. Cut over to Highway 1 at Route 46 at Paso Robles, south of San Simeon.

ACCOMMODATIONS   _Beach House,_ 6360 Moonstone Beach Drive, 927-3136, antiques and sea views, E–EE, CP • _Squib House,_ 5063 Burton Drive, 927-9600, M–E, CP • _Blue Whale Inn,_ 6736 Moonstone Beach Drive, 927-4647, lavish mini-suites, ocean views, and fireplaces, E–EE, CP • _Ollalieberry Inn,_ 2476 Main Street, 927-3222, 1873 Victorian home in town, M–E, CP • _J. Patrick House,_ 2990 Burton Drive, 927-3812, cozy log house above town, rooms with fireplaces, E–EE, CP • _Silvia's Rigdon Hall Inn,_ 4036 Burton Drive, 927-5125, nicely furnished suites in the East Village area, E–EE, CP • _Cambria Pines Lodge,_ 2905 Burton Drive, 927-4200, recently rebuilt rustic lodge, log cabins to fireplace suites, indoor pool, I–M • _Creekside Inn,_ 2618 Main Street, 927-4021, in-town motel, good value, I–M • **Above-average motels across from the beach:** _Sand Pebbles Inn,_ 6252 Moonstone Beach Drive, 927-5600, M–EE, CP • _Blue Dolphin Inn,_ 6470 Moonstone Beach Drive, 927-3300, M–EE, CP • _Sea Otter Inn,_ 6556 Moonstone Beach Drive, 927-

5888, M–E • *Fog Catcher Inn,* 6400 Moonstone Beach Drive, 927-1400, M–E. All zip codes are 93428.

DINING *The Hamlet at Moonstone Gardens,* Highway 1 north of town, 927-3535, ocean views, garden setting, great for lunch as well as dinner, M • *Ian's,* 2150 Center Street, 927-8649, California cuisine, well recommended by residents, M–E • *Robin's,* 4095 Burton Drive, eclectic ethnic menu, M • *Sow's Ear Café,* 2248 Main Street, 927-4865, cozy, dining by the fireside, M • *Moonstone Beach Bar & Grill,* 6550 Moonstone Beach Drive, 927-3859, seafood with ocean views, good bet for Sunday brunch, M • *Brambles Dinner House,* 4005 Burton Drive, 927-4716, generous portions, old-fashioned menu, roast beef and other favorites in a fine local home, M • *Mustache Pete's Italian Eatery,* 4090 Burton Drive, 927-8589, casual, pizza, pasta, good for families, I–M • *Linn's,* 2277 Main Street, 927-0371, restaurant and bakery, serves all three meals, known for pot pies and homemade desserts, especially ollalieberry pie, I.

SIGHTSEEING *Hearst San Simeon State Historical Monument,* off Highway 1, San Simeon, 927-2020; telephone or mail charge-card reservations, MISTIX, P.O. Box 85705, San Diego, CA 92186, (800) 444-4445. Four different 1¾-hour tours offered, including the castle, guest houses, and grounds of the estate of William Randolph Hearst. Tours leave at least once every hour from 8:20 A.M. to 3 P.M. in winter, 8 A.M. to 5 P.M. in summer. Tour One is recommended for first-time visitors. Evening tours last two hours and ten minutes and are offered most Fridays and Saturdays, March through May and September through December. Reservations accepted up to eight weeks in advance. Daytime tours: Adults, $14; ages 6 to 12, $8. Evening tours: Adults, $25; children, $13. *Schoolhouse Gallery,* 880 Main Street, 927-8190. Hours: Thursday to Sunday noon to 3:30 P.M. Free.

INFORMATION *Cambria Chamber of Commerce,* 767 Main Street, Cambria, CA 93428, 927-3624.

The Best of the Best of Northern California

Once in a while, everyone should splurge on an ultimate getaway, a place so perfect that the jangling everyday world disappears into serene silence, a place so at one with nature that beauty surrounds on every side.

Northern California has many fine getaways, but two superb hilltop retreats get this nomination for best of the best: Ventana, on the Big Sur coast, and Timberhill Ranch, in the beautiful backcountry of Sonoma County. Though miles apart in setting, each shares understated good taste and a sense of belonging to its environment. And each offers that rarest of commodities, tranquility.

Timberhill is the creation of two couples who grew weary of the rat race and determined to create on 80 acres of lofty Sonoma hillside the kind of escape they had sought but rarely found. This is their home, and their presence sets the tone for the resort, an unusual blend of sophistication and country warmth.

The drive inland from the coastal highway north of Jenner gives a preview of what's ahead—for 14 miles, the road is all but deserted, winding ever higher past peaceful farms and redwood stands, with occasional glimpses of the sea. When you reach the parking lot at Timberhill, one of the owners greets you personally, transfers your belongings to a golf cart, and takes you to the main lodge for a welcome before you are driven to your room. No more cars to worry about—no more sound of cars to distract you.

The lodge is as comfortable as it is beautiful—a shingled retreat with skylights, lots of wood and windows, antiques, books, a big inviting L-shaped couch in front of the fieldstone fireplace.

On the grounds are a duck pond, pygmy goats, and miniature horses. Deer and pheasants sometimes make an appearance. Green hills and meadows surround the swimming pool and outdoor Jacuzzi; the views from the tennis courts are enough to distract from your game.

Timberhill guest lodgings are 15 individual cedar log cottages scattered around the grounds. Each has a sizable fireplace and walls of natural wood, except for one of sliding glass that opens onto a deck and views of pond or meadows. The only sounds are the songs of the birds and the occasional honks of ducks and geese heading for the pond.

Furnishings are rustic-elegant—handmade quilts in rich colors, wing chairs, antiques, fresh flowers, warm carpeting, and accessories like wooden decoys and whimsical stuffed lambs and geese. Each room also has a refrigerator-bar. A continental breakfast is brought to your door, to be enjoyed before the fire or on the patio.

Elegant candlelit dinners are served in a spacious dining room with a massive fireplace. Afterward guests can mingle over after-dinner drinks or go back to their private decks for stargazing.

Equally outstanding and in touch with its surroundings is Ventana, already mentioned briefly on page 43. Tucked away on a ridge in a mountain meadow 1,200 feet above the Pacific's pounding surf, sheltered by redwood, oak, and bay laurel trees, Ventana admirably captures the spirit of Big Sur—escapist, sensuous, serene. It has been lauded by countless writers and lovers since it opened in 1975.

The main building, a lodge of glass and cedar weathered gray by sea mist, is where you check in and are offered refreshments to be enjoyed in front of the oversize fireplace, where complimentary wine and cheese are served to guests every afternoon.

Once again, cars are left behind until you leave. The rooms are in long lodges tucked into the trees. Two secluded swimming pools are screened by weathered wood fencing. Adjoining saunas and Japanese baths have chambers marked "his," "hers," and "ours."

The restaurant is located down the hill, where cars won't disturb resident guests. It is open to the public and extremely popular, especially the big deck with heavenly views. This is the only part of the complex where you remember that the rest of the world exists.

Ventana's guest rooms are spacious and airy, paneled with natural wood and furnished with wicker and pine. The colors are soft earth and rose tones, with splashes of color added in the duvets and matching hand-painted headboards. Every small detail seems perfect, from the ceramic tile of the fireplace to the unusual polished wooden floor tiles to tables made from tree trunks. The bathrooms are huge and equally tasteful. Some rooms offer private hot tubs on the deck.

Room views are of coastline or forest, and there's something to be said for each. With an ocean view, you can wake to watch the sea and hills emerge as the mist slowly gives way to sunshine, casting a golden glow on the hillside. Facing the tall trees means extra privacy and an enchanted feel when you wake to birds singing on your balcony. You can walk to the main lodge or the library for breakfast, or ask for a tray to share with the birds. If you're like most guests at Ventana, you'll wish you could stay forever.

Needless to say, neither of these sublime escapes is inexpensive, but in a world where the ordinary often comes high, they are worth every cent.

ACCOMMODATIONS AND INFORMATION *Timberhill Ranch,* 35755 Hauser Bridge Road, Cazadero, 95421, (707) 847-3258, EE, MAP • *Ventana,* Highway 1, mile 28.1S, Big Sur, 93920, (408) 667-2331 or in California (800) 628-6500, EE, CP; dinners, E.

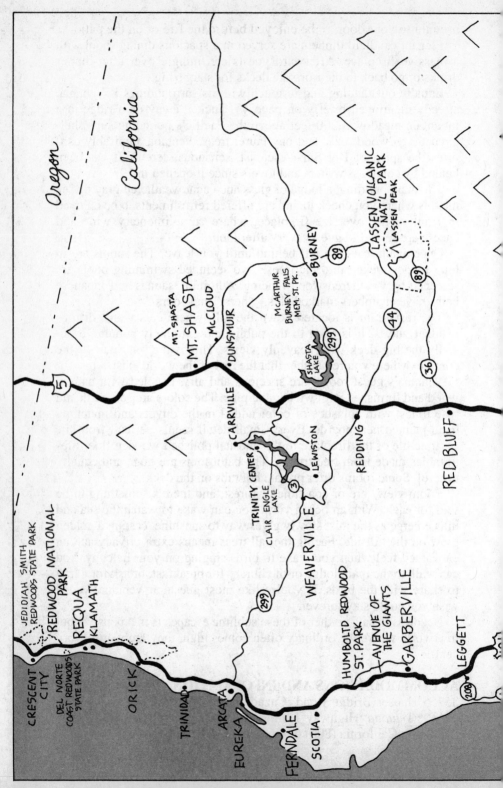

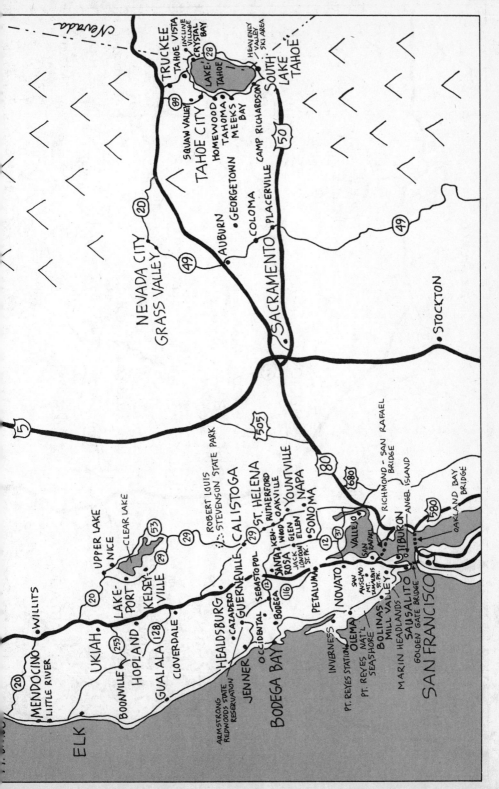

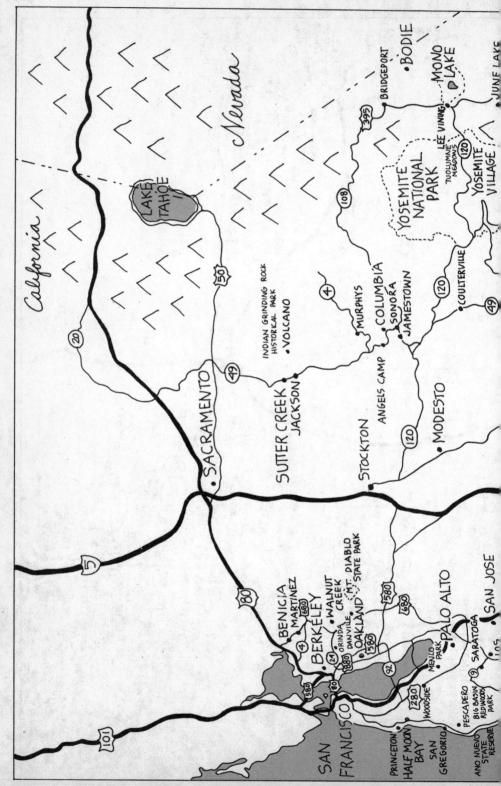

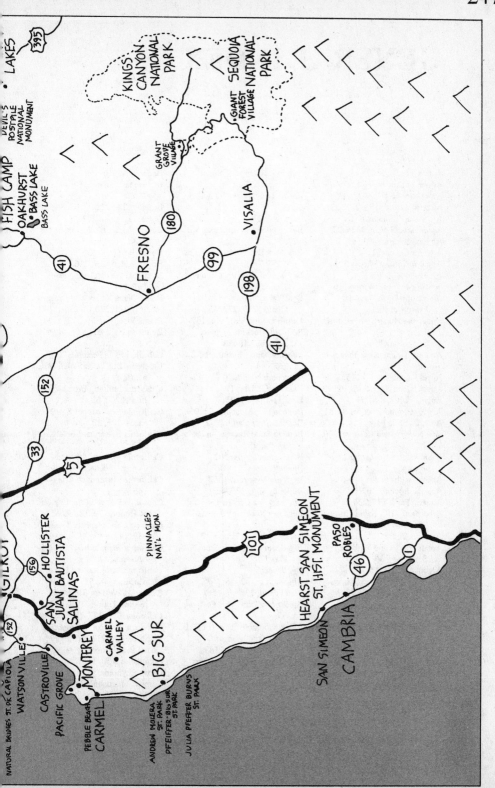

GENERAL INDEX

CATEGORY INDEX